TUCSON

TIM HULL

Contents

Maps

SEE MAP 3

W SPEEDWAY BLVD

De Anza Park

Estevan Park

Catalina Park

DUNBAR SPRING

4th Avenue

WEST UNIVERSITY

Oury Park

Santa Cruz River Park

DOWNTOWN

EL PRESIDIO

El Presidio Real de San Agustín del Tucson

Tucson Museum of Art and Historic Block

SEE MAP 5

El Presidio Park and Pima County Courthouse

Alvarado Park

St. Augustine Cathedral

San Augustine Plaza Park

Tucson Amtrak

Military Plaza Park

ARMORY PARK

Santa Cruz River Park

Tucson Convention Center

El Tiradito Shrine

Barrio Histórico

Verdugo Park

BARRIO SANTA ROSA

Santa Rosa Park

Santa Rita Park

0   300 yds
0   300 m

DISTANCE ACROSS MAP
Approximate: 2.9 mi or 4.6 km

SEE MAP 6

© AVALON TRAVEL

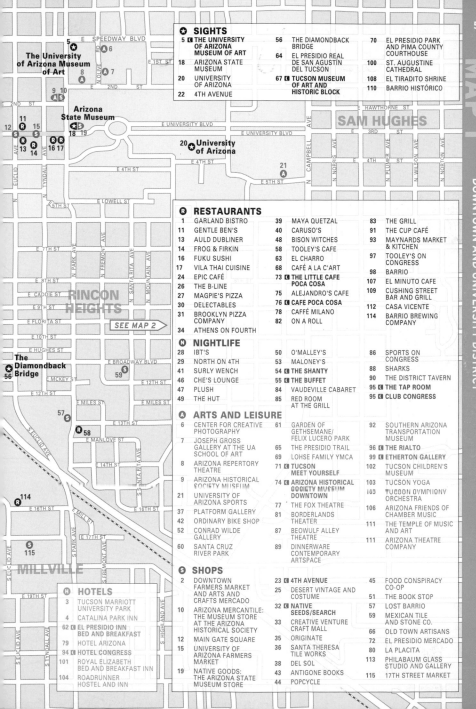

SIGHTS

5	THE UNIVERSITY OF ARIZONA MUSEUM OF ART	56	THE DIAMONDBACK BRIDGE	70	EL PRESIDIO PARK AND PIMA COUNTY COURTHOUSE
18	ARIZONA STATE MUSEUM	64	EL PRESIDIO REAL DE SAN AGUSTÍN DEL TUCSON	100	ST. AUGUSTINE CATHEDRAL
20	UNIVERSITY OF ARIZONA	67	TUCSON MUSEUM OF ART AND HISTORIC BLOCK	108	EL TIRADITO SHRINE
22	4TH AVENUE			110	BARRIO HISTÓRICO

RESTAURANTS

1	GARLAND BISTRO	39	MAYA QUETZAL	83	THE GRILL
11	GENTLE BEN'S	40	CARUSO'S	91	THE CUP CAFÉ
13	AULD DUBLINER	48	BISON WITCHES	93	MAYNARDS MARKET & KITCHEN
14	FROG & FIRKIN	58	TOOLEY'S CAFE	97	TOOLEY'S ON CONGRESS
17	VILA THAI CUISINE	63	EL CHARRO	98	BARRIO
24	EPIC CAFÉ	68	CAFÉ A LA C'ART	107	EL MINUTO CAFE
26	THE B-LINE	73	THE LITTLE CAFE POCA COSA	109	CUSHING STREET BAR AND GRILL
27	MAGPIE'S PIZZA	75	ALEJANDRO'S CAFE	112	CASA VICENTE
30	DELECTABLES	76	CAFE POCA COSA	114	BARRIO BREWING COMPANY
31	BROOKLYN PIZZA COMPANY	78	CAFFÉ MILANO		
34	ATHENS ON FOURTH	82	ON A ROLL		

NIGHTLIFE

28	IBT'S	50	O'MALLEY'S	86	SPORTS ON CONGRESS
29	NORTH ON 4TH	53	MALONEY'S	88	SHARKS
41	SURLY WENCH	54	THE SHANTY	90	THE DISTRICT TAVERN
47	CHE'S LOUNGE	55	THE BUFFET	95	THE TAP ROOM
47	PLUSH	84	VAUDEVILLE CABARET	95	CLUB CONGRESS
49	THE HUT	85	RED ROOM AT THE GRILL		

ARTS AND LEISURE

6	CENTER FOR CREATIVE PHOTOGRAPHY	61	GARDEN OF GETHSEMANE/ FELIX LUCERO PARK	92	SOUTHERN ARIZONA TRANSPORTATION MUSEUM
7	JOSEPH GROSS GALLERY AT THE UA SCHOOL OF ART	65	THE PRESIDIO TRAIL	96	THE RIALTO
8	ARIZONA REPERTORY THEATRE	69	LOHSE FAMILY YMCA	99	ETHERTON GALLERY
9	ARIZONA HISTORICAL SOCIETY MUSEUM	71	TUCSON MEET YOURSELF	102	TUCSON CHILDREN'S MUSEUM
21	UNIVERSITY OF ARIZONA SPORTS	74	ARIZONA HISTORICAL SOCIETY MUSEUM DOWNTOWN	103	TUCSON YOGA
37	PLATFORM GALLERY	77	THE FOX THEATRE	105	TUCSON SYMPHONY ORCHESTRA
42	ORDINARY BIKE SHOP	81	BORDERLANDS THEATER	106	ARIZONA FRIENDS OF CHAMBER MUSIC
52	CONRAD WILDE GALLERY	87	BEOWULF ALLEY THEATRE	111	THE TEMPLE OF MUSIC AND ART
60	SANTA CRUZ RIVER PARK	89	DINNERWARE CONTEMPORARY ARTSPACE	111	ARIZONA THEATRE COMPANY

SHOPS

2	DOWNTOWN FARMERS MARKET AND ARTS AND CRAFTS MERCADO	23	4TH AVENUE	45	FOOD CONSPIRACY CO-OP
10	ARIZONA MERCANTILE: THE MUSEUM STORE AT THE ARIZONA HISTORICAL SOCIETY	25	DESERT VINTAGE AND COSTUME	51	THE BOOK STOP
		32	NATIVE SEEDS/SEARCH	57	LOST BARRIO
12	MAIN GATE SQUARE	33	CREATIVE VENTURE CRAFT MALL	59	MEXICAN TILE AND STONE CO.
15	UNIVERSITY OF ARIZONA FARMERS MARKET	35	ORIGINATE	66	OLD TOWN ARTISANS
19	NATIVE GOODS: THE ARIZONA STATE MUSEUM STORE	36	SANTA THERESA TILE WORKS	72	EL PRESIDIO MERCADO
		38	DEL SOL	80	LA PLACITA
		43	ANTIGONE BOOKS	113	PHILABAUM GLASS STUDIO AND GALLERY
		44	POPCYCLE	115	17TH STREET MARKET

HOTELS

3	TUCSON MARRIOTT UNIVERSITY PARK
4	CATALINA PARK INN
62	EL PRESIDIO INN BED AND BREAKFAST
79	HOTEL ARIZONA
94	HOTEL CONGRESS
101	ROYAL ELIZABETH BED AND BREAKFAST INN
104	ROADRUNNER HOSTEL AND INN

SEE MAP 3

To 2 Tucson Racquet & Fitness Club

RICHLAND HEIGHTS EAST

WINTERHAVEN

McCormick Park

VISTA DEL MONTE

Campbell Plaza

La Madera Park

COUNTRY GLEN

OAK FLOWER

Tucson Botanical Gardens

Tahoe Park

PALO VERDE

MIDTOWN

University Medical Center

BLENMAN-ELM

University of Arizona

Himmel Park

Adoration Sanctuary Hospital

PETER HOWELL

SEE MAP 1

SAM HUGHES

El Con Mall

Broadway Village

SAN CLEMENTE

ARROYO CHICO

Randolph Golf Course

Hi Corbett Field

Gene C. Reid Park

Reid Park Zoo

SAN GABRIEL

Randolph Plaza

SEE MAP 6

H	HOTELS		
34	ARIZONA INN	77	DOUBLETREE HOTEL AT REID PARK
39	FOUR POINTS BY SHERATON TUCSON UNIVERSITY PLAZA	82	LODGE ON THE DESERT
64	SAM HUGHES INN BED AND BREAKFAST	86	EMBASSY SUITES

DISTANCE ACROSS MAP
Approximate: 6.5 mi or 10.5 km

0   0.5 mi
0   0.5 km

© AVALON TRAVEL

SEE MAP 3

◎ SIGHTS

26	TUCSON BOTANICAL GARDENS	75	REID PARK ZOO

◎ RESTAURANTS

1	GHINI'S FRENCH CAFFE	32	FRANK'S
3	NICO'S	38	MISS SAIGON
4	ROSA'S	40	ALI BABA
5	PASTICHE MODERN EATERY	41	EEGEE'S
6	BEYOND BREAD	43	THE DISH BISTRO-BAR
7	LOVIN' SPOONFULS VEGETARIAN RESTAURANT	45	FRONIMO'S, GREEK CAFÉ
8	THE INDIA OVEN	48	GUILIN HEALTHY CHINESE RESTAURANT
9	YOSHIMATSU HEALTHY JAPANESE EATERY	49	COFFEE TIME
11	BLUE WILLOW	51	IKE'S COFFEE & TEA
12	LUCKY WISHBONE	53	GEE'S GARDEN BISTRO
13	RAGING SAGE	54	FEAST
14	KARUNA'S THAI PLATE	60	CASA MOLINA
15	KINGFISHER	63	ROCCO'S LITTLE CHICAGO
19	GOVINDA'S NATURAL FOOD BUFFET	69	AUSTIN'S
29	LUKE'S	80	SUSHI GARDEN
32	FRANCISCO'S	81	OLD PUEBLO GRILLE
		85	THE HUNGRY FOX
		89	SERI MELAKA FINE MALAYSIAN CUISINE

◎ NIGHTLIFE

17	DANNY'S BABAQUIVERI	70	ELLE: A WINE COUNTRY RESTAURANT
20	CATAVINOS	73	AIN'T NOBODY'S BIZNESS
28	THE SHELTER	83	SMOKE CIGAR PATIO AND BAR
37	DIRTBAGS	84	KON TIKI
59	DV8	87	CACTUS MOON CAFÉ
65	BOB DOBB'S	90	BAR TOMA
68	EL PARADOR		

◎ ARTS AND LEISURE

2	TUCSON RACQUET & FITNESS CLUB	42	HIMMEL PARK	62	3RD STREET BIKE ROUTE	74	GENE C. REID PARK
21	LIGHTHOUSE/ CITY YMCA	42	HIMMEL PARK TENNIS CENTER	67	MID-VALLEY ATHLETIC CLUB AND WELLNESS CENTER	76	RANDOLPH GOLF COURSE AND DELL URICH GOLF COURSE
23	FORT LOWELL MUSEUM	47	THE LOFT CINEMA	71	LAFFS COMEDY CAFFE	78	RANDOLPH RECREATION CENTER
23	FORT LOWELL TENNIS CENTER	52	PROVIDENCE INSTITUTE			78	RANDOLPH CENTER SKATE PARK
						79	RANDOLPH TENNIS CENTER

◎ SHOPS

10	PLAZA LIQUORS	25	POTTERY BLOWOUT	35	THE BUFFALO EXCHANGE	55	SPEEDWAY ANTIQUES DISTRICT	66	RINCON MARKET
16	THE MEXICAN GARDEN	27	GRANT ROAD ANTIQUES DISTRICT	36	MORNING STAR TRADERS	56	SUMMIT HUT	72	BROADWAY VILLAGE
20	CLUES UNLIMITED	30	MRS. TIGGYWINKLE'S TOYS	44	THE RUMRUNNER	57	COPPER COUNTRY ANTIQUES	72	BON BOUTIQUE
22	PLAZA PALOMINO	31	THE KID'S CENTER	46	GADABOUT SALON AND SPA	58	TOM'S FINE FURNITURE AND COLLECTIBLES	72	TOQUE DE PASIÓN
22	GREY DOG TRADING COMPANY	33	CRIZMAC TUCSON MARKETPLACE	50	ZIA RECORD EXCHANGE	61	BOOKMANS	72	BOHEMIA
24	PDQ RECORDS AND CDS							88	PARK PLACE MALL
								91	THE SHOPS AT EL MERCADO

Tohono Chul Park
2
3
4
8
INA RD
Casas Adobes Plaza
5
6
7
To N 1 World Sports Grille
77
LOS ALTOS RD
To S 9 Antigua de Mexico
Oracle Plaza
LAVERY LN
RUDASILL RD
10
11
Quail Canyon Golf Course

SKYLINE DR
NA RD
SKYLINE DR
SUN JOAQUIN
ORANGE GROVE RD
LA ZORREA
MIRAVAL
CAMPBELL AVE

INA RD
CAMPBELL AVE
CORONADO DR
ALVERNON WAY

13 14 15
12 S
16
R
19 R
18 17
A

Canyon Hill 20
R
21
22
S
Golf Course

E SUNRISE DR
VALLEY VIEW RD

23 24
R
HACIENDA DEL SOL RD

THE FOOTHILLS

SUMO
HACIENDA DEL SOL
PONTATOC RD

RIVER RD
RIVER RD

35 A
Rillito Downs Park
36
A
37 R
38 St. Phillip's in the Hills Episcopal Church
39 R 43
40
41
H
42

33 34 Tucson Mall
Tucson Place
WETMORE RD
LIMBERLOST DR
77

45 N
ROGER RD
LIMBERLOST
PASTIME RD
46 N
THURBER RD
PRINCE RD

SEE MAP 5

AMPHI
NAVAJO RD
48 N
49 N
KLEINDALE RD
50 S

MIRACLE MILE STRIP

HENDRICK ACRES

MIRACLE MANOR
KEELING
51
GRANT RD
ALTURAS ST

SAHUARO ST
52 R
53
Mansfield Park
JEFFERSON PARK
54 R H
56

DEL ARIZONA
CAMPUS FARM

ROGER RD
Tucson General Hospital
North Central District Park

RICHLAND HEIGHTS EAST
47 R

STONE AVE
FONTANA AVE
GLENN ST

Campbell Plaza
PARK AVE

1ST AVE
COPPER ST
SILVER ST

WATER ST
EDISON ST
WAVERLY ST
LESTER ST
University Medical Center
ADAMS ST
A
57 BE ST

Tahoe Park

BLENMAN ELM

CHERRY AVE

ROGERS AVE

PRINCE RD
OIVER RD

ROGER RD

44 A

RILLITO

KLEINDALE RD
FORT LOWELL RD
PRESIDIO RD
BLACKLIDGE DR
MONTE VISTA DR
GLENN ST
BERMUDA ST
FLOWER ST

VISTA DEL MONTE
McCormick Park

GRANT RD
GRANT RD

PIMA ST
SEE MAP 2
Tucson Botanical Gardens
MIDTOWN

80

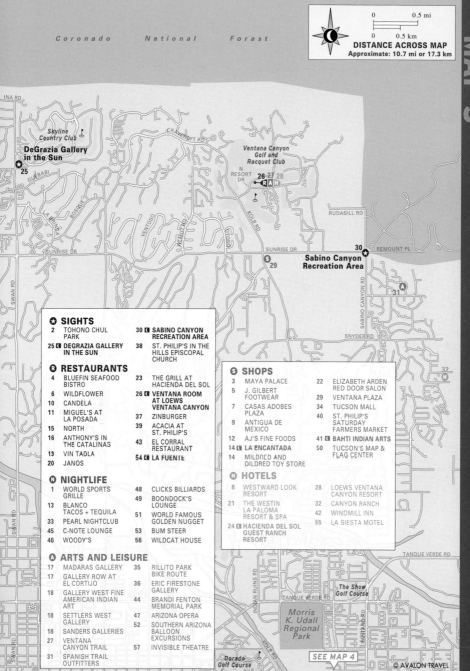

Coronado   National   Forest

DISTANCE ACROSS MAP
Approximate: 10.7 mi or 17.3 km

Skyline Country Club
DeGrazia Gallery in the Sun
Ventana Canyon Golf and Racquet Club
Sabino Canyon Recreation Area

☼ SIGHTS
2 TOHONO CHUL PARK
25 ◖ DEGRAZIA GALLERY IN THE SUN
30 ◖ SABINO CANYON RECREATION AREA
38 ST. PHILIP'S IN THE HILLS EPISCOPAL CHURCH

🍴 RESTAURANTS
4 BLUEFIN SEAFOOD BISTRO
6 WILDFLOWER
10 CANDELA
11 MIGUEL'S AT LA POSADA
15 NORTH
16 ANTHONY'S IN THE CATALINAS
19 VIN TABLA
20 JANOS
23 THE GRILL AT HACIENDA DEL SOL
26 ◖ VENTANA ROOM AT LOEWS VENTANA CANYON
37 ZINBURGER
39 ACACIA AT ST. PHILIP'S
43 EL CORRAL RESTAURANT
54 ◖ LA FUENTE

🌙 NIGHTLIFE
1 WORLD SPORTS GRILLE
13 BLANCO TACOS + TEQUILA
33 PEARL NIGHTCLUB
45 C-NOTE LOUNGE
46 WOODY'S
48 CLICKS BILLIARDS
49 BOONDOCK'S LOUNGE
51 WORLD FAMOUS GOLDEN NUGGET
53 BUM STEER
56 WILDCAT HOUSE

🎭 ARTS AND LEISURE
17 MADARAS GALLERY
17 GALLERY ROW AT EL CORTIJO
18 GALLERY WEST FINE AMERICAN INDIAN ART
18 SETTLERS WEST GALLERY
18 SANDERS GALLERIES
27 VENTANA CANYON TRAIL
31 SPANISH TRAIL OUTFITTERS
35 RILLITO PARK BIKE ROUTE
36 ERIC FIRESTONE GALLERY
44 BRANDI FENTON MEMORIAL PARK
47 ARIZONA OPERA
52 SOUTHERN ARIZONA BALLOON EXCURSIONS
57 INVISIBLE THEATRE

🛍 SHOPS
3 MAYA PALACE
5 J. GILBERT FOOTWEAR
7 CASAS ADOBES PLAZA
9 ANTIGUA DE MEXICO
12 AJ'S FINE FOODS
14 ◖ LA ENCANTADA
14 MILDRED AND DILDRED TOY STORE
22 ELIZABETH ARDEN RED DOOR SALON
29 VENTANA PLAZA
34 TUCSON MALL
40 ST. PHILIP'S SATURDAY FARMERS MARKET
41 ◖ BAHTI INDIAN ARTS
50 TUCSON'S MAP & FLAG CENTER

🏨 HOTELS
8 WESTWARD LOOK RESORT
21 THE WESTIN LA PALOMA RESORT & SPA
24 ◖ HACIENDA DEL SOL GUEST RANCH RESORT
28 LOEWS VENTANA CANYON RESORT
32 CANYON RANCH
42 WINDMILL INN
55 LA SIESTA MOTEL

The Show Golf Course
Morris K. Udall Regional Park
Dorado Golf Course
SEE MAP 4
© AVALON TRAVEL

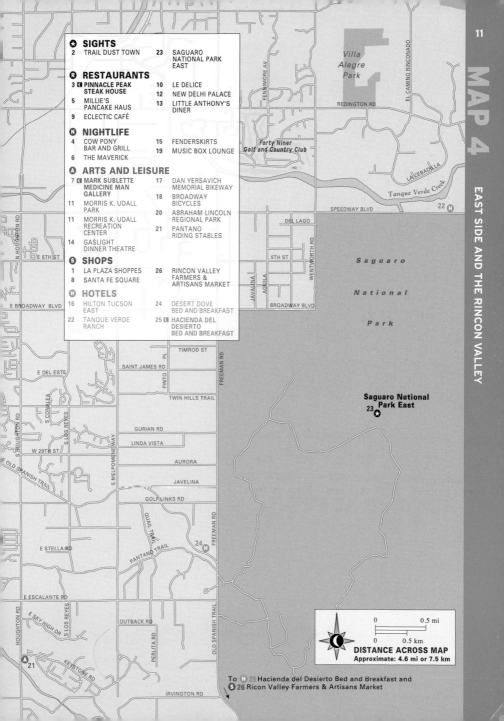

☉ SIGHTS
2 TRAIL DUST TOWN
23 SAGUARO NATIONAL PARK EAST

℞ RESTAURANTS
3 PINNACLE PEAK STEAK HOUSE
5 MILLIE'S PANCAKE HAUS
9 ECLECTIC CAFÉ
10 LE DELICE
12 NEW DELHI PALACE
13 LITTLE ANTHONY'S DINER

Ⓝ NIGHTLIFE
4 COW PONY BAR AND GRILL
6 THE MAVERICK
15 FENDERSKIRTS
19 MUSIC BOX LOUNGE

Ⓐ ARTS AND LEISURE
7 MARK SUBLETTE MEDICINE MAN GALLERY
11 MORRIS K. UDALL PARK
11 MORRIS K. UDALL RECREATION CENTER
14 GASLIGHT DINNER THEATRE
17 DAN YERSAVICH MEMORIAL BIKEWAY
18 BROADWAY BICYCLES
20 ABRAHAM LINCOLN REGIONAL PARK
21 PANTANO RIDING STABLES

Ⓢ SHOPS
1 LA PLAZA SHOPPES
8 SANTA FE SQUARE
26 RINCON VALLEY FARMERS & ARTISANS MARKET

Ⓗ HOTELS
16 HILTON TUCSON EAST
22 TANQUE VERDE RANCH
24 DESERT DOVE BED AND BREAKFAST
25 HACIENDA DEL DESIERTO BED AND BREAKFAST

Villa Alegre Park

REDINGTON RD

Forty Niner Golf and Country Club

LA CEBADILLA

Tanque Verde Creek

SPEEDWAY BLVD 22 Ⓗ

EL CAMINO RINCONADO

DEL LAGO

WENTWORTH RD

5TH ST

DEL LAGO

Saguaro

National

Park

JAVALINA
AGUILA

BROADWAY BLVD

Saguaro National Park East
23 ☉

FENNIMORE AV

N HOUGHTON RD

E 5TH ST

E BROADWAY BLVD

TIMROD ST

SAINT JAMES RD

PINTO

PL

FREEMAN RD

E DEL ESTE

TWIN HILLS TRAIL

S COMLEA
S LOS REYES

S HOUGHTON RD

GURIAN RD

LINDA VISTA

W 29TH ST

S MELPOMENE WAY

AURORA

JAVELINA

OLD SPANISH TRAIL

GOLF LINKS RD

QUAIL TRAIL

FREEMAN RD

E STELLA RD

PANTANO TRAIL

24 Ⓗ

E ESCALANTE RD

HOUGHTON RD

E SKY HIGH DR
S LOS REYES

OUTBACK RD

PERLITA RD

OLD SPANISH TRAIL

A 21

KEYSTONE RD

IRVINGTON RD

0   0.5 mi

0   0.5 km

DISTANCE ACROSS MAP
Approximate: 4.6 mi or 7.5 km

To Ⓗ 25 Hacienda del Desierto Bed and Breakfast and
Ⓢ 26 Ricon Valley Farmers & Artisans Market

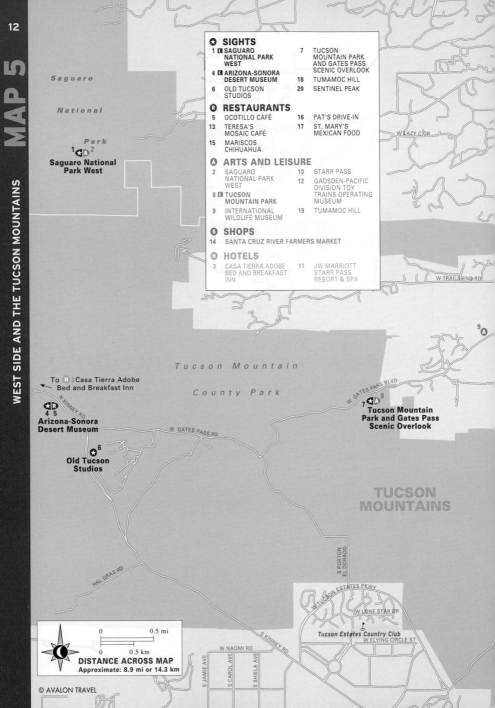

○ SIGHTS

1 **SAGUARO NATIONAL PARK WEST**
4 **ARIZONA-SONORA DESERT MUSEUM**
6 OLD TUCSON STUDIOS
7 TUCSON MOUNTAIN PARK AND GATES PASS SCENIC OVERLOOK
18 TUMAMOC HILL
20 SENTINEL PEAK

ℝ RESTAURANTS

5 OCOTILLO CAFÉ
13 TERESA'S MOSAIC CAFÉ
15 MARISCOS CHIHUAHUA
16 PAT'S DRIVE-IN
17 ST. MARY'S MEXICAN FOOD

Ⓐ ARTS AND LEISURE

2 SAGUARO NATIONAL PARK WEST
8 **TUCSON MOUNTAIN PARK**
9 INTERNATIONAL WILDLIFE MUSEUM
10 STARR PASS
12 GADSDEN-PACIFIC DIVISION TOY TRAINS OPERATING MUSEUM
19 TUMAMOC HILL

Ⓢ SHOPS

14 SANTA CRUZ RIVER FARMERS MARKET

Ⓗ HOTELS

3 CASA TIERRA ADOBE BED AND BREAKFAST INN
11 JW MARRIOTT STARR PASS RESORT & SPA

Saguaro

National

Park

Saguaro National Park West

Tucson Mountain County Park

TUCSON MOUNTAINS

To Casa Tierra Adobe Bed and Breakfast Inn

Arizona-Sonora Desert Museum

Old Tucson Studios

Tucson Mountain Park and Gates Pass Scenic Overlook

Tucson Estates Country Club

W LAZY C DR

W TRAILS END RD

W GATES PASS BLVD

W GATES PASS RD

N KINNEY RD

HAL GRAS RD

W TUCSON ESTATES PKWY

S PORTON EL DORADO

W LONE STAR DR

W FLYING CIRCLE ST

S KINNEY RD

W NAOMI RD

S JAMIE AVE

S CAROL AVE

S SHIELA AVE

0   0.5 mi
0   0.5 km

DISTANCE ACROSS MAP
Approximate: 8.9 mi or 14.3 km

© AVALON TRAVEL

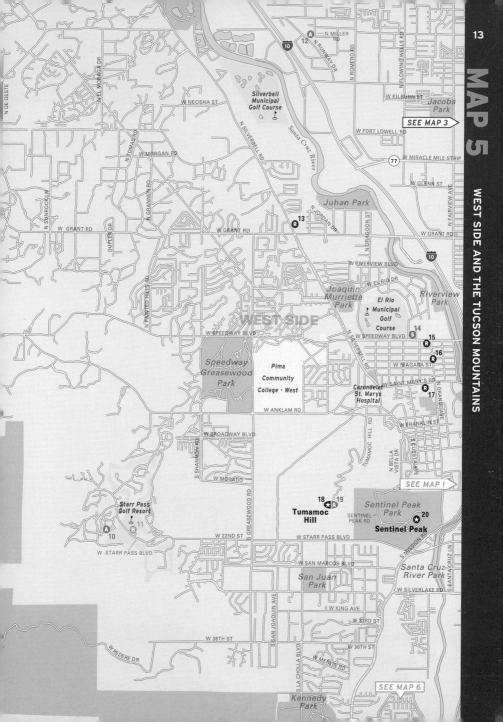

N DE OESTE

N EL MORAGA DR

W NEOSHA ST

Silverbell
Municipal
Golf Course

N TOMAS RD

N SUNROCK LN

N GRANNEN RD

W MORGAN RD

DUPLER DR

W GRANT RD

N SILVERBELL RD

Santa Cruz River

12 N MILLER RD

10

N RUNWAY DR

N ROMERO RD

N FLOWING WELLS RD

W KILBURN ST

Jacobs
Park

SEE MAP 3

W FORT LOWELL RD

77

W MIRACLE MILE STRIP

W GLENN ST

N FAIRVIEW AVE

Juhan Park

13

N JORDAN DR

N DRAGOON ST

W GRANT RD

10

W RIVERVIEW BLVD

W GRANT RD

N PAINTED HILLS RD

Joaquin
Murrietta
Park

N EL RIO DR

El Rio
Municipal
Golf
Course

Riverview
Park

WEST SIDE

W SPEEDWAY BLVD

N SILVERBELL RD

W SPEEDWAY BLVD

14

15

16

Speedway
Greasewood
Park

Pima
Community
College - West

W NIAGARA ST

N SAINT MARY'S RD

Carondelet
St. Marys
Hospital

17

N GRANDE AVE

W ANKLAM RD

W FRANKLIN ST

S SHANNON RD

W BROADWAY BLVD

TUMAMOC HILL RD

N BELLA
VISTA DR

SEE MAP 1

W MONDO

S GREASEWOOD RD

18 19

Sentinel Peak
Park

20

Starr Pass
Golf Resort

A

H 11

10

Tumamoc
Hill

SENTINEL
PEAK RD

SENTINEL
PEAK RD

Sentinel Peak

S MISSION RD

W 22ND ST

W STARR PASS BLVD

W STARR PASS BLVD

W SAN MARCOS BLVD

Santa Cruz
River Park

W SILVERLAKE RD

S SANTA CRUZ LN

San Juan
Park

S JOAQUIN AVE

W KING AVE

W 93RD ST

S LA CHOLLA BLVD

W 36TH ST

W 36TH ST

W MERLIN RD

W REDERE DR

SEE MAP 6

Kennedy
Park

STARR PASS BLVD

Sentinel Peak Park

Santa Cruz River Park

Jardín de César Chávez

20TH ST

Santa Rita Park

SEE MAP 1

210

SAN MARCOS BLVD

San Juan Park

SILVERLAKE RD

SEE MAP 5

KING AVE

34TH ST

36TH ST

44TH ST

Kennedy Park

AJO WAY

RAVENNA

MISSION RD

SILVERLAKE RD

32ND ST

35TH ST

36TH ST

40TH ST

44TH ST

Santa Cruz Plaza

R 2 **R** 3

R 4

Quincie Douglas Park

Euclid Ave

Park Ave

Kino Pkwy

19

Tucson Veterans

Administration Hospital

AJO WAY

Benson Hwy

10

☉ SIGHTS
1 JARDÍN DE CÉSAR CHÁVEZ
12 ☚ SAN XAVIER DEL BAC
13 PIMA AIR AND SPACE MUSEUM

☻ RESTAURANTS
2 LA CAVE'S BAKERY
3 ☚ MI NIDITO
4 TAQUERIA PICO DE GALLO
9 EL GUERO CANELO

Ⓝ NIGHTLIFE
5 WOODEN NICKEL TAVERN
7 ☚ NIMBUS BREWING COMPANY

Ⓐ ARTS AND LEISURE
8 TUCSON RODEO PARADE MUSEUM

Ⓢ SHOPS
6 COMMUNITY FOOD BANK FARMERS MARKET

Ⓗ HOTELS
10 HOLIDAY INN EXPRESS
11 DESERT DIAMOND HOTEL AND CASINO

PRESIDENT ST
PALMDALE ST

OHIO ST

Tucson Rodeo Grounds

A 8

IRVINGTON RD

Pima County Rodeo Park

R 9 NEBRASKA ST

BANTAM RD

CANADA DR

Mission Park

MISSIONDALE RD

19

ALVORD RD

BILBY RD

VALESKA RD

Sunnyside Park

VALENCIA RD

HEADLEY RD

PINTA AVE

SANTA CLARA AVE

VALENCIA RD

MEDINA RD

NOGALES HWY

MISSION RD

INDIAN AGENCY RD

19

ACADIA DR

TETON RD

ERIC ST

CORONA RD

ELVADO RD

LOS REALES RD

Tucson International Airport

To ☉ 12 San Xavier del Bac

SAN XAVIER LOOP RD

H

19

EASTLAND ST
22ND ST
Randolph Park
Randolph Park Golf Course
22ND ST
SEE MAP 2
Randolph Plaza
22ND ST
22ND ST
SEE MAP 4
COUNTRY CLUB RD
TREAT AVE
ALVERNON WAY
COLUMBUS BLVD
SWAN RD
26TH ST
26TH ST
SILVERLAKE RD
FAIRLAND STRA
AVIATION HWY
5
N
31ST ST
Freedom Park
FERRY DR
32ND ST
CRAYCROFT RD
SAHUARA AVE
GOLF LINKS RD
GOLF LINKS RD
210
SUNGLOW RD
6
PALO VERDE RD
DODGE BLVD
7
N
44TH ST
1ST ST
3RD ST
6TH ST
QUILOTA BLVD
86
AJO WAY
Kino Veterans Memorial Sports Arena
CONTRACTORS WAY
Davis-Monthan
Air Force Base
6TH ST
7TH ST
8TH ST
YUMA ST
PHOENIX ST
RAMSGATE RD
General Blanchard Golf Course
PICACHO ST
COUNTRY CLUB RD
MILBER ST
MICHIGAN ST
ILLINOIS ST
GAS RD
TENNESSEE ST
SOUTH SIDE
IRVINGTON RD
BELVEDERE AVE
UTAH ST
TUCSON BLVD
FAUX BLVD
ALVERNON WAY
BENSON HWY
SWAN RD
NEBRASKA ST
ARCADIA AVE
CANADA ST
HOLLADAY ST
DREXEL RD
MILTON RD
ALVORD RD
BONNEY AVE
BELVEDERE AVE
REX ST
DREXEL RD
CROYCROFT RD
OLD V'AIL RD
10
GANLEY RD
BILBY RD
13
Pima Air and Space Museum
VALENCIA RD
PALO VERDE RD
ALVERNON WAY
EAST ST
CRAYCROFT RD
MELODY AVE
VAN BUREN AVE
E. MEDINA RD
10
ELVIRA RD
TUCSON BLVD
CORONA RD
AIRPORT DR
LOS REALES RD

0   0.5 mi
0   0.5 km
DISTANCE ACROSS MAP
Approximate: 18 mi or 29 km

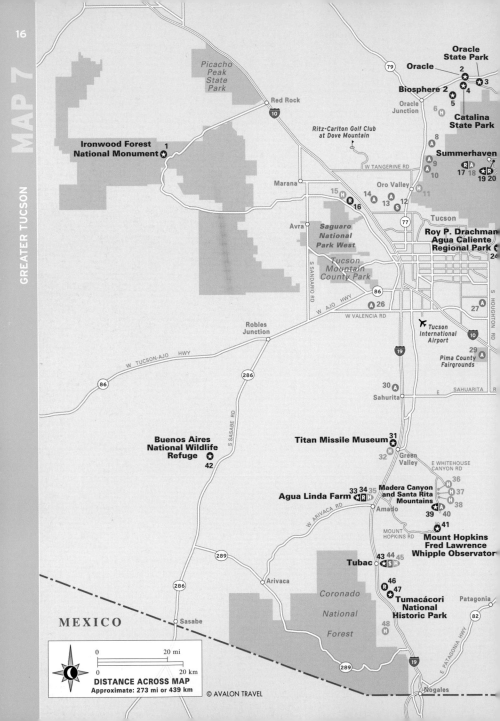

Picacho
Peak
State
Park

Red Rock
10

Oracle
State Park
79   Oracle   2
Biosphere 2   3
4
Oracle
Junction   5
6

Ritz-Carlton Golf Club
at Dove Mountain

Catalina
State Park

Ironwood Forest
National Monument   1

W TANGERINE RD

8
Summerhaven
9
A
10   17 18   19 20

Marana

Oro Valley

15 14   11
16   13 12
S

Avra   Saguaro
National
Park West   77   Tucson

Tucson
Mountain
County Park

Roy P. Drachman
Agua Caliente
Regional Park
24

86

A 26   27
W VALENCIA RD

Robles
Junction

286

S SANDARIO RD

W AJO HWY

S HOUGHTON RD

Tucson
International
Airport   10
19
29
A
Pima County
Fairgrounds

86

W TUCSON-AJO HWY

30 A
Sahurita

E   SAHUARITA R

S SASABE RD

Buenos Aires
National Wildlife
Refuge
42

Titan Missile Museum 31
A
32   H   Green
Valley

E WHITEHOUSE
CANYON RD

36
H
37
H
38
39 40
A
41

33 34 35
Agua Linda Farm   R H

Madera Canyon
and Santa Rita
Mountains
Amado

289

286

W ARIVACA RD

MOUNT
HOPKINS RD

Mount Hopkins
Fred Lawrence
Whipple Observatory

Arivaca

43 44 45
Tubac   S R

Coronado

46
R   47
Tumacácori
National
Historic Park

Patagonia

82

MEXICO

Sasabe

National

Forest

48
H

E PATAGONIA HWY

289   19   Nogales

0   20 mi
0   20 km
DISTANCE ACROSS MAP
Approximate: 273 mi or 439 km
© AVALON TRAVEL

Mammoth

77

San Manuel

7
Peppersauce Canyon

21
Ski Valley

22
Sky Island Scenic Byway

Coronado National Forest

23

Reddington Pass
25

Saguaro National Park East

28
Colossal Cave Mountain Park

Mountain View

10 Benson

90

83

S SONOITA HWY

Kartchner Caverns State Park

82 Whetstone

Sonoita

90

Fairbank

80

90

Sierra Vista 90

Nicksville

92

McNeal

Bisbee

80

191

N REDINGTON RD

Redington

N CASCABEL RD

✪ SIGHTS

1	IRONWOOD FOREST NATIONAL MONUMENT	25	REDDINGTON PASS
2	ORACLE	28	COLOSSAL CAVE MOUNTAIN PARK
3	ORACLE STATE PARK	31	TITAN MISSILE MUSEUM
4	CATALINA STATE PARK	33	AGUA LINDA FARM
5	BIOSPHERE 2	39	MADERA CANYON AND SANTA RITA MOUNTAINS
7	PEPPERSAUCE CANYON	41	MOUNT HOPKINS FRED LAWRENCE WHIPPLE OBSERVATORY
19	SUMMERHAVEN		
21	SKI VALLEY	42	BUENOS AIRES NATIONAL WILDLIFE REFUGE
22	SKY ISLAND SCENIC BYWAY		
24	ROY P. DRACHMAN AGUA CALIENTE REGIONAL PARK	43	TUBAC
		47	TUMACÁCORI NATIONAL HISTORIC PARK

✪ RESTAURANTS

16	LI'L ABNER'S STEAKHOUSE	34	COW PALACE RESTAURANT
17	IRON DOOR RESTAURANT	34	LONGHORN GRILL
20	MOUNT LEMMON CAFÉ	46	WISDOMS

✪ ARTS AND LEISURE

8	50-YEAR TRAIL	23	BRAD P. GORMAN MEMORIAL BIKEWAY
9	PUSCH RIDGE RIDING STABLES	26	ANSELMO VALENCIA TORI AMPHITHEATER
10	VISTA DEL RIO CULTURAL RESOURCE PARK	27	FANTASY ISLAND
13	NORTHWEST YMCA	29	TUCSON RACEWAY PARK
14	ARTHUR PACK REGIONAL PARK	29	SOUTHWESTERN INTERNATIONAL DRAGWAY
18	MOUNT LEMMON AND THE SANTA CATALINA MOUNTAINS	30	ASARCO MINERAL DISCOVERY CENTER
18	MOUNT LEMMON	40	MADERA CANYON

✪ SHOPS

12	THE FOOTHILLS MALL	44	TUBAC

✪ HOTELS

6	MIRAVAL RESORT & SPA	35	AMADO TERRITORY INN
11	HILTON TUCSON EL CONQUISTADOR GOLF & TENNIS RESORT	36	SANTA RITA LODGE
		37	MADERA KUBO
15	WHITE STALLION RANCH	38	CHUPAROSA INN
		45	TUBAC GOLF RESORT
32	THE INN AT SAN IGNACIO	45	TUBAC INN
		48	ESPLENDOR RESORT

186

Discover Tucson

Over the past two centuries, Tucson has grown from an adobe-hut village on the far edge of the Spanish frontier into a major Sunbelt city, and yet through all that time and change the Old Pueblo has held on to the disparate cultural ingredients that have made it one of North America's most unique destinations.

In Tucson, visitors will find the true Southwestern experience, one that is neither encased under glass nor petrified through architectural uniformity; the Southwestern lifestyle is lived, not merely marketed. And what is this lifestyle? Well, it definitely involves a dedication to cultural mixing and a concentration on an active life lived outdoors on the saguaro-lined trails of the desert. This lifestyle is casual and laid-back, with flip-flops and shorts sufficing for dinner-wear, and a friendly margarita-and-sunshine-inspired smile sufficing for a general greeting.

If you're looking for extreme pampering, holistic pool-side navel-gazing, brisk hikes into the cactus foothills, and horseback rides along ancient trails, there are numerous world-famous resorts at which to stay and play. If you're longing for physical proof of the myths of the Old West, you'll find it in many of the city's museums and historic buildings. If you want to experience the Sonoran Desert, one of the continent's most exotic natural landscapes, you'll find it within a short drive of your hotel. This Old Pueblo is bustling with life, the Southwestern life – one lived just a bit off center, a bit slower, with a mild sunburn and a big happy smile.

Planning Your Trip

▶ WHERE TO GO

Downtown and University District

The downtown area is where Tucson began and where its heart still beats today. Although downtown usually becomes a bit deserted after 5 P.M. on Friday, the University district and 4th Avenue—the city's bohemian-chic enclave, sometimes called a smaller version of Berkeley, California's Telegraph Avenue—are busy most hours of the day. History is everywhere here, and it's the only truly pedestrian-friendly section of the city.

Midtown

Tucson's midtown neighborhood is where most of the Old Pueblo's real-life living takes place. The Fort Lowell Museum in the northern part of this district preserves the artifacts of the military's role in Tucson, and the Tucson Botanical Gardens are the best place to learn about the unique local flora that thrives on aridity. The small but prestigious Reid Park Zoo is a must for families.

The Foothills

The foothills area features artist Ted DeGrazia's romantic DeGrazia Gallery in the Sun and renowned architect Josias Joesler's imprint on Tucson. And at Sabino Canyon Recreation Area, the desert meets the mountains and a cool-water creek rushes down from the peaks to create one of the state's most beautiful and popular desert riparian areas.

East Side and the Rincon Valley

The top draw here is Saguaro National

an impressionistic portrait of the ubiquitous Virgin of Guadalupe at DeGrazia Gallery in the Sun

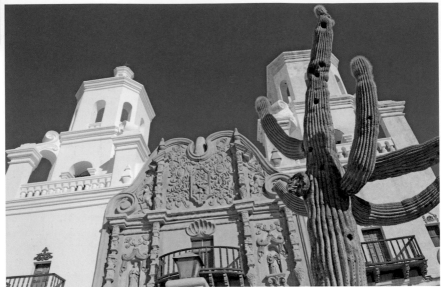
San Xavier del Bac

Park East, the park's largest and oldest section. You can walk, bike, or drive through a thick saguaro forest, one of the best and most accessible portions of the Sonoran Desert and the very best place to learn about and witness the desert's fauna and flora. Head east from the park to tour Colossal Cave Mountain Park, where Old West outlaws used to hide out.

West Side and the Tucson Mountains

This rugged desert land, west of central Tucson, is where you'll find Tucson's premier attraction, the world-renowned Arizona-Sonora Desert Museum. Here you'll see mountain lions and black bears lounging on warm rocks, and watch baby bighorn sheep negotiating the man-made cliffsides. But before you even reach the museum, you'll rise and descend over spectacular Gates Pass, looking down across a sweeping saguaro-dotted landscape.

South Side

The South Side holds one of Tucson's top sights, San Xavier del Bac (the "white dove of the desert"), one of the nation's finest remaining examples of mission architecture. Lovers of Mexican food in all its varieties will want to return to the small incorporated city of South Tucson again and again, for it is here that you'll find the region's best enchiladas, tamales, and carne asada.

Greater Tucson

Greater Tucson includes the forested heights of the Santa Catalina range, whose highest peak, Mount Lemmon, reaches above 9,000 feet and holds the nation's southernmost ski run. The mountains feature such a different ecosystem that the trip along the twisting Sky Island Scenic Byway is like driving from Mexico to Canada in about an hour. To the south is the lush Santa Cruz Valley, where you can learn all about the nuclear missiles that once ringed the city.

► WHEN TO GO

The Tucson calendar can be divided into just three seasons: spring, summer, and second spring. In January, the average high is about 64°F. February is the Old Pueblo's so-called "golden month," with an average daily high of 70°F. At least three major events—the Gem, Mineral, and Fossil Showcase, the Fiesta de los Vaqueros, and the Accenture Match Play golf tournament—have the hotels booked solid during this time. Unless you're coming to town for one of these popular events, I'd recommend staying away from town in February, despite the near-perfect weather.

In March, the average high is about 73°F, and in April, Tucson and Southern Arizona is a paradise, with an average daily high of 81°F.

the desert in bloom

The high season, during which prices are highest and tourists are everywhere, runs from February to the end of April. This is the first spring, and it is the most popular time of the year. You need to plan ahead and get a reservation if you're coming to town during this time. The spring months also feature the multicolored bloom of all the desert's cacti, trees, and wildflowers.

It's very hot in the desert in the summer (often over 105°F), but it's perfect in the mountains, and in July and August Tusconans can usually count on near-daily late-afternoon thunderstorms.

mighty saguaros

Explore Tucson

▶ THE THREE-DAY BEST OF TUCSON

The following suggested itinerary is meant to guide you to the city's very best—the essential Old Pueblo experience. You'll need your own car, a camera, a hat, and a comfortable pair of walking shoes.

Day 1

▶ Try to get an early start for sightseeing, especially during the hot months, when you only have a few hours before the weather gets unbearable. If you're an early riser I'd suggest heading downtown to the St. Augustine Cathedral before 7 A.M. You can stand across the street and watch as the rising sun lights up the Spanish revival cathedral, and the tall, skinny imported palm trees cast their shaggy shadows against the glowing building. It's a perfect Southwestern scene.

▶ Head downtown to the Hotel Congress and have a big breakfast at The Cup Café and take a look around the historic old hotel.

a palo verde tree and a colorful mural, downtown

▶ Hop in the car and head west from downtown into Tucson Mountain Park, stopping to enjoy the view of the desert below at Gates Pass. Then spend a few hours exploring the Arizona-Sonora Desert Museum, just down the hill.

▶ Next, head back over the Tucson Mountains to downtown and stroll, shop, eat a late lunch or early dinner, and take a trolley ride on 4th Avenue and nearby Main Gate Square.

▶ If you have it in you, forget about going back to the hotel and bar-hop around 4th Avenue and Main Gate Square, taking in a few bands at The Hut, Che's Lounge, and Plush along the way.

Day 2

▶ Drive to midtown for a filling greasy-spoon breakfast at Frank's.

▶ On your way back downtown, stop by the Arizona Inn and have a look around the lush grounds.

▶ Then drive to the El Presidio district downtown and explore the Tucson Museum of Art and Historic Block and El Presidio Real de San Agustín del Tucson for a few hours.

▶ For lunch, go to El Charro right near the museum, or to Little Cafe Poca Cosa, a short walk away, then take a short drive south on I-19 and check out San Xavier del Bac.

▶ In the late afternoon, drive into the foothills to Sabino Canyon Recreation Area and take a tram ride up into the canyon or hike one of the trails.

▶ As the sun dips behind the Santa Catalinas, head on over to Hacienda del Sol for drinks and appetizers (or dinner) on the patio overlooking the city.

▶ Hit El Parador (assuming it's a Friday or Saturday night) for salsa dancing, or kick back a few at The Tap Room and dance or watch a band at Club Congress.

SOUTHWEST STYLE

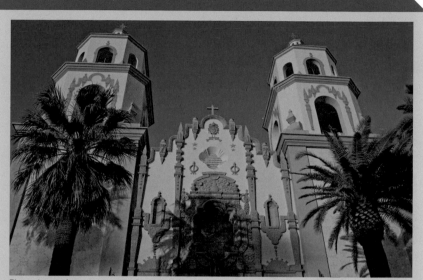

The early morning sun warms the Spanish revival St. Augustine Cathedral.

There are many Southwest art and architectural styles in Tucson, from Spanish realism to Spanish revival, pueblo chic to adobe row house, mission revival to railroad hacienda, to dryland art nouveau.

- The top draw, of course, is the "white dove of the desert," **San Xavier del Bac,** a mission that dates back to the 1600s. A bit south of San Xavier, the half-ruin **Mission Tumacácori** awaits at **Tumacácori National Historical Park.**

- Take a look around the elegant old hotels from the golden age of Southwestern tourism, such as the **Arizona Inn** and **Hacienda del Sol.**

- Two churches warrant a look: **St. Augustine Cathedral,** a Spanish revival church that

puts on a mariachi mass every Sunday; and the Josias Joesler-designed, Mexican-influenced **St. Philip's in the Hills Episcopal Church.**

- Several buildings on the **University of Arizona** campus reflect both revival and territorial styles.

- To really get an idea about the various styles that influence Tucson, visit the **Tucson Museum of Art and Historic Block.**

- Lovers of Western art should visit the **galleries in the foothills** around the intersection of Campbell and Skyline. The most essential gallery in town for Southwestern art lovers is the **Eric Firestone Gallery,** housed in a Joesler-designed adobe.

Day 3

▶ Depending on your personal inclinations, you should either tour Kartchner Caverns State Park near Benson, or head north up the Sky Island Scenic Byway into the Santa Catalina Mountains. Both trips are scenic and fun and take about two hours of driving time round-trip; it just depends on whether you prefer sweeping mountain views or otherworldly underground sights.

▶ If you're headed up to the mountains, stop at the Rincon Market on your way out of town and pick up a picnic lunch. If you take a trip to the caverns, stop afterwards at the Horseshoe Café in Benson for lunch. Either way you go, you'll likely get back to town in the late afternoon if you get an early start.

▶ Once back downtown, head to Old Town Artisans to have a few drinks in the lush courtyard and check out the shops.

▶ For your final dinner in Tucson, go to Mi Nidito or La Fuente, where you'll be sent home with the brassy sounds of mariachi ringing in your sunburned ears.

SONORAN DESERT ADVENTURES

There are myriad ways to experience the Sonoran Desert's unique landscape. At the top of the list should be a visit to the **Arizona-Sonora Desert Museum.** On your way to the museum you'll drive through **Tucson Mountain Park,** where some of the largest saguaro stands in the world are protected.

Both sections of **Saguaro National Park** have some of the oldest and largest saguaros in the desert. Consider hiking the many desert trails around the park, or visit one of Tucson's many stables, where you can hire a horse to do the work for you.

To see how just a small but steady amount of water can change the desert into a relatively verdant Eden, make sure to visit **Sabino Canyon Recreation Area.**

To learn about the various ways the indigenous peoples of Southern Arizona have adapted to life in the desert, check out the **Arizona State Museum;** and to learn how other cultures have learned (or failed to learn) to live in this harsh land, check out the **Arizona Historical Society Museum.**

For gifts, souvenirs, food, and other items related to the desert, make sure to visit **Native Seeds/SEARCH,** and if you want to eat a gourmet meal prepared with ingredients unique to the desert, try the high-end restaurants **Janos** and the **Ventana Room at Loews Ventana Canyon.**

Saguaro National Park East and the Santa Catalina Mountains

SIGHTS

Many of Tucson's attractions are meant to provide easy access to, and to put a human-made frame around, the exotic natural beauty of the Sonoran Desert, one of the rarest and strangest landscapes in North America. Even the Old Pueblo's most urban sights—art museums and galleries, historic neighborhoods, the ruins of lost civilizations—must be seen and judged within the context of how their creators, residents, and builders adapted and responded to the area's unique, often harsh environment.

Sightseeing in and around Tucson, you'll discover not only the arid beauty of a mythic landscape, but also a kind of living timeline of a region that has been home to many different, often contradictory cultures going back at least 12,000 years.

You'll see the left-behind evidence of the Hohokam, desertland farmers who lived here long before the Spanish came to the New World. You'll learn the lifeways of the Tohono O'odham, and the Apache, who fought the Spanish, the Mexicans, the Americans, and each other for the right to make a life in this forbidding land. You'll see the remains of the Spanish, who were building whitewashed missions and ranching the region's fertile river valleys back when Jamestown was just somebody's crazy idea. Everywhere you go you'll feel and see the influence of Mexico, just an hour or so south of the city: The language, the culture, and the food of that dynamic nation infuse Tucson and its environs quite thoroughly. And you'll also see evidence of

HIGHLIGHTS

LOOK FOR TO FIND RECOMMENDED SIGHTS.

(Best Museum: See the art and artifacts left behind by the many cultures who have called this desert home at the **Tucson Museum of Art and Historic Block** (page 33).

(Best Time Spent for Free: The **University of Arizona Museum of Art** has an excellent collection and it's all for free (page 35).

(Best In-Town Walk: At the **Tucson Botanical Gardens,** stroll through the varied gardens that are cool and quiet, yet right in the heart of town (page 36).

(Best Artist-Built Gallery: Even if you aren't a fan of famous artist Ted DeGrazia's impressionistic work, you must visit the **DeGrazia Gallery in the Sun** to see the romantic home he built in the desert (page 37).

(Best Place to See Water in the Desert: At **Sabino Canyon Recreation Area,** a famous riparian area will change your idea about aridity (page 38).

(Best Place to Learn About the Desert: The world-famous **Arizona-Sonora Desert Museum** is both a museum and zoo, where you can learn about the general struc-

ture and the minute details of the surrounding desert and see live native animals in a tame environment (page 42).

(Best Place to See the Desert: At **Saguaro National Park West** you can really get to know the saguaro and its desert compatriots; also check out the eastern section of the park (page 44).

(Best Historical Site: **San Xavier del Bac,** called the "white dove of the desert," is considered by many to be the foremost example of mission architecture remaining in the United States (page 48).

(Best Adventure With Kids: At **Colossal Cave Mountain Park** you can tour an old cave (once a hideout for Old West bandits), ride horses, say hello to ancient tortoises, and much more (page 51).

(Best Place to Outrun the Heat: On the **Sky Island Scenic Byway,** an hour-long scenic drive takes you from the desert to an ecosystem akin to Canada's (page 58).

(Best Reminder of the Cold War: Learn about Tucson's past as a nuclear missile hot spot at the **Titan Missile Museum** (page 59).

© TIM HULL

A mountain lion relaxes at the Arizona-Sonora Desert Museum.

the American pioneers, who began moving into the valley about 150 years ago, and their generations-long efforts to create a pretty typical American city in a decidedly atypical environment. Most of all, though, you will see the land. Its secrets may seep into your soul, and you may find yourself irrevocably changed because of it.

SIGHTS

Downtown and University District   Map 1

ARIZONA STATE MUSEUM

1013 E. University Blvd., 520/621-6302,
www.statemuseum.arizona.edu
HOURS: Mon.-Sat. 10 A.M.-5 P.M., Sun. noon-5 P.M.
COST: $3 pp suggested donation

Established in 1893, the Arizona State Museum is the oldest anthropology museum in the Southwest. Here you'll find several rooms of fascinating displays on the state's various Native American tribes, and the world's largest collection of Southwest Indian pottery, including many contemporary pieces that prove pottery-making is certainly not a lost art. Every year in February the museum's grassy grounds play host to the Southwest Indian Art Fair, one of the more important and well attended of such events in the Southwest. A permanent exhibition inside the stately old building explains the origins and histories of 10 of Arizona's Native American groups, including the Hohokam, the O'odham, and the Apache, all of whom ruled Southern Arizona at one time or another.

BARRIO HISTÓRICO

Bordered by Stone Ave., I-10, Cushing St., and 18th St.

The photogenic Sonoran-style row houses in the Barrio Histórico district on the southwest edge of downtown are well adapted to

The Arizona State Museum has a large collection of Native American arts and artifacts.

© TIM HULL

THE HISTORY AND FUTURE OF DOWNTOWN TUCSON

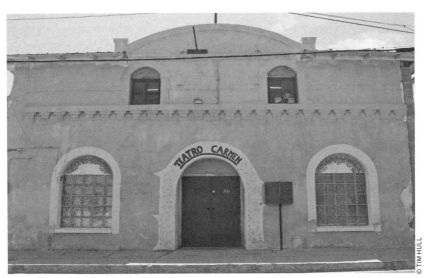

© TIM HULL

an old theater in the Barrio Histórico

Downtown Tucson, where the Old Pueblo began its life as a far-flung outpost of the Spanish crown a year before the eastern colonies declared their independence from the English crown, is a rather contradictory place. While it is overstuffed with all manner of fascinating historical landmarks, plaques, and mini-attractions, not to mention dozens of restaurants, bars, and clubs, most weekdays it's typically as deserted as the farthest corner of the scrubby desert come 5 P.M.

For well over a decade there has been a sometimes robust, often half-hearted, but always vigorously publicized city and state effort to "revitalize" Tucson's downtown and nearby historic districts. The effort, branded Rio Nuevo, has moved along in fits and starts, and in these times of economic belt-tightening it faces, at best, a slow down, and at worst a full-fledged firing squad.

The truth of it is, there's really nothing wrong with downtown that needs fixing. It's already a pretty cool place, if you know where to look. Plus, Tucson doesn't have a good record with urban renewal. Back in the 1960s and '70s, as Tucsonans were increasingly shopping at malls out in the sprawl instead of downtown, the city decided to demolish many blocks of the Barrio Libre in favor of a sprawling convention center. Today, Barrio Histórico, basically what's left of the once large and dynamic Barrio Libre, is among the city's most aesthetically interesting and representative – and certainly most photographed – neighborhoods. Revitalization, as many developers and bureaucrats imagine it, can often be at odds with a city's best interest, which usually can be found not in demolishing and replacing, but in fixing up, patching, building on, and most importantly preserving history.

the desert environment. Their front entrances hug the property line (unlike their Anglo counterparts with large front and back yards) to make space for central courtyards hidden from the street, which provide a shaded outdoor living space within the home. Many of the adobes here have been lovingly and colorfully restored and now serve as offices, working galleries, and private residences. Sometimes called Barrio Viejo (the Old Neighborhood), the barrio has been on the National Register of Historic Places since the 1970s. It dates from the mid-1850s and, as its dominant architecture suggests, has traditionally been a Mexican enclave. Many similar neighborhoods once sprawled out to the edge of the El Presidio district, a large quarter referred to as Barrio Libre (Free Neighborhood), due either to the anything-goes atmosphere in some corners or because the Mexican population was mostly left alone to follow its own rules and culture. Much of the quarter was razed in the late 1960s to make way for the "urban renewal" program that built the Tucson Convention Center. The best examples of the adobe rowhouses can be found along Myer, Main, and Cushing. Along Myer look for the old Teatro Carmen, a now-empty Spanish-language theater that opened in 1915. The adobe building, which over the years would become a movie house, a boxing arena, and an Elks Lodge, still retains the charm and historic interest that once pervaded this district.

THE DIAMONDBACK BRIDGE

Spanning Broadway Blvd. near Euclid

Artist Simon Donovan completed this rather literal work of public art in 2002 to be a kind of memorable entrance to downtown. The Diamondback Bridge, spanning Broadway Boulevard just as the busy street dips into the central city, has since become a popular local landmark, winning in 2003 the prestigious American Public Works Project of the Year. The pedestrian bridge, which looks like a monster-sized rattlesnake taking it easy (albeit

The Diamondback Bridge, at the entrance to Tucson's downtown, always has its jaws open.

with his jaw perpetually stretched open), is 300 feet long and cost about $2.7 million to build. There's a small, pleasant park on either end of the snake. The easiest way to see it is to pull over at Euclid and Broadway, park, and walk across. Just after the snake bridge as you enter downtown, you'll see huge black-and-white photographs on the sides of the underpass. These are actual photos from the 1940s and '50s of Tucsonans walking, shopping, and generally bustling about downtown, back when it used to be a place where people did such things.

EL PRESIDIO PARK AND
PIMA COUNTY COURTHOUSE

115 N. Church Ave.

HOURS: El Presidio Park daily 6 A.M.–10:30 P.M.;
Pima County Courthouse Mon.-Fri. 8:30 A.M.–noon
and 1–5 P.M.

The 80-year-old Pima County Courthouse has a sea-green tiled dome that is a landmark of the Old Pueblo's modest skyline, and it's worth a walk around the grounds of the city's government beehive to take in the Spanish colonial revival touches and, on weekdays, to see downtown at its most industrious. On the weekends, especially in the summer, you'll likely find the area mostly deserted but still inviting. Walk across the front courtyard through a few arches and you'll be in El Presidio Park, with its fountains and memorial to the Mormon Battalion, which occupied the presidio briefly in late 1846. There are also memorials and statues in this large urban government-center park honoring WWII veterans, John F. Kennedy, and various pioneers of the Old West. There's usually a hot-dog cart on the plaza on weekdays, and plenty of opportunities for people-watching and shade.

EL PRESIDIO REAL DE
SAN AGUSTÍN DEL TUCSON

Corner of Washington and Church Sts., 520/884-4214,
www.tucsonpresidiotrust.org

HOURS: Wed.-Sun. 9 A.M.–4:30 P.M.

COST: Free

Experts on the history, lifeways, and architecture

Pima County Courthouse's Moorish dome

© TIM HULL

© TIM HULL

El Presidio Real de San Agustín del Tucson

of the original Spanish settlers of the Tucson valley have re-created a portion of the old Presidio de San Agustín del Tucson at the downtown corner of Washington and Church Streets. Within the newly raised adobe walls there's a large, realistic mural depicting daily life in and around the fort; the details are all historically accurate, and there are a few dark, cool adobe rooms set up in period style to show visitors what life was like on the far, lonely northern edge of the Spanish Empire circa 1776, when an Irishman working for the crown rode north to Tucson from Tubac to establish the fort in an effort to outrun Apache predations. During the week parking is available in a nearby parking garage on Alameda Street; metered parking is available on nearby streets. On weekends, street parking is free.

EL TIRADITO SHRINE

221 S. Main Ave.

Roadside shrines are common in Southern Arizona even in the most out-of-the-way places, but only one is dedicated to a folk saint who was, by the church's standards, an unredeemed sinner. El Tiradito (The Castaway) dates to the 1870s, when Juan Oliveras, a young shepherd, fell in love with his mother-in-law and the two gave in to an illicit passion. They were discovered by her ax-wielding husband, who killed Oliveras and tossed his dead body away on the land that now holds the shrine (such is the tradition, anyway). The church wouldn't allow the doomed lover to be buried on consecrated land, so the people of the barrio interred him where he was "cast away" and erected a shrine. Some say that if you make a wish at the shrine by night and leave a lit candle, and you find it still burning in the morning, your wish will come true—this is why it's sometimes called the Wishing Shrine. Next door to the shrine is La Pilita, an old adobe house that now holds a small museum and store selling handmade items by local school children, with a few exhibits on local history created by neighborhood kids. There's an excellent mural on the south

© TIM HULL

El Tiradito (The Castaway) shrine

wall that tells the story of Tucson's Mexican-American community.

4TH AVENUE
4th Ave., 520/624-5004, www.fourthavenue.org

Lined with chic thrift stores, exotic clothing boutiques, smoke shops, ethnic food restaurants, and cocktail lounges, this is an ideal place to people-watch, and there are some really good places to eat and many treasures to be found in the quirky shops. Beware the young men and women of the bohemian persuasion who spend their days panhandling along the street. Twice a year, in spring and fall, the area closes to vehicle traffic for a street fair featuring artisan booths, concerts, and greasy food galore. Located between downtown and the university district, 4th Avenue is just a short walk from campus, and on Friday and Saturday nights you can expect hordes of college kids out looking for inebriation. It's best to avoid driving in this area on weekend nights altogether. The **Old Pueblo Trolley** (520/792-1802, 6–10 p.m. Fri., noon–midnight Sat., $1 adult each way, $0.50 kids 6–12), a historic electric streetcar, runs from 4th Avenue to University Boulevard and on to the University of Arizona's Main Gate. The trolley also runs noon–6 p.m. on Sunday, when the fare drops to $0.25 each way for everyone. You can board the trolley at various marked stops along the route.

ST. AUGUSTINE CATHEDRAL
192 S. Stone Ave., 520/623-6351,
www.staugustinecathedral.com

Facing Stone Avenue on the eastern edge of Barrio Histórico in downtown, this cathedral dedicated to Tucson's patron saint was built in 1896 and remodeled several times over the years. The facade has stone-carved yucca, saguaro, and horned-toad flourishes, and there are statues of the Virgin Mary and the titular saint near the big heavy-wood entrance. Catholics or anyone interested in regional variations on the Mass may want to attend the lively mariachi mass at 8 a.m. every Sunday. Inside,

© TIM HULL

The craftsmen who built St. Augustine Cathedral spared no detail.

one of the bells formerly used in the Spanish-era cathedral is preserved in the vestibule.

◖ TUCSON MUSEUM OF ART AND HISTORIC BLOCK

140 N. Main Ave., 520/624-2333,
www.tucsonmuseumofart.org
HOURS: Tues.-Sat. 10 A.M.-4 P.M., Sun. noon-4 A.M.
COST: $8 adult, $6 senior, $3 student

The Tucson Museum of Art's permanent collection is heavy with mysterious artifacts of the Americas prior to Columbus's arrival in the New World, the art of the American West, and contemporary art with a Latin flavor. This is a good place to introduce yourself to that tri-cultural mixing that makes Southern Arizona unique. Together known as the "historic block," five historic homes built in the last half of the 19th century survive next to the museum. Just beyond the museum's wide Main Avenue entrance is the oldest of the historic block's buildings (and probably the oldest building in Tucson), La Casa Cordova, its

two west rooms built several years before the Gadsden Purchase made Tucson part of the United States in 1854. The home is a perfect example of the style of Mexican townhouse that once lined the city's core, with its central courtyard and entrance right on the street. A shady courtyard behind the museum's main building, the Plaza of Pioneers has a wall honoring Tucson pioneers from the Spanish, Mexican, and American periods.

UNIVERSITY OF ARIZONA

Campbell Ave. and 3rd St. (eastern entrance), Park Ave. and University Blvd. (western entrance), 520/621-2211, www.arizona.edu

Since it was founded in 1885 as the first institution of higher learning in the Arizona Territory, the University of Arizona's fate and that of its host pueblo have been inextricably linked. It's difficult to imagine what Tucson would be without the shady central campus. A "Public Ivy" land-grant school that has educated countless Arizona leaders and citizens, UA has nearly 37,000 students (more than the number of residents of most Arizona towns) and is active in the U.S. space program, specifically in Mars exploration. Not surprisingly, the school is world-renowned for its arid land research, and has an allopathic medical school founded by best-selling healer-doctor Andrew Weil. It's also the place where anthropology, archaeology, and many other disciplines were revolutionized through the discovery of tree-ring dating.

The university is also becoming known for contributing to space exploration in a big way. Check out the displays on the HiRISE Mars Camera, the Phoenix Mars Lander, and Cassini mission to Saturn at the **Sonett Visitor Center** (northwest corner of University Blvd. and Cherry St., 520/626-7432, Mon.–Fri. 9 A.M.–5 P.M.).

On campus you'll find a number of museums and galleries, and the entire campus itself is an arboretum. Indeed, the green central campus claims to be the "oldest continually maintained green space in Arizona." Flora enthusiasts can stroll around the campus and take in a cactus garden, a collection of rare tropical trees, and

HOWARD HUGHES IN TUCSON

Everybody's heard about those weird few years that Howard Hughes spent hiding out on the top floor of a Las Vegas hotel, going mad.

Well, there are hints that the Old Pueblo could have been the site of Hughes's infamous hideout instead of Vegas. Bob Maheu, Hughes's right-hand man and official public face during the Vegas years, told Geoff Schumacher, author of the 2008 book *Howard Hughes: Power, Paranoia, and Palace Intrigue,* that in the mid-'60s, before moving to Vegas, Hughes first considered moving to Tucson, where he'd already set up a manufacturing plant in 1951.

Hughes loved the desert, considering it free of the germs that stalked him. There's a great scene in *The Aviator* in which the young Hughes, played by Leonardo DiCaprio, sees a stand of saguaros in a film he's watching and whispers something like, "So clean..." Ultimately, though, Hughes soured on the desert around Las Vegas due to his inability to stop nuclear testing at the Nevada Test Site, fallout from which he obsessively feared.

While he never moved to Tucson, Hughes did of course have a presence here. Hughes Aircraft, employing thousands of workers, built the Falcon, the world's first air-to-air guided missile, and many other missiles and weapons here. Hughes Missile Systems was eventually bought up by Raytheon, which is today Southern Arizona's largest private employer.

various arid land species that have been brought to UA from all over the world. If you want to learn more about the campus's natural wonders, go by the **Campus Arboretum** at Herring Hall (520/621-7074, http://arboretum.arizona.edu, Mon.–Fri. 9 A.M.–5 P.M.). Don't miss the Joseph Wood Krutch Cactus Garden in the center of the campus's long, grassy mall.

There are also numerous public art installations on campus. One that should not be missed is the hulking border commentary called **Border Dynamics,** created by artists Alberto Morackis and Guadalupe Serrano. It's not always easy to find parking on campus, and it's impossible during sporting events. Visitors can pay to park at the Park Avenue Garage at

University of Arizona campus from above

© TIM HULL

Border Dynamics, by artists Alberto Morackis and Guadalupe Serrano, on the University of Arizona campus

the corner of Park and Helen Street, and at the Main Gate Parking Garage at Euclid Avenue and East 2nd Street.

◖ THE UNIVERSITY OF ARIZONA MUSEUM OF ART

UA campus near Park Ave. and Speedway Blvd., 520/621-7567, www.artmuseum.arizona.edu

HOURS: Tues.-Fri. 9 A.M.-5 P.M., Sat.-Sun. noon-4 P.M.

COST: Free

This museum's permanent collection has mostly minor (but still worth seeing) works by Tintoretto, Piazzetta, Goya, Bruegel, Rodin, Picasso, Hopper, Pollock, Rothko, O'Keeffe, and many more. Asian and Latin American traditions are also well represented. Special shows often feature the work of well-known local artists and artists from Mexico. The museum has an impressive collection of Spanish Medieval art, the signature piece of which is the 26-panel Retablo of the Cathedral of the Ciudad Rodrigo, an altarpiece depicting the sweep of biblical events from Genesis through the life of Jesus Christ to the Last Judgment.

Midtown   Map 2

REID PARK ZOO

100 S. Randolph Way, 520/791-4022, www.tucsonzoo.org

HOURS: Daily 9 A.M.-4 P.M.

COST: $6 adult, $4 senior, $2 child 2-14

Take Broadway Boulevard east to Randolph Way at Reid Park to Tucson's small but prestigious zoo. The zoo specializes in anteater research, and there are several of these strange beasts to look at here. There's also a polar bear, Boris, who seems to be very happy living in what you'd think would be the absolute opposite circumstances in which a polar bear would want to find himself. Not so, zookeepers say. The arctic, a cold desert, is actually drier than Tucson, so as long as they keep the air-conditioning pumping and his water hole cold he'll be staying for years. Make sure to take the kids to the giraffe habitat, where for $1 they can buy some treats to feed the long-necked residents, who stick out their long, purple tongues, dripping with saliva, to capture the treat—much to the squealing delight of the feeders. A gift shop sells all kinds of zoo-related stuffed animals, shirts, and books, and a fast food–style eatery serves hamburgers, corn dogs, and the like. If you get there early enough you might catch a glimpse of the elegant black jaguars, sisters born at a wildlife park outside of Phoenix, lounging in the cool of the morning. The zoo is small enough that little kids aren't likely to get too tired out. Plan about three hours, less if you don't have kids.

◀ TUCSON BOTANICAL GARDENS

2150 N. Alvernon Way, 520/326-9686,
www.tucsonbotanical.org
HOURS: Daily 8:30 A.M.–4:30 P.M.
COST: $7 adult, $3 child 4-12

Gardeners and anybody who appreciates beauty should stop at this midtown oasis for a few hours. Flat walking trails wind around the nearly six-acre property, which feels secluded and hidden away even though it's right in the path of busy midtown. There are benches throughout on which to sit and contemplate the various gardens—16 in all, each one showcasing a different gardening tradition. Especially lovely is the Mexican-influenced garden, Nuestro Jardín (Our Garden), with its shrine of the Virgin of Guadalupe and found items. A cactus and succulent garden has examples of cacti not just from the nearby deserts but also from around the world, and the xeriscape garden demonstrates how you can grow desert-adapted plants without using a lot of water. If you go between October and March you'll get to see Butterfly Magic, a live tropical butterfly exhibit. Call ahead for times and availability.

Included in the price of admission you can take advantage of one of several tours of the gardens. Different tours are offered throughout the month, and not every tour is offered every day, so it's best to call ahead or check the website. The Garden Gallery has rotating art shows that can be viewed daily 8:30 A.M.–4:30 P.M.

© TIM HULL

Tucson Botanical Gardens

The Foothills

Map 3

DEGRAZIA GALLERY IN THE SUN

6300 N. Swan Rd., 520/299-9191, www.degrazia.org

HOURS: Daily 10 A.M.-4 P.M.

COST: Free

I used to turn up my nose at Ettore "Ted" DeGrazia. His little sad-eyed native children are ubiquitous here, on mugs and Christmas ornaments and whatever else, and all the work seemed to me to look the same and offer little in the way of depth. A visit to DeGrazia's amazing foothills home and gallery, which he largely built himself, changed my opinion of the artist. When you see the home he built, and get a close-up look at the more serious paintings that hang throughout the gallery— epic cycles about the Mexican Revolution, the "founding" of the Southwest by Cabeza de Vaca and his doomed companions, and the lives and traditions of Tohono O'odham, to name just a few—you may conclude, as I did, that, far from being a hack, DeGrazia actually created some of the most enduring impressionistic visions in the Southwest. A native of Southern Arizona, DeGrazia attended the UA and published his first work in *Arizona Highways* magazine. He went on to study in Mexico with muralists Diego Rivera and Jose Clemente Orozco. He died in 1982 at the age of 73, but the DeGrazia Foundation carries on his memory at the Gallery in the Sun, DeGrazia's first studio and gallery in Tucson, built in honor of Padre Kino and dedicated to Our Lady of Guadalupe. A mission on the grounds features DeGrazia murals, with a roof open to the sky. The gallery has a gift shop stocked with DeGrazia reproductions for sale. Even if you can't muster an appreciation of this admittedly overexposed artist's work, go for the native architecture and design to be found at his Gallery in the Sun, which may, after all, be DeGrazia's greatest work of art.

Ettore DeGrazia's work room at DeGrazia Gallery in the Sun

Ettore DeGrazia built this chapel near his studio and dedicated it to the Virgin of Guadalupe.

SIGHTS

◖ SABINO CANYON RECREATION AREA

520/749-8700, www.fs.fed.us/r3/coronado/forest/recreation/camping/sites/sabino.shtml

HOURS: Recreation area daily sunrise-sunset; visitors center and bookstore Mon.-Fri. 8 A.M.-4:30 P.M., Sat. 8:30 A.M.-4:30 P.M.

COST: $5 per car for one day, $10 for a week, $20 for annual pass

Though in the range's foothills, Sabino Canyon is inextricably linked to the Santa Catalinas because without the mountains there would be very little water to fill up Sabino Creek, and without Sabino Creek this Edenic desert canyon would be just another rugged notch dominated by saguaro. As it is, though, Sabino Creek starts as springs high up in the mountains, gathering snowmelt and runoff as it descends into the foothills, where it rushes through Sabino Canyon with sometimes-deadly vigor, creating a riparian oasis of cottonwoods, willow, walnut, sycamore, and ash, while saguaro, barrel cactus, prickly pear, and cholla dominate the rocky canyon slopes away from the creek's influence. It is a truly spectacular place that should not be missed. Sabino Canyon Recreation Area, about 13 miles northeast of downtown Tucson, is easily accessible, user-friendly in the extreme, and heavily used—best estimates say 1.25 million people visit every year. Many locals use the canyon's trail system for daily exercise, and hikers, picnickers, and sightseers usually pack the canyon on any given day in any given season. A paved road, closed to cars since 1978, rises nearly four miles up into the canyon, crossing the nearly always-running creek in several places. During Southern Arizona's summer and winter rainy seasons, it is nearly impossible to cross the small overflowing bridges without getting your feet wet. It's a relatively easy walk along the road to the top of the canyon and access to trails that go far into the Santa Catalinas. The Sabino Canyon Visitors Center and Bookstore has trail guides and sells gifts and books. There are bathrooms, drinking fountains, and dozens of tucked-away picnic areas throughout the canyon, and many of the trails link up with one another, so it is easy to cobble together a loop hike that will take you through all of the various life zones. Bikes are allowed in the canyon only before 9 A.M. and after 5 P.M., never on Wednesday and Saturday, and never on trails that lead into the Pusch Ridge Wilderness Area. If you don't feel like walking to the many

SABINO CANYON SHUTTLE

If you don't feel like walking to the many popular trailheads in the Sabino Canyon Recreation Area, or if you don't want to walk up the paved road to see the upper reaches of the gorgeous riparian canyon, consider a ride on the Sabino Canyon Shuttle (520/749-2861, www.sabinocanyon.com, $8 adult, $4 child 3-12, free under 2). The shuttle runs 45-minute narrated trips into the canyon all day, pausing at nine stops along the way to pick up or drop off hikers at various trailheads. From July through mid-December the shuttle runs Monday-Friday 9 A.M.-4 P.M. and Saturday-Sunday and holidays 9 A.M.-4:30 P.M. From mid-December to June it runs daily 9 A.M.-4:30 P.M. At the last tram stop 3.8 miles into the canyon, hikers can get off and take an easy stroll down the road, crossing the creek at nearly every turn, or try the Phoneline Trail, which winds along the canyon slopes overlooking the riparian beauty below. Perhaps the most popular trail in the entire Tucson valley is the hike through nearby Bear Canyon to Seven Falls, a wonderful series of waterfalls and collecting pools. You can access the Bear Canyon Trail from just outside the visitors center, or take the shuttle to a trailhead 1.5 miles on. From the trailhead to the falls it's a total of 3.8 miles one-way, and worth every step. The Bear Canyon shuttle leaves the visitors center every hour on the hour, daily 9 A.M.-4 P.M. ($3 adult, $1 child 3-12).

© TIM HULL

Sabino Canyon Recreation Area

popular trailheads here, consider a ride on the Sabino Canyon Shuttle (520/749-2861, www.sabinocanyon.com, $7.50 adult, $3 child 3–12, free under 2).

ST. PHILIP'S IN THE HILLS EPISCOPAL CHURCH

4440 N. Campbell Ave., 520/299-6421, www.stphilipstucson.org

This church was originally designed in 1936 by Josias Joesler, a Swiss-born architect who designed the majority of the tony foothills structures and is responsible for the amalgam of native and revival architecture sometimes known as the Tucson Style. Joesler's structures can be counted on to mimic Mexican, Spanish, and Moorish styles with upscale flourishes, many of them stylish desertland haciendas on the bajada of the Catalinas, an area long reserved for the region's wealthy. A longtime Tucson architect once told me that Tucson, at least when it came to architecture,

divorced itself from Mexico (and thereby Spain and its Moorish traditions) too quickly; these styles, with their courtyards and native materials and passive solar heating, are ideal for living in the hot, dry Sonoran Desert, certainly much better than the cheaply built tract homes that proliferate in the valley these days. Very few Tucsonans build homes in the Joesler style anymore (to do so, or to live in one that's already extant, is out of the financial question for most of us), and that's too bad, because Joesler, like the originals he was inspired by, had it right. St. Philip's, my favorite of all Joesler's structures in Tucson, is along the busy River Road corridor and yet retains a peaceful atmosphere with gardens and fountains and thick, silent walls. The building and grounds have been added to and changed over the years, but always with respect to the original vision. Church officials welcome visitors and students of architecture and anybody else who wants to look around. It's best not to go on a Sunday if you're just

© TIM HULL

St. Philip's in the Hills Episcopal Church, designed by Josias Joesler, is one of many Mexican- and Spanish-inspired buildings in Tucson.

looking, and it's best to go before 4 P.M. week-days if you want to talk to someone about the church and its history.

TOHONO CHUL PARK

7366 N. Paseo del Norte, 520/742-6455,
www.tohonochulpark.org
HOURS: Daily 8 A.M.–5 P.M.
COST: $5 adult, $4 senior, $3 student, $2 child 5-12

This 49-acre desert preserve is worth the short drive north on Oracle Road out into Tucson's sprawl. Turn left on Ina Road, and then right on Paseo del Norte, and you'll find native-plant gardens with easy trails punctuated by interpretive signs. The Ethnobotanical Garden, with rows of maize and other crops once planted by the O'odham and the Spanish settlers, demonstrates the different methods used by each group to coax subsistence out of the dry ground. Kids will love floating little boats shaped like fish on the miniature stream in the Garden for Children, where they can also see some old desert tortoises lolling about. If you stay quiet and sit by one of the many fountains or other water features on the grounds, you might get a glimpse of the many bobcats or javelina that call the preserve home.

One night a year, in June or July, the gar-den's night-blooming cereus comes to life, an event so rare and spectacular that there's a hotline (520/575-8468) for visitors to keep up-to-date on the expected bloom. There are gift shops and galleries on the property, and exhibits generally feature Native American and Mexican folk and fine arts. Don't miss the locally famous scones at the **Tohono Chul Park Tea Room** (520/797-1222, daily 8 A.M.–5 P.M., $2.95–12), a perfect place to lounge after exploring the grounds.

East Side and the Rincon Valley — Map 4

SAGUARO NATIONAL PARK EAST

3693 S. Old Spanish Trail, 520/733-5153

HOURS: Daily 7 A.M.-sunset, visitors center daily 9 A.M.-5 P.M.

COST: $10 per car, receipt valid for seven days, good at both sections

The eastern portion of Saguaro National Park is backed by the 8,600-foot Rincon Mountains. At the visitors center are a bookstore and exhibits about the desert. The easiest way to see this section is to stroll, bike, or drive very slowly along the paved Cactus Forest Drive, an eight-mile one-way that begins at the visitors center and winds up and across the bajada. The desert here is gorgeous, especially after a rainstorm or early in the morning during the bloom months (Mar.–May, July–Aug.). There are more than 100 miles of trails here, including one that goes to Rincon Peak above 8,000 feet. The park's newspaper guide has a full description of the major trails.

TRAIL DUST TOWN

6541 E. Tanque Verde Rd., 520/296-5442, www.traildusttown.com

HOURS: Daily 5-8 P.M.

COST: $1-2 for each attraction

The best way to visit Trail Dust Town, an Old West–themed family attraction on the east side, is to wrap it up with a cowboy steak-and-beans dinner at Pinnacle Peak Steak House. But if you don't have kids, rethink the entire venture. I'm not saying that there's nothing for the adult at Trail Dust Town; anyone interested in the more popularized notions of Old West culture might get a kick or two here—there's

© TIM HULL

Saguaro National Park East

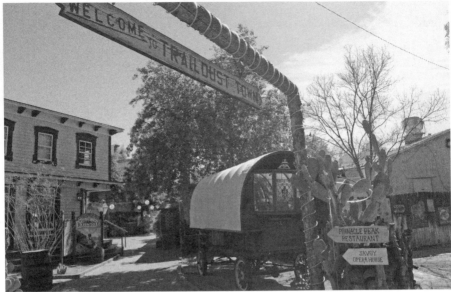

Trail Dust Town is an Old West-themed family attraction.

some movie set–style buildings, a miniature train that circles the property, a few on-cue gunfights in the dusty streets, and various shops and displays featuring touristy gifts and frontier artifacts; there's a gold-panning game, a shootout gallery, and a lot of other commotion. If you have young or even youngish children, though, you and the spouse can sit in the saloon and wait for your table while the kids explore the attractions.

West Side and the Tucson Mountains   Map 5

◀ ARIZONA-SONORA DESERT MUSEUM
2021 N. Kinney Rd., 520/883-2702,
www.desertmuseum.org
HOURS: Mar.–Sept. daily 7:30 A.M.–5 P.M. (until 10 P.M.
Sat. June–Aug.), Oct.–Feb. daily 7:30 A.M.–5 P.M.
COST: $12 adult, $4 child 6-12

A big part of the fun of a visit to the Arizona-Sonora Desert Museum is the getting there. Driving west out of Tucson over dramatic Gates Pass, you'll see thousands of sentinel-like saguaros standing tall on the hot, rocky ground below, surrounded by pipe cleaner–like ocotillo and fuzzy cholla, creosote, and prickly pear. But the saguaro forests of Tucson Mountain

Park and Saguaro National Park West, both of which surround the Desert Museum, are only one of several distinctive desert life zones you'll see and learn about at this world-famous museum and zoo, where native mammals, birds, reptiles, amphibians, fish, and arthropods live in displays mimicking their open-desert habitats. This is the best place to learn about both the general structure and the minute details of the surrounding desert, and probably your only realistic chance to see all of the unique creatures that call it home. Easy trails wind through the beautiful 21-acre preserve, passing exhibits on semidesert grasslands and

© TIM HULL

© TIM HULL

A bighorn sheep relaxes in the shade at the Arizona-Sonora Desert Museum.

mountain woodlands similar to those surrounding and growing on the Sonoran Desert's high mountain ranges. The Desert Loop Trail leads through a lowland scrub and cacti landscape with javelina and coyote. In Cat Canyon, a bespeckled ocelot sleeps in the shade and a bobcat lounges on the rocks. A mountain lion can be seen close up through a viewing window, and a black bear strolls along a man-made stream and sleeps on a rock promontory. There are also rare Mexican wolves, white-tailed deer, bighorn sheep, and adorable prairie dogs with which to commune. A riparian habitat has beavers and otters, water lovers that were once abundant in the Southwest. There's a desert garden exhibit, a cactus and succulent garden, and a butterfly and wildflower display. There are also displays on desert fish, dunes, and a walk-in aviary that holds dozens of native birds. Docents are scattered throughout the complex to help with questions and give presentations on special topics. All this, plus a restaurant, snack bars, and a gift shop that sells excellent Pueblo and Tohono O'odham crafts

make the Desert Museum Tucson's very best attraction. If you're planning on doing any exploring in the desert, do so after a trip to the Desert Museum, where you'll get a comprehensive mini-course in desert ecology.

OLD TUCSON STUDIOS

201 S. Kinney Rd., 520/883-0100, www.oldtucson.com
HOURS: Daily 10 A.M.–6 P.M.
COST: $16.95 adult, $10.95 child 4-11

Since 1939 Old Tucson has been the setting for more than 400 film productions, the majority of them Westerns. It was originally constructed to make the film *Arizona,* starring Jean Arthur and William Holden, which tells the story of Tucson's early days before and after the Civil War. In the 1950s, impresario Bob Shelton bought the disused property and rebuilt its circa-1860s town, again drawing productions west from Hollywood, several starring Shelton's friend John Wayne. It remained popular as a movie set as long as Westerns were popular at the box office, and so went through boom and bust periods along with the genre. Shelton

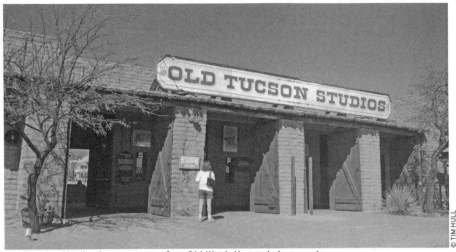

© TIM HULL

Old Tucson Studios is now more of an Old West-themed show park.

added gunfight shows and other family-oriented tourist attractions to ride out the lean times. Today a rebuilt Old Tucson (the town burned to the ground in the 1990s) concentrates on re-creating a movie-house version of the Old West for tourists. Make sure to check out the collection of vintage posters from the films produced at the studio. Tours talk about the history of the studio and the stars who walked its dusty streets, and musical acts and vaudeville-style revues go on all day. There are several restaurants on-site, including Big Jake's, which serves up good barbecue and beans, and El Vaquero, offering Southwestern-style entrées and a wide variety of specialty drinks. Unless you're a Western-film buff, Old Tucson is a little stale. If you're into the genre you'll find the film-related aspects worth a look. Kids might enjoy it, but the entry price is rather expensive for what you get.

SAGUARO NATIONAL PARK WEST
2700 N. Kinney Rd., 520/733-5158, www.nps.gov/sagu
HOURS: Daily 7 A.M.–sunset, visitors center daily 9 A.M.–5 P.M.
COST: $10 per car, receipt valid for seven days, good at both sections
This is where the icon of arid America holds court. The split Saguaro National Park has a western section at the base of the Tucson Mountains and a larger eastern section at the base of the Rincon Mountains. Both are worth visiting, but if you have time only for one go to the eastern section, which is older and larger. Together they protect about 91,300 acres of magnificent Sonoran Desert landscape, including large and crowded saguaro forests surrounded by a thick underbrush of ocotillo, prickly pear, cholla, mesquite, and palo verde. If you want to see an accessible and wondrous example of the Sonoran Desert at its best, there are few better places to go. The place to start your tour of the western park is the **Red Hills Visitor Center,** where you can learn about the ancient symbiotic friendship between the Tohono O'odham and the saguaro. Here you'll find a guide to the park's 40 miles of trails, and you can also book a tour with a naturalist and peruse the bookstore stocked with titles on local history and nature. A good way to see the park, especially in the heat of summer, is to drive the six-mile Bajada Loop through a thick saguaro forest. The route is graded dirt and it can get dusty; you can also walk or bike the loop. Or you can drive the loop and stop at the Valley View Overlook Trail, an easy one-

THE SAGUARO AND OTHER NATIVE CACTI

To the native inhabitants of the Sonoran Desert – be they cactus wrens, coyotes, screech owls, or Tohono O'odham tribespeople – the saguaro (pronounced sa-WAH-ro) is much more than a strange-looking plant. It is so supremely adapted to the arid environment, in which moisture from the sky comes but twice a year, that it anchors an entire busy community of living things, providing food and shelter to all sorts of desert creatures. The great cactus-tree grows slowly, and only during the summer rainy season. After living, shaded and protected by a mesquite tree, for 15 years, a saguaro is still only about a foot tall. But, then again, these ribbed green ribbed giants can live to be 150 years old or more, so there's really no hurry. Not until it reaches 75 years old does a saguaro even begin to sprout its identifying arms; so when you see a tall, fat one with many arms, know that it is a venerable old guy, deserving of respect and awe.

The saguaro looks like it does because it is perfect: Every form has a function. Its green skin allows for photosynthesis, normally the job of leaves on less individualistic plants. Its spongy flesh and ribbed contours encourage water storage; from a single rainfall the saguaro can collect and store up to 200 gallons of water, which is enough to get it through the year. Its telltale needles protect it from the incessant gnawing of hungry desert creatures. Its splashy white blossoms (Arizona's official state flower, seen in April, May, and June), and its juicy red fruits (eaten for eons by the desert's native inhabitants) assure the rising of another generation. The best place to commune with these perfectly adapted desert plants is Saguaro National Park near Tucson.

You'll see various other species of cactus throughout the lower and into the upper Sonoran zones. Most cacti are easily recognizable if you know their names: Organ pipe, barrel, beaver tail, claret cup, and hedgehog cactus generally look like their sobriquets suggest, albeit spiky and standoffish versions. The famous prickly pear cactus can be identified by its red fruit-blooms, which are turned into jellies and even maragarita mix.

© TIM HULL

---

mile round-trip trail off the loop road that rises to an expansive view of the Avra Valley, the saguaro-lined desert, and the skulking rock mountains. A half-mile round-trip walk to the Signal Hill Picnic Area offers a look at ancient petroglyphs. Both trails can be accessed off the Bajada Loop drive and are well marked. There are also a few very short, paved walks around the visitors center featuring interpretive signs about the saguaro and other desert fauna.

SENTINEL PEAK AND TUMAMOC HILL

498 S. Sentinel Peak Rd. (Sentinel Peak), Tumamoc Hill Rd. (Tumamoc Hill)

HOURS: Mon.-Sat. 8 A.M.-8 P.M., Sun. 8 A.M.-6 P.M.

Also called "A" Mountain for the large

© TIM HULL

Sentinal Peak (right) and Tumamoc Hill (left)

white—or, since September 11, 2001, red, white, and blue—"A" repainted on its face every year by University of Arizona students (a tradition that began in 1915), Sentinel Peak served the early populations of the Tucson valley with spring water and black basalt. When Father Kino first rode into the valley in the 1690s, he found the native population living in the small peak's shadow, and it was surely an important landmark in the basin for eons before that. During the presidio days it earned its name as a promontory from which soldiers would scan the desert for Apaches. Now there's a park on the peak, reached by a paved, winding road to the top: Take Congress Street west under I-10 and follow the signs. There are a few short trails around the park, a little rock shelter to sit under, charcoal barbecues, and some great views of the valley. The hill just to the north of Sentinel Peak is called Tumamoc (horned-lizard) Hill, and is home to a living-desert laboratory founded in 1903. For thousands of years indigenous residents of the Tucson valley farmed on and around Tumamoc Hill, as evidenced by numerous archaeological sites found there. Among the legends of the Tohono O'odham is the story of a giant horned lizard that threatened to devour the tribe had not the god I'itoi, in response to

prayers, turned the great reptile into a hill—hence the name Tumamoc Hill.

TUCSON MOUNTAIN PARK AND GATES PASS SCENIC OVERLOOK

Take Speedway west from downtown over Gates Pass to Kinney Rd.

HOURS: Daily 7 A.M.–10 P.M.

Robert Gates was a typical Southwestern frontier entrepreneur: He did a little mining, a little ranching, a bit of saloon keeping, some homesteading. In 1883, in order to connect his Avra Valley mine with his other interests in Tucson, he set about building a precipitous route over the Tucson Mountains, and in the process set the stage for local officials, about 50 years later, to establish one of the largest public parks of its kind in the nation. Thus we have the 37-square-mile Sonoran Desert preserve called Tucson Mountain Park. The 20,000 acres of wild desert features one of the largest saguaro forests in the world, and has something like 62 miles of trails for hiking and mountain biking. The park has a rifle and pistol range, and three large picnic areas with grills, ramadas, and picnic tables; also within park boundaries is the world-renowned Arizona-Sonora Desert Museum. If all these activities seem a bit sweaty and active for your taste, at least make it to the top of the road named for the man who conquered the comparatively short Tucson Mountains at Gates Pass. You can drive to the pass and park at a large lot with bathrooms and a ramada and two little stacked-rock huts decorated inside with eons of graffiti. There are short trails out to a promontory from which you can see the whole sweeping expanse of the desert below. It's one of the best views in Arizona—a state that has no shortage of sweeping views. If you want to stay the night at the park, the **Gilbert Ray Campground** (8451 W. McCain Loop, off Kinney Rd., 520/883-4200, $10–20) has sites with RV hookups and picnic tables, plus restrooms and a dumping station.

South Side
Map 6

JARDÍN DE CÉSAR CHÁVEZ
Stone Ave. and 6th St.
HOURS: Sunrise-sunset

This tiny park on the edge of South Tucson is dedicated to the Mexican-American labor organizer and human-rights activist (a native of Yuma, Arizona) and is worth seeing for its brilliant mural depicting ancient Aztec gods lounging around and seemingly passing stern judgment on all who pass. Artist Melchor Ramirez, known for painting the heroes and legends of the Aztec and Maya, painted the mural in vibrant yet earthy colors, and the names and dates of well-known human-rights advocates—Tolstoy, Ghandi, etc.—are scrawled alongside the oversized figures. There isn't a parking lot here, but you can park along a small road on the west side of the park. As you drive south on Stone Avenue, look to your right as you approach 6th Street. There are several benches perfect for sitting and contemplating the fascinating paintings as the traffic zips by.

PIMA AIR AND SPACE MUSEUM
6000 E. Valencia Rd., 520/574-0462, www.pimaair.org
HOURS: Daily 9 A.M.–5 P.M.
COST: $11.75 adult, $9.75 senior/military, $8 child 7-12

One of the largest museums of its kind in the West, the Pima Air and Space Museum has interesting exhibits and an impressive

© TIM HULL

mural by Melchor Ramirez at Jardín de César Chávez

number of decommissioned aircraft that tell the story of our fascination with defying gravity. Nearly 300 rare airplanes, many of them ·military—among them Kennedy's Air Force One and the Blackbird spy plane—rest on the grounds and in six different hangars. The Air and Space Museum is operated by the same group that operates the Titan Missile Museum near Green Valley, and for one price you can see both attractions. Warplane enthusiasts will have to take the hour-long bus tour to the Aerospace Maintenance and Regeneration Center (AMARC) to see the hundreds of dust-gathering planes ending their days in this "boneyard."

◖ SAN XAVIER DEL BAC

1950 W. San Xavier Rd., 520/294-2624, www.sanxaviermission.org

HOURS: Daily 8 A.M.–5 P.M.

COST: Free; donations encouraged

Founded in 1692 by Father Eusebio Francisco Kino and then built slowly over decades by other priests, missionaries, and natives, the mission sits pure white against the perpetually blue sky about nine miles south of Tucson on the Tohono O'odham's San Xavier Indian Reservation. It is considered by many to be the foremost example of mission architecture remaining in the United States, blending elements of Moorish, Byzantine, and late Mexican Renaissance architecture. Few Arizona landmarks have received as much worldwide attention as the "white dove of the desert," which has also been called America's answer to the Sistine Chapel. Mass is still celebrated daily in the church (check website for times), but non-Catholic visitors are encouraged and welcomed. Most days there are tables and booths set up in the mission's plaza selling burritos, fry bread, and other delicious eats, and across the wide plaza to the south is San Xavier Plaza, with a snack bar and several shops selling Native American crafts. Statues and paintings of St. Francis Xavier and the Virgin of Guadalupe decorate the cool, dark interior of the domed church. A continuous videotape about the mission runs throughout the day as a self-guided tour, and there's a gift shop on-site that sells religious items and

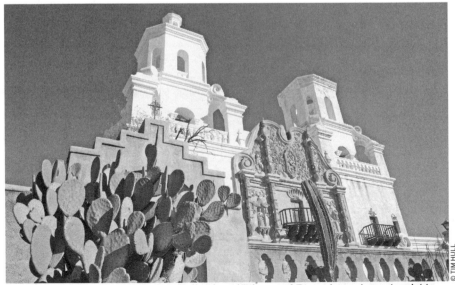

© TIM HULL

San Xavier del Bac (the "white dove in the desert") is one of Tucson's most popular sights.

© TIM HULL

There is a memorial dedicated to the spirit of Native Americans inside San Xavier del Bac.

© TIM HULL

statue of Father Kino at San Xavier del Bac

books about the history of the mission and the region. A small museum presents the history of the area's native inhabitants and the construction and ongoing rehabilitation of the mission. The mission is continually being worked on, but the seemingly ever-present scaffolding doesn't detract too much from its grandeur. In late 2008, the front of the mission was finally revealed again after years of being covered with scaffolding.

Greater Tucson   Map 7

AGUA LINDA FARM

2643 E. Frontage Rd., Amado, 520/398-3218, www.agualindafarm.net

HOURS: Sat. 9 A.M.–3 P.M., Sun. noon–3 P.M.

COST: Free except during festivals

A local leader in the Community Supported Agriculture movement, this small riverside farm in the lush Santa Cruz Valley south of Tucson sells fresh seasonal crops from a farm store open on the weekends. The family-owned farm also puts on several festivals throughout the year, including one in fall involving pumpkin patches and hayrides. There isn't always something going on at Agua Linda, and often the farm is used for private events like weddings. If you're interested in looking around and touring the farm, picking your own vegetables, and generally communing with the fertile land, check the farm's website to make sure there's something happening.

BIOSPHERE 2

32540 S. Biosphere Rd., Oracle, 520/838-6200, www.b2science.org

HOURS: Daily 9 A.M.–4 P.M.

COST: $20 adult, $13 child 6–12

In the early 1990s eight scientists took up

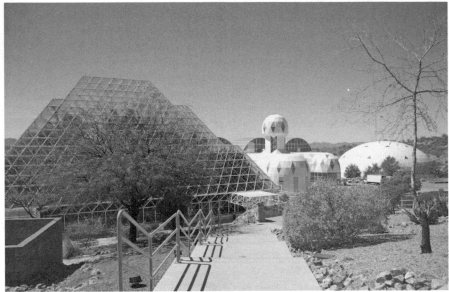

© TIM HULL

Biosphere 2

residence in this 3.14-acre simulation of the earth in hopes of lasting two years and gaining important knowledge about how humans will survive in the future. They weren't able to remain self-contained owing to problems with the food supply, but two members of the team fell in love at least.

The unique laboratory may yet save the world, however, as the UA is now running experiments under the dome and researching ways to combat climate change. While the science is fascinating—there are actually small savannas, rainforests, deserts, and even an ocean under the glass—many who take the tour seem more intrigued by the doomed experiments in togetherness. The tour takes you into the "Biospherians'" apartments and kitchen and guides field more questions on this part of the tour than all the others. The tour lasts about 45 minutes and is not wheelchair-accessible. The Biosphere is in a beautiful 35-acre desert setting about 30 minutes north of Tucson near the small town of Oracle.

BUENOS AIRES NATIONAL WILDLIFE REFUGE

Hwy. 286, milepost 7.5, Sasabe, 520/823-4251, ext. 116, www.fws.gov/southwest/refuges/arizona/buenosaires

HOURS: Refuge open daily 24 hours; visitors center daily 7:30 A.M.–4 P.M., closed weekends June 1–Aug. 15

This remote 118,000-acre refuge preserves large swaths of endangered semidesert grassland, home to the pronghorn. The refuge's flagship program was once the reintroduction of the rare masked bobwhite quail to the grasslands, but the program was transferred to a private organization in 2007. Its proximity to the U.S.-Mexico border has caused some trouble on the refuge, and portions are indefinitely closed to the public because of smuggling activity. One of the most accessible portions of the refuge is the Arivaca Cienega, a swamplike desert wetland just outside the tiny village of Arivaca. The easy two-mile loop trail includes boardwalks over the wetter portions, and birds, frogs, and snakes abound. Take Arivaca Road about 20 miles from I-19 exit 48 until you see the sign for the Cienega, just east of Arivaca. At the western end of town turn at the Y and drive 2.5 miles to Arivaca Creek, also managed by the refuge, where there's easy creekside hiking among cottonwoods and mesquite. Keep on Arivaca Road to Highway 286 and turn left at milepost 7.5 to get to refuge headquarters. Far off to the northwest in the Baboquivari Mountains is Brown Canyon, a riparian area accessible only with a guide and by appointment.

CATALINA STATE PARK
Hwy. 77, milepost 81, Oro Valley, 520/628-5798,
www.azstateparks.com
HOURS: Daily 5 A.M.–10 P.M.
COST: $5 per car

This popular desert preserve just north of Tucson (about 14.5 miles from midtown) in the saguaro-dotted north-side foothills of the Santa Catalinas is heavily used, especially on weekends—hikers shouldn't be surprised to pass large families carrying coolers and bags of chips up the trail. The 5,500-acre park has eight trails—most of them range in difficulty from easy to moderate—picnic areas, charcoal grills, and a small gift shop. It's an easily accessible place to see the desert, lush here thanks to the runoff and snowmelt that barrels down from the mountains through boulder-strewn washes. In the early spring and late summer there are many natural pools that fill up with runoff, some of them deep enough to be called swimming holes. The seven-mile Romero Canyon Trail will take you to an array of natural pools—and you don't have to hike the whole trail to get there. If you want to get off the beaten track a little, veer right about a mile into the trail near a bench and pick your way down into the wash, then head up the wash following a footpath that leads to some out-of-the-way, less-used pools. For an easy walk, take the 0.5-mile round-trip Romero Ruin Interpretive Trail to an ancient Hohokam site. The ranger station–gift shop has a guide to all the park's trails, some of which link to other trails going all the way up into the mountains.

⬛ COLOSSAL CAVE MOUNTAIN PARK
16721 E. Old Spanish Trail, 520/647-7275,
www.colossalcave.com
HOURS: Mar. 16–Sept. 15 daily 8 A.M.–5 P.M.,
Sept. 16–Mar. 15 daily 9 A.M.–5 P.M.
COST: Park entry $5 per car with up to five people; cave tours $8.50 adult, $5 child 6–12

Sure it's a "dead cave," and certainly in recent years it has become but a poor country cousin to the living underground wonderland that is Karchner Caverns State Park just a few dozen miles to the southeast, but Colossal Cave Mountain Park near Vail, about a half-hour drive through the desert east of Tucson proper, has many charms nonetheless. The cave has been used as a shelter, an altar, a hideout, and a tourist attraction by various bands of natives and colonists for the last 1,000 years or so, according to prehistoric artifacts and historic local newspaper accounts. In the 1930s the Civilian Conservation Corps built a few structures near the cave's entrance in that inimitable stacked native-stone style, and installed lights and railings through about a half mile of the sprawling grotto. The typical tour follows this route, while the guide narrates a general natural history of the cave with a bit of human history (including a tale of outlaws) peppered in. It's all very basic, but interesting and really fun, especially with kids. Those looking for a more adventurous route should check out the Saturday-night **Ladder Tour** (5:15–9 P.M., $35 with dinner, must be at least 12 years old and fit, reservations required), on which you'll shimmy and squeeze through passageways far off the tourist path in a helmet and headlamp. After the cave tour, there's a gift shop and a café and long views of the desert. A few miles down the road but still within the park the 130-year-old La Posta Quemada Ranch offers more activities, particularly for children. In addition to trail rides and a gift shop, the ranch features a large sundial, displays on the cave and the CCC's work in the park, and a habitat for two old Desert Tortoises, Henry and Big Nasty. It's unlikely you'll see either tort unless you arrive in the morning, especially during the hotter months. There are plenty of shady and peaceful places to picnic here, and you can even camp if you make a reservation.

SIGHTS

IRONWOOD FOREST NATIONAL MONUMENT

I-19 north to Avra Valley Rd., Marana, 520/258-7200, www.blm.gov

The long-lived tree that lends its name to this 129,000-acre Sonoran Desert preserve about an hour's drive northwest of Tucson is likely to appear a bit underwhelming to the uninitiated. The gray-green monotony of the surface-level desert tends to blur the vision, and one bushy little tree tends to look a lot like another. As it usually is, however, the truth is in the details. The ironwood, which can live 800 years or more, is an anchor for a deceptively busy desert ecosystem, providing shade and succor for a whole host of flora and fauna unique to the region. Like most of Arizona's BLM-monitored National Monuments, Ironwood Forest is a vast and empty place, inviting to hikers and hunters and campers and other outdoor types. There's no visitors center, no campgrounds, no rangers. It is a perfect place for a long daytime drive through the desert on its dirt roads, which are mostly smooth and accepting of regular cars, although an SUV is best. More so than even Saguaro National Park, Ironwood is a place where the wild desert is there for you

to discover—unvarnished, uncultivated, and unforgiving. It's not a good idea to venture out here in the summer. If you want to head out to this wilderness, the easiest way to see it is to drive slowly along the dirt roads that traverse part of the monument, stopping here and there to look into the details. The best way to do this is to take I-19 north to Avra Valley Road, continue southwest on Avra Valley Road until it turns to dirt around the waste-pile remainders of the Silverbell Mine. Just follow the road through the monument, passing the mine, the Silverbell Mountains, Ragged Top Mountain, and Wolcott Peak. Take Silverbell Road out of the monument and back to the interstate. The whole trip could take all day if you stop often to look around. Archaeologists say that people have been living out here for about 5,000 years, though these days there's usually only campers and hunters hanging around this glorious desert outback.

MADERA CANYON AND SANTA RITA MOUNTAINS

Madera Canyon Rd., east of Green Valley

COST: $5 per-car user fee, $20 annual pass

Black bears, mountain lions, ringtailed cats,

The Ironwood Forest National Monument, a vast and empty desert northwest of Tucson, features the ironwood tree, which reaches 800 years old or more.

© TIM HULL

LESSER-KNOWN CAVES OF THE SANTA RITA MOUNTAINS

There are two caves in the Santa Rita Mountains southeast of Tucson that are actually quite well known to spelunkers far and wide, though not compared to the tourist-friendly "show-cave" confines of Colossal Cave and Kartchner Caverns. And they are certainly not as accessible as those two attractions; indeed, they are nearly off-limits to all but the most dogged cave lovers.

The Cave of Bells, in Sawmill Canyon on the eastern side of the Santa Ritas, has a warm natural lake just 80 meters below its entrance, which is now gated and locked, the key jealously controlled by the U.S. Forest Service – too many a Neanderthal (not the extinct cave-dwelling kind, mind you) spray-painted his name alongside that of his lover; too many stalactites were knocked down and shattered. If you want to make an investment of time and effort, however, you just might be able to get a hold of that key. You have to get a permit from the Forest Supervisor's Office at 300 West Congress Street in Tucson, or call the National Cave coordinator at 520/388-8497. You'll have to put down a $100 refundable deposit, and each member of your party has to sign a liability release. Then you'll need to use a four-wheel-drive vehicle to get

there: Take scenic Highway 83 south from I-10 just east of Tucson, then Forest Road 183 to Forest Road 4086 to the wondrous cave.

Another Santa Rita Mountain cave, **Onyx Cave,** is just a few miles ahead on Forest Road 4086, but its key is guarded by the Escabrosa Grotto, a group of Tucson-area cavers who leased Onyx and gated its entrance in 1974 in an effort to protect it from the unconscionable vandalism that had left it graffiti-scarred and nearly ruined. If you plan far enough ahead, you might be able to get the keys to both caves and make an epic trip out of it, but the folks at the Escabrosa Grotto aren't easy to impress.

"Onyx Cave is a complex and beautiful cave, but requires considerable caving experience and a guide to explore safely," says a warning on the group's website (www.escabrosa.org). To get the key to Onyx Cave, you must contact the Grotto's conservation chair and fill out a key-request form. Even then it's not a sure thing. Merely doing the paperwork "does not ensure that your request will be granted," the group says. "The conservation of the cave and the safety of all those who enter it are among [our] top priorities." That's as it should be, and it's an attitude that will make gaining access to these rarely visited caves all the sweeter.

deer, and too many birds to count call this sky island range home, where mining and logging once were legitimate pursuits but now outdoor recreation rules. The range's highest peak is 9,453-foot Mount Wrightson. Most visitors to the Santa Ritas head to Madera Canyon and its trails to the peak's summit. A classic example of the kind of pine-oak woodland that grows in the sky island regions, Madera Canyon is the part-time home to many subtropical bird species that stop off on their migrations north to mate along a cool mountain creek in conditions not dissimilar from more tropical climes to the south. Consequently the canyon is a kind of mecca for serious bird-watchers fulfilling their life lists. It is one of

a very few places in North America one can see the fat green-and-red elegant trogan, a relative of the quetzal and the source of much thrill and consternation for birders visiting from points far away. The great variety of hummingbird species flitting about the canyon also draws visitors from far and wide. A paved two-lane leads from the desert floor up to about 6,000 feet, where well-used and relatively steep trails climb the slopes of Mount Wrightson all the way to its bare and rocky peak. During the summer rainy season, the usually small Madera Creek becomes a torrent. The average summertime temperature in the canyon is about 85°F, about 15 to 20 degrees cooler on any given summer day than

© TIM HULL

Madera Creek in full swell rushing through Madera Canyon

it is down in the valley. It gets cold in the high country October–April, and it regularly snows up there in deep winter. Madera Canyon is an extremely popular day-use area and hiking destination for Tucson and Santa Cruz Valley residents, so expect to see quite a few people on the trails and using the three developed picnic areas, all of which have tables, charcoal grills, and bathrooms. You can pick up a trail map at any of the lodges in the canyon, or you can get one at the welcome station at the canyon's entrance, but it is staffed irregularly.

MOUNT HOPKINS
FRED LAWRENCE WHIPPLE
OBSERVATORY
Mount Hopkins Rd., Amado, 520/670-5707,
http://cfa-www.harvard.edu/flwo
HOURS: Mon.-Fri 8:30 A.M.-4:30 P.M.
COST: $7 adult, $2.50 child 6-12
The Smithsonian Institution operates this observatory atop 8,550-foot Mount Hopkins, where astronomers take advantage of the dark Southern Arizona sky to scan space for very

faint objects. The MMT, the largest single-mirror telescope in North America, is one of four you can see up close during a six-hour tour of the facility offered Monday, Wednesday, and Friday mid-March through November. It's a good idea to call far in advance for reservations. The visitors center near Amado has displays about the work being done on the mountain and the history of the telescope. No kids under six.

ORACLE
From midtown in Tucson take Rte. 77 (Oracle Rd.) to the northeastern slopes of the Santa Catalina range
This small historic town about 30 miles north of Tucson has a few historic buildings and a proliferation of high desert–dwelling artists. The **Acadia Ranch Museum** (825 Mount Lemmon Rd., 520/896-9609, Fri.–Sat. 1–5 P.M., free) tells the colorful history of the ranch—once a sheep ranch and later a sanatorium for suffers of TB and other ailments—and the town, which today has about 3,500 people, many of them artists and other desert runaways. The **Oracle Union Church** (695 E. American Ave.) is on the National Register of Historic Places and is worth a look, as is nearby Oracle State Park. There are several restaurants, including a historic steak house, and even a few little bed-and-breakfasts if you'd rather stay out here in the relative cool of 4,000 feet.

ORACLE STATE PARK
3820 Wildlife Dr., Oracle, 520/896-2425,
www.azstateparks.com
HOURS: Thurs.-Mon. 7 A.M.-3 P.M.
COST: $6 per car in winter, $5 per car in summer
This small state park about 40 miles north of Tucson preserves about 4,000 acres of oak woodlands and rare semidesert grasslands. This is a great place to see the high desert, with a picnic and a hike on some of the 15 miles of trails within the park. The whole area was once a ranch, and the historic, architecturally thrilling Mediterranean-style **Kannally Ranch House** is preserved in the park and open for tours Saturday–Sunday 10 A.M.–2 P.M. There's probably not enough here to inspire a trip just to the

SIGHTS

park, but it should definitely be wrapped into a car trip north into Pinal County and the northeast foothills—a trip best taken in the summer, when the higher elevations here provide a welcome respite from the sweating lowlands.

PEPPERSAUCE CANYON

Six miles southeast of Oracle on Forest Rd. 38, 520/749-8700, www.fs.fed.us/r3/coronado/forest/ recreation/camping/sites/peppersauce.shtml
HOURS: Open year-round
COST: $10 per car to picnic and/or to camp overnight

If you're up for yet another dirt-road drive into the mysterious desert landscape, consider the easy and smooth—albeit dusty—drive six miles southeast of Oracle (about 40 miles northeast of Tucson proper) to Peppersauce Canyon and Campground. This beautiful riparian area, with shady cottonwood and walnut trees guarding an intermittent stream, has 18 camping spaces and is a good place for picnics and general creek-side rambling. If you go during the rainy seasons you might even see the creek rushing. The lushness of the riverine environment in the canyon is quite shocking compared to the aridity of the oak scrublands around it, making the bustling green life of the creek and canyon all the more inviting.

FIRE ON FROG MOUNTAIN

The Coronado National Forest had barred campfires and smoking by mid-June of 2003, saying it would take just one careless spark to send flames surging through the brush-choked, bone-dry Santa Catalina Mountains.

But the precautions weren't enough to keep the worst from happening. On June 17, 2003, a hiker dropped a cigarette on the Aspen Loop Trail in the range's Pusch Ridge Wilderness. A month later 84,750 acres had turned black, and 333 structures, including much of the mountain village Summerhaven, had turned to ash. It cost $16.3 million to put the fire out; it was finally "contained" (stopped from spreading to new ground) on July 15.

At the fire's peak, some 1,270 firefighters and support workers battled the blaze, and half a dozen air tankers rumbled through great plumes of black smoke to drop their deep-red fire retardant on the forest. The smoke, and at night the flames, were visible across Southern Arizona, especially in Tucson, where residents sat outside on hot nights to watch their mountains burn.

President George Bush declared the fire a federal disaster on July 14, and a month later he visited the Santa Catalina Mountains. By August 2, when the public was allowed back on Mount Lemmon to survey the damage for the first time, Summerhaven's residents had already started to rebuild, and later came a promise of funding help from Pima County.

Crews began mulching and reseeding the burned areas from the air before the fire was even out, and that rehabilitation would continue until the spring of 2004.

Six years on, the mountain is alive with new growth, though it looks much different than it did before the fire. Especially in Mount Lemmon's upper reaches, trails lead through large stands of burned-out husks, and you can't help but get black smudges on your arms and hands if you lean on one for balance. Summerhaven promised to come back better than ever, though now the village, born in the 1940s, has a just-built look where it used to seem like an inevitable part of the mountain environment. As everything in nature runs in cycles, Summerhaven may be just starting to look snug and lived-in again in another 60 years or so – just about in time for another historic conflagration.

A few months after life got back to normal in Tucson, a young college student was charged with making false statements to law enforcement. Police had questioned the young man about allegations that he'd been smoking in the area where investigators believed the fire had started, on the day it started. He originally denied the accusation, but then later pled guilty to lying to police. He was sentenced to six months of probation and 200 hours of community service.

There are a few trails around here as well, and if you're into mounting a larger expedition, you can drive to Peppersauce from high in the Catalinas along four-wheel-drive-friendly routes. Otherwise, coming from Oracle, you can reach the canyon in a regular old sedan. From Tucson take Oracle Road for 27 miles to Highway 77, then turn right and go 10 miles to the town of Oracle. Take the first Oracle exit and then drive four miles through the tiny town to Forest Road 38, then on to Peppersauce Canyon.

REDDINGTON PASS
Tanque Verde Rd. (at Wilmont and Grant Rds.) to Reddington Rd.

Take Tanque Verde Road, which eventually turns into Reddington Road, as far as it will go—until it turns to dirt—and you'll be in the pass between the Santa Catalinas and the Rincons, a wild saguaro-crowded desert with some dramatic views. Unless you're a hiker or a desert rat, there's not a lot to do out here, but it's a great place to look back on the city, especially at night with all the lights in the valley twinkling. One of the huge mansions you'll see right before the road turns to dirt (you can guess which one it is; it's fairly obvious I think) belongs to Sir Paul McCartney, and is where Linda McCartney died on April 17, 1998, with Paul and her children by her side.

ROY P. DRACHMAN
AGUA CALIENTE REGIONAL PARK
12325 E. Roger Rd., 520/749-3718

HOURS: Park daily 7 A.M.–sunset; visitors center and art gallery Nov.–Apr. Wed.–Fri. 1–4 P.M., Sat.–Sun. 8 A.M.–4 P.M.

Approaching the shock of wet greenery among the otherwise gray-green of the foothills, it's easy to see why this spring-fed oasis has been a popular spot for humans for the last 5,000 years or more. Now a 100-acre public park with a visitors center, gallery, nature shop, and wildlife-attracting springwater ponds, the site has over the millennia been a stopover for

One of the oldest trees in the area, this huge, sprawling mesquite in Roy P. Drachman Agua Caliente Regional Park supports a whole ecosystem of its own.

© TIM HULL

hunter-gatherers and the farming Hohokam culture, as well as a ranch and a resort built to exploit the supposedly curative powers of the springs. Much of the vegetation here, as well as the fish and the log-lounging turtles you'll see everywhere, are decidedly nonnative. The shaggy palms, encircling the ponds like at some Spice Road camp, were planted long ago, but the 200-year-old mesquite tree next to the former ranch house, a tree that hosts a whole ecosystem of its own, is native to the area and one of the oldest mesquites in the valley. This is a contemplative, peaceful spot, a good place for a walk, a picnic, or a long talk by the 87-degree ponds, with lazy turtles listening in.

SKI VALLEY

10300 Ski Run Rd., Summerhaven, 520/576-1321, snow report 520/576-1400

HOURS: Daily 9 A.M.–4 P.M.

COST: $11-32

Just up a bit from Summerhaven and near the peak of Mount Lemmon, the highest in the Santa Catalina range, are the 22 runs of Ski Valley, the nation's southernmost ski hill. The ski season runs, roughly, from mid-December to early April in a very good year. But if you happen to arrive in "winter" and are expecting to get a few runs in, don't make too many set-in-stone plans. While the ski run does open from time to time, and provides some acceptable skiing and snowboarding, it's not to be counted on. In late 2008, for example, it snowed up on the mountain and the TV newscasters and everybody else in the valley headed up to play in the white stuff. About a month later, it was 91 degrees Fahrenheit on the valley floor and there was not a patch of dirty snow left. My advice is to get your skiing in elsewhere; the chairlift, however, operates year-round, and a cool, refreshing, and scenic ride up to nearly 10,000 feet in August, while everybody else sweats or breathes in the packaged air in their office building, is one of the best rides to be had in Southern Arizona.

© TIM HULL

Even when there's no snow, which is most of the time, riding a ski lift up green and cool Mount Lemmon is a fun way to spend an hour or so.

◖ SKY ISLAND SCENIC BYWAY

E. Catalina Hwy. to Summerhaven, Santa Catalina
Mountains, 520/749-8700 (Palisade Visitor Center)
HOURS: Daily 8:30 A.M.–4:40 P.M.
COST: $5 per car

About 50 miles—an hour or so up a twisty paved two-lane road from the desert floor northeast of midtown—and you're at nearly 10,000 feet. This two-lane road is known as the Sky Island Scenic Byway, a nod to the fact that the 10,000-foot, forested peaks look like lonely islands in an endless dried-up sea. The trip, it is often said, is like traveling from Mexico to Canada in one short scenic drive. Until the 1930s Tucsonans couldn't reach the cool heights in great numbers. But then former U.S. Postmaster General Frank Hitchcock called in some federal favors and secured money and convict labor to begin building a road into the mountains; the indomitable Civilian Conservation Corps eventually finished the job. There are dozens of trails on the range, and there are several public bathrooms, campgrounds, and lookout points. It's a good idea to stop at the Palisade Visitor Center (milepost 19.6) at 7,200 feet, which has trail maps, a bookstore, and displays about the mountain's ecology. To begin your drive, take either Broadway Boulevard or Speedway Boulevard east to Wilmot Road, which becomes Tanque Verde Road. Head northeast on Tanque Verde Road for about 10 miles, and then turn left at

THE LEMMON ROCK LOOKOUT

Arizona still has 72 active or semi-active fire lookouts, meaning they are staffed at least intermittently, especially during fire season or times of high-risk and emergency.

Only Oregon, with 106, and Florida, with 130, have more active fire lookouts than Arizona, according to the Forest Fire Lookout Association, a group that advocates for the preservation of lookouts and their traditions. What's more, Arizona has a higher ratio of active to standing lookouts than most states – 72 active or semi-active out of 83 still standing. Contrast that with California, where 198 lookouts still stand but just 50 of those are active.

Only a small handful of lookouts classified as active are still staffed full-time for the entire fire season – roughly April 1 to September 1 – and one of these rare huts happens to be lashed to a rock overhang in the Santa Catalinas above Tucson, overlooking the Wilderness of Rocks and beyond that the unfurled basin and range territory as far as the urban haze will allow. The Lemmon Rock Lookout, at 8,820 feet, has been occupied for about five months a year for going on 70 years. On the face of the 14-foot-by-14-foot lookout shack, the side that stares down on the vast pine and boulder land below, someone stenciled long ago the words No Diving, as if aware of the risks of so much war with oneself.

Fire lookouts like Lemmon Rock have been around, in one form or another, for a very long time, but they really started to proliferate in the 1930s with the advent of the Civilian Conservation Corps (CCC) and the U.S. Forest Service's all-or-nothing suppression policy. Responding to several huge, unprecedented backcountry forest fires that plagued the nation during the first third of the 20th century, government foresters enacted the 10 A.M. policy, decreeing that every fire on public lands must be quelled by 10 A.M. the morning after its initial spark. The fire lookout was an integral component of that policy. There is still some debate about the scientific efficacy of suppression, and we are, in many ways, paying for it now with overgrown, drought-ridden forests just waiting for a slash of dry lightning or a tossed cigarette to molt and be reborn, in the process ripping through the million-dollar homes we build in the forest hoping old Smokey the Bear will keep us safe from nature's cycles. Around the same time as the lookout was first constructed, the stock market crashed and so too the job market, hence the birth of the New Deal and the CCC, which put thousands of out-of-work Americans in the national forests building trails, fire breaks, and, in some of the most remote areas in the country, fire lookouts. Lemmon Rock was built

East Catalina Highway, which rises into the Santa Catalina Mountains. At various points, East Catalina Highway becomes the General Hitchcock Highway and the Mount Lemmon Highway (the name most locals use for the route). The road ends at the tiny village of Summerhaven.

SUMMERHAVEN
End of the Sky Island Scenic Byway

People began building and buying cabins in this mountain village at 7,840 feet in the 1940s, and by the early 2000s Summerhaven had a wonderful sort of lived-in look that made it especially romantic to desert dwellers. Then it burned down in the summer of 2003 after a careless hiker left his cigarette burning. That which burned was soon rebuilt bigger and better and newer; the oversized "cabins" on slopes cleared by wildfire don't provide the same aesthetic pleasures that the funky pre-fire cabins once did, but it's still a fun place to spend a few hours looking around a few gift shops and maybe having a bowl of chili or a hamburger.

◖ TITAN MISSILE MUSEUM
1580 W. Duval Mine Rd., Sahuarita, 520/625-7736, www.pimaair.org

HOURS: Daily 9 A.M.–5 P.M.

COST: $8.50 adult, $5 child 7-12

This deactivated missile site, one of several missile facilities that were staffed with

by a CCC crew in the early 1930s, replacing a more primitive lookout on Mount Lemmon that had stood since 1913.

You can take a look at the Lemmon Rock Lookout for yourself, and, during the summer months, even sit down and have a high-altitude chat with the friendly current occupant of the little hut. To get there, drive up the Sky Island Scenic Byway to Ski Valley and park at the trailhead parking lot at the top of Mount Lemmon (keep going past the ski slopes and take the dirt road after the pavement ends). Once you park, pick up the short Lemmon Rock Trail.

© TIM HULL

The fire lookout on Mount Lemmon was built in the 1930s.

© TIM HULL

Titan Missile Museum

underground-dwelling Cold Warriors in what was once referred to as the Titan Valley, had its Titan II aimed squarely at the USSR from 1963 to 1982. The site was decommissioned in 1986 and became a National Historic Landmark in 1994. The one-hour tour takes you deep underground, where volunteer guides, some of them former crew members, explain what daily life was like working at the silo. The highlight of the tour for many is seeing an actual Titan II waiting there in the launch duct. Guides also simulate the launch sequence that crewmembers hoped they would never have to complete. The visitors center provides context with a Cold War timeline and artifacts from the era, and a gift shop sells souvenirs and books.

TUBAC
I-19 south to Tubac exit

This small village along the Santa Cruz is steeped in the history of the Spanish adventurers in Pimería Alta. Padre Kino established the mission at nearby Tumacácori in 1691, and Tubac, an Akmiel O'Odham

village, became a mission farm and ranch. By the 1730s Spanish colonists had arrived from the south to farm and ranch the fertile river valley. In 1751 the violent Piman revolt convinced the Spanish crown to establish the Presidio San Ignacio de Tubac, which was founded the next year. The famous Basque Juan Bautista de Anza II was the second commander of the presidio, and in 1776 he led the first of two overland journeys to establish a fort at San Francisco, California, taking along about 60 colonists from Tubac. In 1860 silver strikes nearby briefly made Tubac the largest town in the Arizona Territory. It eventually fell into obscurity but was discovered again as an artists' colony during the second half of the 20th century, and today its many galleries and shops are a draw for tourists and locals alike. Crowds flock to Tubac during the weeklong Tubac Festival of the Arts in February, during which artisans and artists from around the country set up booths and music and the smell of greasy, delicious food fills the village. **Tubac Presidio State**

MISSION TUMACÁCORI

When the Jesuit missionary Eusebio Francisco Kino visited the Akimel O'odham village of Tumacácori in January 1691, he did little more than say mass and promise the natives immediate and lasting salvation. But since he arrived there a day before he did the same in nearby Guevavi, technically the Mission Tumacácori is the oldest, though not the most famous nor most visited, Spanish colonial mission in Arizona.

In 2007 some 45,000 visitors walked the shady grounds of Mission Tumacácori. That's a far cry from the approximately 200,000 that flocked to San Xavier del Bac, its more famous and prettier sister to the north. But the experience at Tumacácori is very different from the still-living traditions available at San Xavier. It's as much about experiencing a long-lost landscape as it is about seeing a crumbling church ruin.

For many years the church was an adobe hovel on the east side of the Santa Cruz River, which back in those days flowed seasonally and gave the O'odham their lives. While the same river today flows north from Mexico past the same land, now it has surface water year-round; it's a few inches deep with reclaimed wastewater and high levels of E. coli and coliform bacteria, so much so that you wouldn't want to dip your feet in it.

It wasn't until after the coming of the Franciscans that construction on the church we can all visit today got under way on the west side of the river, in about 1800. Then the narrow adobe church with the fired-brick bell tower was renamed in honor of St. Joseph, Jesus of Nazareth's step-dad. In 1908 Teddy Roosevelt, who more than any other president saved Arizona from Arizonans, established Tumacácori National Historic Park.

To celebrate its momentous hundredth birthday, in early 2009 the park opened a new $400,000 museum. Eight years in the making, the museum is a long leap forward from the somewhat dusty early-1970s exhibits that used to tell the mission's history. One of the most striking elements of the new museum is a huge photo of the bajada stretching west from the Santa Rita Mountains; it has been digitally cleaned of the many homes that now dot the area, showing visitors what the valley looked like when Kino first saw it. There are also large digitally illustrated panels featuring photo-realistic scenes of native life along the Santa Cruz circa 1690; they reportedly took the artist two years to complete. The new museum is organized around three intricate wax-figure dioramas made in the 1930s that were part of the old museum but now seem fresh in their sleek new surroundings. And for the first time since 1840 a striking statue of Jesus is on display. In late 2008, the statue was returned to Tumacácori from San Xavier del Bac, where it had been kept for more than 150 years.

© TIM HULL

Historic Park (520/398-2252, www.pr.state. az.us, daily 8 A.M.–5 P.M., $3 adult, $1 child 7–13), Arizona's first state park, founded in 1959, preserves the history and foundations of the Presidio San Ignacio de Tubac. You can see the fort's original foundation and peruse a museum that explains what life was like for the natives, settlers, and soldiers. Guided tours and hands-on interpretation programs are available on request. The park's annual Anza Days celebration around the third week of October honors the fort's most famous commander with historical re-creations, music, and food. The Tubaquenos, a historical reenactment society, put on living-history demonstrations at the park on Sundays October–March, 1–4 P.M.

A good place to start your Tubac visit is the **Tubac-Santa Cruz Visitor Center** (4 Plaza Rd., 520/398-0007, www.toursanta-cruz.com, Mon.–Fri. 9 A.M.–4 P.M., Sat.–Sun. 10 A.M.–4 P.M.), just to the left as you enter the village by the big Tubac sign.

TUMACÁCORI NATIONAL HISTORIC PARK

Three miles south of Tubac on the east-side frontage road, 520/398-2341, www.nps.gov/tuma

HOURS: Daily 9 A.M.–5 P.M.

COST: $3 adult, free child under 16

Padre Kino founded the Mission San Jose de Tumacácori in 1691, and much of it stills stands today on this 310-acre national park. You can explore the mission and its grounds, which include an old graveyard, an orchard, and a re-created Piman shelter. A museum tells the history of the mission and Pimería Alta, and most days you can buy tortillas and refried beans made right before your eyes in the traditional fashion. A gift shop sells a wide assortment of books on local history. The mission at Tumacácori still holds masses on holidays, but the two other missions protected by the park are mostly in ruins. The ruins of **Mission San Cayetano de Calabazas,** normally closed to the public, can be visited on monthly guided tours for $10 per person; reservations are required (520/398-2341).

© TIM HULL

Though not as popular as San Xavier del Bac, Mission Tumacácori in Tumacácori National Historic Park has charms all its own.

RESTAURANTS

The Old Pueblo's culinary scene is famously dominated by the ranchland comfort food available at the dozens of Mexican eateries in town, most of them serving classic variations of a cuisine formed in Mexico's arid northern states and on the hot, dry coastlines of the nearby Sea of Cortez. While such home-style Mexican food represents one of the most popular cuisines in America, in Tucson it has a kind of authenticity and diversity of taste that's available nowhere else—except perhaps just across the border, about an hour's drive from the city.

While you could spend a lifetime here eating carne asada, chiles rellenos, and enchiladas exclusively, you'd not only join the ranks of the obese but you'd miss out on sampling the work of some of the most creative, adventurous chefs and restaurateurs in the Southwest. The amorphous hodge-podge that is New American cuisine thrives in Tucson through an impressive array of mid- to high-end locally owned "Tucson originals," many of which combine spices, flavors, ingredients, and crops common to the borderlands with American, French, and other culinary traditions to create a new hybrid that goes by the inexact term Southwestern.

To be totally honest, though, when you've got year-round outdoor patio dining—with gentle heaters when its chilly, and cold water-spitting "misters" when it's hot—and the sky above that patio is ever blue and clear, and the views from that patio are of looming high

HIGHLIGHTS

LOOK FOR TO FIND RECOMMENDED RESTAURANTS.

⟨ Best Gourmet Mexican Food: Don't miss the creative and adventurous gourmet Mexican food at **Cafe Poca Cosa,** one of Tucson's top eateries, which is often featured in gourmet and lifestyle magazines (page 70).

⟨ Best Lunch with a Hug: At **The Little Cafe Poca Cosa** the music is loud, the waitresses kiss and hug their customers, and a bit of attitude comes with every plate of some of the best chiles rellenos in town (page 71).

⟨ Best Coffee House: Ike's Coffee & Tea serves a great cup of joe and offers free wireless Internet, delicious baked goods, and a perfect central location (page 76).

⟨ Best Late-Night Fast Food: Beans, meat, cheese, salsa, and tortillas – is there any better late-night menu? There's a **Nico's** on nearly every corner, and they're always open and serving the best Mexican fast food in town (page 78).

⟨ Best Breakfast: Francisco's, the Old Pueblo's best diner, has tasty and filling American and Mexican breakfasts that will definitely fuel you up for a day of fun (page 81).

⟨ Best Vegetarian Food: Enjoy a tasty, expertly prepared, and inexpensive all-you-can-eat vegetarian and vegan buffet at **Govinda's Natural Food Buffet** (page 84).

⟨ Best Music While You Eat: At **La Fuente,** the airy tropical interior, always-festive atmosphere, and the loud expert mariachi bands strolling among the tables make for a perfect night out (page 89).

⟨ Best Use of Sonoran Desert Ingredients: The prickly pear sorbet in a saguaro cactus seed cone, Arizona jojoba beef tenderloin, and Tohono O'odham white tepary bean coulis are just a few of the desert-influenced dishes available at the high-end **Ventana Room at Loews Ventana Canyon** (page 91).

⟨ Best Cowboy Steak and Beans: If you're hankering for a nice piece of mesquite-grilled meat, a big bowl of beans, and a festive, tourist-friendly atmosphere, there's no better place than **Pinnacle Peak Steak House,** a popular ranch-style family eatery (page 95).

⟨ Best Mexican Food: There's a reason why there is always a line to get into **Mi Nidito,** where you'll find classic Sonoran food cooked to perfection and colorful decor (page 98).

© TIM HULL

The Little Cafe Poca Cosa

mountains and sweeping desert valleys, the quality of the food in front of you often becomes a secondary issue. Whenever you can, barring something unlikely like rain or cold, ask to sit on the patio or in the Spanish-style courtyard—scores of restaurants here have them, and al fresco dining in, say, February is one of the great joys of desert living.

PRICE KEY

⑤ Entrées under $10

⑤⑤ Entrées $10-20

⑤⑤⑤ Entrées over $20

Downtown and University District Map 1

RESTAURANTS

You'll find breakfast, lunch, and dinner choices from all over the globe in the Old Pueblo's downtown and university district. Some of the restaurants downtown exist primarily to serve the lunch crowd in the business and government districts, but most of the best places keep the same hours as restaurants in other neighborhoods. If none of the suggestions given here appeal, stroll up and down 4th Avenue or head over to Main Gate Square; both areas have dozens of restaurants, one of which is sure to whet your appetite. I can't think of a single place in this neighborhood where the "Tucson Casual" dress code (shorts or jeans and whatever shoes you desire, including sandals—basically an emphasis on staying cool and comfortable and on active, outdoor living), or lack thereof, wouldn't be acceptable.

AMERICAN
THE B-LINE ⑤
621 N. 4th Ave., 520/882-7575,
www.blinerestaurant.com
HOURS: Mon.-Thurs. 7:30 A.M.-9 P.M.,
Fri.-Sat. 7:30 A.M.-10 P.M., Sun. 7:30 A.M.-8 P.M.
This café on 4th Avenue has huge breakfast burritos, a full coffee bar, and free wireless Internet. For lunch and dinner they offer soups, salads, and sandwiches, along with creative Southwestern-style burritos, quesadillas, and tacos, and some interesting pasta dishes. Everything is delicious, and the fresh ingredients are given center stage. Make sure to check out the art on the walls. The bar seating

along the front window is a perfect place to kick back, watch the people pass by, and have a plate of fresh guacamole and one or more of the dozen or so craft brews on offer from California, Colorado, and Mexico.

DELECTABLES ⑤
533 N. 4th Ave., 520/884-9289, www.delectables.com
HOURS: Sun.-Thurs. 11 A.M.-9 P.M., Fri.-Sat. 11 A.M.-11 P.M.
This bistro is a 4th Avenue institution, serving light, fresh lunches and dinners in the gourmet mode. My favorite sandwich is the jalapeño BLT on freshly made French bread. There are vegetarian dishes like the awesome asparagus crepes, and bistro plates with all kinds of top-shelf meats and cheeses and fresh fruit. After 5 P.M. they serve hearty dinners like rib eye, wild Pacific salmon, and chicken picatta, and they have a wide range of pasta dishes. They serve a good selection of craft brews and wine, and there's usually some fascinating, or at least intriguing, art on the walls, most of it by local artists.

MAYNARDS MARKET & KITCHEN ⑤
400 N. Toole Ave., 520/545-0577,
www.maynardsmarkettucson.com
HOURS: Sun.-Wed. 11 A.M.-10 P.M.,
Thurs.-Sat. 11 A.M.-midnight; market, pastry, and coffee service daily 10 A.M.-7 P.M.
This café, bar, and market in the refurbished old Southern Pacific train depot downtown serves some excellent sandwiches—the Cuban pork with garlic mayo, cilantro, caramelized

The old train depot in downtown now houses Maynards Market & Kitchen.

© TIM HULL

onions, and grilled jalapeños captures the pan-American chic of the place perfectly. If you're a vegetarian, try the roasted eggplant sandwich with an olive tapenade—it'll change your relationship with the eggplant. The four-cheese mac and cheese is filling and tasty, and their creative pizzas are good anytime. The bar is cool and stylish and looks out on the railroad tracks. They serve their menu late into the night on the weekends.

BAR AND GRILL
AULD DUBLINER 💲💲

800 E. University Blvd. No. 10, 520/206-0323, www.aulddubliner.com

HOURS: Daily 11 A.M.–2 A.M.

Corporate-bred Irish pubs have been popping up all over the Southwest over the last few years, and many of them have a pre-fab look to them that is somewhat insulting, like some kind of Irish World at Disneyland. For the patron who's looking for a bit of authentic atmosphere and a good pint of Guinness in Tucson, however, there's the Auld Dubliner at Main Gate. While it is indeed part of the recent pub trend, it stands above the others with

a deceptively worn-in and comfortable atmosphere (the wood interior was hand-crafted in Ireland) and top-notch eats like fish-and-chips, bangers and mash, and curry fries. They've got the usual Irish pub beers on tap, including the always-refreshing Boddingtons and the hard-to-find Magners Irish Cider. This is a perfect place to spend a day chatting and drinking, and on most Sunday nights there's a pick-up Irish music jam in a back room. The menu has a lot more to offer than pub fare, by the way, and this is a good place for a nice dinner as well.

BARRIO BREWING COMPANY 💲

800 E. 16th St., 520/791-2739, www.barriobrewing.com

HOURS: Sun.-Thurs. 11 A.M.–10 P.M., Fri.-Sat. 11 A.M.–close

The same folks that own Gentle Ben's brewery also operate this cavernous bar and grill and brewery in an old warehouse district just off downtown. It's worth a visit just to see the building, an ancient Quonset hut–style warehouse. Barrio Brewing serves the same style of bar food and microbrews as Gentle Ben's, but the crowd is a bit older.

FROG & FIRKIN 💲💲

874 E. University Blvd., 520/623-7507,
www.frogandfirkin.com

HOURS: Sun.-Thurs. 11 A.M.-1 A.M., Fri.-Sat. 11 A.M.-2 A.M.

This British-influenced pub has a front patio that's very popular with the college crowd at Main Gate Square. There's usually an acoustic set going down outside on the weekends, and the tables seem to always be full and festive. Come here for the beer—it has one of the most complete selections in town, with brews from all over the world, including the rare Belgian Lindeman's Framboise and several hard ciders as well. Most of the beers are offered in bottles, but there's a wide selections of drafts here too. They have a full bar, plus pub food, pizzas, and burgers.

TUCSON ORIGINALS

Though you might find a few grumpy, over-fed, heartburn-haunted food critics who turn up their sunburned noses at the Old Pueblo's food scene – claiming that culinary life in Tucson is too obsessed with chimichangas and melted cheese, or else declaring it a kind of developing nation relative to other, more sophisticated markets – the truth is that this big city that still thinks it's a small town has been, for at least the last 25 years, a regional leader in developing locally owned and locally focused restaurants.

And while the worldwide economic slowdown of 2008 sunk a few beloved local eateries (including one, Terra Cotta, which many considered to be a major local pioneer of the New American, Mexican, and French hybrid called Southwestern), there are still dozens of Tucson-owned eateries doing their part to make the Mexican food capital of the nation into an even more diverse and exciting place to fill up your stomach. Many of these locally owned eateries have gathered together in a group called Tucson Originals (www.tucson-originals.com), marketing themselves as the "authentic flavors of Tucson."

Just over a decade old, Tucson Originals now boasts something like 40 different restaurant members – eateries from the world-renowned, upscale **Janos** to the decidedly, and proudly, downscale **Frank's/Francisco's.** There are typically Tucson Mexican joints among the membership, like **El Charro,** as well as restaurants serving cuisines developed far, far away from the desert, like **Vila Thai.** And, of course, the membership swells with cutting-edge New American joints, where these days just about anything goes – Old Pueblo favorites like **The Cup Café, Barrio,** and **Acacia.**

Every year, since 2003, Tucson Originals has put on the exciting and flavorful **Tucson Culinary Festival** (www.tucsonculinaryfestival.com), a charity event that includes all kinds of tastings and competitions, including the Margarita Challenge to see who can make the best version of the Old Pueblo's signature cocktail. The final-night Grand Tasting ($85 pp) at the Loews Ventana Canyon Resort features food from all 40 or so members of Tucson Originals. The festival typically takes place over four days in early October, but you can sample the very rich and diverse Tucson culinary scene any time you're in town by patronizing one or more of the Tucson Originals.

Quite a few member restaurants are listed in this book; if you want to try others, check the Tucson Originals website or pick up one of their brochures – which has a map pinpointing the location of each member restaurant – at the **Tucson Visitor Center** at La Placita Village downtown (110 S. Church Ave., 520/624-1817, Mon.-Fri. 9 A.M.-5 P.M., Sat.-Sun. 9 A.M.-4 P.M.), or at most hotels and attractions around town.

Frank's/Francisco's

RESTAURANTS

GENTLE BEN'S $$

865 E. University Blvd., 520/624-4177,
www.gentlebens.com

HOURS: Mon.-Sat. 11 A.M.-1 A.M., Sun. noon-9 P.M.

Serving pub eats, burgers, sandwiches, and the obligatory Southwestern-inspired dishes, Gentle Ben's at Main Gate Square has been a favorite student and former-student hangout since the 1970s. While the food is more than edible, the real attractions here are the eight craft brews made on-site. The top three, from my seat, are the Red Cat Amber, the Tucson Blonde, and MacBlane's Oatmeal Stout, but all are excellent. On weekend nights when school's in session both floors of Gentle Ben's are likely to be crowded with frat boys and other UA types.

COFFEE AND TEA
EPIC CAFÉ $

745 N. 4th Ave., 520/624-6844, www.epic-cafe.com

HOURS: Daily 6 A.M.-midnight

The best coffee house on 4th Avenue serves all the usual coffee drinks, chai, ice cream floats, and juices, plus homemade pie and other desserts, including many that are vegan-approved. There's an omelet bar on the weekends from 8 A.M. to 1 P.M., and there's always a changing selection of soups, sandwiches, salads, bagels, and hummus plates. The café has free Internet and all kinds of comfortable couches and coffee tables, plus a few outdoor sidewalk tables. The crowd is a typically Tucson mix of the young, the hip, and the college crowd, with old hippies, assorted downtown artists, writers, musicians, and desert rats.

TOOLEY'S ON CONGRESS $

278 E. Congress St., 520/203-8970,
www.tooleyscafe.com

HOURS: Mon.-Sat. 6:30 A.M.-11 P.M., Sun. 6:30 A.M.-late

Owned by the same folks who operate the other Tooley's in the Lost Barrio, this small coffee house on Congress Street serves fresh-baked scones and pastries along with a pretty good cup of joe; the place is cozy and popular, with big, comfy chairs and free Internet.

DELI
BISON WITCHES $

326 N. 4th Ave., 520/740-1541, www.bisonwitches.com

HOURS: Daily 11 A.M.-midnight

This small deli-bar on 4th Avenue has over-stuffed sandwiches, soup in bread bowls, and good beers on tap. It gets a little crowded around lunchtime and on the weekends, but is worth the wait. There's a patio outside in the back that's pleasant on a temperate day. The waitresses here are usually hot-girl college students, and the service can be a bit indifferent, even condescending if it's really busy. Still, the food is great, and filling. If you're not a championship eater, consider ordering the half-sandwich-and-soup combo—that's plenty here for even the biggest belly around.

GREEK
ATHENS ON FOURTH $$

500 N. 4th Ave., 520/624-6886,
www.athenson4th.com

HOURS: Tues.-Sat. 11 A.M.-10 P.M.

The best place in Tucson to find sweetbreads, spiced lamb, tzatziki sauce, stuffed grape leaves, baklava, and other delectable Greek offerings is Athens on Fourth, a longtime favorite temple for those of us who never met an olive-and-cheese plate we didn't love.

ITALIAN
BROOKLYN PIZZA COMPANY $$

534 N. 4th Ave., 520/622-6868,
www.brooklynpizzacompany.com

HOURS: Mon.-Sat. 11 A.M.-11 P.M., Sun. noon-10 P.M.; slices served Fri.-Sat. 11 P.M.-2:30 A.M.

There's nothing better than a greasy slice of authentic New York–style pizza after a night of hitting the bars, and this 4th Avenue joint serves them late into the night (or rather, morning) on the weekends. The pizza here rivals anything you can find back East, and the meatball subs, calzones, and gelato are the best in town. If you're staying downtown, they'll deliver—even beer and cigarettes, not a common occurrence in Tucson. What's more, the little pizza place has recently gone solar-powered.

© TIM HULL

Brooklyn Pizza Company

CAFFÉ MILANO ⑤⑤
46 W. Congress St., 520/628-1601, www.caffemilano.us
HOURS: Mon.-Thurs. 8:30 A.M.-3:30 P.M.,
Fri. 8:30 A.M.-3:30 P.M. and 5:30-9:30 P.M.,
Sat. 5:30-9:30 P.M.

Located on Congress not far from the Pima County Courthouse, this elegant and bustling Italian café serves breakfast, lunch, and dinner, offering pastries and coffee, omelets, pizza, salads, panini, bruschetta, and dinners like veal scaloppine and *pollo al marsala*. All of it is excellent and creatively prepared, and there are a few tables on the sidewalk out front.

CARUSO'S ⑤⑤
434 N. 4th Ave., 520/624-5765,
www.carusositalian.com
HOURS: Tues.-Sun. 11:30 A.M.-11 P.M.

The Zagona clan has been serving delicious Italian favorites on and around 4th Avenue since 1938 (the original Caruso's was a block away from the current place). Shaded patio dining next to trickling fountains is the perfect way to enjoy the lasagna, pasta, and pizzas created here. It's nothing fancy—just well-prepared Italian favorites in a laid-back atmosphere with, of course, checkered tablecloths and fat bottles of chianti. There's often a wait to be seated on weekend nights, and you can expect to be eating alongside a lot of families.

MAGPIE'S PIZZA ⑤⑤
605 N. 4th Ave., 520/628-1661, www.magpiespizza.com
HOURS: Mon.-Wed. 11 A.M.-11 P.M., Thurs.-Sat.
11 A.M.-11 P.M.

Magpie's has four other locations around Tucson, but in my opinion the 4th Avenue shop is the best. The pizza, thick and creative and cheesy—nearly to a fault—is a sure bet, having won the *Tucson Weekly*'s Best of Tucson poll every year since 1989. It's not cheap, but pizza lovers should not miss sampling this local legend.

LATE-NIGHT EATS
THE GRILL ⑤
100 E. Congress St., 520/623-7621
HOURS: Daily 24 hours

The Grill, open all the time, is a favorite with the city's bohemians and downtown music scenesters. It's a very cool retro diner with a big menu and a bar called The Red Room that showcases local music. The food is very good if you like the genre, but can be uneven, as can be the service, during the after-bar rush hours on the weekends. The tater tots are addictive, and there's free wireless Internet. Just don't expect prompt service, especially if you choose to sit at the counter, and you won't usually get much small talk from the staff, who seem to be uniformly tattooed and pierced and are more often than not moonlighting artists, musicians, and poets.

MEXICAN AND LATIN AMERICAN
ALEJANDRO'S CAFE ⑤
31 N. Scott Ave., 520/623-3277
HOURS: Mon.-Fri. 7 A.M.-3 P.M.

This ultra-casual Mexican eatery downtown claims to have the best burritos and chimichangas in town, and they may have a point. The deep-fried, enchilada sauce–drenched burritos are big and delicious here, available with various fillings (I prefer simple bean and cheese, but there's chicken, beef, green chile, red chile, etc.), and not as pricey as most other places (the most expensive chimi on the menu is $5.25). This is a popular lunch spot during the week for downtown workers and isn't open on the weekends. If you're in the mood for Sonoran-style Mexican food and you're downtown, this is a quick and inexpensive place to satisfy your cravings.

⬛ CAFE POCA COSA $$$

110 E. Pennington St., 520/622-6400,
www.cafepocacosatucson.com

HOURS: Tues.-Thurs. 11 A.M.-9 P.M., Fri.-Sat. 11 A.M.-10 P.M.

Featured far and wide in gourmet and lifestyle magazines, Cafe Poca Cosa is one of the Old Pueblo's top two or three eateries. Reservations are basically required, and the menu changes twice daily. The day's specials are printed in English and Spanish on a chalkboard, which servers take around to each table. The food is usually an adventurous, learned and creative hybrid—a kind of gourmet Mexican food, created by Chef Suzanna Davila, a native of Guaymas, Sonora, Mexico, on the Sea of Cortez, that you won't find anywhere else in Southern Arizona. If you're looking for the usual enchiladas and burritos, this isn't the place. But if you want something on the far creative edge of Mexican cuisine—a much more varied style than most Americans are led to believe exists—then you must eat here. The interior is done up in a smooth, cool modernism with contemporary Latino art, including a print by the great Daniel Martin Diaz, peppered throughout.

EL CHARRO $$

311 N. Court Ave., 520/622-1922,
www.elcharrocafe.com

HOURS: Mon.-Sun. 11 A.M.-9 P.M.

El Charro serves what is probably the city's most beloved Mexican food, or at least it's always a contender. The food is excellent, especially the huge, filling chimichangas, a dish El Charro is often credited with inventing. The margaritas here may be the city's best. At least half the attraction here is the little house the restaurant is squeezed into—spilling out onto a cool, verdant patio—which was once lived in by Jules Flin, a French stonemason who came to Tucson to work on the cathedral. The restaurant has a bar, ¡Toma!, with half-price drinks and appetizers (delicious Mexican favorites like cheese crisps and quesadillas) daily 3–6 P.M.

EL MINUTO CAFE $

354 S. Main St., 520/882-4145, www.elminutocafe.com

HOURS: Mon.-Thurs. 11 A.M.-10 P.M., Fri.-Sat. 11 A.M.-11 P.M.

This small Sonoran-style café in the Barrio Histórico has been serving up home-style Mexican favorites since 1939. The food is topnotch and recognizable: enchiladas, chiles rellenos, carne seca, and the like—all of it expertly prepared. On the weekends there's often a mariachi group playing, and a lush patio out

© TIM HULL

Gourmet Mexican restaurant Cafe Poca Cosa is one of the city's more renowned eateries.

front is a perfect place for a long springtime lunch, with tequila perhaps. If you were going to check out the El Tiradito Shrine anyway, you might consider combining it with lunch here—it's right next door.

☕ THE LITTLE CAFE POCA COSA ⑤

Stone Ave. at Alameda St., no phone, www.littlepocacosa.com

HOURS: Mon.-Fri. 7:30 A.M.-2:30 P.M.

Do you like loud music while you eat, waitresses who kiss and hug their customers, and a bit of attitude with your chiles rellenos? I would have said no to all of the above until I had lunch at this tiny café on Stone Avenue right in the heart of downtown. The food is so spectacular that I'd be willing to put up with just about anything to get the simple Mexican and Latin American fare at this beloved lunch spot. The food is unassailable, and the hugs and even the cheek-kisses are alright with a belly full of goodness. Make sure to tip big; a large percentage of everything made in this place goes to various causes. They only take cash, no exceptions. Again, I assure you: The food is worth the various idiosyncrasies.

MAYA QUETZAL ⑤

429 N. 4th Ave., 520/622-8207

HOURS: Mon.-Thurs. 11:30 A.M.-2 P.M. and 5-8 P.M., Fri.-Sat. noon-9 P.M.

With so much Mexican food to choose from in the Old Pueblo, restaurants serving other Latin American cuisines tend to get forgotten, but not Maya Quetzal. This colorful eatery on 4th Avenue has been serving delicious Guatemalan food for more than 16 years. The small place opens up onto a shaded back patio with small fountains, and there's a mystic mural on one wall inside that conjures up the romance of Central America. The dishes typically offer a mixture of rice, black beans, beef and chicken, corn tortillas, and vegetables from the exotic to the recognizable. There are several vegetarian dishes, and sauces here tend to be creamier and less spicy than their Mexican counterparts. Make sure to try the cheesy "specialty rice"—a favorite of the house that you won't soon forget.

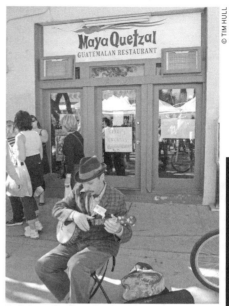

© TIM HULL

Delicious Guatemalan food is served at Maya Quetzal.

TOOLEY'S CAFE ⑤

299 S. Park Ave., 520/203-8970, www.tooleyscafe.com

HOURS: Mon.-Fri. 7 A.M.-4 P.M., Sat.-Sun. 7 A.M.-3 P.M.

Located in the Lost Barrio since 1989, Tooley's is a charming, laid-back family-run place that serves up some of the best Mexican-style breakfasts in town, like corn pancakes with spiced black beans and jalepeño syrup and chipotle pork hash. For lunch or an early dinner, they've got their own versions of burros, tacos, and quesadillas, and a tortilla soup that will delight fans of the genre.

NEW AMERICAN AND SOUTHWESTERN

BARRIO ⑤⑤

135 S. 6th Ave., 520/629-0191, www.barriofoodanddrink.com

HOURS: Mon. 11 A.M.-9 P.M., Tues.-Thurs. 11 A.M.-10 P.M., Fri. 11 A.M.-midnight, Sat. noon-midnight, Sun. 5-9 P.M.

Located downtown on the bottom level of the historic Oddfellows Hall building, Barrio offers a true dining experience in an elegant space. With fresh fish and beef specials and unique desserts, as well as a full bar and private, romantic booths, Barrio is the ideal place for a special couple's night out. Barrio also offers a well-stocked wine list and specialty drinks. This place is perfect for dinner before or after the theater or opera (both venues are located nearby), or a long, luxurious lunch. They offer both appetizers and entrées, the former being about half the price of the latter. One of the better little plates is the Barrio Tostada, with grilled chicken, tomato concasse, and white cheddar on a whole-wheat tortilla—a departure indeed from the usual Sonoran-style fare at other more pedestrian places. Reservations are recommended.

CAFÉ A LA C'ART $$

140 N. Main Ave., 520/628-8533,
www.tucsonarts.com/visit/cafe.php

HOURS: Mon.-Fri. 11 A.M.-3 P.M.

A little French-inspired café at the Tucson Museum of Art, Café a la C'art is housed in a historic building with patio dining, and serves the perfect fare for an art-and-lunch outing. The best items on the menu are under the "Artistry with Bread" heading—a grilled

eggplant sandwich with caramelized onions, or a salmon club with chipotle aioli, both on fresh-baked focaccia bread. An inspired selection of salads is also on the menu, and the freshly made lemonade is worth the trip in itself.

THE CUP CAFÉ $$

311 E. Congress St., 520/798-1618

HOURS: Sun.-Thurs. 7 A.M.-10 P.M., Fri.-Sat. 7 A.M.-11 P.M.

Inside the Hotel Congress downtown, The Cup is a popular weekend breakfast destination, as well as a perfect choice for lunch or dinner anytime. They serve an eclectic blend of American food with a dash of several ethnic traditions, jumping from hummus to nachos, with entrées like *borracho* (drunk) pork tenderloin, marinated in tequila and chipotles and served with a sweet-potato gratin, country green beans, and a red-onion marmalade.

CUSHING STREET BAR AND GRILL $$

198 W. Cushing St., 520/622-7984,
www.cushingstreet.com

HOURS: Tues.-Sat. 4 P.M.-close

On the edge of the Barrio Histórico, this family-owned place has been operating out of its circa-1860s historic building since 1972. It's

The Cup Café is an eclectic café off the lobby of the historic Hotel Congress in downtown.

© TIM HULL

a charming space, with garden patio dining available when the weather permits (which is most of the time). Cushing Street Bar and Grill is known for its carefully made *mojito* ($8), concocted with loads of fresh mint. Many of the entrées have a Southwestern flair—try the gulf tacos, with fish fresh from the Sea of Cortez, just a few hundred miles south. Reservations are recommended.

SPANISH
CASA VICENTE ⊖⑤
375 S. Stone Ave., 520/884-5253, www.casavicente.com

HOURS: Tues.-Wed. 4-10 P.M., Thurs. 11 A.M.-2 P.M. and 4-10 P.M., Fri. 11 A.M.-2 P.M. and 4-10:30 P.M., Sat. 4-10:30 P.M.

Though it was once owned by the Spanish Crown, the Old Pueblo these days clings to its Mexican roots more than its Spanish when it comes to culinary traditions; there aren't many places in town to sample the latest and greatest of the cuisine of Spain. Luckily Casa Vicente is here, offering a seemingly unending parade of tapas and other delights, with flamenco dancing, guitarists, and other entertainment all week. They also have an excellent wine list.

SUSHI
FUKU SUSHI ⑤
940 E. University Blvd., 520/798-3858

HOURS: Daily 11 A.M.-midnight

Open every day, and late at that, Fuku Sushi is popular with the college crowd around Main Gate Square. They serve fresh sushi and traditional Japanese fare as well as their own creative signature rolls. It's a perfect spot for a quick light lunch or a long fish-eating, sake-drinking marathon. Not as pricey as On a Roll, but just as good to my way of thinking.

ON A ROLL ⑤⑤⑤
63 E. Congress St., 520/622-7655, www.onarollsushi.com

HOURS: Mon.-Wed. 11 A.M.-10 P.M., Thurs.-Fri. 11 A.M.-2 A.M., Sat. 4 P.M.-2 A.M.

Most of Tucson's many (and always cloning) sushi joints are closed on Monday; On a Roll,

an upscale eatery on Congress downtown, is one of just a few places serving spicy tuna rolls to buck that trend. The rolls here are very creative and weak-at-the-knees delicious, but they are usually a few ticks up on the price scale from other local sushi places. The interior is cool and sleek, and the waitstaff wear stylish soccer jerseys. This isn't the place to go for a quick bite, unless you go during the cheaper happy hour times (Mon.–Fri. 4–6 P.M. and 10 P.M.–close). This is the place to go for a special dinner that you won't soon forget, especially after the bill comes.

THAI
VILA THAI CUISINE ⊖⑤
972 E. University Blvd., 520/393-3489, www.vilathai.com

HOURS: Mon.-Fri. 11 A.M.-9 P.M., Sat. noon-9 P.M.

A cozy art-filled spot upstairs from the American Apparel store at Main Gate Square, Vila Thai serves the best pad thai in town. They also make a wonderful selection of curries, and all kinds of other Thai favorites. They've got an excellent wine list, and serve a selection of Thai beers and other Asian brews. The art on the walls, mostly by local artists, changes monthly and can be challenging, inspiring, and infuriating. The cheap happy hour prices are just short of theft, offered Monday–Thursday 3–6 P.M. There's free wireless Internet and complimentary valet parking.

VEGETARIAN
GARLAND BISTRO ⊖⑤
119 E. Speedway Blvd., 520/882-3999

HOURS: Mon. and Wed.-Thurs. 8 A.M.-3 P.M., Fri. 8 A.M.-3 P.M. and 5-9 P.M., Sat. 8 A.M.-3:30 P.M. and 5-9 P.M., Sun. 8 A.M.-3:30 P.M.; summer hours vary, call ahead

This small house on Speedway serves a wide range of mostly vegetarian ethnic dishes, but there's plenty here for carnivores to enjoy as well. The Garland is particularly popular as a breakfast spot, and they make their own bread. I'd say they make the best Greek salad in town. The decor is eclectic garage-sale chic, and the waitstaff is hippie-friendly.

Midtown

Map 2

The restaurant scene in midtown, the largest neighborhood covered in this book, is extremely varied. You can get just about any kind of food you desire, from American to Middle Eastern, Thai to Greek, Mexican to French, and more. If none of the suggestions here excite your senses, explore Campbell Avenue between Grant and River; there are dozens of eateries in this section of midtown. You'll also come across scores of eateries, mostly chains, while driving along Speedway Boulevard, Grant Road, and Broadway Boulevard within the borders of midtown (roughly Campbell Ave., Wilmot Rd., 22nd St., and River Rd.).

BREAKFAST AND BRUNCH
BEYOND BREAD ❸

3026 N. Campbell Ave., 520/322-9965, www.beyondbread.com
HOURS: Mon.-Fri. 6:30 A.M.-8 P.M., Sat. 7 A.M.-8 P.M.

The two locations of this Tucson original serve delicious omelets and breakfast sandwiches every morning, perfect for a relatively quick bite. They also serve fresh-baked muffins, coffee cake, sweet rolls, and all kinds of other delectables on the sweeter side of breakfast. They also offer an assortment of the usual coffee drinks. Prepare to stand in line, especially on the weekends. This is a great place for a casual lunch as well, with all kinds of creative sandwiches on fresh-baked bread. The second location is also in midtown (6260 E. Speedway Blvd., 520/747-7477).

BLUE WILLOW ❸❸

2616 N. Campbell Ave., 520/327-7577, www.bluewillowtucson.com
HOURS: Mon.-Fri. 7 A.M.-9 P.M., Sat.-Sun. 8 A.M.-9 P.M.

Huge and delicious omelets, salads, and sandwiches can be had at the Blue Willow, which has been serving out of a cute old house with a large covered patio in Campbell Avenue's busy commercial district since 1978. I like it best for breakfast (the apple-smoked bacon haunts my dreams), but after 5 P.M. they serve entrées like black-angus meatloaf. The emphasis here is on fresh, homemade, all natural, and just-baked. A gift shop sells funny stickers, buttons, and knickknacks about politics and gender issues. It's likely to be busy here on weekend mornings.

FRANK'S ❸

3843 E. Pima St., 520/881-2710, www.franksrestaurant.com
HOURS: Mon.-Fri. 6 A.M.-2 P.M., Sat. 7 A.M.-2 P.M., Sun. 8 A.M.-2 P.M.

Frank's is the best greasy spoon in Tucson, and perhaps the greasiest. Their motto, displayed proudly on a roadside sign out front, is Elegant Dining Elsewhere. You can sit at a rickety table inside or on the patio, or belly-up to the bar and watch your hash browns cook on the grill. The breakfast menu has all you'd expect, with the addition of Mexican favorites, which are highly recommended—there's nothing like getting all spiced up early in the

WHAT'S A WILLCOX TOMATO?

At several of the fine-dining establishments in the foothills neighborhood (and at a few other eateries, grocery stores, and farmers markets in the Old Pueblo), you're likely to see some bragging on menus that this or that dish includes Willcox Tomatoes, or Heirloom Willcox Tomatoes.

Don't worry, it's not some newly engineered super-tomato or anything – quite the contrary, in fact. It simply means that the tomato was grown in the Sulphur Springs Valley near Willcox, about 80 miles east of Tucson. It turns out that the climatic conditions around Willcox are ideal for year-round agriculture, and the area is dotted with greenhouses and farms both large and boutique; **Sunzona** and **Eurofresh** are two of the most well known.

A greasy spoon for breakfast, and a Mexican-food joint at night, Frank's/Francisco's has it all.

morning. This small place draws a big crowd on weekend mornings, so have patience.

THE HUNGRY FOX $

4637 E. Broadway Blvd., 520/326-2835,
www.thehungryfox.com

HOURS: Mon.-Thurs. 6 A.M.-2 P.M., Fri. 6 A.M.-2 P.M. and 4-8 P.M., Sat.-Sun. 6:30 A.M.-2 P.M. and 4-8 P.M.

If you need a big old-school breakfast to get your engine running in the morning, you won't find one more traditional than the double-yolk eggs and biscuits and gravy at this Broadway Boulevard home-style eatery. The Hungry Fox's dining room takes country kitsch to a level that teeters on parody, but once you taste the food you'll know that this is a very serious restaurant, despite the decor. You'll likely encounter a crowd of hungry churchgoers on Sunday mornings, but there's a little gift shop in the waiting area to keep you distracted.

CHINESE

GEE'S GARDEN BISTRO $$

1145 N. Alvernon Way, 520/325-5353

HOURS: Mon.-Fri. 11 A.M.-10 P.M., Sat. 10 A.M.-10 P.M., Sun. 10 A.M.-9 P.M.

One of the few options in Tucson for authentic dim sum, Gee's has a kind of gaudy faux temple look on the outside, and its interiors are just as confusing and delightful. The dining room is huge and high-ceilinged and packed with so many red-draped tables that it somehow always feels empty. Nevertheless, the usual favorites are more than acceptable here, if a bit overpriced. The weekend dim sum is excellent, full of exotic dumplings and other teahouse standards.

GUILIN HEALTHY CHINESE RESTAURANT $

3250 E. Speedway Blvd., 520/320-7768

HOURS: Mon.-Thurs. 11 A.M.-9 P.M., Fri. 11 A.M.-10 P.M., Sat. 11:30 A.M.-9:30 P.M., Sun. 11:30 A.M.-9 P.M.

Tucsonans, especially those who have recently migrated from the right and left coasts, are wont to complain about the city's paucity of good Chinese restaurants. And while I can't disagree entirely, I've yet to be disappointed by the food at this midtown fixture. It always tastes fresh and is never too greasy, and the menu is heavy with vegetarian options. I always leave those industrial "Chinese" super-buffets around town feeling sick from grease, MSG, and guilt. Leaving Guilin all I feel is rightly and correctly full.

COFFEE HOUSES
COFFEE TIME ⑨
3401 E. Speedway Blvd., 520/318-3698
HOURS: Mon.-Sat. 5 A.M.-6 P.M., Sun. 6 A.M.-4 P.M.

If you can't be bothered to get out of your car but think you still deserve an excellent latte, get in line at this tiny kiosk along Speedway Boulevard (just across the street from Ike's). Along with top-notch coffee drinks, the friendly staff (who will, after just a few return trips, invariably remember your usual) will make you a panini while you wait behind the wheel. During the morning rush on weekdays the line of cars here can be quite long, but the crack staff usually whittles it down in no time.

◖ IKE'S COFFEE & TEA ⑨
3400 E. Speedway Blvd., 520/323-7205
HOURS: Daily 6 A.M.-midnight

I've never seen Ike's Speedway Boulevard location empty—or even thinned out, for that matter. One can seemingly visit during any of the 18 hours this sleek locally owned coffee house is open every day and hear the gentle tick-tick-tick of patrons at their laptops. It's a popular place for study sessions, business meetings, and general chit-chat, owing to its excellent free wireless network, its open, cool interior, its very good coffee drinks, and a host of delicious fare, mostly of the breakfast and lunch variety. The downtown location (100 N. Stone Ave., 520/792-1800) has truncated hours (Mon.–Fri. 7 A.M.–5:30 P.M.), as it exists primarily to serve downtown workers and their banker's hours.

RAGING SAGE ⑨
2458 N. Campbell Ave., 520/320-5203
HOURS: Mon.-Thurs. 6:30 A.M.-9:30 P.M., Fri.-Sat. 6:30 A.M.-11:30 P.M., Sun. 6:30 A.M.-7 P.M.

Small and a bit cramped on the inside and lacking an Internet connection, Raging Sage would seem to be a marginal coffee house in a neighborhood largely run by college students. Not so, however. The fresh-roasted coffee is so good and the homemade baked goods so delicious (I once had a green-chile scone here that left me weak and confused), that this coffee house remains popular despite a few drawbacks. Besides, the patio tables spread things out a bit, and you can usually glom on to one of the many wireless networks hovering about the area, so there's really no reason not to go.

Ike's Coffee & Tea is a large, easy-going coffee house in midtown.

© TIM HULL

RESTAURANTS

© TIM HULL

You'll see homegrown fast-food eatery Eegee's on nearly every corner in Tucson.

FAST FOOD
EEGEE'S $

2510 E. Speedway Blvd., www.eegees.com

HOURS: Sun.-Thurs. 9:30 A.M.-10 P.M.,
Fri.-Sat.9:30 A.M.-10:30 P.M.

A homegrown enterprise, Eegee's has been a favorite among Tucsonans for more than 30 years. The most popular items on the menu are the frozen drinks—a Styrofoam cup full of flavored shaved ice that goes down very easy on a hot summer day in the desert. My favorite flavor is still the one they started with: lemon. They serve excellent deli-style sandwiches—many of them hot—and french fries and other, similar fare. The ranch fries, a heap of sliced and deep-fried potatoes smothered in ranch dressing and topped with bacon bits, are a delight if you can risk the coronary. There are 21 of these Tucson-only joints throughout the city.

LUCKY WISHBONE $

2545 N. Campbell Ave., 520/323-9329,
www.luckywishbone.com

HOURS: Daily 11 A.M.-9 P.M.

Deep-fried food, nothing more and nothing less—that's what you'll find at this nostalgic

Old Pueblo favorite. They serve deep-fried chicken, steak fingers, shrimp, gizzards, fish, onion rings, fries, and some of the best garlic toast in the world. It's not exactly healthy, and you're likely to feel a bit grease-spritzed afterwards, but a "family feast" from Lucky Wishbone is certainly one of the guilty pleasures to be had in Tucson. The local chain has six restaurants. The other midtown location is at 10 North Swan Road (520/327-5679).

LUKE'S $

4444 E. Grant Rd., 520/321-9236

HOURS: Mon.-Sat. 10 A.M.-9 P.M., Sun. 11 A.M.-5 P.M.

Luke's serves the best hot dogs in town—as long as you're talking about Chicago-style dogs. In Tucson, the famous Sonoran-style hot dog gets all the press, but lovers of Polish sausage, bratwurst, all-beef dogs with the red-hot works, and posters of Chicago-area sports teams from the 1980s and 1990s should not miss lunch at this spot. These guys fancy themselves traditionalists. I once asked them to hold the onions on my Chicago dog and got a look like I had just spit in the mustard. There is a second Luke's location at 101 East Fort Lowell Road (520/888-8066).

🄲 NICO'S ⑤

1855 E. Fort Lowell Rd., 520/327-3190

HOURS: Daily 24 hours

It's three in the morning and you haven't had an enchilada in nearly 12 hours. You can't sleep, and when you do doze off your troubled, shallow dreams are filled with rice and beans, guacamole, carne asada burritos, and chiles rellenos. Don't panic. On nearly every corner in Tucson there's a Nico's taco shop (or some similar joint that is usually passable but not as good in my view), and they exist to fulfill late-night cravings. The food here is a bit on the greasy side, but it is so tasty and filling and satisfying that nobody cares. Not surprisingly, you'll usually find the drive-thru crowded shortly after the bars close down.

FRENCH

GHINI'S FRENCH CAFFE ⑤⑤

1803 E. Prince Rd., 520/326-9095,
www.ghiniscafe.com

HOURS: Tues.-Sat. 6:30 A.M.-3 P.M., Sun. 8 A.M.-2 P.M.

In a tucked-away space in a strip mall at Prince and Campbell, Ghini's French Caffe and La Baguette Bakery bring a bit of French taste to the desert city. Breakfast is the café's claim to fame, served all day on Saturday and Sunday. Ghini's Eggs Provençale, a fry-up of tomatoes and garlic and eggs on a crunchy baguette, is known far and wide, and their omelets are probably the best in town. The lunch menu includes a slew of unique Frenched-up sandwiches and salads, but my favorite is the simple, delicious *soupe a l'oignon.* Every Tuesday from 5 to 7 P.M. the café stays open for an "aperitif hour," during which they serve little plates of escargots, mussels, and other French favorites, and offer discounts on glasses of wine from their smart collection. They also serve appetite-whetting pastis, and various dark and decadent desserts from the bakery.

GREEK

FRONIMO'S GREEK CAFÉ ⑤

3242 E. Speedway Blvd., 520/327-8321,
www.fronimos.com

HOURS: Daily 10 A.M.-9 P.M.

This casual eatery along Speedway serves excellent gyros, souvlaki, lamb shank, and all

Tuesday happy hours at Ghini's French Caffe offer all kinds of small plates.

Excellent Greek favorites can be had at Fronimo's Greek Café.

manner of other Greek and American delights (including burgers and other sandwiches). The Greek salad is always crisp and fresh, and the baklava is a treat. They also make really good onion rings for those of us who care nothing about our bulges. There's a decent selection of Greek wines and beers as well. A gyro with fries or onion rings, hummus, or Fronimo's special rice pilaf makes for a filling, tasty lunch.

ICE CREAM
AUSTIN'S $

2920 E. Broadway Blvd., 520/514-5132
HOURS: Mon.-Thurs. 11 A.M.-10 P.M.,
Fri.-Sat. 11 A.M.-11 P.M., Sun. 11 A.M.-7 P.M.

The burgers and dogs and other diner-style classics served at this local favorite are good, but it's their homemade ice cream that has kept Austin's open and popular in the Old Pueblo since 1959. They make a variety of flavors, and serve it straight up or in one of their signature sundaes or shakes. The restaurant's current east-side location is relatively new; the joint lingered around its original midtown building until it nearly collapsed in on itself. The beloved parlor moved into its current clean and bright digs across from the Park Mall in 2006, thus assuring its existence for at least a few more generations.

INDIAN
THE INDIA OVEN $

2727 N. Campbell Ave., 520/326-8635
HOURS: Daily 11 A.M.-2:45 P.M. and 5-9:45 P.M.

There's nothing better than a well-stocked buffet when you're really craving the outlandishly delicious cuisine of the world's largest democracy. In Tucson, you'll find the best Indian buffet in this small, nondescript eatery along Campbell Avenue. The dishes are always well made, and the buffet is generally kept fresh and full; try not to fill up on the perfect naan and crispy samosas before you get some saucy, spiced-up goodness from the buffet's various traditional Indian meat, lentil, and vegetable dishes. You can order off the menu if you don't want to pile up a multicolored, multiflavored plate.

ITALIAN
ROCCO'S LITTLE CHICAGO $

2707 E. Broadway Blvd., 520/321-1860,
www.roccoslittlechicago.com
HOURS: Mon.-Sat. 11 A.M.-10 P.M.

It's no secret that half the Rust Belt migrates to the Southwest come October. This explains the diversity of Midwestern-style restaurants in Arizona, and Tucson is no exception. Chicagoans missing their beloved pizza styles will find their homesickness cured in this seemingly always crowded little joint along Broadway Boulevard. They serve up thin- and thick-crust pies, calzones, cheesecake, pasta, and sandwiches—all so good and authentic that they've been known to convince a few snowbirds to finally put down roots in the Old Pueblo. After all, why go home if the pizza's this good out West?

JAPANESE
SUSHI GARDEN $

15 N. Alvernon Way, 520/326-4700,
www.sushigarden.com
HOURS: Mon.-Thurs. 11 A.M.-10 P.M.,
Fri.-Sat. 11 A.M.-11 P.M., Sun. noon-10 P.M.

There are two reasons to visit the Sushi Garden: the sushi and the lunch buffet. The nigiri and sashimi is always fresh and delicious, and the house *ura maki* rolls are typically outstanding. You can eat all that fits in your stomach for $20 per person. The lunch buffet ($9 pp, ends at 2 P.M.) includes California rolls and usually a tempura roll of some kind, but the various Japanese noodle dishes, crunchy appetizers, chicken and beef dishes, and miso soup are the real draw. They serve a variety of Japanese beers and, of course, sake. It's a casual eatery with few frills, but the staff is friendly and there are several TVs staring down from the corners showing one sporting event or another.

YOSHIMATSU HEALTHY JAPANESE EATERY $

2660 N. Campbell, 520/320-1574,
www.yoshimatsuaz.com
HOURS: Daily 11:30 A.M.-2:30 P.M. and 5-9 P.M.

The owners of Yoshimatsu, the best Japanese

Popular and obscure Japanese food is served at Yoshimatsu Healthy Japanese Eatery.

restaurant in Tucson, took a disused building along Campbell Avenue that was once a chain family dining joint and turned it into one of the most stylish and popular eateries in midtown. The interior of this casual place is all dark wood, framed Japanese pop-art images, and big, secluded booths for sake parties among friends. The staff is young and friendly, and the food—a variety of popular, traditional, and virtually unknown Japanese dishes unparalleled in Tucson—is fresh, light, and tasty. There's also a warm wood-floored little sushi bar off the main dining room that's a great scene for couples and romance over half-price happy-hour sake and a tempura-fried "jalapeño seven" roll. And yes, of course they have karaoke.

MALAYSIAN
SERI MELAKA FINE MALAYSIAN CUISINE 💲💲
6133 E. Broadway Blvd., 520/747-7811,
www.serimelaka.com
HOURS: Daily 11 A.M.–9:30 P.M.
If you're not familiar with Malaysian cuisine but

want to give it a try, this unique and welcoming restaurant on the east side offers three different prix fixe menus (for $12.95, $14.95, and $18.95) that present a kind of greatest-hits collection. The light but filling, outrageously tasty food here is based on old family recipes from Melaka, Malaysia, an area with a long history of Chinese migration. This explains the many unfamiliar Chinese dishes offered here as well.

MEXICAN
CASA MOLINA 💲
6225 E. Speedway Blvd., 520/886-5468,
www.casamolina.com
HOURS: Daily 11 A.M.–10 P.M.
There are a few places in Tucson called Casa Molina, but this is the only one that matters. Since 1947, the Molina family has been serving up authentic Mexican favorites on the far eastern edge of midtown in a cool old adobe building with a life-size bull and matador battling each other outside. The building itself is an attraction: There's a lush outdoor patio and a perfectly round room (the Redondo

RESTAURANTS

© TIM HULL

Casa Molina has an excellent buffet on Sundays.

Room) with a saguaro-rib ceiling; the hand-made furniture, wall hangings, and murals will keep you entertained until your delicious high-piled plates arrive. Attending the popular Sunday buffet (11 A.M.–3 P.M.) is a good way to sample a variety of Mexican dishes you might not otherwise order. There's a small, friendly cantina inside where they serve a mean magarita.

FRANCISCO'S $

3843 E. Pima St., 520/881-2710,
www.franciscosintucson.com
HOURS: Sun.-Thurs. 5–10 P.M., Fri.-Sat. 5 P.M.-midnight

Everybody in midtown knows Frank's, the small breakfast and lunch joint at Pima and Alvernon that lets diners know from the start that they'll find "elegant dining elsewhere;" but after the sun retires Frank's becomes Francisco's, serving family-style Mexican food from the state of Michoacán. The food here is on the spicier side, and you'll always get a *cebollita asada* (grilled onion) with your dinner. Big plates of carne asada, *birria,* and *pollo asada*—all along side heaps of rice and beans—are served here, as well as many shrimp dishes and the usual enchiladas, burritos, tacos, and tostadas, but with regional twists (pig's-feet enchiladas, anyone?) that you won't find anywhere else in town.

ROSA'S $

1750 E. Fort Lowell Rd. No. 164, 520/325-0362,
www.rosasmexicanfood.com
HOURS: Daily 11 A.M.-10 P.M.

I have generally found that the great Willie Nelson provides a perfect model for the Western man. That's why I started going to Rosa's: The red-headed stranger's autographed photos are plastered all over this small strip-mall eatery at Fort Lowell and Campbell. It's Willie approved, and that's good enough for me. The Sonoran-style dishes here are always cheesy, sauce-slopped, and delicious. Even though the restaurant has expanded it always seems to be hectic and even chaotic at Rosa's, and the service can be either horrendous or perfunctory depending on how busy it is. The food, however, is unassailable.

RESTAURANTS

© TIM HULL

Ali Baba has the best Middle Eastern food in town.

MIDDLE EASTERN
ALI BABA $

2545 E. Speedway, Ste. 125, 520/319-2559,
www.alibabatucson.com

HOURS: Mon.-Sat. 11 A.M.-8 P.M., Sun. noon-8 P.M.

From this ultra-casual storefront in one of Speedway Boulevard's ubiquitous commercial strips comes the best Middle Eastern (including Lebanese and Persian) food in Arizona other than Tempe's Haji Baba. The falafel is crunchy and wrapped together with a perfectly balanced sauce, and the baba ghanoush is the best I've ever had. The Persian dishes are less recognizable to the average American, but no less tasty. Try any of the Persian kabob plates served with rice and tomatoes—though you risk addiction if you do.

NEW AMERICAN
THE DISH BISTRO-BAR $$

3131 E. 1st St. (inside The RumRunner), 520/326-1714,
www.dishbistro.com

HOURS: Tues.-Thurs. 5-9 P.M., Fri.-Sat. 5-10 P.M.

This warm, elegant bistro and wine bar inside

The RumRunner, a popular local wine and spirits shop, is famous for its mussels—a big steaming bowl of them floating in saffron broth with diced tomatoes and oregano. The "big dishes" served in this very small bistro are all over $20 and include duck, salmon, and New York strip creations. The "small dishes," best enjoyed with a glass of wine or two from RumRunner's large inventory, run $8–15 and include lobster tails and warm goat cheese with grilled bread. Reservations are a good idea.

FEAST $$

4122 E. Speedway Blvd., 520/326-9363 or
520/326-6500, www.eatatfeast.com

HOURS: Tues.-Sun. 11 A.M.-9 P.M.

It's easy to buzz by Feast's small storefront, wherein they claim to serve "tasteful takeout." That means the likes of saddle of rabbit with chicken livers, monkfish foie gras, and sunchoke hash—to go. There's no reason to hurry off, though; the small dining room is surprisingly serene and romantic considering the stream of traffic right outside. An adventurous long lunch

RESTAURANTS

Feast offers creative gourmet goodness to go.

can be had here, with maybe a glass of wine or two and a grilled cheese sandwich made with seared Halloumi cheese and honey-roasted eggplant. The menu changes monthly, with some repetitions. They don't take reservations.

KINGFISHER $$

2564 E. Grant Rd., 520/323-7739,
www.kingfishertucson.com
HOURS: Mon.-Fri. 11 A.M.-10 P.M., Sat.-Sun. 5-10 P.M.

A local favorite for fresh and ingeniously prepared seafood, Kingfisher has a thick oyster menu with something like 15 different varieties. For lunch, the pan-fried shrimp cakes are awesome, and the gulf shrimp is always fresh and sweet. For dinner there's a selection of fish, scallop, pasta, and meat dishes, including magnificent baby-back ribs smothered in prickly pear barbecue sauce. The bar usually stays open until 1 A.M. or so, and there's a late-night menu of small plates. Reservations are recommended, especially on the weekends.

PASTICHE MODERN EATERY $$

3025 N. Campbell Ave., 520/325-3333,
www.pasticheme.com
HOURS: Mon.-Fri. 11:30 A.M.-midnight,
Sat.-Sun. 4:30 P.M.-midnight

The very definition of New American, Pastiche is an upscale eatery along Campbell Avenue that dips into culinary styles the world over and dribbles its findings on American-based dishes. The results are typically excellent, and the elegant atmosphere makes you want to stick around for a drink or two. If you're out on the town late, stop by between 10 P.M. and midnight any night, when Pastiche's myriad creative appetizers—fried avocado, coconut shrimp, pot stickers, and much more—are half price. If you're a Guinness drinker, you might want to make a special trip to try the Guinness Steak ($15): ground steak marinated in Guinness, with porter cheddar, pepper bacon, Guinness gravy, and a fried egg on grilled sourdough.

SOUTHWESTERN
OLD PUEBLO GRILLE 💲💲

60 N. Alvernon Way, 520/326-6000,
www.metrorestaurants.com

HOURS: Sun.-Thurs. 11 A.M.-10 P.M.,
Fri.-Sat. 11 A.M.-10:30 P.M.

Ask five people what Southwestern food is and you're likely to get at least three different answers. To many, it's Sonoran-style Mexican food all dressed up; to others it's about recovering the lost food knowledge of the desert peoples. To a late-century Arizona-reared fella like me, Southwestern food was whatever my mom put on the table—usually something fairly predictable and "American" (chicken, fish, or beef, plus potato and veg), but with a little extra spice. That's exactly what they serve at the Old Pueblo Grille. Make sure to try the chipotle mashed potatoes and the green-chile mac and cheese.

THAI
KARUNA'S THAI PLATE 💲

917 E. Grant Rd., 520/325-4129

HOURS: Tues.-Thurs. noon-3 P.M. and 5-10 P.M.,
Fri.-Sat. 5-9 P.M.

This tiny Thai restaurant on Grant, just across the street from Bookmans, is not much to look at (and the staff can be sullen and perfunctory and even grumpy at times), but it serves a reasonably priced and downright delicious buffet of Thai favorites, plus a full menu. The pad thai, curries, and spring rolls here are as tasty as they get, and everything is kept relatively fresh at the buffet. This is a perfect budget-minded or takeout lunch or dinner spot in midtown.

VEGETARIAN
🌙 GOVINDA'S NATURAL FOOD BUFFET 💲

711 E. Blacklidge Dr., 520/792-0630,
www.govindasoftucson.com

HOURS: Wed.-Sat. 11:30 A.M.-2:30 P.M. and 5-9 P.M.

Some of the best vegetarian eats in town can be found at Govinda's, where on Thursday night everything is vegan, and on Tuesday authentic Indian food is served. Sunday brunch is served 11 A.M.–2:30 P.M., featuring pancakes, home fries, and scrambled tofu. The restaurant is located at the Chaitanya Cultural Center, and its name refers to one of Krishna's many incarnations; you will be among Tucson's Hare Krishna community here, in a peaceful and

Karuna's Thai Plate

© TIM HULL

© TIM HULL

Some of the best, most creative vegetarian food in Arizona can be had at Lovin' Spoonfuls Vegetarian Restaurant.

RESTAURANTS

always friendly atmosphere that may spark a meditative mood—post-buffet, of course.

LOVIN' SPOONFULS
VEGETARIAN RESTAURANT $

2990 N. Campbell Ave., Ste. 120, 520/325-7766, www.lovinspoonfuls.com

HOURS: Mon.-Sat. 9:30 A.M.-9 P.M., Sun. 10 A.M.-3 P.M.

I know a few vegetarians in Tucson who'd like to eat all their meals at Lovin' Spoonfuls: For breakfast it'd be a Southwestern tofu scramble. For lunch, a portobello griller or maybe a soy burger. For dinner it'd be the lasagna with mock Italian sausage. The atmosphere here is calm and friendly and homegrown in the best possible sense, and if you go once you will likely return again and again.

VIETNAMESE
MISS SAIGON $

1072 N. Campbell Ave., 520/320-9511

HOURS: Mon.-Sat. 10:30 A.M.-9:30 P.M., Sun. 11:30 A.M.-9:30 P.M.

This popular Vietnamese eatery just east of the UA campus packs them in for the best *pho* in town. The traditional noodle soup is served with the freshest herbs and bean sprouts and jalapeños on the side, and the spring rolls are light and delicious when dipped liberally in Miss Saigon's awesome peanut sauce. Think about getting the small bowl of *pho*—it's big enough, believe me. They also serve rich and decadent slushes with either coconut-jelly or tapioca, and other exotic desserts and drinks.

The Foothills Map 3

In the foothills of the Santa Catalina Mountains north of midtown you'll find high-end, high-concept eateries that define the cutting edge of Tucson's culinary scene. Nearly all of the upscale restaurants in this neighborhood offer patio dining with gorgeous views of the valley and the mountains. While still casual at heart, the scene in the foothills requires a bit more dressing up than it does elsewhere in the Old Pueblo. You can still wear jeans, but maybe replace those flip-flops with a pair of loafers.

CONTINENTAL

ANTHONY'S IN THE CATALINAS $$$

6440 N. Campbell Ave., 520/299-1771,
www.anthonyscatalinas.com

HOURS: Daily 5:30-10 P.M.

The foothills of the Santa Catalina Mountains have been a place for culinary

TALKING WITH TUCSON CHEF AND AUTHOR JANOS WILDER

While studying political science at the University of California–Berkeley in the late 1960s, Tucson chef Janos Wilder learned to break every received notion down to its ideal, primary form. A James Beard Award-winning chef and a longtime regional leader in the trend toward growing, buying, and eating local foods, Wilder still uses such methods in the kitchen.

Consider, for example, the chile relleno, a

© TIM HULL

Janos Wilder, a James Beard Award-winner, is one of Tucson's most popular chefs.

touchstone of Tucson's regional cuisine on which Janos wrote an entire cookbook, *The Great Chiles Rellenos Book* (Ten Speed Press, 2008). He didn't really like the dish when he first tried it. It was generally not well made, and full of some lesser cheese imported all the way from Wisconsin. So, Janos re-created it. The first one he made had lobster and brie stuffed in an Anaheim chili, dipped in beer batter and covered with a French cream sauce. Is that Southwestern food?

"It's a departure from our sense of place, but totally grounded in the history of the region," the chef said when I sat down with him at his J Bar, which is attached to his main endeavor in life, world-renowned restaurant Janos, on the grounds of the Westin La Paloma Resort in the foothills.

"What we do is extremely optimistic," he continued. "We take ancient foods and ancient ingredients and cook them with an eye toward the future, saying: This is what can be; this is what is possible."

It's an approach toward authenticity that Wilder learned, in part, from members of the Gila River Indian community when he was researching the native foods of the Gila River basin as part of his consulting work for Kai, a fine-dining restaurant on the Gila River Reservation at Wild Horse Pass, in Phoenix, about an hour and a half up I-10 from Tucson.

adventurism since 1998—at least since (now-defunct) Terra Cotta and Janos moved from downtown to the high-end north end. But long before that, Tucson's wealthy had a more traditional non-resort fine-dining destination on the scenic bajada in the pink-walled Spanish revival structure that is Anthony's. This is your grandfather's fine-dining restaurant. If you're hankering for a bit of conservatively prepared chateaubriand, beef Wellington, grilled quail, or lamb chops, accompanied by a long and distinguished wine list, then this is your place. There is absolutely no way you are going to leave Anthony's without spending at least $60 per person, but you're likely to remember the experience for a while afterwards. You will definitely remember the view. Reservations are strongly recommended.

JANOS ⑤⑤⑤

3770 E. Sunrise Dr., 520/615-6100, www.janos.com
HOURS: Mon.-Thurs. 5:30-9 P.M.,
Fri.-Sat. 5:30-9:30 P.M.

The James Beard Award–winning chef and author Janos Wilder mixes French culinary

Wilder sat in on meetings with the tribal elders, people who had lived on the reservation and among each other all their lives. "I asked them, what did you eat when you were growing up?" Wilder explained. "The conversation went on for hours, and became really animated. There was a lot of, 'your mom used to make this, and I used to go to your house and eat this'; and I'm scribbling notes furiously and everybody is laughing and I am thinking these are wonderful memories – I can really use this stuff."

But then, at the end of the conversation, Wilder remembered to ask the simplest question of all: So how *was* the food? "Oh, it sucked," they all said. "Our mothers couldn't cook worth a damn!"

"I realized then," Janos said, "that these were great memories, but they weren't the memories people were going to spend money to have; it reinforced what had been my take on it from the beginning, which is, let's move forward, but with the past still in hand. It was funny; but it is also reminded me, don't take what you are doing too seriously."

Wilder's interest in local foods began pragmatically. He was working at the Gold Hill Inn above Boulder, Colorado, at 8,300 feet and the end of a dirt road; not a lot of distributors were willing to deliver there.

"In the course of doing that I realized that there were some foods that were being pro-duced right around me in the mountains," he said. "If we had a neighbor who was growing rhubarb, we would trade meals for it, and in the process of going into town every day I started seeing that there were trout farms and mushroom foragers and all kinds of other local products that I could get, and I always made up my menu for the day in the truck on the way back to the restaurant."

In 1983, after a sojourn in France living on the far edge of local, artisan cooking, he opened the first Janos in downtown Tucson, and immediately started looking for local farmers and other producers from which to purchase his ingredients. And he hasn't looked back. He still prints all of his menus in-house, and he is still dedicated to the local foods movement – a movement that he helped create.

When I asked him to summarize his philosophy of cooking, he had this to say: "Be serious about your craft; take that seriously, of course – the craft of cooking and the craft of service – but don't take yourself too seriously or what you are doing too seriously," he told me. "Having people in for dinner is fun, it's not a downer. I'm not trying to make sure everybody who eats here 'gets it.' *I* need to get it, you just need to like it. If I have done my job right you will taste it and it will come through the food; it's not about high culinary concept at the table, though it may be in the kitchen."

ideals with traditional Southwestern and Latin American ingredients at this popular high-end eatery on the grounds of the Westin La Paloma Resort. The result is usually something heretofore unconsidered, such as grilled beef tenderloin with *churrasco*-style wild licensed Mexican shrimp, duck-confit *papas rellenos,* and *chiles rajas.* Janos is all about sustainable, local ingredients, and he works with regional farmers and the folks at Native Seeds/SEARCH to find the freshest, most sustainable, and most interesting regional ingredients he can. The menu changes pretty regularly—it's printed in-house, allowing for maximum flexibility in responding to seasonal variations. Dining here is an adventure, and usually an expensive one, but well worth it. Next door to the main restaurant is the more casual and less expensive, but still relatively experimental, **J Bar** (Mon.–Sat. 5 –9:30 P.M., happy hour Mon.–Sat. 5–6:30 P.M.), with excellent creative cocktails, Latin American–inspired bar foods, and great views of the city down below. Reservations are strongly recommended for the main restaurant.

ITALIAN
NORTH ⑤⑤⑤
2995 E. Skyline Dr., 520/299-1600,
www.foxrestaurantconcepts.com
HOURS: Sun.-Thurs. 11 A.M.-3 P.M. and 5-10 P.M.,
Fri.-Sat. 11 A.M.-3 P.M. and 5 P.M.-midnight

Another one of Scottsdale-based Fox Restaurant Concepts' upscale eat-and-drink playhouses in the foothills, North, at La Encantada (Skyline and Campbell), has a huge patio with comfortable furniture, heat in the winter and misters in the summer, and commanding views of the Santa Catalina range hovering close above and the valley below. The food, billed as modern Italian cuisine, is generally delicious, especially their appetizers and pizzas. For dinner, the "plates of the day" feature all sorts of Italian favorites done a bit differently. This place seems perfect for sitting around the patio with a group of friends, drinking wine, chomping on antipasti and bruschetta. They serve a limited bar menu 3–4:30 P.M. every day. Reservations are recommended.

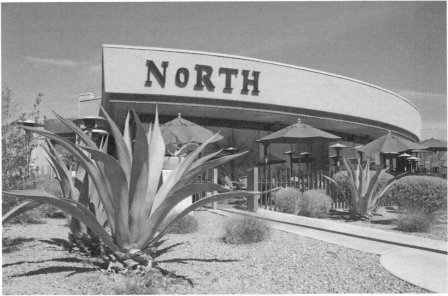

© TIM HULL

North serves high-end Italian food.

© TIM HULL

If you're ready for a change from Mexican food, try the Peruvian cuisine at Candela.

LATIN AMERICAN
CANDELA $$

5845 N. Oracle Rd., 520/407-0111

HOURS: Daily 11 A.M.–9 P.M.

Candela, an easily overlooked small strip-mall restaurant on Oracle just north of River Road, serves excellent Peruvian food—delicate and savory empanadas, intricately spiced shrimp and beef dishes with rice, fried plantains, and even Inca Kola, a Peruvian soft drink that tastes like a mixture of Mountain Dew and cream soda. Candela, with its yellow and red exterior, may not look like much from the outside, but the small dining room and bar are decorated with fascinating Peruvian artifacts, folk art, and murals.

MIGUEL'S AT LA POSADA $$

5900 N. Oracle Rd., 520/887-3777, www.miguelstucson.com

HOURS: Mon.-Thurs. 3-10 P.M., Fri.-Sun. noon-11 P.M.

Not your typical Tucson refried bean–slingers, the chefs at Miguel's at La Posada, on Oracle Road, serve a more varied and intricately prepared style of south-of-the-border cuisine than the comfort food offered at most Old Pueblo Mexican restaurants. New Latin American cuisine, one might call it. That's not to say you can't get an enchilada here, it's just that it will be filled with wild mushrooms. You can get beans and rice, too, only they'll be black beans and creamy Oaxacan rice. The chile relleno is filled with fresh seafood from the Sea of Cortez; the Guaymas prawns are wrapped in bacon and slathered with a horseradish and brown-sugar sauce. Get my drift? They also have something like a hundred different kinds of tequila in their cozy cantina (the margaritas here are among the best in town), where they serve a limited but delicious bar menu all day. Reservations are recommended.

MEXICAN
◖ LA FUENTE $$

1749 N. Oracle Rd., 520/623-8659, www.lafuenterestaurant.com

HOURS: Mon.-Thurs. 11 A.M.-9 P.M., Fri. 11 A.M.-10 P.M., Sat. noon-10 P.M., Sun. 11 A.M.-9 P.M.

The airy, tropical interiors at La Fuente, a

© TIM HULL

La Fuente is one of the best places in town to hear mariachi music with your meal.

popular Old Pueblo eatery since 1959, add to what always seems to be a busy, festive air in this popular Mexican restaurant on Oracle just north of downtown, but it's the loud and brassy mariachi band strolling among the tables (Thurs.–Sun.) that really brings in the crowds. The food here is excellent, if a bit pricey; the fresh guacamole, prepared before your eyes right at table, is among the best in town—and the atmosphere can't be beat. A champagne brunch is served Sunday 11 A.M.–2 P.M.

NEW AMERICAN
ACACIA AT ST. PHILIP'S $$$
4340 N. Campbell Ave., 520/232-0101,
www.acaciatucson.com
HOURS: Mon.-Thurs. 11 A.M.-3 P.M. and 5-9 P.M., Fri.-Sat. 11 A.M.-2 P.M. and 5-10 P.M., Sun. 10 A.M.-2 P.M. and 5-9 P.M.

The best thing about Acacia is its patio looking out on the shops and oversized garden statue of, one assumes, the titular saint at St. Philip's Plaza, a small shopping and eating center at Campbell and River on the edge of the foothills. That's not to say that the food takes a

back seat to the atmosphere, which is all about upscale but casual elegance, the foothills' go-to aesthetic. The food here also follows the neighborhood tradition of mixing local and sustainable boutique ingredients, many of them with a Southwestern and Latin bent, with high-style culinary methods to create something new and wonderful. The Guaymas Shrimp Cocktail, made with big sweet shrimp from the Sea of Cortez just a few hundred miles to the south and mixed with peppadew chile, mango, and horseradish, is one of the best variations on the classic that I've ever had. Not too many of the high-dollar foothills eateries serve lunch; Acacia does, and it's a good way to sample the fare without having to take out a loan.

THE GRILL AT HACIENDA DEL SOL $$$
5601 N. Hacienda del Sol Rd., 520/529-3500,
www.haciendadelsol.com
HOURS: Daily 5:30-10 P.M.,
Sun. brunch 10 A.M.-1:30 P.M.

Tucson, especially its foothills, is known for its

© TIM HULL

Acacia offers excellent patio dining at St. Philip's Plaza.

year-round patio dining and sweeping views of the city, with twinkling lights from the valley like signal fires in the darkness below. The best patio out of them all is the Terraza del Sol bar, inside The Grill at Hacienda del Sol, a charming historic resort in the foothills. Terraza del Sol serves a relatively low-priced bar menu ($7–26) of creative small plates, and features live music Thursday–Sunday. Inside at the Grill, dinner consists of entrées on the order of pork osso buco with a bing-cherry shallot confit, and Tasmanian ocean trout with a roasted beer and potato carpaccio. You know, the usual. Reservations are strongly recommended.

◖ VENTANA ROOM AT LOEWS VENTANA CANYON ⑤⑤⑤

7000 N. Resort Dr., 520/615-5494,
www.ventanaroom.com

HOURS: Tues.-Thurs. 6-9 P.M., Fri.-Sat. 6-10 P.M.

The tasting menu at this famous foothills restaurant, part of the world-renowned Loews Ventana Canyon Resort, is a masterpiece of locavore chic. For $85 per head you're invited to a feast both ancient and completely new—creative New American cuisine with several dashes of Southwestern flavor, combined with a commitment to use fresh, local, and even historical ingredients. This is true for all of the dishes at this AAA five-diamond, four-star restaurant that's been serving locals and visitors from around the world for 25 years, but the tasting menu's delights really sum up what's going on here. Consider this series of dishes: slow-roasted Willcox tomato soup; New England diver scallops dusted with mesquite flour (mesquite trees, found all over the desert, produce beans from which natives have long made flour and more); and a saguaro syrup gastrique, all with paired wines and dessert. I think it's safe to assume that you won't find this exact meal offered anywhere else in the world. It's a Sonoran Desert original, just like the restaurant that serves it. Reservations are a must.

RESTAURANTS

VIN TABLA $●●●$

2890 E. Skyline Dr., 520/577-6210, www.vintabla.com

HOURS: Daily 5-9 P.M., happy hour daily 4-6 P.M.

The food at this high-end wine shop and restaurant at the Plaza Colonia shopping center (Skyline and Campbell) is all over the map, from Italian (baked macaroni and cheese, and pizzettas cooked in a wood-burning oven), to New American (slow-roasted pork belly with buttered braised cabbage, smashed Yukon Gold potatoes and pear relish), to Sino-French (Peking duck confit with steamy buns and plum sauce). The award-winning wine cellar, and knowledgeable sommelier, make this warm and comfortable upscale eatery a destination for wine-and-food adventurers.

WILDFLOWER $●●$

7037 N. Oracle Rd., 520/219-4230,
www.foxrestaurantconcepts.com

HOURS: Mon.-Thurs. 11 A.M.-3 P.M. and 5-9 P.M.,
Fri.-Sat. 11 A.M.-3 P.M. and 5-10 P.M., Sun. 5-9 P.M.

This delightful upscale New American eatery in Casas Adobes Plaza was the first in local success story Sam Fox's Southwestern restaurant empire (Scottsdale-based Fox Restaurant

Concepts), an empire that now markets 11 different restaurant concepts (27 total restaurants) in Arizona, Texas, Colorado, and Kansas, including North, Sauce (next door to Wildflower), Zinburger, Blanco Tacos & Tequila, and many more. It all began with Wildflower at Casas Adobes in 1998, and it's still one of the better restaurants in town, with a charming patio and familiar but dressed-up lunches like roasted meatloaf and a excellent grilled chicken BLT with aged gouda and honey mustard. For dinner they offer steaks, seafood, duck, and even variations on pad thai and bok choy; my favorite dish is the brown-sugar braised short ribs—call it meat-candy. Reservations are recommended.

ZINBURGER $●●$

1865 E. River Rd., 520/299-7799,
www.foxrestaurantconcepts.com

HOURS: Sun.-Thurs. 11 A.M.-10 P.M., Fri.-Sat. 11 A.M.-11 P.M.

For those of us who could exist on beef alone, and who believe that beef is best served ground, in patty form, and between two warm buns, there is Zinburger, Fox Restaurant Concepts' gourmet homage to the good old burger joint.

The high-end burgers, fries, and shakes at Zinburger are worth savoring.

Not surprisingly, the $14 Kobe Burger (with cheddar cheese and wild mushrooms) is quite popular, but I like the Samburger, with maple bacon, American cheese, and thousand island dressing—a kind of dressed-up Big Mac. The sides are worth a visit alone: sweet-potato chips, zucchini fries, double truffle fries. Thick shakes, crème brûlée, and bananas Foster are among the perfectly paired desserts offered in this sleek and bright, young and hip, yet relatively affordable upscale burger house. There's a happy hour daily at 4 P.M.; the bar closes an hour after the restaurant.

SEAFOOD
BLUEFIN SEAFOOD BISTRO 💲💲
7053 N. Oracle Rd., 520/531-8500,
www.bluefintucson.com
HOURS: Sun.-Thurs. 11 A.M.-9 P.M., Fri.-Sat. 11 A.M.-11 P.M.
There are at least half a dozen restaurants in and around Casas Adobes Plaza, and each is a decent place to spend your time and money. But if, like most of us, your upscale or even midscale dining resources are rather limited, I'd recommend handing them first to this charming seafood bistro. Operated by the folks

from midtown's Kingfisher, Bluefin has a cozy open-air patio-bar that looks out on a courtyard with a fountain. They serve great fish-and-chips and clam chowder for lunch, and for dinner they bring out the Alaskan king crab, Maine lobster, and all kinds of creative seafood creations; I like their Sunday brunch (until 3 P.M.) and the poached lobster Benedict the best. They've also got an oyster bar, and serve a limited late-night menu until midnight. Reservations are recommended, especially for dinner and brunch.

STEAK HOUSE
EL CORRAL RESTAURANT 💲💲
2201 E. River Rd., 520/299-6092,
www.elcorraltucson.com
HOURS: Mon.-Thurs. 5-10 P.M., Fri.-Sun. 4:30-10 P.M.
Maybe it's Southern Arizona's ranching heritage, but there's something about being in Tucson that makes you crave beef. This charming historic restaurant on the edge of the foothills is the best place in town to get prime rib, a thick steak, and a big bowl of cowboy beans. This restaurant, in a low-ceiling stone-and-wood-beam territorial ranch house

A wonderful patio and a mean bowl of clam chowder await you at Bluefin Seafood Bistro.

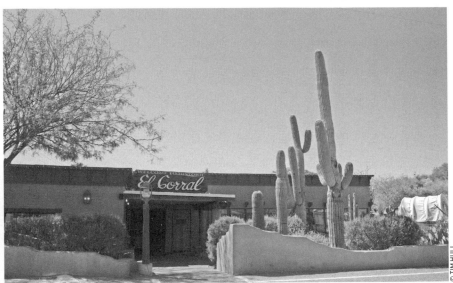

© TIM HULL

The best steaks and prime rib in town are available at the historic El Corral Restaurant.

with flagstone floors, has been a Tucson institution for more than 60 years. The setting is almost as inviting as the sizzling beef and barbecue ribs, with Technicolor portraits of movie-house cowboys on the walls and several rooms that offer romantic fireside dining.

It's also a great place to take the kids, with an inexpensive children's menu and a friendly, helpful staff. The prices are reasonable, and you'll likely agree as soon as you sink your teeth into a perfectly prepared juicy hunk of the best beef in town.

East Side and the Rincon Valley   Map 4

The sprawling east side has several excellent dining options, and the Eclectic Café offers patio dining with beautiful views of the mountains.

AMERICAN
LITTLE ANTHONY'S DINER $

7010 E. Broadway Blvd., 520/296-0456,
www.littleanthonysdiner.com

HOURS: Mon. 11 A.M.–9 P.M., Tues.-Thurs. 11 A.M.–10 P.M.,
Fri. 11 A.M.–11 P.M., Sat. 7:30 A.M.–11 P.M., Sun. 7:30 A.M.–9 P.M.

Located in the same east-side strip mall as the Gaslight Dinner Theatre, this '50s-style diner plays the part perfectly. The servers all wear

period get-ups, Elvis is ever on the radio, and there's a classic car show in the parking lot, featuring fins and chrome as far as the eye can see, at least twice a month (check website for dates). The food is just about perfect, as long as you like classic diner fare—and if you don't, you need to think about revising your opinions.

BREAKFAST AND LUNCH
MILLIE'S PANCAKE HAUS $

6530 E. Tanque Verde Rd., 520/298-4250

HOURS: Tues.-Sun. 6:30 A.M.–3 P.M.

If there's a wait at this county-style eatery at the east-side La Plaza Shoppes (as there often is for breakfast on weekends), you can always window shop around the few art galleries and boutiques near at hand. Once you're inside, try the pancakes. I mean, you can get a good omelet here, and the bacon is excellent, but if you're at a place called the "pancake haus," why not try the pancakes? You won't be disappointed if you do, and they have all sorts of flavors and syrups.

FRENCH
LE DELICE $$$

7245 E. Tanque Verde Rd., 520/290-9714, www.le-delice.com

HOURS: Breakfast daily 7 A.M.-10:30 A.M., lunch Tues.-Sat. 11 A.M.-4:30 P.M., dinner Tues.-Sat. 5-8 P.M., bakery Sun.-Mon. until 2 P.M.

The walls are covered with paintings by local artists, keeping you busy while they ladle out your vichyçoise and gather up your prosciutto and melon—all part of the plan at this east-side bistro, which claims to be "like Paris only closer." They've certainly got the food part down, anyway. The homemade quiches come in several varieties, including seafood, and the lunchtime sandwiches come on fresh baguettes (made on-site along with a variety of baked goods and pastries). The dinner menu includes, of course, canard à l'orange, and you can even get steak tartare if you order it two days in advance. On Sunday they offer brunch beginning at 11 A.M.

INDIAN
NEW DELHI PALACE $

6751 E. Broadway Blvd., 520/296-8585, www.newdelhipalacetucson.com

HOURS: Daily 11:30 A.M.-2:30 P.M. and 5-10 P.M.

The 18-item daily lunch buffet at this comfortable restaurant is outstanding, with all the favorites—curry, tandoori, vindaloo, tikka masala, samosas, etc. At dinner, they serve big plates of traditional dishes from all over India, including dishes cooked in Karhai style. They stock a full bar with a great selection of bottled beer—there's nothing like a cold India pale ale alongside a spicy heap of Indian food.

NEW AMERICAN AND MEXICAN
ECLECTIC CAFÉ $$

7053 E. Tanque Verde Rd., 520/885-2842, www.eclectic-cafe.com

HOURS: Mon.-Fri. 11 A.M.-9 P.M., Sat. 8 A.M.-9 P.M., Sun. 8 A.M.-8 P.M.

Part of the mini-empire of Tucson restaurants owned by the folks at Frank's/Francisco's in midtown, this casual east-side favorite serves a delicious, creative mixture of Mexican and New American dishes—everything from sugar-cured pit ham sandwiches to crab quesadillas to quiche Lorraine—in the Tanque Verde Shopping Center, on the northwest corner of Tanque Verde and Sabino Canyon. The tortilla soup here is excellent, as is the always freshly made guacamole; then again, so are the hamburgers and the chicken crepes. On Saturday (8 A.M.–noon) and Sunday (8 A.M.–1 P.M.) they serve a diverse breakfast, and I can assure you that their green chile and cheddar omelet is a perfectly acceptable way to start the day.

STEAK HOUSE
◖ PINNACLE PEAK STEAK HOUSE $$

6541 E. Tanque Verde Rd., 520/296-0911, www.pinnaclepeaktucson.com

HOURS: Mon.-Fri. 5-10 P.M., Sat.-Sun. 4:30-10 P.M.

Located in Trail Dust Town, the Old West theme park, Pinnacle Peak is a typical (and that means tasty, fun, and affordable) cowboy steak-and-beans hall that packs in families, tourists, and locals dining with out-of-town friends. It always seems like there's a celebratory atmosphere here. I guess that has something to do with the stage-dressing buildings and the loud cap-gun fights in the dusty streets out front. This is a fun place to bring kids—they can check out the harmless attractions while the adults have a few margaritas in the saloon before dinner. The steaks are well made and always fresh and hot, and the ranch beans go down easy on the side. There's also good prime rib and a low-priced kid's menu.

West Side and the Tucson Mountains Map 5

The west side, being a primarily wild desert and residential area, doesn't have as diverse an array of restaurants as other neighborhoods in Tucson, but many of the eateries here are long-established Old Pueblo institutions popular with locals.

FAST FOOD
PAT'S DRIVE-IN $

1202 W. Niagara St. at Grande Ave., 520/624-0891
HOURS: Mon.-Sat. 11:30 A.M.-10 P.M.,
Sun. 11:30 A.M.-9 P.M.

Fans of the chili dog will want to try this long-time local favorite, a throwback to the early days of fast food in both style and substance. It's usually busy here at lunch time, there isn't a lot of parking, and the staff can get over-whelmed on occasion, but it's worth the trouble if you like hot, flavorful chili over a hot dog with mustard and onions. The fries, onion rings, and burgers are pretty good too.

MEXICAN
MARISCOS CHIHUAHUA $$

1009 N. Grande Ave., 520/623-3563
HOURS: Daily 9 A.M.-9 P.M.

Tucsonans like to get away to a little Sea of Cortez resort town called Puerto Penasco (Rocky Point) to play in the ocean, drink, and eat shrimp, among other activities. If you can't make the trip south, however, a visit to one of the four Mariscos Chihuahua locations around the Old Pueblo is the next best thing. Their shrimp cocktail is as good as anything served in a *palapa* bar on the beach, and they offer a host of other *mariscos* (shellfish) favorites in the Mexican style and all manner of other treasures from the gulf. All the locations (2902 E. 22nd St., 520/326-1529; 999 N. Swan Rd., 520/881-2372; 356 E. Grant Rd., 520/884-3457) are great, but the ambience of the restaurant on Grand Avenue is the best. No credit cards are accepted.

Mariscos Chihuahua offers some of the best Mexican seafood dishes in Tucson.

© TIM HULL

ST. MARY'S MEXICAN FOOD $

1030 W. Saint Marys Rd., 520/884-1629

HOURS: Mon.-Sat. 8 A.M.-6:30 P.M.

This tiny Mexican joint is a good place to stop for a quick burrito for lunch if you're in the neighborhood, but it's the tortillas that keep me coming back. They've been voted best in town by readers of the *Tucson Weekly* many times, which is quite an accomplishment considering the depth of the local competition. Order up a dozen, wait while they're prepared fresh, and then just try to get to your destination before you reach in and grab one. (It won't happen.)

TERESA'S MOSAIC CAFÉ $

2455 N. Silverbell Rd., 520/624-4512

HOURS: Mon.-Sat. 7:30 A.M.-9 P.M., Sun. 7:30 A.M.-2 P.M.

This classic Sonoran-style restaurant on the west side serves up exactly what is expected of it—delicious northern Mexico favorites with a dash of individuality. The green-corn tamales are excellent here, and Alfonso's Plate—a heap of grilled beef and pork with an enchilada or one of their well-made chiles rellenos—will fill you up for at least a few days. The service here can be somewhat lackadaisical. I wouldn't drive to the west side specifically to go here, but if you're on your way back from the desert preserves out this way and are hungry for a chimichanga, this is a fine place to stop.

SOUTHWESTERN

OCOTILLO CAFÉ $$

2021 N. Kinney Rd., Arizona-Sonora Desert Museum, 520/883-2702,

www.desertmuseum.org

HOURS: Lunch Dec.-Apr. daily 11 A.M.-3 P.M., dinner June-Aug. Sat.

The café at the Arizona-Sonora Desert Museum isn't always open, but when it is it serves dishes like charred salmon with prickly pear wasabi glaze and Sonoran Niçoise salad (with a serrano pepper vinaigrette). The brand of Southwestern fusion served at Ocotillo Café is fresh and light and inventive, and of course you can't beat the setting. Their hours vary according to season; before you make the half-hour drive out to the desert, call to make sure they're serving.

RESTAURANTS

South Side   Map 6

The south side is where the best Mexican restaurants are located, and a drive down South 6th Avenue or South 4th Avenue looks a bit like a drive through a similarly sized Mexican town. If none of the Sonoran-style places listed here sounds good, head down South 4th Avenue and you'll see several Mexican places along both sides of the road.

BAKERY

LA CAVE'S BAKERY $

1219 S. 6th Ave., 520/624-2561

HOURS: Tues.-Fri. 7:30 A.M.-6 P.M., Sat. 7:30 A.M.-5 P.M., Sun. 7:30 A.M.-1 P.M.

This South 6th Avenue bakery is the best place in town to get Mexican wedding cookies and other South Tucson delicacies, but I keep coming back for the simple glazed doughnuts, the best in town hands-down. A variety of other freshly made pastries and breads are available throughout the day at this longtime local favorite. If you're going in the early morning, remember that that they don't serve coffee—just absolutely perfect doughnuts.

MEXICAN

EL GUERO CANELO $

5201 S. 12th Ave., 520/295-9005,

www.elguerocanelo.com

HOURS: Mon.-Sat. 7 A.M.-midnight, Sun. 7:30 A.M.-midnight

The carne asada and the Mexican (sometimes called Sonoran) hot dogs are the specialties of the house here, and the 12th Street semi-outdoor location replicates better than any other

Old Pueblo Mexican restaurant the atmosphere of casual eating south of the border. It has the feel of a taco stand, but with a huge menu and shaded patio seating. The beans here are different than many places, served whole instead of in the usual refried mash. If you're a fan of the hot dog, you really have to try the Mexican variation—a skinny grilled dog hidden in a thick and rich soft white bun, slathered with beans, mayo, salsa, and whatever else you want to add. It's amazing, but it rarely sparks ambivalence—people seem to either love it or hate it. There is also a second El Guero Canelo location (2480 N. Oracle Rd., 520/882-8977).

MI NIDITO ⑤
1813 S. 4th Ave., 520/625-5081, www.minidito.net
HOURS: Wed.-Thurs. 11 A.M.-10:30 P.M.,
Fri.-Sat. 11:30 A.M.-2 A.M., Sun. 11 A.M.-10:30 P.M.
If you only have the time or inclination to eat at one of Tucson's famous Sonoran-style Mexican restaurants, consider Mi Nidito ("my little nest"). Bill Clinton did. While on a short stopover in Tucson during his presidency, Clinton, known for his love of food (especially the comfort variety), stopped here and sampled pretty much one of everything. His order is still preserved as a special on the menu. It's difficult to say what it is about this bright South 4th Avenue restaurant, with its tropical decor and friendly albeit always harried staff, that sets it apart from the dozens of other similar eateries in the Old Pueblo. It is the best, that's all there is to it. *Tucson Weekly* readers invariably name it the top (or at least among the top) Sonoran joints in town in that publication's annual Best of Tucson poll, and you shouldn't be surprised to see a line of people waiting to be seated at 10:45 A.M. on a Wednesday. On a weekend night, figure on at least an hour on the porch, waiting anxiously for your name to be called.

TAQUERIA PICO DE GALLO ⑤
2618 S. 6th Ave., 520/623-8775
HOURS: Mon.-Sat. 9 A.M.-9 P.M., Sun. 10 A.M.-5 P.M.
The distinctive fruit and chili concoction that gives this south-side taqueria its name is something to behold. In many places, *pico de gallo* ("beak of a rooster") is a chunky mixture of tomatoes, peppers, onions, and lime heaped on tacos; here it's a cup of fresh fruit cut in big chunks and doused with salty chili powder. The tortillas, made fresh for each order, are what set this place apart from other taquerias. This is a good place to get takeout; the dining room is serviceable but hardly comfortable.

Greater Tucson   Map 7

Outside of the Tucson metro area the number of restaurant choices declines precipitously. There are a few that are definitely worth trying, however. While I wouldn't make a special trip to any of the places listed here, if you're nearby sightseeing, hiking, or shopping, all of them will more than do.

AMERICAN
COW PALACE RESTAURANT ⑤⑤
28802 S. Nogales Hwy., Amado, 520/398-1999
HOURS: Daily 8 A.M.-9 P.M.
Across the street from Longhorn Grill, a statue of a Hereford announces the locally beloved Cow Palace Restaurant, serving a wide variety of favorites from chicken-fried steak to spaghetti. Despite its long history as a cowboy bar—and it's said that even John Wayne ate here back in the day—the Cow Palace has a family-friendly atmosphere with a ranch theme. On weekends there is often a crooner playing the piano during dinner hours.

IRON DOOR RESTAURANT ⑤
10300 E. Ski Run Rd., Mount Lemmon, 520/576-1321
HOURS: Mon. and Thurs.-Fri. 10:30 A.M.-4 P.M.,
Sat.-Sun. 9 A.M.-4 P.M.
Right across the road from the nation's

southernmost ski run (and run by the same company), the Iron Door offers a menu of hearty fare for high altitudes. The selection here isn't that big, but the quality is typically high. They serve a bratwurst platter with a delicious applesauce that is the perfect accompaniment to the forested highland atmosphere. Service is patchy, and most likely you'll have to wait for a table, especially on weekends and on the rare occasions that there's snow on the mountain.

LONGHORN GRILL $$

Exit 48, Amado, 520/398-3955

HOURS: Mon.-Fri. 11 A.M.-9 P.M., Sat.-Sun. 7 A.M.-11 P.M.

You'll know you've made it to Amado, a former ranching center, when you see the building-sized cow skull on the west side of I-19 about 10 miles south of Green Valley at exit 48. The skull serves as the facade for the Longhorn Grill, which serves Southwestern food, ribs, and even pizza. The restaurant has a casual, family atmosphere, but there is a separate bar area. The service is friendly, though sometimes spotty depending on the size of the crowd. A mix of tourists, locals, and retirees from Green Valley frequent this classic borderland restaurant.

MOUNT LEMMON CAFÉ $

12976 Sabino Canyon Rd., Summerhaven, 520/576-1234

HOURS: Mon., Wed., and Fri. 11 A.M.-9 P.M., Sat.-Sun. 11 A.M.-5 P.M.

Summerhaven, a tiny summer-cabin village on the slopes of Mount Lemmon, has few restaurants. This is the oldest one still standing, and is known for its delicious homemade pies. The food is pretty good—your basic burgers and dogs and sandwiches—and the chili goes down especially easy on a cool mountain day. The staff, however, often seem overwhelmed and distracted by the constant stream of hungry tourists, and the food is expensive for what you get. You might just as well think about bringing your own picnic lunch with you.

MEXICAN
WISDOMS $

1931 E. Frontage Rd., Tumacácori, 520/398-2397, www.wisdomscafe.com

HOURS: Mon.-Sat. noon-3 P.M. and 5-8 P.M.

Open since 1944 and still run by the same family, Wisdoms may be the best restaurant in the Santa Cruz Valley, serving Mexican food from passed-down family recipes. Don't miss the famous deep-fried fruit burrito for dessert. The chile relleno, encased in a thick cocoon of batter, is the best in the Tucson area as far as I'm concerned. To get there, head south on the frontage road from Tubac toward the Tumacácori Mission and look for the big chicken statue out front.

STEAK HOUSE
LI'L ABNER'S STEAKHOUSE $$

8500 N. Silverbell Rd., 520/744-2800

HOURS: Sun.-Thurs. 5-10 P.M., Fri.-Sat. 5-11 P.M.

As you approach this Western-style steak house, you can see cord upon cord of mesquite stacked in the backyard, just waiting for the flame to turn it into flavor. The steaks and ribs and chickens here are cooked over a big open pit outside, and on the weekends there's often music and dancing. Many years of patron graffiti mark the walls inside, giving the place a friendly, casual air that could easily turn celebratory with the right mix of meat, music, and alcohol.

RESTAURANTS

NIGHTLIFE

Tucson's nightlife and entertainment scene is casual and mixed, drawing drunken college kids, post-college slackers and go-getters, thirty-something urban workers, hip parents who still haunt the alt-rock shows, and professors and professionals of indeterminate age. There's really something for everybody out there.

Tucson's youngest and sloppiest nightlife takes place on three blocks within easy walking, or stumbling, distance of each other: Congress Street downtown, 4th Avenue, and Main Gate Square near the UA. There are always plenty of cabs waiting around outside the bars in these neighborhoods, especially on the weekends. When school's in session these areas are fairly packed with college students. That doesn't mean that townies don't go out; in fact, some of the bars in these districts are just as busy during Spring Break and summer as they are when the students are in town. For more upscale watering holes, try the bars at the restaurants in the foothills.

Most of Tucson's nightlife is relatively low-tech, so to speak, meaning that, save for a few places, the bars in the Old Pueblo are mostly neighborhood joints where locals go to drink and socialize. There isn't a lot of importance put on the way you look and the way you dress. People here are friendly and laid-back, and they seem to be even more so once they've got a few margaritas in them.

There is no smoking in bars or restaurants in Tucson, but most have built outdoor patios to accommodate smokers. For a generation Arizona's bars closed at 1 A.M., but in 2007 the state legislature put off last call until 2 A.M.; however, many bars close much earlier than that on weekdays.

HIGHLIGHTS

LOOK FOR ◖ TO FIND RECOMMENDED NIGHTLIFE.

◖ **Best Neighborhood Pub: The Shanty** is the best place in town to become a regular. Its large patio lined with greenery and choice of a 100 different beers invites a mixed crowd of locals (page 102).

◖ **Best Dive Bar: The Buffet,** the oldest bar in town still in its original location, is the epitome of the great American shot-and-beer dive. It has been welcoming hard-core drinkers since the 1930s (page 105).

◖ **Best Student Hangout: Dirtbags** is a longtime favorite student bar, just a few steps from campus, that is famous for its candy-like shot concoctions (page 106).

◖ **Best Bar Decor:** The Kennedy pop-portraits, memorabilia of Cold War culture, and looping cult films make **The Shelter** a fun hideaway (page 108).

◖ **Best Historic Watering Hole: The Tap Room,** a cramped little watering hole off the Hotel Congress lobby, has been serving drinks to thirsty desert travelers since 1919 (page 108).

◖ **Best Margarita:** Fresh-squeezed lime juice, top-shelf tequila, and some ineffable skill make the refreshing margaritas at **Bar Toma** the best in town (page 109).

◖ **Best Cocktail Menu:** Beat the heat with a tropical cocktail inside **Kon Tiki**'s cool, dark interior. Sip away at something pink, blue, or frozen, or try the Polynesian-style cocktail served in a bowl bigger than your head (page 110).

◖ **Best Dance Club:** Salsa night at **El Parador** starts every Friday at 10:45 P.M.,

featuring dance lessons for $5; then you can try out what you've learned in front of the powerful, brassy, fun-loving band Descarga (page 112).

◖ **Best Place to See Local and National Bands:** The intimate space at **Club Congress** in the historic Hotel Congress packs in local music lovers with a constant stream of home-grown and national touring acts (page 114).

◖ **Best Local Microbrew:** Whether purchased on tap at this local brewery's on-site bar or in six-pack form at the supermarket, the varied flavors of Tucson's finest craft beer will have you coming back to **Nimbus Brewing Company** for more (page 115).

© TIM HULL

Bars

PUBS
BOB DOBB'S
2501 E. 6th St., 520/327-3767, www.bobdobbs.net
HOURS: Daily 10 A.M.-1 A.M.
Map 2

Despite its name, this popular Sam Hughes neighborhood bar and grill is not connected with the founder of the Church of the Subgenius, J. R. "Bob" Dobbs. It is, however, a casual, popular place that attracts aging jocks, UA sports fans, and college kids. It has a great patio looking out on 6th Street, and the food—burgers, dogs, and other pub fare—goes down easy. The walls are covered with several generations of graffiti, and it's easy to get sucked into reading all the drunken scrawls.

THE DISTRICT TAVERN
260 E. Congress St., 520/791-0082,
www.thedistricttavern.com
HOURS: Sat.-Thurs. 6 P.M.-2 A.M., Fri. 4 P.M.-2 A.M.
Map 1

A cool old-school drinker's bar on Congress, the District Tavern is a fine place to spend an hour or five drinking on the cheap and sitting back in cushy booths. They offer wine tasting on Friday 5–7 P.M., and the mixed drinks are always under $3. You can also always get a can of PBR for $1, and they've got what must be a professional drinker's dream special: a bottle of Miller High Life and a shot for $3, all the time.

MALONEY'S
213 N. 4th Ave., 520/388-9355
HOURS: Daily 11 A.M.-2 A.M.
Map 1

A large, popular bar on 4th Avenue flanking the railroad tracks, Maloney's—part of a regional chain—draws a mostly college-age crowd for general drinking and eating revelry. They offer half-price drinks and appetizers weekdays from 4 to 7 P.M., and they have a good selection of beers. There are black-and-white still shots from famous movies and pictures of your favorite stars of yesterday and today throughout the place, and the lonely whistle of the passing train lends this rather typical college-town tavern a somewhat melancholy air. The food is edible—burgers and sandwiches and the usual beer-soaking bar food.

O'MALLEY'S
247 N. 4th Ave., 520/623-8600
HOURS: Daily 11 A.M.-2 A.M.
Map 1

Just across the parking lot from Maloney's, O'Malley's is a laid-back bar popular with the college crowd, offering live cover bands several nights a week and a cozy enclosed patio for smoking. They serve food of the bar-menu variety; it's palatable, especially with a beer or two to wash it down. There are TVs scattered throughout playing sports events; the bartenders are friendly and efficient; and there are a few pool tables and video games scattered around the place.

◖ THE SHANTY
401 E. 9th St., 520/623-2664
HOURS: Sun.-Wed. noon-1 A.M., Thurs.-Sat. noon-2 A.M.
Map 1

The Shanty is an old railroad bar turned Irish pub turned college-kid hangout. It's on the edge of the Iron Horse neighborhood (where the railroad workers used to live) just off 4th Avenue. It has a large patio lined with greenery and is usually crowded on the weekends with, as in most Tucson bars, a mixture of the young and the not-so-young, all drinking together. They've got between 80 and 100 different beers, with most of the exotic stuff in bottles; they certainly pour a good Guinness. Several pool tables get heavy use. There's no food other than free bar-top popcorn. Though it has moved once since it opened, the Shanty actually holds the oldest liquor license in Tucson.

© TIM HULL

The Shanty serves up 100 different beers.

SURLY WENCH

424 N. 4th Ave., 520/882-0009,
www.surlywenchpub.com

HOURS: Mon.-Fri. 5 P.M.-2 A.M., Sat.-Sun. 2 P.M.-2 A.M.

Map 1

The Surly Wench is a cool 4th Avenue pub with a kind of punkabilly vibe. The holy trinity here is "booze, burlesque, and bands," but they also serve pretty good burgers, sandwiches, fried stuff, and a few Mexican dishes. This is the only place in town where you can see the tattooed and pulse-quickening bombshells that make up the Black Cherry Burlesque troupe (there's an up-to-date schedule of shows—and photos—on the website), and they are certainly something worth seeing.

WOODEN NICKEL TAVERN

1908 S. Country Club Rd., 520/323-8830

HOURS: Daily 11 A.M.-2 A.M.

Map 6

On the south end of Country Club below 22nd Street, this casual and fun tavern has cheap drinks and good food; every day at lunch you can get a burger and a pint for $6. On Friday and Saturday nights they push the pool tables to the corners and a DJ spins dance music. Fridays it's Tejano music, popular with the city's Mexican and Latino population, and on Saturday it's hip-hop, which brings in a younger crowd. Outside there's a covered patio for smokers.

SPORTS BARS AND BILLIARDS

CLICKS BILLIARDS

3325 N. 1st Ave., 520/887-7312, www.clicks.com

HOURS: Daily 11 A.M.-2 A.M.

Map 3

Some of us need only a well-made cocktail and a view, but others require more distraction—like all those games pubgoers have always played to pass the time until the dreaded last call. This large, clean, and well-lit pool hall (part of a national chain) on 1st Avenue just south of Prince offers 20 pool tables, darts, foosball, eight televisions scattered throughout, and plenty of other distractions to go with the relatively low-priced beer and cocktails.

NIGHTLIFE

TEQUILA: A SHORT GUIDE

Tucson's best restaurants are its many authentic Mexican eateries, and many of them offer hundreds of different kinds of tequila, an alcohol made in the state of Jalisco, in a city called Tequila. Tequila is made exclusively from just one species of the agave plant, the blue agave. Another drink, mezcal, is made from 100 percent agave, but is prepared in a different way than tequila, giving it an earthier, almost "dirty" taste that some borderlanders – including your author – prefer over the more popular and widely available tequila. The southern Mexican state of Oaxaca (pronounced wa-HA-kah) is known for producing superior mezcal, but it is also made in other regions of Mexico; whereas tequila, by law, is made only in Jalisco. A simple rule to go by is this: All tequila is mezcal, but not all mezcal is tequila. Mezcal is probably best known in the United States as the drink with the worm at the bottom of the bottle. Contrary to myth, the worm has no hallucinogenic properties (trust me – I've eaten dozens of them). Not too many restaurants and bars in the Old Pueblo serve mezcal, although you can usually find one or two brands at some of the better-stocked liquor stores in Tucson. Try **The RumRunner** on Speedway east of Tucson Boulevard, or **Plaza Liquors** on Campbell just north of Grant Road. Of course, if you make a short drive to Nogales, Sonora, Mexico's tourist area just across the border, there are many stores that sell Oaxacan mezcal. I recommend the brand Gusano Rojo ("red worm").

As for tequila, there are several different kinds to choose from, not to mention myriad brands. For my money, the top tequila bar in the Old Pueblo is **Bar Toma** at the downtown historic Court Avenue location of El Charro.

Now, if you're having a margarita, a popular tequila-based cocktail with lime juice and other flavors, it's not overly important that it be made with the most expensive, best tequila (although it certainly doesn't hurt). Usually an *oro* (gold) tequila, which has colors and flavors added to it, will do. If you're a bit confused by all the different kinds of tequila available, remember: *Blanco* (white or silver) tequila is bottled less than 60 days after being distilled in stainless-steel barrels; *reposado* (rested) has been aged anywhere from two months to one year in oak barrels; and *añejo* (aged) has been aged for at least one year. If you want to drink your tequila straight (with a bit of lime and salt added), it's best to choose a brand made from 100 percent agave, with no sugars or other ingredients added. Or just ask your bartender – I've found that they are usually very nice, understanding people.

COW PONY BAR AND GRILL
6510 E. Tanque Verde Rd., 520/721-2781
HOURS: Daily 11 A.M.–2 A.M.
Map 4

This east-side joint is pure Tucson: a little bit country, a little bit rock and roll, and all casual, inexpensive, and fun. The name suggests a honky-tonk, but the Cow Pony has something for everybody—which is proven most weekend nights when the place is packed with a cross section of Tucson's drinking, partying crews. There are half a dozen or more TVs in the small place, comfortable half-moon booths perfect for a group of friends, and pool tables and foosball fill up the back.

FENDERSKIRTS
140 S. Kolb Rd., 520/722-1214
HOURS: Daily 11 A.M.–2 A.M.
Map 4

There's always something going on here—free pool on Sunday and Monday, poker tournaments on Thursday and Saturday, karaoke, live bands, and dancing on weekends, and even the odd wet T-shirt contest. This is a regular's kind of joint, with friendly bartenders and a welcoming vibe, especially during the after-work hours. It's also a good place to watch sports, with several televisions looking down from the corners and local fans gathered around the bar cheering.

SPORTS ON CONGRESS

254 E. Congress St., 520/622-1116

HOURS: Daily 11 A.M.-2 P.M.

Map 1

A small, laid-back sports bar on Congress, this bar has pretty good food (burgers and sandwiches and the like) and an excellent selection of beers. The sports are always on, and there are often live bands playing throughout the week. Check out their happy hour 4–7 P.M. weekdays, when they take a dollar off their already reasonably priced drinks and appetizers. This place isn't as sleek and media-saturated as some of the high-concept sports bars in town, but it's a friendly, comfortable, and relatively inexpensive place to hang downtown.

WORLD SPORTS GRILLE

2290 W. Ina Rd., 520/229-0011,
www.worldsportsgrille.com

HOURS: Daily 11 A.M.-2 A.M.;
must be 21 or older after 11 P.M.

Map 3

This huge high-concept restaurant, sports bar, and family gaming center at the Foothills Mall is a good place to take the kids, especially if you want them to leave you alone while you watch the game on a 103-inch flat-screen TV, choose from among scores of draft beers, and play a few games of pool. The video, old-school, and interactive games here are legion, which is not surprising given that the World Sports Grille model was developed by Sega—they've got more than 50 to choose from, including classic arcade and Japanese games.

DIVE BARS
(THE BUFFET

538 E. 9th St., 520/623-6811

HOURS: Daily 6:30 A.M.-2 A.M.

Map 1

The oldest bar in town still in its original location, the Buffet has been welcoming drinkers to the Iron Horse neighborhood since the 1930s. This is a shot-and-beer kind of place most of the day, the local professional drinkers' home bar. As such, it opens as early as 6:30 A.M., and there are numerous UA traditions that involve imbibing at the Buffet at that ungodly hour. This is a place where frat

NIGHTLIFE

© TIM HULL

The Buffet is a popular dive bar and one of the oldest watering holes in Tucson.

boys slum it with 80-year-old retired miners on oxygen, knocking back tequila. Settle in and order a cheap shot and a beer, and pretty soon you won't want to leave. There are no windows to speak of, and with that too-earnest Tucson sun blacked out and forgotten the day just slips away on bar time. Make sure you're there around 6 P.M. for "Happy Minute," when the barkeep goes around and gives everybody one more of whatever they're having, on the house. At 11 P.M., refills are a mere dollar. The only food offered is cheap hot dogs cooked in Coors, which is the only beer offered on tap. They've got a few brews in the fridge that are more drinkable, but that's not really the point here, is it?

BUM STEER

1910 N. Stone Ave., 520/884-7377

HOURS: Mon. noon-1 A.M., Tues.-Sat. 11 A.M.-1 A.M., Sun. 11 A.M.-midnight

`Map 3`

Cluttered with a few generations worth of quirky junk and an arcade's worth of mostly retro video and pinball machines, the Bum Steer has been a favorite drinking and burger-eating joint for UA students since the 1970s. The burgers are outstanding, and the beer is cold and cheap. The party here usually follows the undergrad pattern—drinking to excess and then dancing the night away—but early in the evening and on most weekdays it's a fine place for families: The kids will love the food and the games, and the prices are just right. A recent remodel and clean-up made the place even more inviting without sacrificing the slummy charm.

DANNY'S BABAQUIVERI

2910 E. Fort Lowell Rd., 520/795-3178

HOURS: Mon.-Sat. 2 P.M.-2 A.M., Sun. 6 P.M.-2 A.M.

`Map 2`

Named for the mountains where the Tohono O'odham believe their creator dwells, this near-dive bar near Fort Lowell and Country Club is the perfect place to hide out from the heat, or anything else you might be running from. It's cool and cozy and dark, with a low ceiling and

big cushy Naugahyde booths along the wall. The jukebox is excellent, the drinks are cheap, and there are a few pool tables in the back. It's one of the few bars in Tucson that hasn't added a semi-covered patio for smokers since a 2006 state law banned lighting up even at your favorite watering hole. Smokers at Danny's stand around outside under the front awning, watching traffic.

◖ DIRTBAGS

1800 E. Speedway Blvd., 520/326-2600, www.dirtbagsbar.com

HOURS: Mon.-Sat. 11 A.M.-2 A.M.

`Map 2`

The typical drinker at Dirtbags is a twenty-something undergrad with, depending on gender, a skimpy summer outfit and bleached blonde hair or a baseball cap, cargo shorts, and flip-flops. This small, popular watering hole is on the corner of Speedway and Campbell, within easy stumbling distance of most University of Arizona dorms and frat houses. Dirtbags is famous for its shot concoctions,

Dirtbags is a favorite hangout of students from the nearby University of Arizona.

TUCSON'S CASINOS

Near Tucson are three casinos owned and operated by Native American tribes, and all of them offer slots, poker, blackjack, and plenty of other games of chance to separate you from your money. Though it's not exactly Vegas, the "Indian casinos," as most locals call them, are generally clean and fun places to spend your time. The completely rebuilt **Desert Diamond Casino & Hotel** (7350 S. Nogales Hwy., 520/294-7777, 866/332-9467, www.desertdiamondcasino.com) has excellent accommodations and several restaurants on-site – including a steak house and Vegas-style all-you-can-eat buffet. The hotel-casino, operated by the Tohono O'odham, also has the **Monsoon Nightclub,** which brings in a mixed crowd of dancing revelers that skews a bit older than other dance clubs in town.

About 20 miles south of downtown Tucson, along I-19, the O'odham operate a second **Desert Diamond Casino** (520/294-7777, www.desertdiamondcasino.com) near the small bedroom town of Sahuarita and just a hop and a skip to the retirement community of Green Valley. As such, you're likely to see a few retirees hanging around the blackjack tables, poker tournaments, and slots spending their Social Security checks. The New American cuisine served at the elegant **Agave Restaurant** (Mon.-Thurs. 11 A.M.-10 P.M., Fri.-Sat. 11 A.M.-11 P.M., Sun. 11 A.M.-7 P.M.) is always tasty, and the all-you-can-eat buffet is delicious, fresh, and stocked with more food than anybody needs. There's also a constant stream of talent moving through the **Diamond Entertainment Center,** an intimate concert theater that has hosted top-name acts like Willie Nelson and Bob Dylan.

A Mediterranean-influenced funland with poker, slots, bingo, blackjack, and keno, **Casino del Sol** (5655 W. Valencia Rd., 800/344-9435, www.casinodelsol.com) is operated by the Pascua Yaqui. About 17 miles southwest of downtown Tucson, the casino offers delicious high-end continental cuisine at **Bellissimo** (daily 5-11 P.M.), and live music in the **Paradise Bar and Lounge.** Check the website for the schedule of bands playing at the intimate **Anselmo Valencia Tori Amphitheater,** which welcomes national touring acts, many of them stars from the 1960s, '70s, and '80s.

NIGHTLIFE

most of them mixed up to taste like cookies and candies. Consider the Sicilian Whore, a *pitcher* of pineapple-flavored shots made from eight different liquors that, according to the owners, "can only be served to a close group of friends."

NORTH ON 4TH
536 N. 4th Ave., 520/770-1161
HOURS: Daily 1 P.M.-2 A.M.
Map 1

This is one of the divier joints on 4th, with little or no atmosphere and a mixed crowd pounding back very cheap drinks—including beer that's less than $1 on Thursday nights. There are a few pool tables and comfortable booths, and a few video games scattered around. Otherwise, it's really a place built for one activity alone: drinking, and doing so cheaply and deeply.

This isn't the place you're likely to meet your soul mate, but you will see the less hipster-chic side of 4th Avenue and downtown, and when you're done you can take a few steps next door and get a slice at Brooklyn Pizza.

WORLD FAMOUS GOLDEN NUGGET
2617 N. 1st Ave.
HOURS: Daily 9 A.M.-2 A.M.
Map 3

You probably won't find a cheaper, stronger drink in town than here at the Golden Nugget, where all of Tucson's subcultures and classes mix it up for the sake of economy and value. There's nothing I can say to recommend the Nugget other than that it is a *real* bar in the classical sense, nothing more and nothing less. Everybody's friendly, and there are well-used pool tables and shuffleboard games and a good jukebox. They don't take credit cards, and they don't have a big selection of draft beer, but otherwise this is a great place to go at either the start or the sloppy end of an Old Pueblo night out. Be careful with the mixed drinks, though; they truly are stronger than any other place in town—believe me, I've done the research.

HISTORIC BARS
(THE SHELTER
4155 E. Grant Rd., 520/326-1345
HOURS: Daily 3 P.M.-1 A.M.
Map 2

The Tucson valley played a major role in the Cold War: For years ICBMs ringed the city, locked and loaded beneath the desert and aimed directly at various targets in the USSR. While there's a museum south of town where you can learn all about the Old Pueblo's atomic-age bona fides, The Shelter is the best place to celebrate, so to speak, the era and its two coolest cold warriors. It's dark and cool like a shelter should be, and there's plenty of good booze and always a campy cult film playing

out silently on a TV in the corner. The walls are covered with Jack and Bobby, and the pinball machines ding and flap. I could last out the nuclear winter in here no problem. Happy hour is daily from 3 to 7 P.M.

(THE TAP ROOM
311 E. Congress St., 520/622-8848,
www.hotelcongress.com
HOURS: Daily 11 A.M.-2 A.M.
Map 1

This cramped old bar (it has been around since 1919) still packs them in, especially when there's a band playing at Club Congress, to which The Tap Room serves as a kind of hideout from the crush and noise. But if you belly-up here of an afternoon, or on a slow midweek night, you'll notice the details: the retro booths and stools; the scratchy juke in the corner; and especially the cowboy-life art of Pete Martinez, one of several lauded Western artists who once called Tucson home. Martinez, who lived in Tucson from 1935 until his death in 1971, was neighbor to the painter and illustrator Maynard

Go back in time to the Cold War era at The Shelter.

© TIM HULL

NIGHTLIFE

© TIM HULL

The Tap Room has been in Tucson since 1919.

Dixon and friend to Ted DeGrazia, and he reportedly spent a good deal of his time drinking at The Tap Room. Martinez's art can be seen on the bar's walls. People always used to say that he would from time to time trade his work for his drinks, and that's how they got there. But the management says that's just a rumor, and that the artist gifted the paintings to his favorite bar.

LOUNGES
☾ BAR TOMA
6310 E. Broadway Blvd., 520/745-1922,
www.elcharrocafe.com
HOURS: Mon.-Fri. 11 A.M.-9 P.M., Sat. 10:30 P.M.-2 A.M.
Map 2

El Charro, one of the Old Pueblo's oldest and best-loved restaurants, has five locations around town, each of them with a version of Bar Toma, from which the local chain serves some of the best margaritas available anywhere. Weekdays 3–6 P.M. those margaritas are sold for half their usual price, as are the restaurant's distinctive Mexican appetizers. Bar Toma

offers a long list of premium tequilas (all the *añejos, blancos,* and *reposados* you'll ever need) and, of course, all the usual beers and cocktails as well. The Bar Toma on East Broadway Boulevard is larger and wilder than some of the other locations. This venue offers dancing every Saturday night, playing everything from club to Norteño.

BLANCO TACOS + TEQUILA
2905 E. Skyline Dr., 520/232-1007,
www.foxrestaurantconcepts.com
HOURS: Sun.-Thurs. 11 A.M.-10 P.M., Fri.-Sat. 11 A.M.-11 P.M.
Map 3

A sleek, high-style Mexican place in the urban mode, with a delightful patio looking over the valley from a foothills perch at high-end La Encantada, Blanco Tacos + Tequila usually attracts a youngish and necessarily moneyed crowd; even a few drinks and appetizers on the patio is going to cost you $50 at least. They serve some delicious signature margaritas and cocktails, the best of which are the white peach and hibiscus margarita ($9); their Sangria Rojo (made with

NIGHTLIFE

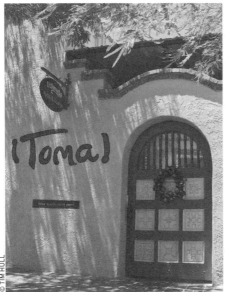

© TIM HULL

Bar Toma serves some of the best margaritas in the city.

red wine, raspberries, strawberries, plums, and currants, $8); and the distinctive black-and-blue mojito, with fresh blackberries and raspberries mixed in ($10). A daily happy hour (4–6 P.M.) puts the excellent drinks here somewhat within the normal person's price range.

CHE'S LOUNGE

350 N. 4th Ave., 520/623-2088, www.cheslounge.com
HOURS: Daily noon-2 A.M.
Map 1

Not exactly a hangout for revolutionaries in the Che Guevara mode, Che's Lounge is instead a small, inviting hangout for a vast array of 4th Avenue denizens, from college kids to fortysomethings. They don't charge much for their drinks, and if you're broke you can always find somebody with $1 to buy you a PBR or one of the round-robin of $1 drafts they serve nightly. Bands set up in the cramped corners most weekend nights, and there are a few classic arcade games scattered throughout and an excellent fully stocked juke.

KON TIKI

4625 E. Broadway Blvd., 520/323-7193,
www.kontikitucson.com
HOURS: Mon.-Sat. 11 A.M.-10 P.M., Sun. 4-9 P.M.
Map 2

The ancient recipe of fruit juice mixed with booze is at the heart of this retro-realistic spot on Broadway Boulevard, a favorite among the Arizona tiki-culture crowd since it opened way back in 1963. The drinks at Kon Tiki are a far cry from a red plastic cup full of "jungle juice" ladled out in some dorm room, however. Even if you claim to be a tough-guy shot-and-beer type, it's hard to resist escaping to Kon Tiki's cool, dark interior to sip away at happy hour (when tasty pupus, with amazing booze-soaking power, are half price), trying something pink, something blue, something red, something frozen, something served in a Polynesian-style bowl bigger than your head. Make sure to say hello to the huge, languid iguana hanging out behind glass.

MUSIC BOX LOUNGE

6951 E. 22nd St., 520/747-1421
HOURS: Mon.-Sat. 11 A.M.-2 A.M., Sun. 11 A.M.-9 P.M.
Map 4

A fun place to hang out on the far east side, the Music Box offers all the games and events that the contemporary bargoer has come to expect: karaoke, beer pong, Wii, and a DJ spinning top-40 dance hits on Friday and Saturday nights. The drinks are cheap, with well and domestic beers usually under $3. There's a nice smoking patio, and the place has a friendly, regulars' vibe. They serve chili dogs and burgers throughout the night.

SMOKE CIGAR PATIO AND BAR

2959 N. Swan Rd., 520/327-7463
HOURS: Mon.-Thurs. 11:30 A.M.-11 P.M.,
Fri.-Sat. 11:30 A.M.-midnight, Sun. 5 P.M.-9 P.M.
Map 2

This very comfortable and stylish climate-controlled smoker's patio-lounge is at McMahon's Prime Steakhouse. The steak house isn't among my recommendations, but if you're a smoker looking for fellow travelers and a high-end place

NIGHTLIFE

© TIM HULL

Escape the heat in Kon Tiki's cool, retro interior.

to relax with a drink, an appetizer, and a clean ashtray at the ready, this is the place for you. It's a bit pricey all around, but they offer daily drink and food specials, and a half-price happy hour weekdays 3–7 P.M. The cigar selection runs from as low as $2.50 to as high as $36, with most falling in the $8–15 range. While nearly all Tucson's bars have added enclosed climate-controlled patios since an ordinance banned smoking in bars otherwise, this is by far the nicest.

Dance Clubs

CACTUS MOON CAFÉ
5470 E. Broadway Blvd., 520/748-0049,
www.cactusmoon.net
HOURS: Tues. 8 P.M.-2 A.M., Wed.-Fri. 5 P.M.-2 A.M.,
Sat. 6 P.M.-2 A.M.
COST: Varies
Map 2

This is where the cowboys and cowgirls, urban or otherwise, hang out. It has a huge central dance floor surrounded by booths and tables, and a cavernous space that can fit hundreds of Western-clad revelers. It's not all line-dancing and honky-tonk shuffling, though; DJs will mix up the broadcast with disco and urban dance music as well. A large UA student contingent is usually part of the crowd on weekends. Country line-dancing lessons are offered Thursday 6–7 P.M. and Saturday 6:30–7:30 P.M. On Wednesday, couples can take dance lessons from 6:30 to 7:30 P.M.

C-NOTE LOUNGE
1302 W. Roger Rd., 520/407-1000
HOURS: Daily 10 A.M.-2 A.M.
COST: Free
Map 3

If Hank Williams were alive and playing honky-tonks today, would he do a set or two at the C-Note? Perhaps. This neighborhood country-western bar, as close to the classic honky-tonk as you're likely to find in Tucson, offers dance-friendly live country music Thursday–Sunday beginning around 9 P.M. There's never a cover, but they might want to start charging people to watch the popular karaoke sessions offered from 9 P.M. to close, where the emphasis seems to be on channeling Patsy Cline.

DV8

5851 E. Speedway Blvd. #D, 520/885-3030
HOURS: Wed.-Thurs. 9 P.M.-2 A.M., Fri.-Sat. 8 P.M.-2 A.M.
COST: Women free before 10 P.M.; otherwise varies
Map 2

This is a fun dance club for a mostly young college-age set, with a premium on dressing to impress, dancing wildly, and hooking up. Thursday nights get dangerous, with a $10 cover charge sufficient to get you penny drinks all night. Friday nights welcome the 18-and-over crowd with $1 mixed drinks all night if you can prove your age. DJs spin a mix of dance, hip-hop, top 40, and classic alternative dance beats. This is definitely a dress-up kind of place, but that means something different in Tucson than it does elsewhere. If you're clad in the fashions of the day you're likely to pass muster.

◖ EL PARADOR

2744 E. Broadway Blvd., 520/881-2808,
www.elparadortucson.com
HOURS: Fri. and alternating Sat. 10 P.M.-2 A.M.
COST: $7
Map 2

With Tucson's deep Latino roots, it's no surprise that salsa dancing is all the rage, and the best place to learn the steps, find a partner, and cut a *caliente* rug is the colorful jungle-like atmosphere of El Parador. Every Friday starting at 10:45 P.M. a salsa master offers dance lessons for an extra $5; then you can try out what you've learned in front of powerful, brassy, fun-loving band Descarga until the wee hours. This is a great place to commune with Tucson's Latino community; on many weekend nights, young men and women up from Ambos Nogales crowd the dance floor, dressed to impress and swinging and kicking and sweating to the music. On alternating Saturdays the band Salsarengue plays a more traditional brand of salsa.

You can learn how to salsa at El Parador.

THE MAVERICK

6622 E. Tanque Verde Rd., 520/298-0430,
www.mavericktucson.com
HOURS: Tues.-Sat. 5 P.M.-2 A.M.
COST: $5 Thurs.-Sat.
Map 4

This east-side country-western nightclub has been calling in cowboys and cowgirls from all over Southern Arizona for nearly 50 years. A rotating lineup of three tight house bands plays country dance music Tuesday–Saturday. The sound system is excellent, and if you can't even two-step it's fun to watch those who can from comfortable sidelines, which include a whiskey lounge. The kitchen serves burgers, sandwiches, fried foods, and appetizers until 11 P.M., but if you get to dancing you'll likely be on the floor long after that.

PEARL NIGHTCLUB

445 W. Wetmore Rd., 520/888-8361,
www.pearltucson.com
HOURS: Wed.-Sun. 9 P.M.-2 A.M.
COST: Varies
Map 3

Pearl bills itself as a "Las Vegas–style" nightclub, meaning that there's a concentration here on how you look, how you dress, and your relative hotness. It's not cheap, and it's not meant to be—quite the opposite, actually. They offer all the high-end perks, like concierge service and limos, and they require—demand, really—that you be dressed to their stylish specifications or you won't get in. I'd say check out the website before showing up just to make sure your attire fits their dress code specifications. If you do get in you'll likely be impressed by the stylishness of the place, the thumping beats, and the expensive drinks.

SHARKS

256 E. Congress St., 520/791-9869
HOURS: Daily 5 P.M.-2 A.M.
COST: Varies
Map 1

Mexican rock bands have found fervent fans here in the borderlands for as long there's been Mexican rock-and-roll, and it's been around nearly as long as the American kind—long before bands like Santana, Los Lobos, and Los Lonely Boys broke into the mainstream. At Sharks nightclub downtown the tradition continues every Friday night, when rock *en español* draws a crowd. Other nights the mostly youngish

The Maverick, very popular with the cowboy and cowgirl set, features nightly music and dancing.

crowd hits the small, sweaty dance floor with the help of DJs playing a mix of rock, hip-hop, and dance music, and on Tuesday there's karaoke.

WILDCAT HOUSE
1801 N. Stone Ave., 520/622-1302,
www.thewildcathouse.com
HOURS: Tues.-Wed. and Fri.-Sat. 11 A.M.-2 A.M.,
Mon. and Thurs. 11 A.M.-9 P.M., Sun. 11 A.M.-6 P.M.
COST: Women free before 10 P.M., $6 after;
men $5 before 9 P.M., $6 after
`Map 3`

This is a decadent joint where college-age bacchanalia goes down nightly—everything from dancing to wrestling to bikini contests. They have a huge menu of food, but the real draw here is the dance floor and the DJs, along with drink specials intent on getting everybody lubricated and making bad decisions. During happy hour, Monday–Wednesday 4–8 P.M., you can get a mixed drink for $2 and a pint for $3; Thursday during the same time period mixed drinks are $1 and so is the beer, while on Friday during happy hour you can get a good margarita for $2. Have a couple of these cheap drinks and see if you can stay off the dance floor, where scantily clad young women dance in groups. Fridays they play alternative dance and the place usually gets packed, while Saturday nights it's Tejano dance music. On the weekends the dancing usually starts around 10 P.M. and goes until 1 A.M.

Live Music

BOONDOCK'S LOUNGE
3306 N. 1st Ave., 520/690-0991,
www.boondockslounge.com
HOURS: Mon. noon-2 A.M., Tues.-Sat. 10 A.M.-2 A.M.
COST: $5
`Map 3`

When you see the two-story bottle of chianti near 1st Avenue and Prince, you'll know you've found Boondock's Lounge, a friendly place with lots of pool tables and dartboards, a cast of regulars, and a stage that welcomes roots rock, reggae, and country bands throughout the week. The in-house Range Rider's Grille serves good burgers, sandwiches, and finger foods, and five nights a week there's a dinner special for a mere $5–6 a plate. It's an all-around fine place to spend your time.

◖ CLUB CONGRESS
311 E. Congress St., 520/622-8848,
www.hotelcongress.com
HOURS: Sun.-Mon. 9 P.M.-1 A.M., Tues.-Sat. 10 P.M.-1 A.M.
COST: Varies
`Map 1`

This small club inside the historic Hotel Congress is the city's premier spot for touring alternative rock and alt-country bands. Most nights, if there's not a band playing there's a DJ and dancing. Music geeks and college-town rock-and-rollers frequent the shows here, and it's a kind of headquarters for the thriving downtown music scene—the stage new local bands aspire to. If you're not in the mood for sweaty crowds, guitars, or break-beats, there's a somewhat quieter lounge in the lobby, but the music is the club's reason for being, and thank the gods for that. Check their website for the live music schedule and show times.

THE HUT
305 N. 4th Ave., 520/623-3200,
www.myspace.com/thehuttucson
HOURS: Mon.-Fri. 4 P.M.-2 A.M., Sat.-Sun. noon-2 A.M.
COST: Varies
`Map 1`

This faux-tropical bar features roots rock, rock, blues, reggae, and even spoken-word performance art. It has a kind of slum-tiki vibe, laid-back and beach-bound with a lot of frozen drinks on the menu. A three-story cement tiki head saved from a beloved but defunct miniature golf course in east Tucson was installed at the bar's entrance in 2008, adding one more reason to visit this classic watering hole.

🎵 NIMBUS BREWING COMPANY

3850 E. 44th St., No. 138, 520/745-9175,
www.nimbusbeer.qwestoffice.net

HOURS: Mon.-Thurs. 11 A.M.-11 P.M., Fri.-Sat. 11 A.M.-1 A.M., Sun. noon-9 P.M.

COST: $3-5

`Map 6`

The home of the best craft beer in the state also books local and touring rock, folk, blues, and country bands into the same ultra-casual brew-house setting from which they produce 22,500 barrels of delicious elixir every year. If you don't like beer, and you don't like to rock, you'll find there's not much to do here. But if you do like beer, especially European-style ales (Nimbus makes six different flavors), then you must go here. The bands are usually excellent and a lot of fun. They offer a small menu of tasty "munchies" to help soak up a few pints.

PLUSH

340 E. 6th St., 520/798-1298

HOURS: Mon.-Sat. 4 P.M.-2 A.M., Sun. 6 P.M.-2 A.M.

COST: Varies

`Map 1`

A well-appointed, comfortable club frequented by downtown artists and musicians, hipsters, and students, Plush is the place on 4th to experience Tucson's vibrant music scene, as well as nationally known alternative rock and alt-country acts. There are often acts playing in the front living-room area and on a stage in the back; there's also a patio for smoking.

RED ROOM AT THE GRILL

100 E. Congress St., 520/623-7621

HOURS: Daily 24 hours

COST: Free

`Map 1`

The Grill is a downtown classic—the greasy-spoon headquarters of the art and music scenes in Tucson. So it stands to reason that they book a few bands throughout the week into the small Red Room cocktail lounge off the main dining room. This is a great place to see a band, because from anywhere in the room you are within whispering distance of the singer. As such, the sets here are often acoustic, and

the bands on the folksy, singer-songwriter side of things.

VAUDEVILLE CABARET

110 E. Congress St., 520/622-3535,
www.vaudevillecabaret.com

HOURS: Daily 4 P.M.-2 A.M.

COST: Varies

`Map 1`

Just west of the Hotel Congress downtown, Vaudeville bills itself as Tucson's "only punk bar." That's not to say that it's a stinking mess in here or anything—far from it. The bands that play here are typically on the harder side of pop-punk and bar rock, and a large selection of the patrons are likely to be tattooed and pierced; but one could say that about any of the bars downtown. If you are into bar bands and possibly discovering something unknown and exciting, stop in here on a Saturday night. The cover varies for the entrance to the back room, where the top-billing bands perform. Access to the front room, where there's often an acoustic act, is free.

Vaudeville Cabaret puts on a good show most weekends.

Gay and Lesbian

AIN'T NOBODY'S BIZNESS

2900 E. Broadway Blvd. No. 118, 520/318-4838,
www.thebiztuc.com

HOURS: Daily 5 P.M.-2 A.M.

Map 2

If a bar has an Erotic Dancer Appreciation Night you know you're in a friendly place, and "The Biz" in midtown, which has theirs on Mondays, is surely that. A mostly younger crowd of women with a few guys mixed in hits the dance floor nightly with the help of DJs playing primarily hip-hop and club music. They've got a comfortable smoking patio, and there's always something going on, from beer-pong tournaments to open-mic night. Saturday nights always have a Latin flavor, and on Wednesday ("kennel night") a fence goes up around the bar (to which access is age-restricted) and they let in the 18-and-over crowd.

IBT'S

616 N. 4th Ave., 520/882-3053, www.ibts.net

HOURS: Daily noon-2 A.M.

Map 1

Tucson's most popular gay bar is a bit bigger inside than it looks to be from the outside, but not by much. Follow the revelers toward the back and you'll find a dance floor and a smoking patio. There's usually a fun mix of dudes and chicks here—college kids, young professionals, and older folks even, with everybody dancing to the beats. There are often live DJs, karaoke (Sundays), drag shows, and other revelry as announced. IBT's is the perennial Best Gay Bar winner in the *Tucson Weekly*'s annual poll. It's not a fancy place by any means—the usual Tucson casual, or even less, will do.

WOODY'S

3710 N. Oracle Rd., 520/292-6702,
www.mywoodysaz.com

HOURS: Daily 11 A.M.-2 A.M.

Map 3

Woody's has friendly servers and bartenders, a mixed clientele of various ages, and what is quite possibly the longest happy hour in town (daily 11 A.M.-8 P.M.). The patio bar opens most nights at 8 P.M., and amateur voices fill the air during the nightly karaoke sessions, with one of the better songbooks in town, from 9 P.M. to 1 A.M. There are usually DJs spinning, and they have a few pool tables and other games. On Sunday they serve brunch with a Bloody Mary bar.

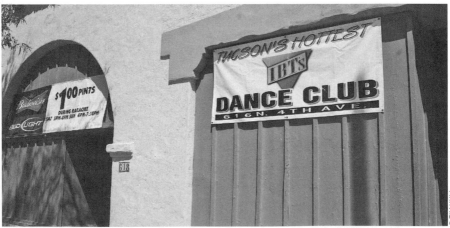

IBT's is considered Tucson's most popular gay bar.

Elle usually features 30 or 40 different international wines.

Wine Bars

CATAVINOS

3063 N. Alvernon Way, 520/323-3063,
www.catavinoswines.com

HOURS: Tues. 11 A.M.–6 P.M., Wed.-Sat. 11 A.M.–8 P.M.

Map 2

This locally owned cozy wine shop and tasting room on Alvernon Way is the most affordable destination in town for wine lovers, with hundreds of great wines from around the globe offered for under $15 a bottle. The themed wine tastings (Thurs.–Sat. 4–8 P.M.) feature a different flight of six wines every week, and include cheese and crackers for just $10 per person ($8 if you buy a bottle for $10 or more). CataVinos also features a rotating gallery of local and regional art to look at while you're worshipping the grape.

ELLE: A WINE COUNTRY RESTAURANT

3048 E. Broadway Blvd., 520/327-0500,
www.ellerestaurant.com

HOURS: Mon.-Thurs. 11:30 A.M.–9 P.M.,
Fri.-Sat. 11:30 A.M.–10 P.M., Sun. 4-9 P.M.

Map 2

The bar at Elle, located at the historic Josias Joesler designed Broadway Village, concentrates on an international selection of wines that's always changing (they have about 30 or 40 available by the glass at any one time), but you can also get an excellent and unique cocktail here as well. Glasses of wine here run from $5 to $15, with most on the higher end of the scale. There's happy hour daily 4:30–6:30 P.M., when their bar-food menu—pâté, ceviche, fried brie, bruschetta, and the like—is half price.

ARTS AND LEISURE

It's certainly true that Tucson is an active, out-doorsy, sunburned kind of place. On any given weekday, let alone during the crowded, busy weekends, you'll see Tucsonans decked out in colorful, skin-tight Lycra outfits, pedaling with all their might up and down the steep mountain roads and along the bike routes through the city; you'll also see them hiking on desert trails among the saguaro forests, and exploring the sky island mountain ranges that encircle the valley. If you're coming to Tucson to find some similar action, you won't have to look far.

Tucson is also a cultural center; it is, when all's said and done, the cultural capital of Arizona, and one of the top art towns in the Southwest. There are scores of galleries and museums in town, and, contrary to popular opinion, not all of them are dedicated exclusively to paintings of

cowboys and Indians and howling coyotes. The festival seasons in Tucson are pretty much the opposite of everywhere else. There's little going on here in the summer, but come February suddenly the calendar is full with arts fairs, cultural festivals, and sporting events.

Let's say you want to get some exercise but you don't feel like jogging or biking or walking in the wild desert. Fear not, for as much as I've tried to show that Tucson is indeed an exotic city with a wholly unique setting, the truth is that much of the town is as normal and American as can be. That means there are myriad green-grass parks within easy distance of all the neighborhoods. Here you can play all the tennis, golf, and pick-up basketball that you want to, only you don't have to take it inside when the summer ends.

HIGHLIGHTS

LOOK FOR **(C** TO FIND RECOMMENDED ARTS AND ACTIVITIES.

(C Best Place to Brush Up on Tucson's History: Visit the **Arizona Historical Society Museum Downtown** to learn about the history of Tucson's city center from the dusty-street territorial days to the advent of suburban sprawl in the 1960s (page 121).

(C Best Contemporary Art Gallery: **Etherton Gallery** concentrates on photography – from the classic 19th-century chroniclers of the West to today's shutterbugs, as well as regional and local artists of the highest caliber (page 126).

(C Best Southwestern Art Gallery: At the huge east-side **Mark Sublette Medicine Man Gallery** you can view all the famous images and tropes from the Southwest's history beside the best interpretations of the region by today's artists (page 127).

(C Best Live-Music Venue: Open since 1920 and over the years a vaudeville house, a silent movie theater, and a porn theater, **The Rialto** now operates as a nonprofit organization showing the best concerts in town (page 129).

(C Best Movie Theater: The Loft Cinema, a nonprofit art house, shows the best in contemporary and classic cinema, along with craft-brewed beers and gourmet pizza (page 131).

(C Best Festival: Make sure you're hungry when you attend the annual multicultural **Tucson Meet Yourself** festival at downtown's El Presidio Park. Members of dozens of cultural clubs – from Colombians to Navajos – cook up and sell their national cuisine (page 135).

(C Best Urban Park: The cool green grass, duck ponds, shade trees, and state-of-the-art playgrounds at **Gene C. Reid Park** will make you forget you're in a desert (page 138).

(C Best Hiking in the Mountains: About an hour's drive from Tucson's downtown, **Mount Lemmon and the Santa Catalina Mountains** are green and lush and about 10 degrees cooler than the desert floor far below (page 147).

(C Best Hiking in the Desert: Tucson **Mountain Park** is a huge public park west of downtown that has dozens of desertland trails with some of the largest saguaro forests in the world (page 149).

(C Best Mountain Biking: A fantastic system of single-track trails on a swath of scrubby state-trust land southeast of midtown, **Fantasy Island** is indeed a mountain biker's dream come true (page 153).

© TIM HULL

Tucson Mountain Park

The Arts

The creative class is well represented in Tucson. Indeed, there are probably more artists and artisans living in or near the Old Pueblo than in any other Arizona locale save the Navajo and Hopi Reservations. Many of the top galleries in Tucson also have sister galleries in Santa Fe, New Mexico, or in Sedona in Northern Arizona. You don't have to appreciate the sometimes overly romantic depictions of the famed Old West to enjoy looking at art in Tucson. There are all kinds of galleries, especially in the downtown area, that show art from a more experimental, contemporary Southwest, and there are few cowboys left these days. But if you do love Western and Southwestern art, from the conservative to the experimental, there are few better places to be. Head to the foothills neighborhood around Campbell and Skyline for galleries showing the best of the genre.

MUSEUMS

You'll find the largest and best of the city's museums in the *Sights* chapter. Described here are some of Tucson's smaller, more specific museums, for those with an interest in Arizona history, mining history, rodeo, archaeology, trains, photography, art and other subjects.

ARIZONA HISTORICAL SOCIETY MUSEUM

49 E. 2nd St., 520/628-5774,
www.arizonahistoricalsociety.org
HOURS: Mon.-Sat. 10 A.M.-4 P.M., Sat.-Sun. noon-4 P.M.
COST: $5 adult, $4 student
Map 1

Just south of the Main Gate wall along North Campus Drive is the largest of the Arizona Historical Society's three Tucson museums. Exhibits include a full-scale reproduction of the cramped canvas-tent homes early miners lived in, and a walk through a dark underground mine. There's also an old Studebaker on display; this make of car was once so popular with Arizona's sheriffs that the car company sent an author to the young state to write a public relations pamphlet that included exciting stories of frontier law enforcement. This is an interesting stop for Arizona history buffs, and there are several hands-on exhibits for the kids.

The Arizona Historical Society Museum features displays about the history of Tucson and Arizona.

© TIM HULL

Arizona Historical Society Museum Downtown

◖ ARIZONA HISTORICAL SOCIETY MUSEUM DOWNTOWN

140 N. Stone Ave., 520/770-1473,
www.arizonahistoricalsociety.org

HOURS: Mon.-Fri. 10 A.M.-4 P.M.

COST: $3 adult, $2 student 12-18 and senior

Map 1

Until shopping malls began to proliferate in midtown starting in the 1960s, downtown Tucson was the commercial and social heart of the city, a fact that this small museum celebrates. While there are ongoing attempts to revitalize downtown through a project called Rio Nuevo, it's unlikely the once-bustling mixed-use area will ever return to its former glory, when locally owned department stores, barber shops, boutiques, hotels, restaurants, and theaters lined the narrow streets, the sidewalks crowded with people working, shopping, living, and playing all within the same few blocks. The museum, tucked away in a few rooms off the lobby of the Wells Fargo building on Stone Avenue—a still-busy, business-minded downtown district crowded on the weekdays but largely deserted after 5 P.M. Friday—shows artifacts from the early days of downtown through to its desertion, with large, rare photographs and saved ephemera from different eras of the city's history. An especially interesting installation tells the history of the Dillinger gang's capture in Tucson in the 1930s.

ASARCO MINERAL DISCOVERY CENTER

Exit 80 off I-19 west of the casino, 1421 W. Pima Mine Rd., Sahuarita, 520/625-8233, www.mineraldiscovery.com

HOURS: Tues.-Sat. 9 A.M.-5 P.M.

COST: Exhibitions free, mine tour $6 adult, $4 child 5-12

Map 7

The Discovery Center explains, using exhibits, old mining equipment, and films, how all the huge piles of dirt flanking the valley's west side got there. The copper in the Santa Cruz Valley is of the porphyry variety, meaning it's very low grade and takes a lot of earth moving to get at; a one-hour bus tour offered five times a day on Tuesday, Thursday, and Saturday will take you up into the hills to the sprawling Mission Mine to show you how it's done. From the bus you'll see the vast pit and the post-apocalyptic landscape created by large-scale copper mining, and you'll drive through a working mill. Back at the Discovery Center there's a gift shop that sells souvenirs.

ARTS AND LEISURE

Fort Lowell Museum tells the story of what military life was like on the dusty frontier.

CENTER FOR CREATIVE PHOTOGRAPHY

1030 N. Olive Rd., 520/621-7968,
www.creativephotography.org
HOURS: Mon.-Fri. 9 A.M.-5 P.M., Sat.-Sun. noon-5 P.M.
COST: Free
Map 1

UA's Center for Creative Photography has one of the largest photography collections in the world; it holds the archives of Ansel Adams, Edward Weston, and dozens more major artists. The center mounts a few exhibitions a year, so it's a good idea to check the website in advance to see what's on display. You can even make an appointment to personally view a few of the 80,000 prints accessible to the public.

FORT LOWELL MUSEUM

2900 N. Craycroft Rd., 520/318-0219,
www.oflna.org/fort_lowell_museum/ftlowell.htm
HOURS: Wed.-Sat. 10 A.M.-4 P.M.
COST: $3 adult, $2 child under 18
Map 2

This small museum is dedicated to the stories of the Apache wars of the late 19th century. There are still a few crumbling adobe ruins left behind that give a sense of what the fort was like just before it was abandoned in 1891, after the end of the struggle between the army and various Apache tribes. Displays inside the reconstructed commanding officer's quarters tell the whole history of the those wars and show what life was like then, with pictures, artifacts, and text.

GADSDEN-PACIFIC DIVISION TOY TRAINS OPERATING MUSEUM

3975 N. Miller Ave., 520/888-2222,
www.gpdtoytrainmuseum.com
HOURS: Sept.-June second and fourth Sun. of the month 12:30-4:30 P.M., closed July and Aug.
COST: Free
Map 5

This north-side toy-train museum is open only rarely, but if you're an enthusiast of miniature trains you'll want to see it. The museum's main warehouse building features several large, intricate toy-train cities, and there's a historic caboose waiting in retirement on the grounds. The museum isn't open in July and August, and it's only open to the public two weekends a month otherwise, so it's a good idea to call ahead if you want to visit. It's located two blocks west of Price and Romero Roads, on Miller Avenue.

INTERNATIONAL WILDLIFE MUSEUM
4800 W. Gates Pass Rd., 520/629-0100,
www.thewildlifemuseum.org
HOURS: Mon.-Fri. 9 A.M.-5 P.M., Sat.-Sun. 9 A.M.-6 P.M.
COST: $7 adult, $2.50 child 4-12
Map 5

As you drive west toward Gates Pass and the Tucson Mountains, off on the north side of the road, partly obscured by the thick desert, a large castle-esque building holds the impressive taxidermy collection of this private nonprofit natural-history museum. There are more than 400 stuffed and preserved mammals, birds, insects, and spiders here, including "Big Terror," a stuffed tiger who still looks a bit hungry. The mighty beast was killed in 1969 in India, after he'd reportedly devoured between 8 and 12 people. This is a fun and educational place to bring kids, but if you have limited time I'd recommend skipping it in favor of the Arizona-Sonoran Desert Museum a few miles up the road, where the mountain lions, rattlesnakes, beavers, and scorpions are all indigenous—and alive.

MAYNARD DIXON: MASTER PAINTER OF THE TUCSON VALLEY

Maynard Dixon (1875-1946) was a popular artist and illustrator who mixed the Southwest's exotic landscape and peoples with the aesthetic tropes of modernism. He lived and painted in Tucson in the 1930s and '40s with his wife, the photographer Dorothea Lange.

Dixon had a very successful career as an illustrator for magazines, books, and advertising – he was there among the leading lights of the Golden Age of Illustration like Wyeth, Parrish, and, especially, Remington – before settling down to paint the desert and its peoples full-time. In his commercial work he wandered, as many illustrators do, among realism, fantasy, and stereotype, and his paintings, mostly oils and watercolors, similarly teeter back and forth between pure recordings of bouncing-light landscapes and an almost social realism in some of his portraits of Native Americans.

Others of his paintings are mythic and border on a kind of romantic fantasy. In 1922, two decades after he first visited Arizona, Dixon lived at Walpi on First Mesa, in the land of Hopi Indians in northeastern Arizona, for four months. His hosts were "two Hopi snake priests, Namoki and his blind brother Loma Himna." One of the more powerful and evocative of Dixon's paintings from this era is "The Witch of Sikyatki," an arresting scene from Hopi mythology in which the titular witch is locked in an unnerving glance at the viewer.

In Tucson, Dixon primarily painted the desert landscape, and I don't think anybody painted it better. The overwhelming feeling one gets after spending time with Dixon's work is one of being overwhelmed – by jutting rock, by deep canyons, by endless blue sky. In his paintings, the desert is nearly always much bigger than the people in it. And that's as it should be.

"Maynard Dixon's love for the simplified forms and colors in the west he wandered, explored and mined for subject matter, is what distinguishes him from other Western artists and makes him essential in every sense of the word," says a 2009 catalogue for the prestigious Scottsdale Art Auction, in which Dixon's painting "Prairie Mother" was expected to go for between $150,000 and $200,000. "It is Dixon," the catalogue continues, "who bridges modernism and the characteristic realism of Western art."

Here in the Old Pueblo, Dixon's work is very popular. In 2008 the Tucson Museum of Art put on the largest single show of his work ever, collecting each of Dixon's Arizona paintings in one place for the first time. At the essential Medicine Man Gallery in east Tucson, there's a permanent display of much of Dixon's work collected at the Maynard Dixon Museum. The gallery's owner, Mark Sublette, also presents a lot of information on Dixon's life and many images of his work at www.maynarddixon.org.

SOUTHERN ARIZONA TRANSPORTATION MUSEUM

414 N. Toole Ave., 520/623-2223,
www.tucsonhistoricdepot.org
HOURS: Tues.-Thurs. 11 A.M.-3 P.M.,
Fri.-Sat. 10 A.M.-4 P.M., Sun. 11 A.M.-3 P.M.
COST: Free
Map 1

When the railroad reached the isolated town of Tucson in the 1880s, it transformed the city and the region. This small museum at the refurbished old rail depot downtown explains all the myriad ways the railroad, and later the car and the interstate system, changed Tucson and the Southwest, opening it up to visitors and settlers and linking it more with the United States rather than with Mexico, as it had been before the train's arrival. There's a life-like statue of Wyatt Earp and Doc Holliday nearby, and a plaque that tells the story of a bit of revenge and/or murder that went down here back in the old violent days. Also, an old locomotive of the kind that used to haul goods and folks across the nation is preserved and on display.

TUCSON CHILDREN'S MUSEUM

200 S. 6th Ave., 520/792-9985,
www.tucsonchildrensmuseum.org
HOURS: Tues.-Sat. 10 A.M.-5 P.M., Sun. noon-5 P.M.
COST: $7 adult, $5 senior and child 2-18
Map 1

My favorite thing about the Tucson Children's Museum is the historic downtown Carnegie Library building it's been housed in since 1991. But if you have kids, you're sure to appreciate the creativity and attention to detail of the operators of this nonprofit interactive learning center. There are 12 permanent exhibits here, all of them hands-on and featuring some kid-mesmerizing subject like dinosaurs, electricity, ocean life or trains. There's also an "enchanted rainforest" geared toward preschoolers. It's not always easy to find parking because the museum has no lot of its own. There are metered spaces around the museum, and $1 in change will get you about two hours during the week; on weekends parking is free.

TUCSON RODEO PARADE MUSEUM

4823 S. 6th Ave., 520/294-1280,
www.tucsonrodeoparade.org
HOURS: Jan. 5-Apr. 11 Mon.-Sat. 9:30 A.M.-3:30 P.M.
(hours vary during rodeo week Feb. 21-Mar. 2)
COST: $5 minimum donation, free child under 16
Map 6

In a circa-1918 hangar on the south side, a fabled "surrey with the fringe on top" used in the 1955 film *Oklahoma*—filmed in the Santa Cruz Valley south of Tucson—is preserved in near-mint condition along with scores of other original buggies and wagons from the days before the internal combustion engine took over the world. Many of the buggies and wagons are hitched up to horses and rattled through the streets in late February during the annual Rodeo Parade, the longest non-motorized parade in the nation. Other highlights include a carriage once owned by industrialist Andrew Carnegie; a U.S. Army freight wagon from the days when the Army occupied the Arizona Territory; and a carriage that was used for a time by Emperor Maximilian, whom the French set up as their puppet leader of Mexico in 1864. There's also a re-creation of what Tucson's main street might have looked like in the 19th century, including a blacksmith shop and a bunkhouse.

VISTA DEL RIO CULTURAL RESOURCE PARK

7575 E. Desert Arbor St.
HOURS: Daily dawn-dusk
Map 7

Before the Spanish arrived in Southern Arizona, before the Mexicans, before the Americans, even before the Tohono O'odham and the Apache ruled this desert, it was home to the Hohokam people, arid-land farmers who lived in the Sonoran Desert's river valleys, building a highly complex culture that survived for centuries. Though the Tucson valley doesn't have any spectacular Hohokam ruins on the order of Casa Grande just off I-10 halfway between Tucson and Phoenix, this four-acre east-side archaeological park preserves the humbler ruins of a village occupied by the Hohokam from about A.D. 1000 to 1150. Even if you're less than fascinated by the dirt-mound ruins, this is a quiet and peaceful park with walking paths and sitting areas, perfect for relaxation and contemplation among the ghosts of a long-lost nation.

GALLERIES

Check with the **Tucson-Pima Arts Council** (www.tucsonpimaartscouncil.org) for a complete calendar of all the arts-related stuff going on in town at any given moment.

CONRAD WILDE GALLERY

210 N. 4th Ave., 520/622-8997,
www.conradwildegallery.com
HOURS: Tues.-Sat. 11 A.M.-5 P.M.
Map 1

An emphasis on abstraction and the mysterious power of color pervades this 4th Avenue gallery. Emerging and established artists have common cause here, but most of the colorful, challenging work is by artists (many of them regional) with long resumes. Collectors especially shouldn't miss popping into Conrad Wilde if

they are in town. Contemporary paintings, sculpture, and works on paper are all well represented, and the works often have an experimental quality that will make you scratch your head and lose your breath at the same time.

DINNERWARE CONTEMPORARY ARTSPACE

264 E. Congress St., 520/792-4503,
www.dinnerwarearts.com
HOURS: Tues.-Sat. 11 A.M.-6 P.M.
Map 1

This contemporary art gallery has been showing the best work by Southern Arizona artists for nearly 30 years. The work is usually eclectic, with an emphasis on artists' responses to the desert landscape and the unique history of the region, but with a contemporary, multicultural twist that you certainly won't find at other galleries in town. A case in point: One exhibition featured works by the growing number of Asian artists working in the Tucson region. If you want to know what emerging, avant-garde, and cutting-edge artists are doing in Tucson, Dinnerware is the place to find out.

Dinnerware Contemporary Artspace features work by local and regional artists.

© TIM HULL

ARTS AND LEISURE

The Eric Firestone Gallery is housed in an old adobe designed by Josias Joesler.

© TIM HULL

ERIC FIRESTONE GALLERY

4425 Campbell Ave., 520/577-7711,
www.ericfirestonegallery.com
HOURS: Mon.-Thurs. 10 A.M.-5 P.M.,
Fri.-Sat. 10 A.M.-5 P.M., Sun. noon-5 P.M.
Map 3

Eric Firestone is interested in how modernism, in all its forms, found purchase in the desert Southwest. His main gallery, in a Josias Joesler–designed adobe at the corner of River and Campbell, is set up as if it's the winter home of a very cultured Southwesterner before the population boom, with amazing well-preserved Monterey furniture (along with later Gottschalk and Eames chairs) arranged in each small room. The gallery's collection of paintings—displayed at the main foothills gallery and at a separate exhibition space downtown (266 E. Congress St., 520/903-0997, Wed.–Sat. 11 A.M.–5 P.M.)—is heavy with desertland modernists like Maynard Dixon, Douglas Denniston, Jorge Flick, and Philip Curtis, as well as the more traditional Southwestern styles of artists like Jack Van Ryder and Pete Martinez.

☾ ETHERTON GALLERY

135 S. 6th Ave., 520/624-7370,
www.ethertongallery.com
HOURS: Tues.-Sat. 11 A.M.-5 P.M. (Thurs. until 7 P.M.)
Map 1

Etherton is one of the city's finest galleries and is routinely voted among the best in town in the Old Pueblo's many polls. The downtown gallery, located in the historic Oddfellows Building, concentrates on photography—from the classic 19th-century chroniclers of the West to today's interpreters—and regional and local artists of the highest caliber. The **Temple Gallery** at the Temple of Music and Art (330 S. Scott Ave., 520/624-7370, Mon.–Fri. 10 A.M.–6 P.M.) is also managed by Etherton Gallery and features new work by local artists.

GALLERY ROW AT EL CORTIJO

3001 E. Skyline Dr. (northeast corner of Campbell and Skyline)
Map 3

The best of the contemporary art galleries at Gallery Row at El Cortijo, a collection of five art galleries at 3001 East Skyline at Campbell, is the **Wilde Meyer Gallery** (3001 E. Skyline Dr., Ste. 115, 520/615-5222, www.wilde-meyer.com, Mon.–Fri. 10 A.M.–5:30 P.M., Sat. 10 A.M.–6 P.M., Sun. noon–5 P.M.). Wilde Meyer truly has some of the best paintings in town, and features a large and eclectic selection of contemporary paintings, many but certainly not all by artists dealing with the past, present, and future of the Southwest. Other galleries worth a pop-in here are the **The Max Gallery** (3001 E. Skyline Dr., Ste. 127, 520/529-7349, www.themaxgallery.com, Tues.–Thurs. 10 A.M.–5:30 P.M., Fri.–Sat. 10 A.M.–7 P.M., Sun. 11 A.M.–4 P.M.) and the **Mountain Shadow Gallery** (3001 E. Skyline Dr., Ste. 109, 520/577-6301, www.mountain-shadowgallery.com, Mon.–Sat. 10 A.M.–6 P.M., Sun. 11 A.M.–5 P.M.), both showing paintings and sculptures about the West and its many myths, legends, and iconic landscapes. There are also a few galleries worth perusing in the shopping center just to the south of Gallery Row along Skyline.

GALLERY WEST
FINE AMERICAN INDIAN ART

6420 N. Campbell Ave., 520/529-7002, www.indianartwest.com
HOURS: Mon.-Sat. 10 A.M.-4 P.M.
Map 3

A tiny gallery featuring Native American art and artifacts from the 19th and 20th centuries, Gallery West, one of three excellent galleries of Western art that look out on a shady courtyard at Campbell and Skyline, features Tohono O'odham baskets, Hopi and Pueblo pottery—including rare Hopi tiles—kachinas from the 1950s and 1960s, and Navajo and Pueblo jewelry. They also sell unique reprints of the original 1886 photograph of Geronimo and Chiricahua Apache Chief Naiche by Tombstone photographer C. S. Fly—the only photographer to have photographed these infamous Apache warriors while they were on the run from the U.S. Army. A large (44" x 72") framed digital pigment print reproduced from the original first-generation photograph will set you back about $1,500 (although a small—23" x 28"—unframed reproduction runs as low as $250).

JOSEPH GROSS GALLERY
AT THE UA SCHOOL OF ART

University of Arizona campus, 520/626-4215, http://web.cfa.arizona.edu/galleries
HOURS: Mon.-Fri. 9 A.M.-4 P.M.
Map 1

A small gallery on the UA campus, the Joseph Gross Gallery, and its sister Lionel Rombach Gallery, both free to the public, exhibit works by UA faculty, students, and various regional, national, and international artists working in a variety of media. The work featured here is usually some of the most experimental and cutting edge to be seen in the Old Pueblo, especially during the annual Master of Fine Arts Thesis show in April and May.

MADARAS GALLERY

3001 E. Skyline Dr., at Gallery Row, 520/615-3001, www.madaras.com
HOURS: Mon.-Sat. 10 A.M.-6 P.M., Sun. 11 A.M.-5 P.M.
Map 3

Diana Madaras is among Southern Arizona's most successful and popular artists; her watercolors and acrylics, a mixture of playful realism and expressionistic color, have earned her high-profile commissions—including paintings hanging at the Westin La Paloma, Loews Ventana Canyon, and Mirival—a little bit of fame, and enough money to sustain not just one but two local galleries that feature her work exclusively. The second gallery location is in Midtown at 1535 East Broadway Boulevard (520/623-4000). Her style is instantly recognizable once you see it for the first time, and her various whimsical and romantic interpretations of Southwestern landscapes, people, and culture represent her best work.

◖ MARK SUBLETTE
MEDICINE MAN GALLERY

7000 Tanque Verde Rd., Ste. 16, 520/722-7798, www.medicinemangallery.com
HOURS: Sept.-Apr. Mon.-Sat. 10 A.M.-5 P.M., Sun. 1-4 P.M.; May-Aug. Tues.-Sat. 10 A.M.-5 P.M.
Map 4

For anyone enraptured, as I am, by the classic art of the Southwest—from the photographs of

Edward Curtis to the modernist illustrations of Maynard Dixon; from the ceremonial kachinas of the Hopi people to the elegant yellow-brown pottery of Nampeyo—Mark Sublette's Medicine Man Gallery on the east side is an absolute must-visit. The huge gallery also features the **Maynard Dixon Museum,** with a wide selection of often obscure paintings, illustrations, and ephemera from throughout the great artist's career. There's also a contemporary art gallery here featuring the best in new Western art by the likes of the fabulous Navajo artist Shonto Begay.

PLATFORM GALLERY
439 N. 6th Ave., 520/882-3886, www.platformart.com
HOURS: Tues.-Sat. 2-5 P.M.
Map 1

This contemporary art gallery is in the warehouse arts district on the corner of 6th Avenue and 6th Street and offers a heady mix of paintings, drawings, photographs, and sculptures by emerging and established artists from the Southwest. Here, as in many of Tucson's contemporary art spaces, you'll find artists dealing with the region, and the history of the region's art, in exciting new ways. The owners seem to prefer a mixture of representation and abstraction, and the old utilitarian building (it looks like it might have been a gas station at one time) has been refurbished into something wonderful.

SANDERS GALLERIES
6420 N. Campbell Ave., 520/299-1763,
www.sandersgalleries.com
HOURS: Mon.-Sat. 10 A.M.-5 P.M.
Map 3

One of three longtime galleries looking out on a lush enclosed courtyard overlooking the valley at Campbell and Skyline, Sanders, like its neighbor Settlers West, features the kind of work that often appears in the magazine *Art of the West:* contemporary regional, national, and international artists, many of whom use as their subject matter scenes of Native American life; thrilling landscapes featuring mostly unspoiled Western scenes;

and detailed, ultra-realistic portraits of iconic Western animals—mountains lions, bobcats, mustangs, and the like.

SETTLERS WEST GALLERY
6420 N. Campbell Ave., 520/299-2607,
www.settlerswest.com
HOURS: Mon.-Sat. 10 A.M.-5 P.M.
Map 3

For 30 years Settlers West has shown the best in contemporary and classic Western art. The paintings and sculptures depict romantic, even idealized, scenes of Native American life, many of them non-Southwestern. Wildlife art, depictions of cowboy culture, and landscapes filled with deserts, cacti, and red-rock canyons abound. This is not the place to find experimental or even modernist work—it's all pretty traditional, but always of the highest quality.

CONCERT VENUES
ANSELMO VALENCIA TORI AMPHITHEATER
Casino del Sol, 5655 W. Valencia Rd., 520/838-6700,
www.avaconcerts.com
Map 7

Where else are the likes of Queensryche or Frankie Valli and the Four Seasons going to play when they come to Tucson, the Rialto? Don't be absurd. They're too big to be contained by a roof. We can thank the proliferation of midsized outdoor venues like the 4,470-seat Anselmo Valencia Tori Amphitheater for keeping undead doo-woppers and the skeletal remains of bands we really liked when we were 13 on the touring circuit. This is Southern Arizona's largest concert venue, with six corporate boxes, nearly 2,000 seats, and a lawn for the rest of us.

THE FOX THEATRE
17 W. Congress St., 520/624-1515,
www.foxtucsontheatre.org
HOURS: Box office Mon.-Fri. 11 A.M.-6 P.M.,
Sat. 11 A.M.-2 P.M.
Map 1

From the 1930s to the 1970s, the Fox was the

The 1930s-era Fox Theatre has been restored to its former grandeur.

Built in the 1920s for vaudeville shows, The Rialto now hosts a broad array of performers.

place to go in Tucson to see Hollywood's latest offering, and the theater's art deco style nearly matched the glamour on the screen. Along with many other once-famous and much-used buildings in downtown, the Fox fell into disrepair until the late 1990s, when a group formed to raise money to refurbish the old movie house. Now the theater, beautifully restored to its original grandeur, shows classic films several times a month and hosts concerts and events.

◖ THE RIALTO

318 E. Congress St., 520/740-1000,
www.rialtotheatre.com
HOURS: Box office Mon.-Fri. noon-6 P.M.
Map 1

A cool old theater with a balcony, The Rialto regularly hosts the best alt-rock and alt-country touring bands—acts like Ryan Adams, Son Volt, the Drive-By Truckers, and Shooter Jennings. Across Congress Street from the Hotel Congress downtown, the theater originally opened in 1920. Now it operates as a nonprofit organization showing the best

concerts in town. If you're a serious fan of music—rock, hip-hop, alternative rock, and alt-country—don't come to Tucson without checking the Rialto's website first; you just might find that there's someone coming that you want to see.

THE TEMPLE OF MUSIC AND ART

330 S. Scott Ave., 520/884-4875
Map 1

A group of music-loving Tucsonans called the Saturday Morning Music Club saw to the construction of this wonderful Spanish colonial revival theater downtown, on the edge of the historic Armory Park neighborhood. The theater, known for its stylish interior and excellent acoustics, drew top-name musicians to the Old Pueblo for years. Bands and soloist still play here from time to time, but mostly it is the main stage for the Arizona Theatre Company (box office 520/622-2823, www.aztheatreco.org), which puts on excellent regional productions of top-shelf plays and musicals here and in Phoenix.

PERFORMING ARTS

ARIZONA FRIENDS OF CHAMBER MUSIC

260 S. Church St., 520/577-3769,
www.arizonachambermusic.org

Map 1

This dedicated group of local chamber-music enthusiasts brings the world's top musicians to the intimate Leo Rich Theater at the Tucson Convention Center, and in March presents a festival's worth of the new sounds of various known and unknown small ensembles from all over.

ARIZONA OPERA

3501 N. Mountain Ave., 520/293-4336,
www.azopera.org

Map 1

It's not Santa Fe, but I think the Arizona Opera Company presents some of the best regional opera in the country October–April at the Tucson Convention Center Music Hall. There's usually not a lot of experimenting going on—you'll get the classics that you've heard of, done well. A night out at the opera in Tucson is a good chance to see the city's diversity of style: you'll see a few people in black tie and flowing gowns, and others in jeans and flip-flops. Like the Arizona Theatre Company's productions, operas usually premier in Tucson and then move on to Phoenix.

ARIZONA REPERTORY THEATRE

University of Arizona School of Theatre Arts,
520/621-1162, http:/web.cfa.arizona.edu/theatre

Map 1

The training company for the UA's School of Theatre Arts necessarily puts on a short season of top-name dramas and comedies—works by Neal Simon, Shakespeare, William Inge, and the like, performed earnestly if not always expertly. The UA Fine Arts box office is located at 1025 North Olive, near the southeast corner of Park Avenue and Speedway Boulevard.

ARIZONA THEATRE COMPANY

330 S. Scott Ave., 520/622-2823, www.aztheatreco.org

Map 1

The state's flagship troupe puts on an entertaining season of plays September–May. Most productions debut at the beautiful Temple of Music and Art in Tucson and then move on to Phoenix. Lately the company, like most other regional nonprofits, has been choosing material with somewhat obvious toe-tapping, audience-pleasing potential. Tucson's many ex-hippie boomers were overjoyed with a recent revival of *Hair,* and other recent productions have depicted the lives, and music, of Janis Joplin, Billie Holiday, and Hank Williams.

BEOWULF ALLEY THEATRE

11 S. 6th Ave., 520/882-0555, www.beowulfalley.org

Map 1

This intimate, somewhat charming little theater downtown presents three or four plays every season, typically quite well done and accessible; many of the works are Arizona premiers of off-off-Broadway shows by contemporary playwrights. At the Beowulf, as it is with most of the small theater companies in Tucson, one gets the sense that the players love and need theater in a way that most of us don't understand, and that they would be performing the same play in the same way even without an audience. You can't ask for more than that out of a night at the theater.

BORDERLANDS THEATER

El Centro Cultural de las Americanas, 40 W. Broadway Blvd., 520/882-7406, www.borderlandstheater.org

Map 1

Borderlands, as its name implies, concentrates on theater that explores regional issues and lifestyles, especially Mexican-American and border-region culture. They usually produce between three and six plays a season, some of them by homegrown playwrights, at various small venues around town. Ticket prices are in the $10.75–20.75 range.

GASLIGHT DINNER THEATRE

7010 E. Broadway Blvd., 520/886-9428,
www.thegaslighttheatre.com

HOURS: Box office Mon.-Thurs. 10 A.M.-9 P.M., Fri.-Sat. noon-9 P.M., Sun. noon-9 P.M.; showtimes Tues.-Thurs. 7 P.M., Fri.-Sat. 6:30 P.M. and 9 P.M., Sun. 3 P.M. and 7 P.M.

COST: $19.40 adult; $17.24 senior, student, and active military; $8.59 child 2-12

Map 4

It's certainly not high art, but the melodramas and family comedies put on at this east-side dinner theater are typically fun and often hilarious. The shows change every few months and are usually on the order of the *Ballad of Two-Gun McGraw, or Just Horsin' Around* and *On the Road to the North Pole, or The Snow Must Go On.* The shows last about two hours, and the "dinner" is a pretty good pizza pie ordered and delivered from Grandma Tony's next door. Kids will invariably like the shows; if the adults need a little help getting into it, a modest selection of beer and wine is served.

INVISIBLE THEATRE

1400 N. 1st Ave , 520/882-9721,
www.invisibletheatre.com
Map 1

For nearly 40 years the Invisible Theatre has been offering popular productions of the classics, off-Broadway touring productions, and locally created plays as well. The theater itself is an old building that used to hold a laundry but now holds 80 seats and an intimate stage. Tickets typically range $22–45.

RHYTHM & ROOTS CONCERT SERIES

Various venues, 520/319-9966,
www.rhythmandroots.org

This series brings roots musicians—blues, folk, bluegrass, zydeco, and some bluesy-country rock—to Tucson. Concerts are held at various locations in the downtown area, such as Old Town Artisans, the Lost Barrio, and other places. The music is always good, and the series is responsible for bringing some little-known legends to the Old Pueblo. If you're a fan of the genere(s), you'll want to get the latest scoop from the website before coming to town.

ROGUE THEATRE

Various venues, 520/551-2053,
www.theroguetheatre.org

The only company in Tucson doing the likes of Pirandello and Genet as a regular rule, the Rogue Theatre doesn't have a permanent home but instead puts on about four or five productions a year at various venues around town.

Individual tickets run $20, and you usually get your money's worth as long as you are looking to be challenged, entertained, and inspired.

TUCSON SYMPHONY ORCHESTRA

260 S. Church St., 520/882-8585,
www.tucsonsymphony.org
Map 1

More than 80 years old, this orchestra holds concerts September–May at the Tucson Convention Center Music Hall, with the familiar mixture of classics and pops, from Stravinsky to Bugs Bunny. The orchestra is impeccable most nights, and well worth seeing and hearing—certainly one of the better midsized orchestras in the Southwest.

CINEMA

◖ THE LOFT CINEMA

3233 E. Speedway Blvd., 520/795-7777,
www.loftcinema.com
Map 2

The nonprofit arts organization that runs this landmark theater on Speedway books thoughtful and entertaining films, showing not only the best of today's art-house flicks but also classics and cult films, and you can buy a microbrew and a slice of pizza to go with all the soul searching on the screen. The theater regularly puts on special events with directors, screenwriters, and actors, as well as festivals and one-night-only showings, so it's a good idea to check out the website if you're a traveling cinephile. Before 6 P.M. on weekdays tickets cost $6, otherwise it's $8.75 for an adult, $5.75 for kids 12 and under.

COMEDY

LAFFS COMEDY CAFFE

2900 E. Broadway, 520/323-8669,
www.laffstucson.com
HOURS: Showtimes Thurs. 8 P.M., Fri. 8 P.M. and 10:30 P.M., Sat. 7 P.M. and 9:30 P.M.
COST: $10-15
Map 2

Touring comics from around the country stop in for a set or two at Laffs Comedy Caffe near Broadway and Country Club. There's usually a fun time to be had here—the local-comic emcees are amusing and the touring pros kill more often than not. The staff herds show-goers into a small lounge before each show, and it's easy to forget that the two-drink (or food item) minimum doesn't start until the show does. The full bar serves a range of beers in cans and bottles, and several delicious and insidious high-octane special drinks with names like the Giggler and Laff's Punch. The kitchen serves a full menu of appetizers, grill-style entrées, and desserts, but this is not an ideal place to eat your supper. Calling ahead for a reservation is a good idea but not typically necessary. They may ask you to share your table once the show starts in an effort to fill up the room, but you can just politely say no and they won't ask again.

Festivals and Events

SPRING
ARIZONA INTERNATIONAL FILM FESTIVAL
The Screening Room, 127 E. Congress St., 520/882-0204, www.filmfestivalarizona.com
`Map 1`

For 10 days beginning in mid-April, filmmakers and film lovers from around the world come to Tucson to watch and celebrate independent cinema. This popular local film festival is approaching its third decade, and the most recent event premiered movies from Bolivia, Japan, Germany, South Africa, and even the good old U.S.A. The best films screened at the festival, which takes place at downtown's tiny Screening Room and sometimes at other venues around town, are the entrants in the annual Reel Frontier Film and Video Contest.

4TH AVENUE STREET FAIRS
4th Ave., 520/624-5004, www.fourthavenue.org
`Map 1`

Artists, artisans, street performers, food-booth proprietors, and thousands of Tucsonans converge on 4th Avenue twice a year for this popular event. The street closes down and hundreds of white tents go up, selling jewelry, paintings, photographs, leather goods, glass art, and all kinds of other items you never knew existed. The best part of the two annual street fairs is seeing all the street performers—mostly fiddle and guitar bands and folksingers vying for attention, but there are also usually a few adorable little kids with their violins hoping for a few bucks tossed in their case. It's a crowded, greasy-food good time every year. Usually the spring fair, toward the end of March, is the more popular, what with the gorgeous weather and all. The winter fair is in December.

LA FRONTERA TUCSON INTERNATIONAL MARIACHI CONFERENCE
504 W. 29th St., 520/838-3908, www.tucsonmariachi.org
`Map 1`

Mariachi music is an important part of Tucson's soundtrack; it can be heard everywhere—in one restaurant or another just about every night of the week, and pretty much at any festival or event that draws more than three people. Many public schools in the Old Pueblo offer mariachi classes as part of their music curricula. It's not surprising, then, that one of the most popular annual gatherings of mariachi enthusiasts and professionals takes place in Tucson every April. The weeklong event features concerts and workshops and a final-day fiesta at the Reid Park bandshell—the easiest and least expensive way to take part ($5 adult, free child under 12). Otherwise check the website for performance times, venues, and prices (tickets tend to sell out early).

PIMA COUNTY FAIR

Pima County Fairgrounds, 11300 S. Houghton Rd.,
520/762-3247, www.pimacountyfair.com
COST: $7 adult, $2 child 6-10, $5 parking
Map 7

For 10 days every year beginning in mid-April, myriad cowboys, country folk, 4-H geniuses, and cotton candy–kids converge on the Pima County Fairgrounds southeast of Tucson, where they show off their pigs and goats and prize bulls, their roses, jams, and pumpkins-on-steroids, their gullibility and screaming skills, and quite often the contents of their stomachs. In short, it's the county fair, an ancient American ritual that is different in Southern Arizona only in that there are usually quite a number of families up from Sonora in attendance. The free concerts usually feature one or two superstar Mexican groups along with a few mid-level American country acts.

SPRING ART FAIR

Tucson Museum of Art, 140 N. Main Ave.,
520/624-2333
Map 1

The last weekend in March brings artisans from around the region to the Tucson Museum of Art. You'll find one-of-a-kind handmade treasures and unique decorative items here, and both the fair and entrance to the museum are free. There's a similar market in the fall—a good chance to buy unique holiday presents.

TUCSON FOLK FESTIVAL

El Presidio Park, 520/792-6481
Map 1

The Tucson Kitchen Musicians, a longtime group of folkies and other musical types in Tucson, put on this excellent showcase of local and regional folk and blues music every year in downtown El Presidio Park. It's a chance to discover all the talented singer-songwriters working in the folk, acoustic, and roots traditions in the Old Pueblo, and much of the festival is usually broadcast on KXCI, Tucson's community radio station. There are always a few food booths set up, and the whole event is popular and crowded with families and kids.

UA SPRING FLING

Rillito Downs, 4502 N. 1st Ave., 520/621-5610,
www.springfling.arizona.edu
COST: $5 adult and child over 7, free UA students and active military, $1 parking
Map 3

Instead of showers, which don't usually return to the desert until July or August, April brings the University of Arizona's annual fund-raising carnival to the Old Pueblo. A popular local tradition since 1974, the event features carnival rides, food booths, games, and displays operated by various UA clubs and organizations in need of funding. The revelry lasts for four nights at the beginning of April, each one usually crowded with UA students, families, and packs of wild teenagers.

WA:K POWWOW

San Xavier del Bac, 520/294-5727
Map 6

The Tohono O'odham were dry-farming and gathering juicy saguaro fruit in the Tucson valley long before the Spanish arrived, and they were often considered friendly allies to the Spanish, Mexicans, and Americans, all of whom fought viciously with the Apache, who were the historic enemies of the "Desert People" as well. During the second weekend in March, the O'odham, formerly called the Papago, gather at the large open plaza at San Xavier del Bac for a cultural festival featuring traditional dancing, drumming, arts and crafts, native foods, and other activities.

SUMMER

CINCO DE MAYO

Kennedy Park, 520/292-9326
Map 6

That fateful day when Mexican soldiers routed an army of adventuring, occupying French at the battle of Puebla (May 5, 1862) is celebrated in the Old Pueblo in various ways. For most of us, the many supermarket markdowns on Mexican beer, corn chips, and salsa are enough to get us in the mood; others head over to South Tucson's Kennedy Park for a colorful fiesta featuring mariachi, traditional dances, folk arts, concerts, and, of course, heaps of Mexican cuisine.

DÍA DE SAN JUAN
W. Congress St. at the Santa Cruz River,
www.tucsonaz.gov/sanjuan
Map 1

On June 24 the overheated populous prays for rain during a free festival celebrating John the Baptist and the saint's historical relationship with the desert's summer rainy season. The tradition of celebrating the Baptist's birthday came to the region with the Spanish in the 1600s, and over the centuries was imbued with more localized and indigenous meanings. The event features a parade, food booths, mariachi, and native dancing meant to inspire the summer rains to visit the dry, hot pueblo.

HA:SAN BAK:
SAGUARO HARVEST CELEBRATION
Colossal Cave Mountain Park, 520/647-7121,
www.colossalcave.com
Map 7

Many, if not most, Tucsonans have at least one saguaro within a few feet of their front door, yet few of them see the ubiquitous cactus as a source of sustenance. The Tohono O'odham, on the other hand, have constructed a large part of their culture around the comings and goings of the saguaro's red fruit, and over centuries in the desert have devised myriad uses for every part of the great cactus-tree. In late June, as the annual harvest is in full swing, native volunteers give workshops on the uses and wonders of the saguaro at Colossal Cave Mountain Park near Vail, including making a batch or two of saguaro syrup and other delicacies.

IRONWOOD FESTIVAL
Mason Audubon Center, 3835 W. Hardy St.,
520/744-0004, www.tucsonaudubon.org
Map 7

In early May, just when the sun starts in with the attitude, Tucson's self-admitted tree huggers gather at the Audubon Society's Mason Center (near Arthur Pack Regional Park)

northwest of town to celebrate the long-lived ironwood tree (protected at nearby Ironwood National Monument), and the key role it plays in the desert's astonishingly diverse ecosystem. The festival features fun and educational activities like guided bird walks, natural history displays and lectures, and, once the sun dips away a bit, a lineup of folk-rock bands.

JUNETEENTH FIESTA
Kennedy Park, La Cholla Blvd. and Ajo Way,
520/617-7385, www.youthtogether.org/juneteenth
Map 6

Tucsonans celebrate the nation's oldest African American holiday with a two-day festival at the south side's Kennedy Park. The fun begins on June 18 and continues the next day, known as Juneteenth, the day that far-flung slaves in Galveston, Texas, finally learned that they'd been set free, two years after President Lincoln issued the Emancipation Proclamation. The annual event, now in its fourth decade, features food booths, live music and other entertainment, and loads of stuff for the kids.

WAILA FESTIVAL
Arizona Historical Society, 520/628-5774,
www.arizonahistoricalsociety.org
Map 1

At the end of May, thousands of Tucsonans gather at the UA's Bear Down Field to step and hop to the very danceable sounds of the folk hybrid that is Waila, sometimes called chicken-scratch. The polka-like party-inspiring music was built and adapted by the Tohono O'odham over the years, based on European and Mexican songs they'd heard during interactions with their various colonizers. This is a fun, free party, with young and old dancing and laughing, and good foods (including traditional O'odham fare) sizzling and smoking.

FALL
ALL SOUL'S PROCESSION
Various downtown locations,
www.allsoulsprocession.org
Map 1

Something like 20,000 people participate in

this unique local tradition, now 20 years old, based on the rites and folk art of Mexico's Day of the Dead. A local arts collective organizes the colorful and creative nonmotorized parade through downtown, featuring giant puppets and other Mexican-inspired folk arts hand-made by participants. The whole thing culminates in a big ceremonial fire and a "dance of the dead." The All Soul's Weekend (the first full weekend of November), with the parade and bonfire its finale, features several like-minded events, like arts shows, poetry readings, and a kids' parade.

EL TOUR DE TUCSON
Perimeter Bicycling Association of America, 2609 E. Broadway Blvd., 520/745-2033, www.pbaa.com
Map 7

The Tucson-based nonprofit PBAA puts on several road-bike races in Southern Arizona that raise millions for local charities and bring tough, wiry bicyclists to Tucson from all over the world. The most popular of these is the Tour de Tucson in late November, when the weather here is more like spring than fall. The main 109-mile route takes riders all over the Tucson valley, up into the foothills and mountains and back, as thousands of spectators line portions of the route cheering and holding up signs to egg on the exhausted cyclists. The tour typically draws more than 9,000 riders and includes shorter routes of 80 miles, 67 miles, 35 miles, and even a 4-mile fun ride for kids and families. Another popular local PBAA event is the **Tour of the Tucson Mountains** in late April, with 70- and 27-mile courses, and in October the group puts on the **Cochise County Cycling Classic,** with 45-, 92-, and 157-mile routes, and even an insane 252-mile route that requires riders to have a back-up crew.

OKTOBERFEST
Hi Corbett Field, 3400 E. Camino Campestre, www.tucsonoktoberfest.org
Map 2

Beer and sausage are year-round necessities for many of us, but these and other German imports take center stage at midtown's Hi Corbett Field in early October. Tucson's Oktoberfest takes place over four days and evenings and features scores of arts and crafts booths and food and beer vendors, along with a polka band or 20. A dance always breaks out, and there is a lot for the kids to do. The only thing that separates this local Oktoberfest from one in, say, Wisconsin, is that here you don't need a coat and gloves.

TUCSON MEET YOURSELF
El Presidio Park, 520/792-4806, www.tucsonmeetyourself.org
Map 1

With so much written and filmed about the usual suspects of Southwestern history, it's easy to forget that Tucson is as multicultural as a city can be, albeit on a rather smaller scale than most. Tucson Meet Yourself, an annual festival held October 10–12 at El Presidio Park downtown, shows off just how diverse the city is. If you're going, go hungry. Dozens of cultural clubs—from Colombians to Danes to Koreans to Irish to Poles, Russians, Navajo, and more—cook up and sell their national cuisine, making it possible to have catfish, sweet-potato pie, roasted corn, fry bread, and pickled herring all in one meal. The festival also features folk-art demonstrations.

WINTER
ACCENTURE MATCH PLAY
Ritz-Carlton Golf Club at Dove Mountain, www.worldgolfchampionships.com
Map 7

In late February the keen eyes of the professional golf world are focused squarely on Tucson when Tiger Woods comes to town, bringing along the world's top 64 golfers to battle it out for an oversized $8 million check. Tiger made his 2009 return to professional golf at this popular tournament, which has top golfers competing for each hole instead of an entire round. The international press descends on the ultra-high-end Dove Mountain golf resort northwest of midtown, and tickets aren't too easy to come by.

ARTS AND LEISURE

DILLINGER DAYS

Hotel Congress, 311 E. Congress St., 520/622-8848,
www.hotelcongress.com

Map 1

In 1935 the small little-known desert town
of Tucson made international news when the
infamous Dillinger gang, and later the public
enemy himself, was captured here after a fire
at the Hotel Congress, where most of the gang
members were laying up for the night. Now, in
late January every year, various downtown institutions, especially Hotel Congress, celebrate
that fateful night with a gala event, reenact-
ments of the capture, lectures, tours, old movies from the time, and much more.

FIESTA DE LOS VAQUEROS

4823 S. 6th Ave., 520/741-2233, 800/964-5662,
www.tucsonrodeo.com

COST: Most seats $12-21

Map 6

One of the Old Pueblo's most popular annual events (local school kids get two "rodeo
days" off every year), the "Celebration of the
Cowboys" began way back in 1925 and is today
one of the top 25 outdoor rodeos in the nation. Something like 50,000 people head to
the south side over eight days every February
(usually beginning around February 20) to
watch the dramatic bull riding, steer wrestling, women's barrel racing, and more, and to
eat a few tons of barbecue beef and pork. The
rodeo typically draws more than 600 contes-
tants, among them the best riders, ropers, and
cow-wrestlers in the world, who compete for
$320,000 in prize money.

LA FIESTA DE TUMACÁCORI

Exit 29 on I-19 South, Tumacácori National Historic
Park, 520/398-2341, Tumacácori, www.nps.gov/tuma

Map 7

During the first full weekend in December,
Mission Tumacácori, about six miles south of
Tubac along the frontage road, hosts a festival featuring dozens of food vendors and craft
booths, live music, kids' activities, and a traditional mariachi mass celebrated in front of
the ruin of the 17th-century mission, which
was founded, like its sister to the north San
Xavier del Bac, by Padre Kino during his
legendary forays into the Santa Cruz Valley.
During the festival admittance to the national
park is free.

SOUTHWEST INDIAN ART FAIR

Arizona State Museum, 1013 E. University Blvd.,
520/621-6302, www.statemuseum.arizona.edu

Map 1

This major event brings Native American artists and the people who love their work to
Tucson from all over the Southwest. White-
roofed booths sprawl out on the lawn in front
of the Arizona State Museum on the UA campus, while the smell of fry bread and other delicious, decadent foods fills the air. Artists from
Navajoland, from Hopi, from the pueblos of
the Rio Grande Valley, and elsewhere bring
their fetishes, kachinas, paintings, squash-blossom belt buckles, paintings, and other items to
sell and talk about. It's a great chance to buy
something unique and meaningful and to meet
the artist who made it so.

baskets for sale at the popular
Southwest Indian Art Fair

TUBAC FESTIVAL OF THE ARTS

Tubac, 520/398-2704, www.tubacaz.com/festival.asp

Map 7

For four days in early February the population of the tiny historic village of Tubac, about 45 minutes south of Tucson on I-19, swells tenfold, as hundreds of roaming artists and artisans set up their white tents and offer their unique and often strange visions and creations. Thousands flock from all around—Tucson, Green Valley, and Nogales—to stroll through the village's few streets, ducking in and out of all the crafty shops, eating grilled and fried food, and generally enjoying a 70-degree blue-sky day in late winter.

TUCSON GEM, MINERAL & FOSSIL SHOWCASE

Various locations, 520/322-5773, www.tgms.org

COST: $9

Map 1

The grand dame of Tucson's "golden month," the Gem Show brings visitors from all over the globe to the desert for one of the most popular and prestigious events of its kind. If you're into gems, minerals, fossils, and rocks, you probably know about it already. If your interest is more casual, however, the most affordable and easiest way to join in is to go to the huge Main Show at the Tucson Convention Center on the second full weekend of February, where you'll likely be astounded by the otherworldly colors and patterns in all those mysterious rocks.

WINTERHAVEN FESTIVAL OF LIGHTS

Fort Lowell Rd. and Country Club Dr., Winterhaven, 520/881-4483, www.winterhavenfestival.org

COST: Donation of canned food recommended

Map 2

Every December for the past 60 years or so, the Winterhaven neighborhood—a tree-lined, relatively upscale enclave in midtown—has draped itself in lights for the benefit of the local food bank. After the sun goes down residents invite the public to walk their pleasant streets and take in the show; vendors sell trolley and wagon rides around the neighborhood and various edible holiday treats, and sometimes it's even a bit cold. You might just mistake the whole scene for a sign of winter.

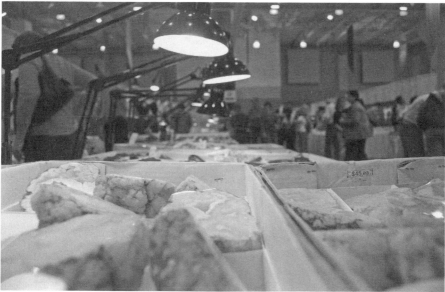

ARTS AND LEISURE

Held during winter, the Tucson Gem, Mineral & Fossil Showcase is the city's biggest event of the year.

Sports and Recreation

PARKS

ABRAHAM LINCOLN REGIONAL PARK

4325 S. Pantano Rd., 520/791-4873,
www.tucsonaz.gov/parksandrec
HOURS: Daily 6 A.M.-10:30 P.M.
Map 4

A 191-acre desert park in southeast Tucson near Davis-Monthan Air Force Base, Lincoln Regional Park features some of the best sand-volleyball courts in town, as well as softball fields, walking trails, a fitness center and swimming pool, playgrounds, picnic ramadas, and more. The lush riparian **Atturbury Bird and Animal Sanctuary** in the lower section of the park features a mile-long loop trail through a water-inspired desert landscape with all kinds of birds and other creatures flitting and scuttling about.

ARTHUR PACK REGIONAL PARK

9101 N. Thornydale Rd., 520/877-6120,
www.pima.gov/nrpr/parks
HOURS: Daily 7 A.M.-10 P.M.
Map 7

A large Pima County–run desert park on the far northwest side of town, Arthur Pack Regional Park has walking trails, picnic areas with shady ramadas, lighted soccer and baseball fields, basketball courts, and an excellent playground. Also on-site is the **Crooked Tree Golf Course** (520/744-3322), a public course with fantastic views of the mountains and the sweeping desert. This park is different from those inside the city in that it has more of a wild desert feel while still offering all the amenities.

BRANDI FENTON MEMORIAL PARK

3482 E. River Rd., www.brandifentonmemorialpark.org
HOURS: Park daily 7 A.M.-10 P.M.; visitor center
Tues.-Fri. 10 A.M.-4 P.M.
Map 3

Kids love the clean and well-designed "splash pad" at beautiful Brandi Fenton Park between River Road and the Rillito, and it's a worry-free good time for parents as well. Just push the button and for 15 minutes at a time cool water sprays out of fountains, falls from buckets, and bubbles and sprays up out of the ground, allowing water-resistant tykes to get the hang of a wet face before tackling the pool. The splash pad is open from mid-April until October 31, and it's free. It's akin to the old lawn-sprinkler method of summertime cooling off, only much better. The park also has covered basketball courts, picnic tables, and more.

GARDEN OF GETHSEMANE/ FELIX LUCERO PARK

602 W. Congress St., 520/791-4873,
www.tucsonaz.gov/parksandrec
HOURS: Daily 6 A.M.-10:30 P.M.
Map 1

On the west bank of the Santa Cruz River downtown, this strange, peaceful sculpture garden holds several handmade religious statues created by Felix Lucero in the 1940s, along with a green and cool spread of vegetation. The concrete sculptures—Jesus in his tomb, a depiction of the Last Supper, and more—were the result, according to the *Arizona Daily Star,* of a battlefield promise the late Lucero made to his God during World War I. Lucero moved to Tucson in 1938 and lived in a handmade shack under a bridge near what is now the park while sculpting the statues using riverbed sand and concrete. You might see a few people praying here, as it's a very calm and obviously inspiring little sanctuary.

GENE C. REID PARK

900 S. Randolph Way, 520/791-4873,
www.tucsonaz.gov/parksandrec
HOURS: Daily 6 A.M.-10:30 P.M.
Map 2

This 131-acre greenscape on the southern end of midtown is probably the city's favorite non-desert playground, with plenty of imported tree–shade and cool bermuda grass for lounging and forgetting. The park has, among dozens of other attractions, two small duck-topped lakes (no swimming), a bandshell and amphitheater for concerts under the stars, and an off-leash dog park. The playground equipment is all cool submarine-style passageways, twisting slides, fire poles, and sky-reaching swing sets, and several layers of soft wood chips and some bouncy outdoor foam flooring provide for soft landings. Hi Corbett Stadium, where the Colorado Rockies train every spring, is located on the park's grounds, as are the Reid Park Zoo, a large modern recreation and aquatics center, a tennis facility, and a golf course.

HIMMEL PARK
1000 N. Tucson Blvd., 520/791-4873,
www.tucsonaz.gov/parksandrec
HOURS: Daily 6 A.M.-10:30 P.M.
Map 2

The Sam Hughes neighborhood is one of midtown's finest, so it stands to reason that its park, a 26-acre grass-covered shade space near Tucson and Speedway Boulevards, is one of the best around. It's crowded with palm and olive trees, and has tennis courts, basketball hoops, playground equipment, and a public pool originally designed in 1936, when the public pool was a very important local institution. On

weekends you can usually catch a league soccer match or two here.

MORRIS K. UDALL PARK
7290 E. Tanque Verde Rd., 520/791-4873,
www.tucsonaz.gov/parksandrec
HOURS: Daily 6 A.M.-10:30 P.M.
Map 4

Named for one of Arizona's best-loved politicians and environmentalists (not to mention secretary of state during the Kennedy administration and onetime presidential candidate), "Mo" Udall, this east-side park is among the best in the city. With 172 acres and a commanding view of the Santa Catalinas, the park features a dog-walking area, human walking and running trails, sports fields, picnic ramadas, a playground, bocce courts, horseshoe pits, sand-volleyball courts, tennis courts, an amphitheater, and much more.

SANTA CRUZ RIVER PARK
South from Grant Rd. to 29th St.
HOURS: Daily 6 A.M.-10:30 P.M.
Map 1

There is neither river nor park here, some might say, but still it's as good a vantage as

SOUTHERN ARIZONA'S BIRDS

Southern Arizona is a mecca for bird enthusiasts, who stalk the region's sky island mountain ranges looking for rare subtropical birds like the **elegant trogan,** a green, red, white, and black bird related to the jungle-loving quetzal. A good guide to get is *Finding Birds in Southeast Arizona,* published by the Tucson Audubon Society and available at its Nature Shop (520/629-0510). If you want to find out which rare birds are making appearances in the area, call the **Rare Bird Alert** (520/798-1005).

Of course not all of the hundreds of bird species in Southern Arizona are rare. Some of the more common avian species you're likely to see around the desert are the small flitting **cactus wren,** which lives among the spiky plants and is the Arizona state bird, and the tall **road run-**ner, which may be the state's most recognizable bird. The **red-tailed hawk** proliferates in the desert sky, hunting rodents. Look for them perched and watching atop telephone poles along the highways. Water birds, including the elegant **great blue heron,** hang around the state's riparian areas, and **wild turkeys** are somewhat common in oak and pine woodlands. One of the most common birds in the desert is the **Gambels quail,** which can often be seen crossing streets followed by a ragged line of tiny offspring. The **turkey vulture** is constantly soaring slowly in the ever-blue dryland sky. Various owl species are common in the woodlands and the deserts, and the **gila** and the **acorn woodpecker** are always tapping away at some tree, saguaro, or woodland home.

any other from which to view what remains. The Santa Cruz, like most Southwestern desert rivers, was never a deep, swollen river, but it at least had a perennial flow. It sustained a few different indigenous communities for eons, and was the green, cool home of beaver, otter, native fish species, and all manner of wild riparian life. Now look at it. It's not *all* our fault; the region is prone to long droughts, and most desert rivers have wildly fluctuating, even intermittent, flows. But it was largely the pumping of groundwater throughout the region that sent the river underground for good a few generations ago. Every now and then, if the late-summer monsoon comes on blessedly strong, the water rises and flows past this pleasant man-made green space just west of downtown, where you can ride your bike or take an early-morning jog, or just gaze at the dry, rocky bed.

GYMS AND HEALTH CLUBS
LIGHTHOUSE/CITY YMCA

2900 N. Columbus Blvd., 520/795-9725, www.tucsonymca.org

HOURS: Mon.-Thurs. 5:30 A.M.-9:30 P.M., Fri. 5:30 A.M.-8:30 P.M., Sat. 7 A.M.-7 P.M., Sun. 9 A.M.-7 P.M.

Map 2

This clean and well-kept YMCA facility on Columbus is on the grounds of the City of

EXERCISING AT 110 DEGREES: HOW TO STAY ACTIVE WHILE BEATING THE HEAT

You must be aware that the incessant sun, the driving reason for most visits to Arizona, can quickly become a dangerous threat to your health. To eliminate this threat, thus allowing you to bask only in the sun's friendly attributes, practice moderation and prevention.

Rather than worship, the sun requires timidity: Stay in the shadows, covered from head to toe. If you're not willing to do this, as most aren't, then at least wear a hat with a wide brim, use high-number sunscreen, cover your neck, and, preferably, wear long sleeves. This applies not only to back-country desert adventurers and hikers; mere sight-seekers, especially those with fresh-faced children in tow, are just as susceptible to sun- and heat-related health issues – more so, in fact: The less fit you are, the higher the danger.

The least of what the sun can do to you is not to be taken lightly. A **sunburn,** which comes on quicker than you'd think, can lead to skin cancer, and that can lead to death. If you get a sunburn there's little you can do save try to make yourself more comfortable. Stay out of the sun, of course, and try to keep cool and hydrated. There are dozens of over-the-counter balms available, but simple aloe works as well as anything. A popular home remedy is to gently dab the burned areas with vinegar. If the burn starts to blister, reaching the dreaded third-degree stage, skin cancer becomes a very real threat. Again, the best way to avoid sunburn is to stay out of the sun; barring that, cover up and follow common sense. Those with fair skin and children should be even more cautious.

Hikers, shoppers, sightseers, golfers, and anybody else exerting themselves under high-heat conditions should watch out for **dehydration.** When your body becomes dangerously depleted of fluids, you'll notice first that you are not urinating regularly and your saliva has dried up. You may become irritable and confused; your skin may turn gray and your pulse race. Children especially can become dehydrated quickly. The best way to avoid dehydration is to limit your exertion during the hottest part of the day and to drink a lot of water. If you feel the symptoms of dehydration coming on, get to a cool, comfortable place, take in fluids, and rest.

Hikers should take along a few packets of electrolyte powder, similar to Gatorade and the like, and a separate water bottle to mix it in – these can be lifesavers. If you exert yourself in the heat and sun and fail to replace the fluids flowing out, your body can become

Tucson's McCormick Park, so after you're done with pilates or swimming laps or punishing yourself on the stair-stepper, you can have a cookout and a softball game. The outdoor pool here is huge and refreshing, at least before July—then you feel like a tea bag dipping in. At any rate, the Lighthouse facility has everything one expects from a YMCA facility, and then some. If you're a member of the YMCA in another city, you can use any Tucson YMCA facility five times a month for free. If you want to use it more, it'll cost you $5 per day. If you're not a member and you're over 22, you can use the facilities for $10 per day.

LOHSE FAMILY YMCA

60 W. Alameda St., 520/623-5200,
www.tucsonymca.org/lohse
HOURS: Mon.-Fri. 5:30 A.M.-8 P.M., Sat. 8 A.M.-5:30 P.M., Sun. 9 A.M.-1:30 P.M.

Map 1

Tucson has some of the best YMCA facilities in the region, all of them bustling and clean, inviting and up-to-date. The Lohse Family branch downtown has all any fitness freak would want: weight machines, cardio equipment, a huge basketball court, free weights, an indoor running track, aerobics and yoga studios, and a six-lane covered and heated swimming pool. There's a parking garage ($2/hr)

depleted of electrolytes and fluids. Such is the path to **heat exhaustion,** a dangerous condition that can turn fatal if not treated. You begin to feel nauseated, dizzy, and weak, and your muscles cramp. Again, if you experience any of these symptoms, get to a cool comfortable place quickly and drink water and something with sodium and potassium in it – like an electrolyte drink.

Dehydration and heat exhaustion, while dangerous and unpleasant, pale when compared to **heat stroke,** sometimes called sun stroke or heat hyperpyrexia, a severe, dangerous health threat that is frequently fatal and, if not fatal, often changes a victim's future health significantly and irrevocably. Heat stroke occurs when the body's temperature-regulating capacity fails; this can be caused by either relatively short exposure to extremely high heat – like, say, a short, strenuous run on a 105-degree July afternoon – or prolonged exposure to relatively high temperatures, as in, a 15-mile hike in 90-degree heat. And that's only if you're in good shape; it would take far less to cause heat stroke in most of us. The first and most important sign of heat stroke is a lack of sweating. If you stop sweating in a situation where you *should* be sweating, take notice. Sweating is your body's way of regulating its

temperature, so it stands to reason that if you stop sweating, there may be something wrong with your body. Your heart rate will speed up noticeably and your skin will become dry; you'll get a headache and become confused. At its worst, heat stroke leads to unconsciousness, convulsions, and death. Once you notice you're not sweating, you must get help immediately: Get to an emergency room as soon as possible.

The mountains in Southern Arizona reach up to 10,000 feet. Though most visitors won't be going that high, you should be aware that a few of the state's mountain towns sit between 5,000 and 8,000 feet above sea level. Lowlanders in relatively good shape may get headaches, a little dizziness, and shortness of breath while walking around Mount Lemmon or other of the region's mountains, but very few will experience serious **altitude sickness** – the result of not getting enough oxygen, and therefore not enough blood flow to the brain. Still, take it easy in the higher elevations if you begin to feel tired and out-of-breath, dizzy, or euphoric. If you have heart or lung problems you need to be more aware in the higher elevations; the best thing to do is to get a prescription for oxygen from your doctor and carry it with you if you plan on spending a lot of time in the mountains.

right next door and metered parking on the street. If you're a member of the YMCA in another city, you can use any Tucson YMCA facility five times a month for free. If you want to use it more, it'll cost you $5 per day. If you're not a member and you're over 22, you can use the facilities for $10 per day.

MID-VALLEY ATHLETIC CLUB AND WELLNESS CENTER

140 S. Tucson Blvd., 520/792-3654,
www.mvactucson.com
HOURS: Mon.-Thurs. 5 A.M.-10 P.M., Fri. 5 A.M.-8:30 P.M., Sat. 7 A.M.-7 P.M., Sun. 9 A.M.-7 P.M.
COST: $10 daily fee
Map 2

A comfortable, clean, and welcoming club near Broadway and Tucson Boulevards, Mid-Valley has all kinds of up-to-date workout and weight machines, pilates and aerobics classes, an excellent pool, and an in-house spa where you can get a massage, a manicure, a pedicure, or a new hairstyle instead of working out. If you're just visiting, you can buy a $10-per-day guest pass and use all the facilities, or it's $70 for a month to reward and punish yourself in equal measure.

MORRIS K. UDALL RECREATION CENTER

7200 E. Tanque Verde Rd., 520/791-4931,
www.tucsonaz.gov/parksandrec
HOURS: Mon.-Fri. 6 A.M.-8 P.M., Sat. 8 A.M.-4 P.M.
COST: $1.25 per day for residents,
$1.75 for non-residents
Map 4

Located on the grounds of the huge east-side Morris K. Udall Regional Park, this clean and popular city-run recreation center has it all—a weight room, cardio equipment, a walking track, three handball and racquetball courts, pool tables, an open gym where people play basketball, volleyball, and badminton, and much more. There's also a seniors' club with all kinds of social and sports activities, and a long schedule of kids' activities like nighttime basketball games and more.

NORTHWEST YMCA

7770 N. Shannon Rd., 520/229-9001,
www.tucsonymca.org
HOURS: Mon.-Sat. 5 A.M.-10 P.M., Sun. 10 A.M.-8 P.M.
Map 7

A gleaming 35,000-square-foot exercise center on the northwest side, the Northwest YMCA features a huge heated pool for lap swimming, and a separate pool area with a slide for the kids. It has clean and well-lit exercise rooms with all the latest cardio and weight-training machines, a large gym for pick-up games, an aerobics room, very clean and comfortable locker rooms, and a day-care area where you can leave the kids while you get in shape.

RANDOLPH RECREATION CENTER

200 S. Alvernon Way, 520/791-4560,
www.tucsonaz.gov/parksandrec
HOURS: Mon.-Fri. 6:30 A.M.-8 P.M., Sat. 8 A.M.-4 P.M.
COST: $1.25 per day for residents,
$1.75 for non-residents
Map 2

One of four large regional recreation centers operated by the City of Tucson, the Randolph Center at Reid Park has a weight room and fitness center, a gym for basketball and volleyball, a gymnastics room, aerobics classes, and even a pottery studio with a kiln. Nonresidents can use weight and fitness machines and the gym for a mere $1.25 per day (for kids under 18 it's $1). There's an outdoor pool that's only open during the summer, and a two-mile outdoor walking-running-biking-rollerblading track that takes you around the entire sprawling midtown park.

TUCSON RACQUET & FITNESS CLUB

4001 N. Country Club Rd., 520/795-6960,
www.tucsonracquetclub.com
HOURS: Daily 24 hours
COST: $10 daily fee
Map 2

A 20-acre oasis for all things active and health-conscious near the dry Rillito River, this tennis and fitness club opened in 1967 and is still the city's finest. The club, which is always open, has 33 lighted tennis courts and 11 indoor racquetball and handball courts. It has two large heated pools, and a state-of-the-art cardio and weight center. Staff members offer pilates, aerobics, tae kwan do, and Thai yoga classes, and there's a restaurant with all kinds of healthful eats and a full-service spa. Out-of-towners, or curious townies, can use all the facilities for $10 per day.

GOLF

It's not easy to justify the existence of golf courses in the arid Southwest, at least not from a perspective that recognizes the region's rather obvious resource deficiencies. It is, however, somewhat easier from the average golfer's point of view, for whom the region's primary deficiency—its aridity—is instead its greatest attribute, allowing one to play 36 holes on Thanksgiving morning with an envy-rotten brother-in-law from Chicago. And so the courses proliferate. The City of Tucson operates five public courses in town, all of them excellent, though older and less dramatic than most of the resort and private courses invading the desert. The City's somewhat humbler courses come with the added benefit of being ecologically defensible: They are all irrigated with reclaimed water. The City maintains a helpful website (www.tucsoncitygolf.com) where you can see maps of all the courses, get rates (they are generally quite low, ranging $15–70 for 18 holes depending on premiums, season, time of day, and residency), and book tee times. All of the city courses have clubhouses, lighted driving ranges, carts, pros, and pro shops.

RANDOLPH GOLF COURSE AND DELL URICH GOLF COURSE

600 S. Alvernon Way, 520/791-4161,
www.tucsoncitygolf.com
HOURS: Daily 5 A.M.-8 P.M.
COST: $23-72 for 18 holes (price depends on season and residency)
Map 2

These side-by-side courses at midtown's Reid Park are the two most popular in Tucson's municipal system. Randolph, the city's flagship

course and the longest at 6,500 yards from the regular tees, has been the site of numerous PGA and LPGA tournaments, and is green, spacious, and tree lined. Dell Urich, a par-70 course a bit to the south of Randolph, was opened in 1996 and is probably the most popular in town. Both make for easily accessible and relatively inexpensive in-town play year-round.

SWIMMING

CITY OF TUCSON AQUATICS PROGRAMS

Various locations, 520/791-4245 or 520/791-5352,
www.tucsonaz.gov/parksandrec/aquatics.php
COST: $1 adult, $0.25 child

Long before air-conditioning became generally available, and before many middle- and upper-class Tucsonans began digging their own backyard pools, the publicly funded swimming hole was a very important Old Pueblo institution. It still is, though to a lesser extent than it was in, say, the 1930s and '40s. The City of Tucson operates 27 public pools all over town. Most of them are only open from May to August, when you almost need a tepid-water pool available to stay sane in the desert. Nine city pools stay open year-round and are heated. The cost to swim is nominal, and you're likely to make a few friends poolside. The best place to find the nearest city pool is the city's comprehensive website (www.tucsonaz.gov/parksandrec/aquatics.php). Most of the city pools have scheduled hours for kids and for lap swimming and other special activities. There are always lifeguards on duty.

TENNIS

FORT LOWELL TENNIS CENTER

2900 N. Craycroft Rd., 520/791-2584,
www.tucsontennis.com
HOURS: Daily 6 A.M.-10:30 P.M.
Map 2

The tennis center at Fort Lowell Park—where the Apache-fighting U.S. soldiers once lived long ago—has eight courts and offers a slew of leagues, tournaments, and classes throughout the year. It's a good idea to call ahead for a reservation as the courts here get regular and heavy use. There's a busy director-pro here to coordinate everything, and the Santa Catalinas loom large and beautiful over the smooth courts.

HIMMEL PARK TENNIS CENTER
1000 N. Tucson Blvd., 520/791-3276
HOURS: Daily 6 A.M.-10:30 P.M.
COST: $2.50 pp for 1.5 hours
Map 2

The eight older and slightly scuffed-up courts at the Sam Hughes neighborhood's Himmel Park offer a bit more laid-back atmosphere for tennis than the huge, serious Randolph Center. You can call ahead and reserve a court, but often you can just show up and there'll be one available. There are several leagues that play here so you might want to call and check before showing up, especially on weekends.

RANDOLPH TENNIS CENTER
50 S. Alvernon Way, 520/791-4896,
www.randolphtenniscenter.com
HOURS: Daily sunrise-9:30 P.M.
COST: $2.50 pp for 1.5 hours
Map 2

The Southwest's largest public tennis facility, this huge gathering of courts, pros, and nets at the corner of Broadway and Alvernon—the northeast corner of sprawling Reid Park—offers 25 lighted tennis courts and 10 lighted racquetball courts. You really must call ahead to reserve a court—it's a very popular place. And, if you're here in the summer, you have to get on the court very early, or after dark, to avoid the heat.

YOGA
PROVIDENCE INSTITUTE
3400 E. Speedway Blvd., Ste. 114, 520/323-0203, 866/280-5713, www.providenceinstitute.com
COST: $5 community classes offered Mon.-Fri. 7:30 A.M.-2:30 P.M.
Map 2

There's certainly no shortage of yoga classes in Tucson, but some of the best are offered by the friendly, earnest folks at this Speedway

Boulevard health and wellness center and school. For a mere $5 a day you can choose from various "community yoga classes" from early in the morning until mid-afternoon weekdays. It's all a bit on the New Age-y side here, but if you're into that you are going to love this place. They also offer all kinds of bodywork, therapy, and massage services.

TUCSON YOGA
150 S. 4th Ave., 520/988-1832, www.tucsonyoga.com
COST: $6 per class or $45 per month for unlimited classes
Map 1

This downtown yoga center offers inexpensive and professionally led classes throughout the day and evening (usually the last class starts around 7 P.M., earlier on weekends). A favorite among Tucson's yogis—it's been voted the best yoga studio in town several times by readers of the *Tucson Weekly*—Tucson Yoga presents at least two or three "basic yoga" classes per week for beginners, as well as classes for experts and everyone in between. They also offer several wellness and spirituality classes and events throughout the month.

GUIDED AND WALKING TOURS
KRUSEARIZONA TOURS
520/881-1638, www.krusearizona.com
COST: $15 pp

Among the few walking tours offered of the Old Pueblo's historic downtown neighborhoods and sights, Alan Kruse's KruseArizona Tours are by far the best. Friendly, animated, and extremely well-versed in the long, fascinating history of Tucson, Kruse dons the typical garb of a frontier teacher to take on the guise of John Spring, the second public-school teacher in Tucson circa 1870. The tours are offered in the mornings throughout the week and on Saturdays; they last about two hours, taking you through Barrio Histórico, the El Presidio Neighborhood, and all around downtown. He also offers "twilight tours" from April through June to avoid the heat of the day.

THE PRESIDIO TRAIL

Starts at Church and Washington Sts.,
Tucson Presidio Trust for Historic Preservation,
520/748-2837, www.tucsonpresidiotrust.org
`Map 1`

Put together by the Tucson Presidio Trust for
Historic Preservation, the Presidio Trail is an
interesting and fun self-guided walking tour of
downtown's historic neighborhoods and landmarks. The 2.5-mile walk is designed as a loop
and takes you past 23 historically significant
sites, most of them marked by plaques. The
walk begins and ends at the intersection of
Church and Washington Streets, right where
the original presidio once stood. The Presidio
Trust has put together a complete guide to the
trail, with a cartoon map that shows the en-
tirety of downtown Tucson's landmarks better than any other—reading the charmingly
drawn map is half the fun. The map is available for free at the Tucson Visitor Center at La
Placita Village (110 S. Church Ave., 520/624-
1817, Mon.–Fri. 9 A.M.–5 P.M., Sat.–Sun.
9 A.M.–4 P.M.).

SKATE PARKS
RANDOLPH CENTER SKATE PARK

200 S. Alvernon Way, 520/791-4560
HOURS: Daily 6 A.M.–10 P.M.
COST: Free
`Map 2`

If you need to shred to live, then grab your
board or your skates and head over to Reid
Park and the Randolph Center Skate Park, with
vertical props, rails, and a host of ramps in an
enclosed 20,000-square-foot asphalt site. Call
ahead for hours; it's not always open. Catalina
High School (E. Pima St., 520/791-4873), near
Pima and Dodge, also has a fenced-in outdoor
roller rink and a skate park that can be used by
the general public after school hours.

HIKING

Tucson and its surrounding sky island ranges
have excellent hiking trails for all experience
levels. Desert trails tend to be rather flat and
rocky, while the mountain trails are steep and
usually offer some spectacular views. I don't
recommend hiking in the desert during the

Take a self-guided walk through historic neighborhoods on The Presidio Trail.

© TIM HULL

ARTS AND LEISURE

height of summer. If you really must, start early in the morning and try to be done by noon. Always take water and salty snacks with you on the trail, always wear a hat, and stay alert to signs of dehydration and heat exhaustion/stroke. If you're hiking in Sabino Canyon or in other areas of the desert that typically receive runoff from the towering mountains above during the rainy season in July and August, remember that just because it's not raining in the desert doesn't meant it isn't raining in the mountains. And rain in the mountains invariably washes down to the desert, sometimes catching lowland hikers unaware and sweeping them off to their deaths. If the trails and hiking areas listed here aren't enough for you, check out local hiking expert Betty Leavengood's *Tucson Hiking Guide.* You can find it online and at many local bookstores.

THE ARIZONA TRAIL

Various trailheads around Southern Arizona, www.aztrail.org

The Arizona Trail is a nearly 800-mile network of mostly existing trails that one could follow

© TIM HULL

The Arizona Trail traverses the entire state, covering 800 miles from south to north.

on foot, horse, or mountain bike (if you want to carry your bike through the Grand Canyon and other federal wilderness areas along the way), from the border with Mexico to the border with Utah. There are 43 different "passages" that make up the trail, each between 11 and 35 miles; more than a dozen of these are in Southern Arizona, within easy reach of Tucson. The trail through Southern Arizona traverses all of the region's biomes, from the scrubby desert to the dry grasslands to the cool, green mountains—it's a great way to get to know all of the natural wonders around Tucson. The nonprofit Arizona Trail Association is responsible for upkeep and trail building, and their website has a complete map and detailed description of the trail.

MADERA CANYON

About 10 miles east of Green Valley on White House Canyon Rd. in the Santa Rita Mountains; managed by the Coronado National Forest's Nogales Ranger District, 303 Old Tucson Rd., Nogales, east from Ruby Rd. exit off I-19, 520/281-2296

`Map 7`

The most popular trail to the top of Mount Wrightson, the 10,000-foot peak of the Santa Rita Mountains, is the 10.8-mile round-trip Old Baldy Trail, which is fairly steep but much shorter than the more gradual, 16-mile round-trip Super Trail. Both trails are well marked, heavily used, and start near the Mount Wrightson Picnic Area at the top of Madera Canyon. Both trails also take you over Josephine Saddle, at about 7,000 feet, and Baldy Saddle at more than 8,000 feet, just below the peak, which make good places to stop and rest. At Josephine Saddle make sure to look at the makeshift memorial to a group of Boy Scouts that got caught in a snowstorm on the mountain in the 1950s and never returned. If you're coming up the Super Trail, stop and rest at Sprung Spring just before you reach the saddle, which has delicious mountain water trickling from a spigot. To see the lushness that a little trickling water can inspire hit the 5.8-mile Bog Spring–Kent Spring Loop, which leads over some old mining roads in the lower reaches of the canyon on to some fairly steep and skinny trails along a windswept ridge, providing pretty spectacular views of the valley below. The trail eventually leads deep into the forest, where sycamores thrive on the edges of green and spongy clearings. Also try the 4.4-mile one-way Nature Trail, a strenuous but easy way to see the entire canyon, from the desert grasslands at its entrance at the Proctor Parking Area, where you can pick up the trail, all the way up to the woodlands at the top. Small signs along the way point out notable flora and fauna, and the highest point on the trail, high above the canyon floor, offers a unique perspective.

◀ MOUNT LEMMON AND THE SANTA CATALINA MOUNTAINS

Coronado National Forest, 520/670-4522, www.fs.fed.us/r3/coronado

COST: $5 per car

Map 7

The dozens of trails around and on 9,157-foot Mount Lemmon, about an hour's drive up the winding Sky Island Scenic Byway from central Tucson and into another world entirely, are beloved among all those Tucsonans sweating away in the hot valley down there, dreaming of a weekend day spent scrambling around the evergreen forests and cool streams up on the mountain. Since there are so many trails to choose from (many of them lead into and branch off one another), you might consider the following eight-mile loop composed of portions of several trails, which is designed to take you through some of the best areas the mountain has to offer.

At Summerhaven, turn onto the Sabino Canyon Parkway and follow it down to **Marshall Gulch;** leave your car at the small streamside parking lot. Start on Trail #3 (Marshall Gulch Trail) behind the bathrooms and follow it up through the shady forest for 1.2 miles to Marshall Saddle, at 7,920 feet. At Marshall Saddle branch off on Trail #44, which will take you down about 700 feet into the beautiful **Wilderness of Rocks** for 1.7 miles. At the junction take Trail #12

The trails on Mount Lemmon are a world away from the desert below.

© TIM HULL

(the Lemmon Rock Lookout Trail) as it rises and rises for about two miles to near the very peak of Mount Lemmon at 9,157 feet, where you'll be among metal towers essential to life down below. Along the way you can stop off at the Mount Lemmon Lookout, which offers one of the best views in the region. You'll see the ski lift near the top, but don't get on. Instead, hike along **Radio Ridge** using the Mount Lemmon Trail (Trail #5) for a mile or so to its junction with Trail #93 (Aspen Trail), then follow that downhill for 1.3 miles to find yourself back at Marshall Saddle—then it's 1.2 miles back to the car. The climbs on this loop can be a bit brutal, but you're definitely rewarded for the effort. For information on other trails and more suggestions on which ones to try, stop by the Palisades Visitor Center on your way up the hill. There you can talk to rangers and pick up a map of the trail system.

JUAN BAUTISTA DE ANZA NATIONAL HISTORIC TRAIL

The Juan Bautista de Anza National Historic Trail, popularly known as the Anza Trail, traces the route the Basque explorer took in 1776 while leading some 240 immigrants west to Alta California to establish a presidio and settlement.

The trail will eventually run from Culiacán, Mexico, to San Francisco, about 1,200 miles over mostly rugged and arid territory.

A rather lush section of the trail, following the Santa Cruz River from the Presidio at Tubac to the Mission at Tumacácori, is already one of the more popular hikes in the valley. The 4.5-mile one-way trail, which can be picked up at well-marked trailheads at the mission and the presidio, provides an intimate look at the riparian habitat along the river, a shady greenway crowded with cottonwoods.

The trail isn't exactly pristine, however. Hikers and horseback riders are likely to see the left-behind evidence of illegal immigration along the trail, and the river itself flows with reclaimed wastewater. Still, it's a beautiful route, and this mostly flat, easy trail is a great option for families.

There's also about a four-mile one-way stretch of the trail near Rio Rico, following the river and winding through mesquite forests. To reach this section of the trail, head south on I-19 to exit 17, Rio Rico/Yavapai Drive. Head north and cross the Santa Cruz, then turn left onto a gravel road and look for the trailhead sign.

A mostly paved section of the Anza Trail runs near downtown Tucson, along the dry riverbed west from Silverlake to Columbus Park, while other stretches are planned for the near future in Green Valley, Canoa Ranch in the Santa Cruz Valley, and northern Pima County.

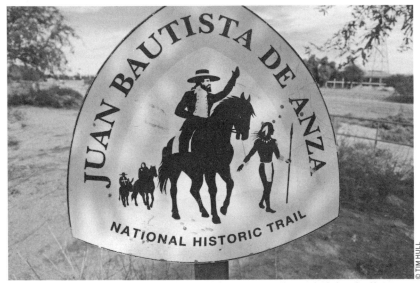

© TIM HULL

Portions of the trail throughout southern Arizona follow the route taken by the Basque explorer in 1776.

© TIM HULL

Tucson Mountain Park is a great place to see the wild desert.

SAGUARO NATIONAL PARK WEST

Red Hills Visitor Center, 520/733-5153,
www.nps.gov/sagu

Map 5

Both sections of Saguaro National Park offer excellent desert hiking. In the Tucson Mountains district west of town, a strenuous but beautiful hike up to 4,687-foot Wasson Peak, the highest in the Tucson Mountains, is a great way to spend a Sonoran Desert morning. You can get there by picking up the King Canyon Trail just across Kinney Road near the Arizona-Sonora Desert Museum. It's about 3.5 miles to the top of the peak hiking on switchbacks though typical bajada desert; then you can make it a loop by heading down the Hugh Norris Trail to its junction with the Sendero Esperanza Trail, then take the Gold Mine Trail back to the car. The whole adventure is about 7.5 miles total. There are certainly easier and less steep trails around the park as well. An easy one to take with kids is the half-mile Signal Hill Petroglyphs Trail, which features a modest climb to a collection of boulders with several petroglyphs on display.

If you continue on from here the flat, easy trail takes you through some wonderful desert with a good chance to see wildlife. In the park's eastern section, at the base of the Rincon Mountains, there are several three- to five-mile loop hikes that will take you through all of the best parts of the sprawling cactus forests; for a short two-mile round-trip walk, the Cactus Forest Trail is an easy, mostly flat trail among the green-armed giants. The visitors centers at both the western and eastern sections have complete trail guides and rangers on duty who can help you decide the best routes, and the park's website has detailed maps and trail guides as well.

◖ TUCSON MOUNTAIN PARK

Enter at Gates Pass Rd., 10 miles west of downtown,
www.pima.gov/nrpr/parks

Map 5

Some of the best desert hiking in the region can be found at this sprawling saguaro-crowded park west of the city. Here the trails are rocky and sandy, moderately flat, and thickly lined with desert vegetation. The nearly five-mile

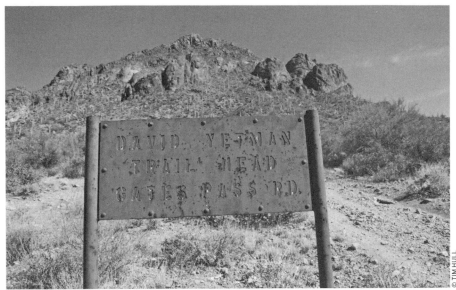

© TIM HULL

One of the more popular trails in Tucson Mountain Park is the David Yetman Trail.

round-trip **Brown Mountain Trail** leads through a cactus forest along the sandy bottomlands between the mountains, then rises gradually to a ridgeline that looks out on the hard country all around. You can access the trailhead at the Brown Mountain Picnic Area or the Juan Santa Cruz Picnic Area, both a bit southeast of the Arizona-Sonora Desert Museum off Kinney Road. Just before you reach the valley after the steep descent from Gates Pass, there's a parking lot and trailhead where you can pick up the five-and-a-half-mile **David Yetman Trail,** named for the host of the PBS show *The Desert Speaks.* There's another trailhead at Camino de Oeste—and if you leave a car at both ends you won't have to do a more-than-10-mile there-and-back trudge. Pima County's Natural Resources Department keeps a map of the trails around Tucson Mountain Park on their website.

TUMAMOC HILL
Enter at the University of Arizona's desert laboratory, www.tumamoc.org
Map 5

For a moderately strenuous climb on smooth asphalt road just a few miles west of downtown, head over to the entrance to the University of Arizona's desert laboratory on Tumamoc Hill (where scientists have been studying the Sonoran Desert for more than 100 years). The gradual rise up the entrance road to the top of the historic hill overlooking Tucson is a 3.1-mile round-trip walk, with an elevation gain of about 730 feet. It's a popular route for Tucsonans looking for some early-evening exercise, and the view from the top can't be beat. A sign at the entrance says that hikers are not allowed on the road Monday–Friday 7:30 A.M.–5:30 P.M. That doesn't mean that you have to wait until Saturday morning, though. Many hikers head up in the evening; bring a flashlight with you because, depending on how in shape you are, the round-trip could take up to three hours. Make sure to stay on the roadway at all times—there are long-term experiments going on in the desert around the route that could be ruined if trampled on or otherwise disturbed. Outside of a small private home at the beginning of the road up the mountain, look for the homemade shrine with a sign encouraging visitors to stop

© TIM HULL

This shrine invites visitants to rest a moment along the road to the top of Tumamoc Hill.

and look. To get to the entrance, head west on Speedway Boulevard from downtown, under I-10 to Silverbell Road. Turn south on Silverbell and drive a short way to West Anklmam Road and turn west; the trailhead is on the left. There is no parking at the trailhead, so either get dropped off or park at nearby St. Mary's Hospital.

VENTANA CANYON TRAIL
Loews Ventana Canyon Resort parking lot,
7000 N. Resort Dr.

Map 3

This tough, steep 13-mile round-trip hike into the Santa Catalina Mountains isn't for the casual hiker, though of course you don't have to go the whole way. The trail ends at the titular *ventana* (window in Spanish), an approximately 15-foot-high, 25-foot-wide naturally worn hole in a jutting rock slab. The trailhead is at the parking lot of the Loews Ventana Canyon Resort in the foothills and is open and accessible to the public during the day. A full day's hike here, or just a few miles up into the steep slopes of the front range, provides

a chance to see how the cactus and mesquite desert changes rather suddenly to become a pine forest as you rise in elevation. Of course, you can always drive up the Sky Island Scenic Byway to see the same phenomenon, and you won't risk exhaustion.

BIKING
Biking, whether of the sleek road or the tough mountain variety, is hugely popular in the Old Pueblo. For years Tucson and Pima County have been recognized as very bike-friendly areas; the region is the only in Arizona to obtain a gold-level ranking from the League of American Bicyclists, and there are something like 630 miles of dedicated bike paths throughout the city and county. The **Tucson Visitor Center** downtown at **La Placita Village** (110 S. Church Ave., 520/624-1817, Mon.–Fri. 9 A.M.–5 P.M., Sat.–Sun. 9 A.M.–4 P.M.) offers free maps to many of the bike paths and trailheads here, or you can download the most up-to-date version at www.dot.co.pima.az.us/tpcbac/, the website of the very active Tucson–Pima County Bicycle Advisory Committee.

ARTS AND LEISURE

FOREST INFORMATION

Most of the public lands around Tucson and Southern Arizona are administered by **Coronado National Forest.** The forest's main office in Tucson (300 W. Congress St., 520/670-4522, www.fs.fed.us/r3/coronado, Mon.-Fri. 8 A.M.-4:30 P.M.) can direct you to a specific field office.

Public wildlands that aren't administered by the U.S. Forest Service are usually administered by the **Bureau of Land Management** (12661 E. Broadway, 570/722-4289, www.az.blm.gov, Mon.-Fri. 8 A.M.-4 P.M.).

If you have any trouble with wild animals or need to report a poaching incident, call the **Arizona Game & Fish Department** (555 N. Greasewood Rd., 520/628-5376, www.azgfd.gov, Mon.-Fri. 8 A.M.-5 P.M.).

A good place to get advice and topo maps is the **Arizona Geological Survey** (416 W. Congress St., Ste. 100, 520/770-3500, www.azgs.az.gov, Mon.-Fri. 9 A.M.-8 P.M., Sat. 9 A.M.-6:30 P.M., Sun. 10 A.M.-6:30 P.M.).

A quick word of warning: The forests, deserts, and grasslands of the Coronado National Forest are extremely susceptible to wildfire, especially in the dry summer months. In fact, fire and smoking restrictions often go into effect early in the summer, if not before, and those who don't follow these restrictions to the letter are liable to end up with a stiff fine or, at worst, a burned-down forest on their conscience. In the worst cases, some forest areas are closed completely during the height of the wildfire season. If you see a wildfire in the forest, call Coronado (520/670-4522) to report it.

Bike Rentals and Shops
BROADWAY BICYCLES
140 S. Sarnoff Dr., 520/296-7819, www.broadwaybicycles.com
HOURS: Mon.-Fri. 10 A.M.-6 P.M., Sat. 9 A.M.-9 P.M., Sun. 11 A.M.-4 P.M.
Map 4

The friendly folks at Broadway Bicycles, off Broadway Boulevard just west of the popular road-bike route on Old Spanish Trail, rent top-brand (Trek and Fisher) late-model road bikes and mountain bikes ($30–50 per day, or $150–250 for seven days) and give out good advice about the best rides and trails in and around Tucson. They also have an expert service department and a full stock of top-of-the-line road and mountain bikes, helmets, clothing, and other equipment.

CYCLE TUCSON
520/245-6011, www.cycletucson.com
The couple that owns this local bike rental and guide service have a combined 35 years in the cycling industry, so they know what they're talking about. They provide rental road and mountain bikes ($50 per day, $120 for three days, plus various packages and specials), and they'll help you decide where to go (or even take you out themselves). Moreover, they bring the bikes to you, take you out to the trail or route, and then pick you up at sunset. They prefer Cannondale road bikes, mountain bikes, and hybrids.

ORDINARY BIKE SHOP
311 E. 7th St., 520/622-6488, www.ordinarybikeshop.com
HOURS: Mon.-Fri. 9 A.M.-7 P.M., Sat. 8 A.M.-5 P.M.
Map 1

Located downtown on 7th Street near 4th Avenue, Ordinary Bikes has been voted the best bike shop in Tucson by the bike-loving readers of the local alternative weekly for nearly a decade straight. The guys here are friendly and helpful, and their service department will fix just about any problem your bike is having. They don't rent bikes, but they do sell used ones from time to time. They have a good selection of new mountain and road bikes, including brands like Bianca, Raleigh, and Diamondback, along with a limited selection of clothing and other equipment.

ARTS AND LEISURE

Trails and Routes
BRAD P. GORMAN MEMORIAL BIKEWAY
Catalina Hwy.
Map 7

A favorite route for road bikers is the long, hard climb up the Catalina Highway, also called the Brad P. Gorman Memorial Bikeway, into the cool heights of the Santa Catalina Mountains. The route is about 38 miles from midtown to the village of Summerhaven, and most of it is uphill. Take Tanque Verde Road to the Catalina Highway, and pedal as hard as you can. Make sure to watch the cars along the road carefully; some of the day-trippers to the mountains will be too busy checking out the views to notice you on your bike.

DAN YERSAVICH MEMORIAL BIKEWAY
Broadway Blvd. to Saguaro National Park E., along the Old Spanish Trail
Map 4

A popular road-bike ride on a warm weekend morning is the Dan Yersavich Memorial Bikeway along Old Spanish Trail from Broadway Boulevard to Saguaro National Park East (about 6 miles). You can ride among the saguaros on Cactus Loop Road or you can continue on the route for another 12 miles to Colossal Cave Mountain Park. Most of the route has a bike lane, but be sure to look out for traffic along the way.

❰ FANTASY ISLAND
South end of Harrison at Irvington
Map 7

While none of the trails and loops at Fantasy Island is very long, they are all fun and relatively easy—it's a great place for beginners and novices to ride. There's a detailed trail map set up at the entrance. Be careful not to stare too much and lose your balance while passing all the strange junk-art objects set up along the trails. You need to purchase a permit to recreate on state-trust land in Arizona, and you should always have it with you while you're riding just in case. To purchase one ($15 for a year) go to www.land.state.az.us.

50-YEAR TRAIL
Golder Ranch area, start at parking lot on Golder Ranch Rd.
Map 7

Some of the best desertland single tracks in Southern Arizona can be found about 25 miles north of Tucson in Golder Ranch area. A series of rocky, undulating trails through desert, the 50-Year Trail is great fun for experts and beginners alike. You'll need your state-trust land permit for this ride (although I've never seen anybody out there checking permits or anything). Take Oracle Road north through Oro Valley and turn right on Golder Ranch Road; follow it until you get to a dirt parking lot and a cattle guard. The trail is just beyond the cattle guard.

MOUNT LEMMON
Palisades Visitor Center, milepost 19.9 on the Catalina Highway
HOURS: Daily 8:30 A.M.–4:30 P.M.
Map 7

If you're not into desert-country mountain biking, head up the Sky Island Scenic Byway to the wooded and green Mount Lemmon and its many difficult, steep, and rocky trails. Consider the **Aspen Draw** (summer only), a popular and technical route, or the **Milagrosa Trail, Green Mountain,** and the **Molino Trail.** Stop at the Palisades Visitor Center on your way up the mountain for a trail map. The air up on the mountain, which rises beyond 9,000 feet, is cooler and thinner, so remember that you probably won't be in top riding condition up here unless you're used to the high altitudes. You can also get information about Mount Lemmon biking trails at the Coronado National Forest Santa Catalina Ranger District (5700 N. Sabino Canyon Rd., 530/749-8700, www.fs.fed.us/r3/coronado, Mon.–Fri. 8 A.M.–4:30 P.M., Sat.–Sun. 8:30 A.M.–4:30 P.M.).

RILLITO PARK BIKE ROUTE
From I-10 east to Craycroft, following the Rillito River
Map 3

This flat and easy 11-mile route following

the sandy-bottomed Rillito is a great route for exercise and commuting across the north end of Tucson. Sure the river is dry on top, but it's still a relatively green and shady route. For north-end bike commuters it's a kind of east–west freeway—one with bunnies and lizards always popping out to keep you sharp. The path runs from near I-10 all the way to Craycroft Road, and along the way it passes several parks, always hugging the parched riverbed, colored here and there with seeping lushness.

STARR PASS
Tucson Mountain Park, start at parking lot
on Clearwell Rd.
Map 5

An eight-mile single-track loop through rocky desert, Starr Pass is a tough ride but fun and beautiful, with sweeping views of the valley below. To get to the trailhead, go west from downtown on St. Mary's Road past Pima College (it turns into Anklam) to Players Club Drive and turn left, heading to a four-way stop with Starr Pass Boulevard, where you turn left again. Take the first right onto dirt Clearwell Road and park in the parking lot. The Starr Pass trails hooks up with the Yetman Trail, which is also a good ride, as are most of the rocky, challenging up-and-down single tracks and old dirt roads in the Tucson Mountains and the cactus-crowded valleys below them.

3RD STREET BIKE ROUTE
Start at 3rd St. at Wilmot
Map 2

This bike route is an easy, flat way to get from midtown to downtown on a bike. It goes from Wilmot on the eastern edge of midtown all the way through the University of Arizona to downtown. The route is designed to avoid high-traffic areas, and most of the time you'll be cruising along empty (except for your biking compatriots) and quiet residential streets. When you go through campus, make sure to follow all of the bike-riding traffic rules.

HORSEBACK RIDING

The horse has been an integral part of daily life in Tucson and Southern Arizona since the Spanish introduced the beast to the Southwest back in the 1500s. The new, useful animal transformed the lives and cultures of the native peoples here virtually overnight, and still today there is a distinct subculture of "horse people" in the Old Pueblo whose lives are dedicated to the care and enjoyment of the equestrian kind. There are quite a few such people who will rent you a usually friendly, docile horse and guide you and your new friend deep into the desert on trails once traversed by conquistadores, cowboys, and Indians. Most places require that kids be at least six years old to ride, and most have a 230-pound maximum weight limit, but call ahead to make sure. Spring rides are the best, obviously, especially when the desert's in bloom. Summer is different—go early in the morning or book one of the fun evening or nighttime rides many places offer. Always wear long pants and closed-toed shoes, and always bring a hat, though it doesn't necessarily have to be the cowboy type.

PANTANO RIDING STABLES
4450 S. Houghton Rd., 520/298-8980,
www.horsingaroundarizona.com
HOURS: Daily 8 A.M.–5 P.M.
COST: $25 one hour, $35 1.5 hours, $45 two hours,
$40 1.5-hour sunset ride
Map 4

About 13 miles southeast of town, out in the shaggy cactus-and-scrub desert not far from Saguaro National Park East, the friendly folks at Pantano Riding Stables will take you out and make you feel like a real cowboy. Along with the usual one- to two-hour trail rides, they offer a fun "campfire ride" where you can dine under the stars as if you're working some kind of round-up. The desert out this way is beautiful and thick, and if you go when the cactus are blooming you are in for a spectacular show. It's a good idea to call ahead for a reservation.

© TIM HULL

Horseback riding is a must for those who want the full Southwestern experience in Tucson.

PUSCH RIDGE RIDING STABLES

13700 N. Oracle Rd., 520/825-1664,
www.puschridgestables.com
HOURS: Daily 8 A.M.–5 P.M.
COST: $35 one hour, $55 two hours, $45 sunset ride
Map 7

In the northwest foothills of the Santa Catalina Mountains, about 20 miles northwest of town near Catalina State Park, Pusch Ridge Riding Stables go out on fun desertland trail rides every hour on the hour every day 8 A.M.–3 P.M. During the busy spring season rides typically include about six to eight riders and a guide. The "moonlight rides" here are particularly enchanting, making one feel a bit like an outlaw on the run. These last 1.5 hours and cost $60 per person with a minimum of four riders. They also offer half-day ($90 pp) and full-day ($150 pp) rides, and private rides ($60 per hour). Call ahead for reservations, especially on the weekends.

SPANISH TRAIL OUTFITTERS

8500 E. Ocotillo Dr., 520/749-0167,
www.spanishtrailoutfitters.com
HOURS: Daily 9 A.M.–5 P.M.

COST: $35 pp one hour, two-person minimum;
$45 1.5 hours; $55 two hours; $55 sunset ride
Map 3

Just a quick nine-mile drive into the Santa Catalina foothills, Spanish Trail Outfitters offers a host of trail-ride options in beautiful desert terrain along Sabino and Bear Creeks. Typically you'll be with five or six other riders and a guide. The earliest rides begin at 9 A.M. and the last ride of the day is a 1.5-hour sunset ride from 5 to 6:30 P.M. Spanish Trail is a perfect option if you're looking to get out into the desert on top of your very own horse without having to travel very far from central Tucson. Call ahead for reservations, especially if you have a large party.

BALLOONING
SOUTHERN ARIZONA BALLOON EXCURSIONS

537 W. Grant Rd., 520/624-3599,
www.tucsoncomefly.com
HOURS: Daily, weather permitting
COST: $175 pp
Map 3

For more than 25 years this local family-owned

ARTS AND LEISURE

company has been taking people high into the blue, cloudless skies over Tucson for a glimpse of the desert from above. For the hour-long rides, offered every day that weather permits (no rain and no strong winds), they'll fill their big balloons for a drift over the Tucson Mountains and the Avra Valley. Depending on the day, you will likely be in a basket with just a few other people or up to eight. The price includes a champagne brunch upon landing, a certificate, and two pictures. Make sure to bring a hat. Calling ahead to make a reservation is a must.

SPECTATOR SPORTS
SOUTHWESTERN INTERNATIONAL DRAGWAY
12000 S. Houghton Rd., 520/762-9700, www.sirace.com
COST: Varies
Map 7

This dragway about 20 miles southeast of midtown, near the Pima County Fairgrounds, hosts a plethora of drag-racing events throughout the year, from professional races with the sport's

big names to weekend-morning high-school races and other amateur events. There's seating here for more than 6,000, and it's always fun to sit in the sun (with a hat on, of course) and watch the cars burn up their rubber on the already near-melting blacktop.

TUCSON RACEWAY PARK
11955 S. Harrison Rd., www.tucsonracewaypark.com
COST: $10 adult; $7 active military, senior, child; free child under 8
Map 7

This small track about 20 miles southeast of midtown, at the Pima County Fairgrounds, puts on street stock, late model, spectator drag, modified, Pro 4, factory stock, and Hornet races throughout the year, along with a host of special events and driving schools.

UNIVERSITY OF ARIZONA SPORTS
McKale Center, 520/621-2287, www.arizonaathletics.com
Map 1

The biggest sports draw in the region are the teams of the University of Arizona. With

University of Arizona students and alumni love their sports teams.

© TIM HULL

SPRING TRAINING AND CACTUS LEAGUE GAMES

One Major League Baseball team or another has been taking advantage of the near-perfect March weather in Tucson since at least 1946; however, it looks increasingly likely that the long tradition of Spring Training in the Old Pueblo could end within the next few years. The Chicago White Sox, one of three MLB teams that trained here in recent years, pulled out of town in 2009, buying out their contract with Pima County in favor of moving up to a new stadium in Glendale, north of Phoenix. That leaves Tucson with the Colorado Rockies and the Arizona Diamondbacks, but with the Sox pull-out both teams can legally break their own contracts with the county; and since the Diamondbacks' AAA team recently relocated from Tucson to Reno, Nevada, the home-state team is widely expected to do its Spring Training elsewhere in the near future. The Rockies would not likely stick around to be the sole team in Tucson, es-pecially since more and more teams – including the Cubs, the Indians, the Dodgers, the Brewers, the Giants, the Padres and others – are locating their training facilities in the Phoenix area, which now rivals Florida as the top spring destination for dedicated baseball fans. For now, as of 2009, two teams are still playing here, and there's a Pima County committee trying to entice a replacement for the Sox and keep the tradition alive in Tucson. For information about Spring Training and Cactus League games in Tucson and the Valley of the Sun, go to www.cactusleague.com, a comprehensive website on the league. Teams play throughout March – 14 teams at 11 different stadiums around Arizona, such as **Tucson Electric Park** (2500 E. Ajo Way, 520/434-1000) and **Hi Corbett Field** (3400 E. Camino Campestre, 530/327-9467; www.cactusleague.com) – and the games nearly always start at 1:05 P.M.

perennial powerhouses in basketball, volleyball, and baseball, and a Pac-10 football team that is usually expected to hold its own in a tough division, there's always something to cheer for on campus. UA basketball is traditionally the top sport not only on campus but in all of Southern Arizona; for years, as now-retired coach Lute Olsen was ever leading the team to the final days of the NCAA tournament every March, the whole town caught the madness en masse. With the Lute era over, it remains to be seen if the team will be as popular locally as it once was, but don't expect getting tickets to be easy regardless of who is coaching. UA basketball is still the top sports draw in town and is likely to remain that way for the time being.

ARTS AND LEISURE

SHOPS

David Puddy asked it on the television show *Seinfeld*: "What can you get at the Gap in Rome that you can't get at the Gap on 5th Avenue?" Use this as your mantra while shopping in Tucson and Southern Arizona. The Old Pueblo has all the chains, more so than most midsized cities. But if you spend your time at the Gap you're going to miss a unique shopping experience—a chance to find that treasure that has eluded you, to return home with an authentic artifact.

You'll find merchants with Mexican imports, folk arts, Western Americana, and Indian jewelry; boutiques with clothes you'll find nowhere else; and galleries featuring the work of artists from Tucson and the rest of the world. Take a short drive south to Tubac—an artist's village that caters to, or better yet exists for, the discriminating treasure hunter—then on across the border to Nogales, Sonora, and you'll find items you never knew you had to have.

A brief scenic journey east and you're among the antiques stores and artisan boutiques of old-town Bisbee. Fear not: Shopping in Southern Arizona isn't just for the moneyed (though it may be easier for them). There are finds for everyone, and for every budget.

If you you're looking for that truly Southwestern gift or souvenir to take home, there are many places to find such items. Some of the most popular items that just scream "Tucson" are the many Day of the Dead *calaveras* available throughout the borderlands and, of course, anything with the beloved visage of the Virgin of Guadalupe will remind you of your time in the desert every time you look at it. There are also many antiques and resale stores here stocked with the former possessions of all those retirees who came to the desert to live out their final days in free and easy style.

© TIM HULL

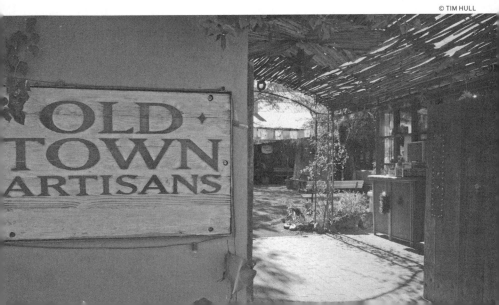

HIGHLIGHTS

LOOK FOR ◖ TO FIND RECOMMENDED SHOPS.

◖ **Best Items Made by Tucson Artists:** The entire inventory at **Bohemia** is made by Tucson artists and artisans (or at least Arizona-based artists), and it is astonishing in its variety, playfulness, and quality (page 160).

◖ **Best Gifts from the Desert:** Take a piece of the Sonoran Desert home with you from **Native Seeds/SEARCH,** where you'll find unique items from and about the desert, including videos, books, crafts, and heirloom seeds (page 161).

◖ **Best Native American Arts:** Bahti **Indian Arts,** the oldest Native American arts shop in Tucson, sells some of the finest examples of Navajo, Hopi, and Pueblo textiles, kachinas, jewelry, basketry, pottery, paintings, and sculptures in the region (page 163).

◖ **Best Bookstore:** Book lovers can't miss **Bookmans,** a popular Southern Arizona chain with an amazing inventory and used books at less than half the original price (page 166).

◖ **Best Music Store:** The East Speedway Boulevard location of **Zia Record Exchange** is stocked full with an eclectic mixture of brand-new and gently used CDS, often for prices similar to, if not below, the big national chains (page 168).

◖ **Best Thrift Store:** "Vintage clothing for New Bohemians" is how the founder of **The Buffalo Exchange** describes her first store, a popular Tucson original that spawned a nationwide chain (page 170).

◖ **Best Shopping District:** With over 100 mostly locally owned stores, restaurants, boutiques, bars, clubs, and coffee houses, the tree-lined **4th Avenue** district downtown is the perfect place to shop, eat, and drink the day away (page 175).

© TIM HULL

◖ **Best Upscale Shopping:** Tucson's answer to the famous high-end shopping mecca of Scottsdale, **La Encantada** is an elegant outdoor mall in the foothills, offering all the most posh chains and a few local boutiques as well (page 175).

◖ **Best Antiques:** Prepare to spend hours in the **Speedway Antiques District,** where the best of the handful of antiques shops is Copper Country Antiques, a huge antiques warehouse with Western- and Southwestern-themed treasures and much, much more (page 179).

◖ **Best Place to Buy Folk Art:** Tubac, Arizona's first settlement, is now an artists colony and shopping village with more than 100 shops and galleries, many of them selling Mexican and South American imports (page 179).

SHOPS

Antiques

COPPER COUNTRY ANTIQUES
5055 E. Speedway Blvd., 520/326-0167,
www.coppercountryantiques.com
HOURS: Mon.-Sat. 10 A.M.-6 P.M., Sun. 11 A.M.-5 P.M.
Map 2

Just head east on Speedway Boulevard past Alvernon and look for the building with the winged buffalos on its roof. There's definitely something a little off center going on at this huge midtown antiques mall; I once saw a homemade sign taped onto their regular sign that said, "will trade antiques for alfalfa hay." Inside they've got all the usual Western- and Southwestern-themed treasures, along with mini-stores dedicated to mid-century modern furniture, war memorabilia, old golf clubs, antique jewelry, and much more. Prepare to spend

hours in here. Don't worry about missing lunch, though; there's a casual little bistro inside.

TOM'S FINE FURNITURE AND COLLECTIBLES
5454 E. Pima St., 520/795-5210
HOURS: Tues.-Sat. 10 A.M.-5 P.M.
Map 2

A labyrinthine store on Pima near Craycroft, Tom's is crammed to the rafters with furniture, antiques, knickknacks, home decor items, and scores of strange, unclassifiable artifacts; there doesn't seem to be any theme here, just rooms of stuff, much of it expensive. I saw a dusty pair of original high-dollar Eames lounge chairs next to a cigar-store Indian next to a Victorian dressing table and on and on—it's a great place to get lost for a while.

Arts and Crafts

FOLK ARTS
C BOHEMIA
2920 E. Broadway Blvd., 520/882-0800,
www.bohemiatucson.com
HOURS: Sun.-Mon. 11 A.M.-4 P.M., Tues.-Sat. 10 A.M.-6 P.M.
Map 2

The Old Pueblo has its fair share of resident artists, and contrary to popular belief not all of them are struggling to find the most evocative pose for a sunset-lit cowboy atop his horse. A stop at this midtown marketplace—selling handmade furniture, jewelry, home decor, fine art, gifts, and many items which are simply unclassifiable—will certainly disabuse one of any preconceived notions about what Southwestern art is.

CREATIVE VENTURE CRAFT MALL
522 N. 4th Ave., 800/543-2610,
www.tucson-creative-ventures.com
HOURS: Mon.-Thurs. 10 A.M.-6 P.M., Fri. 10 A.M.-9 P.M.,
Sat. 10 A.M.-9 P.M.
Map 1

A more than 4,000-square-foot building on

4th Avenue has been converted into a series of small consignment booths from which local artists, artisans, and retailers sell their often-handmade wares. There are many one-of-a-kind items here, and most of them have some kind of Southwestern spirit about them. This is a good family-run place to purchase a fun and unique gift that just says "Southwest," as many of the items here seem to be geared specifically to tourists.

CRIZMAC TUCSON MARKETPLACE
1642 N. Alvernon Way, 520/323-8555,
www.crizmac.com
HOURS: Mon.-Fri. 10 A.M.-5 P.M., Sat. 10 A.M.-4 P.M.
Map 2

A colorful, artistically decorated storefront on Alvernon Way near Pima Street, Crizmac offers an eclectic mix of folk art, art kits, arts and crafts books, jewelry, and kids' books and handicrafts at reasonable prices. They also hold lectures, classes, and workshops on various folk-art topics, and even organize trips for the

All the items at Bohemia are made by Tucson artists.

© TIM HULL

truly dedicated crafter. Here you'll find handi-crafts and artistic discoveries from all over the world, as well as items and advice that will un-doubtedly inspire your own creativity.

DEL SOL

435 N. 4th Ave., 520/628-8765, www.delsolstores.com
HOURS: Mon.-Sat. 10 A.M.-5 P.M., Sun. noon-4 P.M.
Map 1

For more than 30 years the folks at Del Sol, on 4th Avenue, have been scouring Central and South America for the finest in ceramic, wood, metal, glass, and textile handicrafts, clothing made from natural fibers—including hand-woven Guatemalan items—jewelry, and more; it's hard to beat their prices. The same folks own La Zia at Old Town Artisans downtown, selling excellent Native American jewelry and other handicrafts and art purchased directly from the artists themselves.

THE MEXICAN GARDEN

2854 E. Grant Rd., 520/795-4616
HOURS: Mon.-Sat. 9 A.M.-5 P.M., Sun. 10 A.M.-5 P.M.
Map 2

Reasonable prices and a huge inventory are the hallmarks of this friendly, albeit primarily Spanish-speaking, Mexican folk art, ceramic tile, Talavera, and *chimenea* (clay outdoor fire-place) store along busy Grant Road in midtown. There are dozens of similar stores in town, and the village of Tubac, south of Tucson, is rotten with them, but I've found that the prices here are right in line with, if not cheaper than, everybody else. Go here instead of crossing the border and braving the hard-sell in Nogales, Sonora, for a *chimenea,* ceramic tiles with Day of the Dead characters on them, and much more.

(NATIVE SEEDS/SEARCH

526 N. 4th Ave., 520/622-5561, www.nativeseeds.org
HOURS: Mon.-Sat. 10 A.M.-5 P.M., Sun. noon-4 P.M.
Map 1

You won't find any other store in town that has more uniquely Southwestern items, from heirloom seeds for nearly lost regional crops to one-of-a-kind gifts and videos and hand-made crafts and soaps (made of yucca root, for example)—all with a link to the region and its past. A perfect gift to take back home is one of the gift baskets sold here, with all kinds of lo-cally and regionally produced foods, soaps, and

© TIM HULL

You'll find unique Southwestern gifts at Native Seeds/SEARCH on 4th Avenue.

balms. This store also has an excellent selection of books about Tucson and the Southwest.

PHILABAUM GLASS STUDIO AND GALLERY

711 S. 6th Ave., 520/884-7404,
www.philabaumglass.com
HOURS: Tues.-Sat. 10 A.M.-5 P.M.
Map 1

The delicate, colorful glass creations built in this downtown studio are amazing, but more amazing still is watching the artists at work. Most days at this working studio and shop along 6th Avenue (look for the airplane rudder set up outside) you can sit and watch the strange process of glassblowing; be careful though, because you're going to want to buy something once you see how it's done. Glassblowing viewing is available most days, but it's a good idea to call ahead to be sure.

POPCYCLE

422 N. 4th Ave., 520/622-3297,
www.popcycleshop.com

HOURS: Mon.-Sat. 10 A.M.-6 P.M., Sun. 11 A.M.-5 P.M.
Map 1

The concept of "upcycling" is a relatively new one, but it makes a lot of sense in our cluttered world. The artists selling their wares at this charming 4th Avenue boutique take old pop-culture artifacts—record albums, found art, advertising, etc.—and create new and exciting items out of the detritus of the culture. You won't believe what a creative mind can come up with in just a bit of time spent in the attic or thrift store.

POTTERY BLOWOUT

3840 E. Grant Rd., 520/325-6683,
www.potteryblowout.com
HOURS: Daily 9 A.M.-6 P.M.
Map 2

Pottery has always been important in the Southwest; and as a contemporary art form, pottery still thrives in this region. To see the Mexican, South American, and other styles of this essential human art form, head to Pottery Blowout, where there's always at least 1,000 different items in stock, and the prices are usually less than their competitors.

SANTA THERESA TILE WORKS
440 N. 6th Ave., 520/623-1856, 800/862-2198, www.santatheresatileworks.com
HOURS: Mon.-Fri. 10 A.M.-5 P.M., Sat. 10 A.M.-4 P.M.
Map 1

Spend just a little time in the borderlands and you'll notice that everything here is tiled over. Ceramic, Saltillo, Talavera, and other tile styles are ubiquitous in the homes of the Old Pueblo—nobody has carpet here. But tiles are also used as decoration, as knickknacks and gifts. At Santa Theresa Tile Works you'll find the state of the art, where each tile is hand made and hand painted, each one a mini work of art.

NATIVE AMERICAN ARTS AND CRAFTS

ARIZONA MERCANTILE: THE MUSEUM STORE AT THE ARIZONA HISTORICAL SOCIETY
949 E. 2nd St., 520/628-8966
HOURS: Tues.-Thurs. 11 A.M.-3 P.M., Fri.-Sat. 11 A.M.-4 P.M.
Map 1

Inside the Arizona Historical Society's main Tucson museum near the University of Arizona campus, this small gift shop has excellent desert-land gifts, including some really excellent Native American items like Tohono O'odham baskets, Navajo jewelry, and other Southwest-only treasures. There's also a fine selection of books about the state and other gifts for your friends back home, along with replicas of classic 19th- and 20th-century photographs of the romantic Old West, jewelry, and items by local artisans.

◖ BAHTI INDIAN ARTS
4330 N. Campbell Ave., Ste. 72, 520/577-0290, www.bahti.com
HOURS: Mon.-Sat. 10 A.M.-6 P.M., Sun. 8:30 A.M.-4 P.M.
Map 3

First opened by current owner Mark Bahti's father, Tom Bahti, in 1952, Bahti Indian Arts, though no longer in its original location, is now the oldest shop of its kind in the Old Pueblo. The small shop at St. Philip's Plaza, sells some of

finest examples of Navajo, Hopi, and Pueblo textiles, kachinas, jewelry, basketry, pottery, paintings, and sculptures in the state, as well as an assortment of art and artifacts from tribes outside the Southwest. Mark himself is a noted expert on Native American art, as his father was before him.

GREY DOG TRADING COMPANY
2970 N. Swan Rd., Ste. 138, 520/881-6888, www.greydogtrading.com
HOURS: Mon.-Sat. 10 A.M.-6 P.M.
Map 2

An excellent Native American arts boutique at La Plaza Palomino, near Swan and Fort Lowell, Grey Dog carries an amazing array of kachinas, fetish carvings, sand paintings, basketry, pottery, and textiles (mostly by Hopis, Navajos, Zunis, and other Southwestern native artists), as well as a good assortment of books about the Indian arts past and present. I particularly like their selection of contemporary kachinas carved by some of today's greatest Hopi artists, showing that even a largely conservative, religious-based art form can break out of the mold to reveal something new and meaningful.

MORNING STAR TRADERS
2020 E. Speedway Blvd., 520/881-2112, www.morningstartraders.com
HOURS: Mon.-Sat. 10 A.M.-6 P.M.
Map 2

This midtown store has a fabulous collection of high-end Indian arts—kachinas, Navajo textiles, pots and baskets, carvings, and historical artifacts—from the Southwestern traditions and others as well. Next door is **Morning Star Antiques** (Mon.–Sat. 11 A.M.–5 P.M.), which sells Spanish colonial furniture, antique home decor, and other sought-after regional home-arts.

NATIVE GOODS: THE ARIZONA STATE MUSEUM STORE
1013 E. University Blvd., 520/826-5886, www.statemuseum.arizona.edu
HOURS: Mon.-Sat. 10 A.M.-5 P.M., Sun. noon-5 P.M.
Map 1

A visit to the Arizona State Museum is a must

AUTHENTIC NATIVE AMERICAN ART

Despite being hundreds of miles from the Navajo and Hopi Reservations in northeastern Arizona, Tucson has long been known as a center for Native American arts. One of the finest, and now the oldest, dealers of Navajo, Hopi, and Pueblo arts in Tucson is Mark Bahti, owner of **Bahti Indian Arts** (4330 N. Campbell Ave., Ste. 72, 520/577-0290, www.bahti.com). In his small shop, Bahti sells several very useful books and guides on identifying and collecting Native American arts, including his own recent book *Silver + Stone: Profiles of American Indian Jewelers*. Bahti is currently in the process of researching a similar book on Native American pottery artists.

It's often difficult to know what is *authentic* Native American art and what isn't. This has been a problem from the very beginning, but if you learn a bit about the history of the art form, you'll likely conclude that words like authenticity are pretty slippery when it comes to this kind of art. According to Bahti's book, it was during the golden age of Southwestern tourism that the authenticity of Indian jewelry became an issue.

The artists were, of course, encouraged to create work specifically for tourists, who flocked to the reservations and pueblos on the Fred Harvey Indian Detours. Bahti writes that these pieces were often lightweight, with "horses, tipis, arrows, thunderbirds...designed to fit the tourist notion of what Indian jewelry was 'supposed' to look like." But, as Bahti points out, what was Indian jewelry actually "supposed to look like?" Nobody could really say, and they still can't.

By the 1920s, manufactured copies of Indian arts were being made outside the Southwest and then shipped in to be sold as authentic, spurring the native artists to join together in co-ops and guilds, many of which of are still in operation and are still training new artists.

The 1970s brought about a boom in the market for Pueblo and Navajo jewelry, and today there is a really diffuse sense of what is traditional and what is innovative, and innovation – the artist responding not only to tradition but to the world around him or her – can be seen everywhere at Indian markets around the Southwest, including February's popular Indian Arts Fair at the University of Arizona's Arizona State Museum.

Because it's made by Native Americans, many people approach this art with a lot of preconceived notions; especially prevalent are notions about authenticity and tradition. Some people expect every Indian artist and artisan to be adhering to some ancient set of guidelines set down before real time began, a method that washes each squash-blossom necklace and kachina carving with some undeniable spiritual patina. Like most artistic movements, however, the provenance of the Southwestern Indian arts and crafts tradition is far more complex.

Think of these artists as working within similar confines as did painters and sculptors of the Western European tradition before and during the Renaissance. Such artists were bound more often than not to paint and sculpt imagery from the Bible or Greek and Roman mythology, and they could count on their public immediately recognizing the scenes and characters they depicted. However, within this rather narrow tradition, there existed astonishing variety.

Authenticity is a particular concern if you're looking to purchase a katsina doll. Only dolls made by the Hopi and other Pueblo Indians are real katsinas, while those made by the Navajo and other tribes are intended for the tourist trade and will not hold their value. The general rule, unfortunately, is that if a doll is inexpensive, it's probably a fake.

for anyone interested in the native cultures of Arizona and the Southwest, and a visit to the museum is not complete without perusing its excellent gift shop, which sells not only top-shelf Native American arts and crafts but also a great selection of Arizona-related posters, artwork, and books. The store is usually closed for half an hour at noon.

Bath, Beauty, and Spas

ELIZABETH ARDEN RED DOOR SALON
3666 E. Sunrise Dr., 520/742-7866,
www.reddoorspas.com
HOURS: Daily 8 A.M.-8 P.M.
Map 3

Just walking into Tucson's version of the world-famous Red Door Salon, at the Westin La Paloma Resort and Spa lowers your pulse by a few beats, and staff are professional and friendly. They offer just about any massage, facial, or other procedure you're looking for, but it will cost you: The lowest price for a half day or so of pampering is around $350.

GADABOUT SALON AND SPA
3201 E. Speedway Blvd., 520/325-0000,
www.gadabout.com
HOURS: Tues., Thurs., and Fri. 7 A.M.-8 P.M.,
Wed. and Sat. 7 A.M.-6 P.M.
Map 2

Get a cut, style, massage, mani-pedi, a wax, or even a full day of outlandish body-pampering at this branch of this locally owned salon and spa empire. There's even a **Gadabout Male** (2951 N. Swan, 520/325-3300), offering facials, waxing, and something called manscaping.

Locally owned Gadabout Salon and Spa has branches all over Tucson.

SHOPS

Books and Music

ANTIGONE BOOKS

411 N. 4th Ave., 520/792-3715,
www.antigonebooks.com

HOURS: Mon.-Thurs. 10 A.M.-7 P.M.,
Fri.-Sat. 10 A.M.-9 P.M., Sun. noon-5 P.M.

Map 1

A 4th Avenue institution and one of the last independent bookstores in town selling primarily new books, Antigone can get away with it by concentrating on a niche: books about women. There always seems to be some signing or reading going on here, and you'll find an unprecedented selection of books about social justice, gender issues, environmentalism, and left-leaning politics. They also offer a large selection of cards, posters, and book-related merchandise.

BOOKMANS

6230 E. Speedway Blvd., 520/748-9555,
www.bookmans.com

HOURS: Daily 9 A.M.-10 P.M.

Map 2

Book lovers can't miss Bookmans, a Southern Arizona original with an inventory to rival the local Barnes & Noble—only the books here are

gently used and less than half the price. There are three Bookmans stores in Tucson, all of them featuring thousands of used books, CDs, videos, DVDs, and video games, but the relatively new Speedway location has become the firm's flagship store. Prices are cheap compared to smaller boutique-style used-book stores, and the selection is absolutely without compare. This is one of the Southwest's best used-book stores. The other two Bookmans locations are on 1930 East Grant Road (520/325-5767) and 3733 West Ina Road (520/579-0303).

THE BOOK STOP

214 N. 4th Ave., 520/326-6661,
www.bookstoptucson.com

HOURS: Mon.-Thurs. 10 A.M.-7 P.M., Fri.-Sat.
10 A.M.-10 P.M., Sun. noon-5 P.M.

Map 1

One of the last independent bookstores in Tucson, The Book Stop has been around since the late 1960s, but it's only been on 4th Avenue for a few years. They've got a spectacular selection of used and out-of-print books, including a substantial section on the Southwest. The

Bookmans is the best bookstore chain in Arizona.

© TIM HULL

SINGING WIND BOOKSHOP

Take a short, scenic drive north of Benson, a small town east of Tucson, to the verdant ranching country and you'll find an unexpected destination for bibliophiles, or anyone interested in how a bookstore can thrive for more than 30 years in a relatively secluded ranch house.

Winifred Bundy's Singing Wind Bookshop (700 W. Singing Wind Rd., 520/586-2425, daily 9 A.M.-5 P.M., including most holidays) opened 33 years ago in the ranch house where Bundy has lived for 52 years. She still lives in the house, and she's likely to come out and show you around in her stocking feet. Make sure to get the tour, as the stock (mostly new books, with an emphasis on Southwestern and Western themes) is organized according to a slightly individualistic code, and Winifred is a great source for recommendations.

She learned about the Southwest from the great Lawrence Clark Powell, and now publishes several one-of-a-kind editions of his work and also sells tapes of conversations with Powell accompanied by music from Tucson band Calexico. If you plan to buy any books – and it's difficult, many find, to drive all the way out there and not purchase something, there's simply too much great stuff that can't be found elsewhere – take cash or a checkbook; Winifred said she doesn't "mess with credit cards." She encourages book lovers to bring lunch and have a picnic on the ranch, and don't miss saying hello to the mule and beautiful white horse who share a pasture along the road leading

Stop to say hello to the resident mule and white horse at Singing Wind Bookshop.

to the shop. A well-stocked children's reading room makes this a great family destination, especially when Winifred's friendly dog comes out from the back room looking to play. From the tiny town of Benson, along I-10 about 40 miles east of Tucson, take 4th Street (the main drag) to Ocotillo Road, then head north about three miles to Singing Wind Road, a dirt road. Turn east (right) onto the road, drive to a green gate (it may or may not be open; if it isn't, open it yourself), and continue about a quarter of a mile to the ranch house.

books are a bit pricey in comparison to the bigger Bookmans, but when you're inside this classic store you feel a million miles away.

CLUES UNLIMITED

3146 E. Ft. Lowell, 520/326-8533, www.cluesunlimited.com
HOURS: Mon.-Sat. 9 A.M.-5 P.M., Sun. noon-5 P.M.
`Map 2`

Mystery and crime fiction is all they do at Clues Unlimited, a small but very intelligently stocked niche bookstore. They sell an unmatched selection of British imports (everybody knows the Brits write the best mysteries), and there's always some signing or reading featuring crime writers both new and established. A visit here should really be a priority for fans of the genre, or for anyone curious to see what the nearly extinct, locally owned retail bookstore looks like.

PDQ RECORDS AND CDS

2342 N. Dodge Blvd., 520/881-2681

HOURS: Mon.-Sat. 10 A.M.-8 P.M., Sun. noon-6 P.M.

Map 2

A large room with florescent lighting humming down from above, packed full of stack after stack of vinyl, PDQ is a place for record hunters and music nostalgists to disappear for a few hours near Grant and Dodge. PDQ has the largest selection of vinyl in Southern Arizona—maybe in the whole state—most of it ranging from good to near fine condition. You probably won't find a lot of high-dollar, mint-condition records here that haven't already been priced accordingly, but it's a great place to buy listening copies of all those albums you got rid of back when they lied and said that vinyl was dead.

◖ ZIA RECORD EXCHANGE

3370 E. Speedway Blvd., 520/327-3340,

www.ziarecords.com

HOURS: Sun.-Thurs. 10 A.M.-10 P.M., Fri.-Sat. 10 A.M.-midnight

Map 2

This Arizona chain's claim to be "the last real record store" is, sadly, quite true—at least in these arid parts. For a few generations Zia sold an excellent selection of vinyl, cassettes, and CDs, both new and used, to all the state's rock-and-rollers. These days the vinyl and the cassettes are no longer stocked much, but the store's Speedway Boulevard location is stocked full of CDs and DVDs of all stripes, still a mixture of the brand-new and the gently used, and often for prices similar to, if not below, the big chains.

Boutique Grocery and Liquor Stores

Tucson has many industrial-size supermarkets—Fry's, Safeway, Basha's (an Arizona chain), Costco, and more. It also has its fair share of the smaller market chains like Trader Joe's, Sunflower, and, of course, Whole Foods. The best local places to shop for delicacies, delectables, and sprits, however, are the many locally owned (or at least Arizona-based) boutique groceries, delis, and liquor stores. The best of these are gathered here.

AJ'S FINE FOODS

2805 E. Skyline Dr., 520/232-6340,

www.ajfinefoods.com

HOURS: Daily 7 A.M.-8 P.M.

Map 3

This high-end grocery store at the foothills' La Encantada is truly a "purveyor of fine foods," with all kinds of boutique-style foods and imported delicacies available, as well as a good restaurant with outdoor seating.

FOOD CONSPIRACY CO-OP

412 N. 4th Ave., 520/624-4821,

www.foodconspiracy.coop

HOURS: Daily 8 A.M.-9 P.M.

Map 1

This beloved local co-op has been located on busy, bohemian 4th Avenue downtown for years; the produce is all organic, and they stock "as much seasonal, local produce as possible." They also have all kinds of special-diet selections (gluten-free, dairy-free, vegetarian, macrobiotic, low-fat, low-sodium, unrefined foods, etc.) and a good assortment of international foods.

PLAZA LIQUORS

2642 N. Campbell Ave., 520/327-0452

HOURS: Mon.-Sat. 10 A.M.-9 P.M.

Map 2

A perennial winner for best liquor store in town in the *Tucson Weekly*'s Best of Tucson poll, Plaza Liquors is an essential stop for beer lovers. They have the absolute best selection of beer in the Old Pueblo, with hundreds of varieties from all over the world sold by the bottle or can. The small, rather cramped store on busy Campbell Avenue also has a great selection of spirits and wines, and very friendly and helpful staff.

RINCON MARKET

2513 E. 6th St., 520/327-6653, www.rinconmarket.com
HOURS: Mon.-Fri. 7 A.M.-9 P.M., Sat. 7 A.M.-8 P.M.,
Sun. 8 A.M.-8 P.M.

Map 2

In midtown's Sam Hughes neighborhood, Rincon Market is one of the last old-school neighborhood grocery stores in Arizona. They have an excellent butcher, and they sell a lot of kosher foods and prepared dishes, including the best roast chicken in town. The deli here is always good, and they've got a salad bar and a good produce selection. Perhaps the best time to visit the Rincon Market is on the weekend, when they open their **breakfast bar** (Sat. 7 A.M.–noon, Sun. 8 A.M.–1 P.M.), featuring a made-to-order omelet bar, Belgian waffles, and eggs Benedict (Sunday only).

THE RUMRUNNER

3131 E. 1st St., 520/326-0121,
www.rumrunnertucson.com
HOURS: Mon. 11 A.M.-7 P.M., Tues.-Sat. 11 A.M.-10 P.M.,

Sun. noon-6 P.M.

Map 2

This popular midtown liquor store has an excellent selection of wines and spirits from all over the world. Even if you're looking for something a bit obscure, they are bound to have it here. Inside, the Dish Bistro serves up a mean bowl of mussels—the perfect accompaniment to a few glasses of the wine you just picked out.

17TH STREET MARKET

840 E. 17th St., 520/792-2588
HOURS: Mon.-Fri. 9 A.M.-7 P.M., Sat. 9 A.M.-6 P.M.

Map 1

Located in the old warehouse district near downtown's Armory Park neighborhood, this store has a bit of a warehouse feel to it, naturally. It's quite large, and is stacked to the rafters with all manner of food, much of it international in flavor. They have an especially large selection of Asian foods, and excellent always-fresh produce, meats, and seafood. There's also a music shop located inside the store where they sell a great selection of work by Tucson musicians.

Children's Stores

THE KID'S CENTER

1725 N. Swan Rd., 520/322-5437,
www.e-kidscenter.com
HOURS: Mon.-Sat. 9 A.M.-5:30 P.M.

Map 2

The Kid's Center doesn't really look like a toy store from the outside, but more like a school or day-care center, in keeping with its rather scholastic-sounding name. And while there is definitely an emphasis on thoughtful play here, kids from babies to early teens will likely peel away upon entering and commence nosing around and poking through this store's myriad books, science kits, dress-up costumes, puzzles, stuffed animals, toy horses, puppets, art supplies, musical instruments, games, and more, most of

them uncommon and boutique-brand items that you don't usually find at the big boxes.

MILDRED AND DILDRED TOY STORE

2905 E. Skyline Dr. No. 186, 520/615-6266,
www.mildredanddildred.com
HOURS: Mon.-Wed. 10 A.M.-7 P.M., Thurs.-Sat.
10 A.M.-8 P.M., Sun. 11 A.M.-6 P.M.

Map 3

Probably the highest of the high-end toy shops in the Old Pueblo, this cute, playful little boutique at the upscale La Encantada in the foothills sells fun toys, games, and other kids' stuff that you likely won't see too many other places—certainly not at Toys R Us and the like. Many of the toys here are imported, and others are made from recycled products, and others are just weird and fun.

MRS. TIGGYWINKLE'S TOYS

4811 E. Grant Rd., Ste. 151, 520/326-0811, www.tiggytoysonline.com

HOURS: Mon.-Sat. 9 A.M.-9 P.M., Sun. 10 A.M.-5 P.M.

Map 2

Similar to the Kid's Center, Mrs. Tiggywinkles takes an alternative approach to the big-box toy outlets, stocking pricey but long-lasting and unique toys, games, puppets, and stuffed animals, and putting on events for the tykes that like such things. The emphasis here is on fun and "nonsense," but only on the surface; just below the fun and games is a seriousness about childhood and its games that many parents will likely find quite refreshing.

Clothing and Shoes

◖ THE BUFFALO EXCHANGE

2001 E. Speedway Blvd., 520/795-0508, www.buffaloexchange.com

HOURS: Mon.-Sat. 10 A.M.-8 P.M., Sun. 11 A.M.-7 P.M.

Map 2

The Buffalo Exchange has spread to college towns and hipster enclaves from Tempe to Brooklyn, but it all started in midtown Tucson in the early 1970s. At the original store you can still find some gently used or even new higher-end brands here for significantly less than retail, plus a large selection of previously worn shoes and jewelry and other items. Or, you can bring in your unwanted duds and maybe get some cash.

DESERT VINTAGE AND COSTUME

636 N. 4th Ave., 520/620-1570

HOURS: Mon.-Sat. 11 A.M.-6 P.M., Sun. noon-5 P.M.

Map 1

This popular thrift store on 4th Avenue isn't very big, but it's well stocked with clothes from bygone eras. You can find anything you need here to dress up like a disco king or a private eye circa 1945. There are hats, boas, and pass-on jewelry galore. This is one of a few good thrift stores along 4th Avenue; all are stocked with the left-behind fashions of millions of snowbirds, retirees, and longtime natives.

J. GILBERT FOOTWEAR

7041 N. Oracle Rd., 520/531-8385, www.jgilbertfootwear.com

HOURS: Mon.-Sat. 10 A.M.-5:30 P.M., Sun. noon-4 P.M.

Map 3

You probably wouldn't want to wear your high-dollar fancy J. Gilbert boots to the rodeo or out honky-tonkin' (unless you *want* to get them scuffed and dirty), but nobody's better at molding the skin of baby buffalos, gators, caimans, and ostrich into footwear treasures that you're sure to fall in love with. The upscale Casas Adobes Plaza in the foothills has the only J. Gilbert this side of Scottsdale, so check it out and place a special order—they even make them out of python.

MAYA PALACE

7057 N. Oracle Rd., 520/575-8028, www.mayapalacetucson.com

HOURS: Mon.-Fri. 10 A.M.-6 P.M., Sat. 10 A.M.-5:30 P.M., Sun. noon-5 P.M.

Map 3

Fashionable women will want to peruse this high-end clothing store featuring fashions from around the world for work, play, and even formal occasions (their stock of wedding dresses contains many you won't see anywhere else). There's a concentration here on a sartorial globalization, hence the name, and they also stock an ever-changing array of imported gifts and accessories from all over the globe. In addition to this store at the upscale Casas Adobes Plaza in the foothills, the popular Maya Palace has locations at El

Mercado (6332 E. Broadway, 520/748-0817) and Plaza Palomino (2960 N. Swan #133, 520/325-6411), both open the same hours as the store in the foothills.

TOQUE DE PASIÓN
3000 E. Broadway Blvd., 520/881-0411,
www.toquedepasion.net
HOURS: Tues.-Sun. 10 A.M.-6 P.M.
Map 2

A charming, unique store at the Broadway Village, Toque de Pasión ("touch of passion") sells fair-trade and eco-chic clothes, gifts, and accessories. They import all their fashions from South America, where they work only with fair-trade co-ops; there's a good amount of "green" clothing here too, including some amazing outfits made from organic cotton. There's a play area in the back so the tykes can play while you shop, and the owners are a great source of information about fair-trade practices around the world.

Toque de Pasión is the only store in the city that sells free-trade high fashion items.

Home Furnishings

ANTIGUA DE MEXICO
3235 W. Orange Grove Rd., 520/742-7114,
www.antiguademexico.us
HOURS: Mon.-Sat. 10 A.M.-5:30 P.M., Sun. noon-4 P.M.
Map 3

If you're looking to turn your home into a faux Spanish hacienda, there are few better places in the Old Pueblo to shop than Antigua de Mexico. Here you'll find all the usual beautiful and romantic suspects: colonial furniture from Mexico and South America, tinwork, Oaxacan folk art, glassware, Talavera, and even silver jewelry imported from Mexico and elsewhere. There are a lot of stores like this in Tucson, Tubac, and across the border in Nogales, Mexico, but Antigua de Mexico has been family owned for more than 30 years and they have all you need in one place.

BON BOUTIQUE
3022 E. Broadway Blvd., 520/795-2272
HOURS: Mon.-Sat. 10 A.M.-6 P.M.
Map 2

This enchanting, eclectic store sells a mix of home decor, clothes, books, garden supplies, knickknacks, and seemingly just about anything else that appeals to the owners, who have a playful but always elegant, intelligent, and classic sense of style. There's another Bon, this one in a Joesler-designed adobe, at Joesler Village (1825 E. River Rd., 520/615-7690, Mon.–Sat. 10 A.M.–6 P.M., Sun. noon–4 P.M.). You will likely spend a good deal of time in here if you're the kind of shopper that likes to be surprised and intrigued at every corner.

© TIM HULL

Bon Boutique is housed in a Joesler-designed adobe.

MEXICAN TILE AND STONE CO.

1148 E. Broadway Blvd., 520/622-4352,
www.mexicantileandstone.com
HOURS: Mon.-Fri. 8 A.M.-5 P.M.
Map 1

This midtown store has all you need to give your home that Old Pueblo look, selling all kinds of imported and handmade tiles, Talavera sinks, copper items, and all the other special aesthetic touchstones that make the Tucson style so unique. If you can't quite get a grip on what the favored Southwestern design is among those who can afford it, this is the place to peruse. After a few minutes, you're bound to get it.

ORIGINATE

526 N. 9th Ave., 520/792-4207,
www.originatenbm.com
HOURS: Tues.-Fri. noon-6 P.M., Sat. noon-4 P.M.
Map 1

Tucson has been going through a kind of green revolution in recent years, and nowhere has this revolution taken off more thoroughly than in the downtown neighborhood of Dunbar Springs, where you'll see a lot of rain-harvesting, xeriscape, community gardens, solar panels, bicyclists, and alternative building techniques. It's also where you'll find this unique shop, which sells all kinds of green building materials and recycled materials. It's definitely worth a look for anybody interested in the cutting edge of green living.

Maps and Outdoor Gear

SUMMIT HUT

5045 E. Speedway Blvd., 520/325-155,
www.summithut.com
HOURS: Mon.-Fri. 9 A.M.-8 P.M., Sat. 9 A.M.-6:30 P.M.,
Sun. 10 A.M.-6:30 P.M.
Map 2

This locally owned outdoor gear shop has all you need to outfit yourself for a wild desert adventure. You'll find outdoor clothing and backpacking equipment like top-brand backpacks, tents, feather-light stoves and sleeping pads, Chaco sandals, hiking shoes, and other must-have desert-rat gear, plus a large selection of mountaineering equipment. They also sell topographical maps and hiking guides, and there are often lectures and workshops on the local and regional wildlands at both the midtown and northwest locations. Their prices aren't exactly low, but you can usually find some great sales. There is another Summit Hut location in the foothills (4605 E. Wetmore, 520/888-1000).

TUCSON'S MAP & FLAG CENTER

3239 N. 1st Ave., 520/887-4234, www.mapsmithus.com
HOURS: Mon.-Fri. 8 A.M.-5:30 P.M., Sat. 9 A.M.-5:30 P.M.
Map 3

A good selection of Southern Arizona maps, trail guides, and travel books can be found at this midsized store on 1st Avenue; they also stock maps and guides for Arizona and the rest of the world. There is a variety of globes available here, along with flags from nations the world over. They have a decent selection of topographical maps of the region and elsewhere. The prices here are generally on par with the big chain bookstores, which are the only other places in town where you'll find even close to the number of useful guides and road maps that they sell here.

Open-Air Markets

With its year-round growing seasons (save, perhaps, for a few of the hottest months in summer), the Tucson area and Southern Arizona is cultivating an increasingly active appetite for locally grown produce. While you can find vegetables, fruits, eggs, meats, coffee, and other edibles produced in the region at a few Tucson grocery stores, the best place to sample the local land's bounty is at one of many year-round farmers markets held throughout the week at various points around the Old Pueblo.

The best and most popular of these are listed here. For even more, check the monthly news and lifestyle publication *Tucson Green Times,* available free at green-colored racks all over town, which publishes an up-to-date list of all the farmers markets in the Tucson area in every issue.

COMMUNITY FOOD BANK FARMERS MARKET
3003 S. Country Club Rd., 520/622-0525, www.communityfoodbank.com
HOURS: Tues. 8 A.M.-noon
Map 6

Every Tuesday the Southern Arizona Community Food Bank (between Ajo Way and 36th St.) sets up a small farm stand–style market with fresh vegetables and eggs from the food bank's community demonstration garden and elsewhere.

DOWNTOWN FARMERS MARKET AND ARTS AND CRAFTS MERCADO
101 N. Stone Ave., 520/326-7810
HOURS: Wed. 8 A.M.-2 P.M.
Map 1

On the plaza at the Joel V. Valdez Main Library every Wednesday, the Downtown Farmers Market features dozens of booths and tables selling locally grown produce and other foodstuffs, as well as arts and crafts by local artists and artisans. There's even usually a psychic on hand.

EL PRESIDIO MERCADO
255 W. Alameda St. at Church Ave., El Presidio Park, 520/326-7810
HOURS: Fri. 10 A.M.-4 P.M.
Map 1

Every Friday El Presidio Park downtown is taken over by farmers and artisans, selling their vegetables and fruits, coffees, meats, and other homegrown, organic, and healthy alternatives to the age-old supermarket paradigm. All the usual stuff can be found here—from chiles to melons to honey to freshly made tamales and tortillas.

RINCON VALLEY FARMERS & ARTISANS MARKET
13701 E. Old Spanish Trail, 520/591-2276
HOURS: Summer Sat. 8 A.M.-1 P.M., winter Sat. 9 A.M.-2 P.M.
Map 4

On Saturdays year-round folks living in the east-side Rincon Valley set up their homegrown delectables and fresh-roasted coffee and arts and crafts on a lot about four miles east of Saguaro National Park East. It's a beautiful drive, and it's fun to combine a stop off at the market with a slow, easy desert drive out to the national park.

SANTA CRUZ RIVER FARMERS MARKET
Northeast corner of Speedway Blvd. and Riverview Rd., 520/622-0505
HOURS: Summer Thurs. 4-7 P.M., winter Thurs. 3-6 P.M.
Map 5

One of the better farmers markets in town, the

west side's Santa Cruz River Farmer's Market takes place in the late afternoon on Thursdays in a lot between the El Rio Neighborhood Center and the Arizona School for the Deaf and Blind. Here you can find all kinds of fresh vegetables, fruits, and meats in season, as well as prepared Mexican favorites and other delicacies.

ST. PHILIP'S
SATURDAY FARMERS MARKET
4380 N. Campbell Ave., 520/603-8116
HOURS: Sat. 9 A.M.-2 P.M.
Map 3

Probably the Old Pueblo's favorite farmers market, St. Philip's Farmers Market at St. Philip's Plaza in the foothills draws a crowd every Saturday with all the usual fresh seasonal vegetables and fruits, fresh-ground organic coffee, and all manner of other artisanal foods and delicacies, not to mention a fair bit of socializing and meeting of new friends and locavore compatriots.

UNIVERSITY OF ARIZONA
FARMERS MARKET
Main Gate Square btwn. University Blvd. and Park Ave.
HOURS: Fri. 10 A.M.-2 P.M.
Map 1

On Fridays, between September and April, farmers and gardeners, artisans, honey-bee keepers, and coffee roasters, take over Main Gate Square near the University of Arizona campus and sell their wares to the college crowd and anybody else who wants good, wholesome food at a fair price.

Shopping Districts and Centers

BROADWAY VILLAGE
2926 E. Broadway Blvd., 520/321-0392
HOURS: Vary
Map 2

A charming little collection of shops and a restaurant at Broadway Boulevard and Country Club, Broadway Village was designed by Josias Joesler in his always recognizable hybrid of revival styles. There are several home decor stores here, an excellent "wine country" restaurant, and a few boutiques offering fair-trade clothing, gifts, and items unique to the region. There are also a few colonial-style furniture stores and a few other shops worth looking at in the general vicinity between Campbell and Country Club along Broadway Boulevard.

CASAS ADOBES PLAZA
7001-7153 N. Oracle Rd., 520/299-2610,
www.casasadobesplaza.com
HOURS: Mon.-Sat. 10 A.M.-6 P.M., Sun. 11 A.M.-4 P.M.
Map 3

This longtime favorite shopping center of the foothills crowd has six restaurants, including Bluefin and Wildflower, two of the city's best, and a wonderful Spanish colonial style with lots of fountains and patios. There are several decidedly upscale shops and boutiques here, including Maya Palace, a high-end purveyor of designer women's clothing from around the world with three Tucson locations. Many of the stores here sell top-shelf Southwestern styles and gifts, and there's a Whole Foods as well.

THE FOOTHILLS MALL
7401 N. La Cholla Blvd., 520/219-0650,
www.shopfoothillsmall.com
HOURS: Mon.-Sat. 10 A.M.-9 P.M., Sun. 11 A.M.-6 P.M.
Map 7

This sprawling north-side mall has more than 90 stores, many of them designer outlets. Here you'll find the Nike Factory Store, Saks Fifth Avenue Off 5th, a Levi's Outlet, and many more—plus, there's no city sales tax. There are also a number of food court–style restaurants, the usual mall chains, a multistory Barnes & Noble, and Thunder Canyon Brewery, where you can get a well-crafted pint and some tasty appetizers (half-off Mon.–Fri. 3–7 P.M.) after your spending spree.

◖ 4TH AVENUE

4th Ave.
HOURS: Vary
Map 1

Pretty much the opposite of nearby Main Gate Square, nearly all of the shops along 4th Avenue (there are about 100 of them) are locally owned and sell items preferred by bohemian types and the thrift-store-chic crowd. There are also jewelry stores, smoke shops, two bookstores, and numerous coffee houses, restaurants, and watering holes. You could spend all day shopping up and down the avenue, eating and drinking along the way. This is the place to find a unique gift or some treasure that you can only get in Tucson.

GRANT ROAD ANTIQUES DISTRICT

Grant Rd. btwn. Campbell Ave. and Craycroft Rd.
HOURS: Vary
Map 2

There are more than half a dozen antiques and resale shops on both sides of Grant Road between Campbell and Craycroft, the best of which is the **American Antique Mall** (3130 E. Grant Rd., 520/326-3070, www.americanantiquemall.com). A visit here will give you a good idea of the kinds of antiques, collectibles, and generally interesting junk available at most of the Old Pueblo's resale places—a crowded mix of cowboy-life and Southwestern collectibles and kitsch; Native American jewelry and artifacts (not all of them authentic); furniture from the common to the rare, the handmade and the colonial, the retro and modern; old, but not necessarily collectible, books (a *lot* of Westerns); and all the varied possessions and ephemera left behind by several generations of snowbirds and retirees who spent their final days warm and content in the desert.

◖ LA ENCANTADA

2905 E. Skyline Dr., Ste. 279, 520/622-8613
HOURS: Mon.-Wed. 10 A.M.-7 P.M., Thurs.-Sat. 10 A.M.-8 P.M., Sun. 11 A.M.-6 P.M.
Map 3

Tucson's answer to the high-end shopping centers that abound in Scottsdale, just a hundred miles or so up I-10, La Encantada offers all the most posh chains and a few local boutiques as well. It's a two-level outdoor mall, so during summer walking from Bebe to Tiffany & Co. and then back to Louis Vuitton will be a bit uncomfortable. Also here is Crate and Barrel, The Apple Store, a boutique toy store, and the only-for-the-too-rich Muttropolis Dog & Cat Boutique. There are several good places to eat and drink here after a hard day of shopping.

LA PLACITA

110 S. Church Ave., 520/903-9900
HOURS: Vary
Map 1

There are a few shops worth visiting in this multicolored Mexican-style plaza downtown, as well as several restaurants and the must-visit **Tucson Visitor Center** (110 S. Church Ave., 520/624-1817, Mon.–Fri. 9 A.M.–5 P.M., Sat.–Sun. 9 A.M.–4 P.M.), which has all kinds of literature and information on what to do and how to do it in Southern Arizona. La Placita is a great place to sit back and enjoy an invariably beautiful Tucson day, and there's always something going on in the courtyard, whether it's a free lunchtime concert or a classic movie shown

La Placita has several shops and a visitors center.

outdoors at night. Don't miss checking out the 1880s gazebo just off the grassy courtyard.

LA PLAZA SHOPPES
6530 E. Tanque Verde Rd.

HOURS: Vary

Map 4

A small group of stores on the east side just across Tanque Verde from Trail Dust Town, La Plaza Shoppes has a few boutiques and galleries worth a look. There are also three or four good restaurants in and around this small redbrick strip. Make sure to stop into **Covington Fine Arts** (Ste. 140, Tues.–Sat. 10 A.M.–3 P.M.), especially if you're looking for art outside the Southwestern aesthetic so prevalent in Tucson. Covington doesn't have much in the way of the usual cowboy and Indian art, but they carry an impressive selection of American and European paintings and prints ranging from the early 19th century to the 1950s.

LOST BARRIO
Park Ave. south of Broadway Blvd.

HOURS: Daily 9 A.M.–6 P.M.

Map 1

A series of rustic old warehouses tucked away on Park Avenue just before you enter downtown from Broadway, the Lost Barrio has nearly a dozen shops selling hand-crafted and imported furniture, folk arts, antiques, and home decor. Several of the stores sell Mexican and colonial-style furniture and antiques, of course, while others offer treasures from Africa, Asia, and

THE DAY OF THE DEAD

Here in the borderlands it's difficult to find a boutique, gift shop, or gallery these days that doesn't sell *calaveras* (skeletons doing human things), whether on statues, paintings, T-shirts, or all manner of other consumer goods featuring the Day of the Dead aesthetic. Generally these art objects re-create the work, or at least the spirit of the work, of José Guadalupe Posada, a late-19th-century and early-20th-century Mexican printmaker and illustrator whose broadsides and newspaper illustrations employed the *calavera* and Day of the Dead traditions in social commentary. While Posada's work had the immediacy of journalism, it has outlasted its original intent and is more popular today than ever before. His style, and his overt political commentary, influenced the likes of Diego Rivera and other Mexican muralists of the first half of the 20th century.

To see Posada's famous broadsides in the original, as they were distributed on the streets of Mexico City, check out the **University of New Mexico's collection** online at http://elibrary.unm.edu/cswr/posada.

The Day of the Dead, or El Día de los Muertos, falls on November 2, but the celebrations begin on November 1 or even before that. It is roughly meant to coincide with the traditional Catholic holidays of All Saints Day and All Souls Day, but the tradition, most anthropologists believe, is far older than the Spanish conquest of Mexico. Indeed it is, like most New World rites, an amalgam of pre-Columbian and Spanish traditions whose origins reach far back into the mist.

Day of the Dead folk art

© TIM HULL

elsewhere. The oldest and best of the stores here is Rustica, which has gorgeous Mexican and Peruvian furniture and Talavera. You could easily spend several hours exploring these stores and fantasizing about each room of your ideal Southwestern-style bungalow in the desert.

MAIN GATE SQUARE

University Blvd. and Euclid Ave., 520/622-8613, www.maingatesquare.com

HOURS: Vary

Map 1

Here you'll find shopping for the college crowd and those who want to dress young. American Apparel, Urban Outfitters, and the like can be found here, as well as a few homegrown stores. Coffee houses and lunch spots make this a good place for shopping while eating. Main Gate Square is right next to the University of Arizona and so is frequented by students. There are 52 stores and restaurants on this block. Be careful about parking; instead of braving the back-in-only metered parking, go to the Main Gate Parking Garage (815 E. 2nd St.) and leave your car in shade and safety.

OLD TOWN ARTISANS

201 N. Court Ave., 520/623-6024, www.oldtownartisans.com

HOURS: Sept.-May Mon.-Sat. 9:30 A.M.-5:30 P.M., Sun. 11 A.M.-5 P.M.; June-Aug. Mon.-Sat. 10 A.M.-4 P.M., Sun. 11 A.M.-4 P.M.

Map 1

Even if you don't have any room in your

At its heart, the holiday is an explicit admittance that death and the dead have a profound influence on the living, and that the two camps coexist side by side, always. The details of the celebrations vary from region to region, from town to town, from big cities to rural areas. Generally they include feasts, often laid out in graveyards, with a dead relative's favorite dishes prepared and set aside. There are parades and marches, candles and altars, sugar skulls, sweet breads shaped like skulls and skeletons, and, of course, calaveras galore.

For many years the Day of the Dead has been marching north, so much so that it now rivals Cinco de Mayo as the Southwestern Anglo's favorite Mexican import. The spectacles surrounding the holiday have always been a subject of fascination for tourists, especially those from the United States. As far back as the 1970s Mexican observers were complaining that in places like Mixquic and Pátzcuaro, towns famous for their Day of the Dead celebrations, "cameras had come to outnumber candles in the cemeteries."

What would those observers think today if they came to the borderlands and saw the proliferation of consumer goods featuring the Day of the Dead aesthetic? I can't say, but I for one am happy with this proliferation, to a degree.

To me, the Day of the Dead is not so much a holiday, but, as it is to many Mexicans, a year-round way of looking at the world. This way of looking at the world, for me, comes directly from Posada's work. The calavera, especially as it was presented by Posada, is a reminder that we are all mere skeletons; we are all the walking dead, and everything we do and say in this world will one day be forgotten. No matter how much money we have (and Posada's frequent target, along with those in political power, was the rich), no matter how much power we have, we are all equally bones underneath, and we will soon enough be gone. Death is not absent from your life until it comes for you. It is there walking beside you all the time, so you might as well give death its due, and a holiday too.

Usually, throughout November there's a traditional Day of the Dead altar at Tolteca Tlacuilo in the **Old Town Artisans complex** (186 N. Meyer, 520/623-5787) from 9:30 A.M. to 5:30 P.M.; and the **Tucson Museum of Art** (140 N. Main Ave., 520/624-2333) typically celebrates the ancient rite with a family event on November 2, with the usual music, food, arts and crafts, an altar, and a parade and big-head puppets.

Old Town Artisans has a lush courtyard, restaurants, and several unique shops.

budget for pottery, Mexican folk arts, and turquoise jewelry, you should still find time to visit this shady, historic spot across from the Tucson Art Museum downtown. Six shops and galleries are gathered in the 150-year-old adobe structure, each one opening onto the verdant Mexican-style courtyard with a fountain and tables. There's a great restaurant here as well and there are often festivals and live music going on in the courtyard, which is a great place to sit and rest with a beer. The import shop **Tolteca Tlacuilo** (www.toltecatlacuilo.com) here sells some of the best Día de los Muertos items in town.

PARK PLACE MALL
5870 E. Broadway Blvd., 520/748-1222,
www.parkplacemall.com
HOURS: Mon.-Sat. 10 A.M.-9 P.M., Sun. noon-6 P.M.
Map 2

At the eastern edge of midtown and the core of the intensive east-central Broadway commercial sprawlscape, Park Place is probably the most popular mall in the city. It has big anchor department stores like Dillard's and Macy's, popular shops like Abercrombie & Fitch and Old Navy, and all the other usual mid-scale suspects along with a movie theater, a kids' play area, and a food court. The Borders bookstore here is among the top two busiest in Arizona, and always seems to be packed, as do the several square miles of parking lot around this retail temple.

PLAZA PALOMINO
Southeast corner of Swan and Fort Lowell Rds.,
520/320-6344, www.plazapalomino.com
HOURS: Mon.-Sat. 10 A.M.-6 P.M.
Map 2

There are nearly 20 shops and restaurants at this upscale midtown shopping center, including purveyors of Native American arts and crafts, Southwestern-style items and home decor, furniture, jewelry, fine art, and high-style women's clothing. The best time for a visit is during the weekly **Saturday Morning Market** (summer 10 A.M.-2 P.M., winter 9 A.M.-1 P.M.), when there's a farmers market, artisans selling their creations, and live music. There's a complimentary "shopping shuttle" that goes to most Tucson hotels; call 520/327-4674.

SANTA FE SQUARE
7000 E. Tanque Verde Rd.
HOURS: Vary
Map 4

Several shops, galleries, and restaurants can be found at this charming east-side shopping center resembling the faux-adobe uniformity of its namesake. Western-art lovers will already be headed to this shopping center to visit the essential Medicine Man Gallery, and others will find boutiques and shops selling everything from high-style clothes to bicycles to gifts with a regional flavor.

THE SHOPS AT EL MERCADO
6302-6372 E. Broadway Blvd. at Wilmont Rd.
HOURS: Mon.-Sat. 10 A.M.-6 P.M.
Map 2

The Shops at El Mercado is an east-side shopping center with a few boutiques, including the popular but pricey women's clothing store Maya Palace and a gourmet chocolate shop. There's also a sports bar and one of El Charro's many locations. It's different from the other retail blocks in this very busy area in that it has a bit of an enclosed, Spanish-revival feel to it and seems calmer and more secluded than the intense traffic all around would suggest.

◖ SPEEDWAY ANTIQUES DISTRICT
Speedway Blvd. btwn. Country Club Dr. and Wilmot Rd.
HOURS: Vary
Map 2

Though not really recognized locally as such, there is an antiques and resale district along Speedway Boulevard just as there is along Grant Road just a block or so north. Along both sides of busy Speedway, roughly between Country Club and Wilmont, you'll find half a dozen or more shops, both small and large, selling used furniture, antiques, and other used and historic treasures. The best of these is the sprawling Copper Country Antiques at Speedway and Rosemont.

◖ TUBAC
Tubac exit off I-19 south
HOURS: Vary
Map 7

Tubac has more than 100 shops and galleries, many of them selling Mexican and South

Ceramics and other folk arts are available in Tubac.

SHOPS

American imports. The village has a year-round Christmas gallery and several little shops whose wares simply must be seen. There are quite a few working art galleries, including the old adobe gallery of the late Hugh Cabot, a famous local artist. Pick up an illustrated map of the shopping district at any of the shops or at the visitors center.

TUCSON MALL
4500 N. Oracle Rd., 520/293-7330,
www.tucsonmall.com
HOURS: Mon.-Sat. 10 A.M.-9 P.M., Sun. noon-6 P.M.
Map 3

On the north side of town near Oracle and River, Tucson Mall has several old-school department stores like Sears, JCPenney, and Dillard's, along with Eddie Bauer, The Disney Store, and all the others you'd expect. There's a vaguely Arizona-themed row of specialty shops, selling a mixture of tourist throwaways and leather, called Arizona Avenue. As in most malls in America, there are many roving packs of teens patrolling this one's generally clean and well-lit corridors.

VENTANA PLAZA
5425 N. Kolb Rd., 520/444-2006
HOURS: Vary
Map 3

This small, upscale strip mall near Kolb Road and Sunrise Drive features a few boutiques, restaurants, a dance and fitness studio, a day spa and hair salon, and a gallery. This is a perfect place for a couple of girlfriends to spend a few hours—shop for designer handbags and shoes and dip into The Seasoned Woman, a unique shop selling "gifts for the feminine spirit." Then it's time for a sushi lunch, a mani-pedi, and a massage.

HOTELS

If you're just looking for a place to store your gear while you're out exploring the desert, you'll find hundreds of mid-priced chain hotels in and around Tucson. But if you're the kind of person who likes a little style and atmosphere where you sleep and wake up—who takes pleasure in and inspiration from surprising architectural and artistic details, in stories and histories—you'll find a few unforgettable historic hotels, boutique inns, and bed-and-breakfast-style accommodations here as well.

Since the late 19th century, travelers have come to Tucson to find health, rest, and a new lease on life. Those who suffered from TB and other chest ailments came here in droves over the years, sent to the desert by their doctors for the supposed cure provided by the dry air. The first big hotels in Tucson, then, were tent cities thrown up in the streets to house the constant stream of hacking patients. Later, the business community got together and started marketing the sunshine and easy living in the Southwest, and Tucson became what it is today—a world-renowned spa destination and seasonless desert playground for those outrunning the snow and ice. And so the resorts and the hotels and the dude ranches and motor courts began to proliferate, as they still do today.

If you have pockets deeper than the vast majority of Americans, by all means book a week at Canyon Ranch, but try and get beyond the resort walls once in a while. If, like most of us, you fall somewhere in the middle—you want a bit of style and personality, but you don't want to leverage your future to have it—you will likely find what you've been looking for here in the Old Pueblo.

HIGHLIGHTS

LOOK FOR (TO FIND RECOMMENDED HOTELS.

(**Best Bed-and-Breakfast in the City:** With four tasteful rooms in a historic mansion built in the 1880s, **El Presidio Inn Bed and Breakfast** has a cool, lush, and peaceful courtyard garden with a babbling fountain, cobblestone walkways, and shady trees (page 183).

(**Most Affordable Historic Hotel:** Built in 1919 and remodeled only slightly since then, **Hotel Congress,** right in the heart of downtown's nightlife scene, offers charm and atmosphere for only about $79-99 per night (page 184).

(**Best Hotel to Treat Like a Sight:** Stop by the secluded, elegant 1930s-era **Arizona Inn** and walk around the green, shady grounds, taking in the style and history (page 186).

(**Best Resort:** Step into the glory days of Southwestern chic at 1930s-era resort **Hacienda del Sol Guest Ranch Resort.** The history, architecture, and design of the high-style Southwest of yesteryear permeate the desert grounds (page 189).

(**Best Bed-and-Breakfast in the Desert:** A hiker's and bird-watcher's paradise east of town near Saguaro National Park East, **Hacienda del Desierto Bed and Breakfast** is a wonderland of hacienda-style details and quiet comfort for anyone looking to escape to the desert for a few days (page 193).

© TIM HULL

The decor at the Hotel Congress hasn't changed much since 1919.

CHOOSING A HOTEL

There aren't a lot of inexpensive accommodations in Tucson worth taking a chance on. There is one hostel, in a clean and friendly house near downtown, and it's the best choice for budget travelers. On the I-10 frontage road just west of downtown is a long row of chain hotels, some of them inexpensive. This isn't the Old Pueblo's most charming district, however. Throughout midtown and on to the east side there are dozens of big chain hotels to choose from, and of course there are dozens more around the south side near the airport.

For a truly memorable Tucson experience, consider staying in one of the small (though often relatively pricey) bed-and-breakfasts and inns in one of the city's many historic neighborhoods. These include the beautiful Arizona Inn in midtown, and the very affordable Hotel Congress right in the center of the action downtown. There are also inns in the Sam Hughes historic neighborhood in midtown, and in the El Presidio district near downtown.

During the summer months, roughly from late May to late September, nearly all of the hotels, resorts, and inns in Tucson slash their prices—some by as much as 50 percent, but most by around 20 percent. If you're planning on coming to town during those torpid, quiet months, you might just be able to afford to live like a robber baron for a few days. Also, it pays to explore the websites of the larger chains listed in this chapter; most of them offer all kinds of different packages, one of which will likely save you some money. If you're coming to town in February or March, book early and plan to pay a bit more; those two perfect-weather months feature several very popular festivals, events, and conventions in the Old Pueblo, and most places are booked solid.

PRICE KEY

$ Under $150 per night

$$ $150-250 per night

$$$ Over $250 per night

Downtown and University District — Map 1

HOTELS

Many of the inns and hotels in this neighborhood are popular with visiting parents of University of Arizona students, and as such they're often booked up in mid-May for graduation and in October for parents weekend. Staying downtown or around the university is a good idea for anybody visiting Tucson; the neighborhoods all meld together, and they represent the only pedestrian-friendly districts in town. Staying in any of the places listed here will put you right in the center of the action on all fronts.

CATALINA PARK INN $$
309 E. 1st St., 520/792-4541, 800/792-4885, www.catalinaparkinn.com
The Catalina Park Inn ($139–169 d) in the West University historic district was built in 1927 and has beautiful mixed gardens with many native plants in a private, peaceful walled courtyard. There are six rooms, two of which are detached from the main house and open onto the lush courtyard. This inn is close to the UA, downtown, and midtown. Breakfast here is always an elegant, gourmet affair, and wireless Internet throughout the property makes it a great place for combining business and pleasure. Each individually decorated room has a private bath, cable television, a stereo with an iPod dock, big thick bathrobes, and more. Since the inn is popular with parents visiting their kids at the nearby University of Arizona, in mid-May, during graduation, and in early October, for parents weekend, they require a

three-night minimum stay and raise the rates on their rooms by about $120–130 (double occupancy) per night. This is true during Gem Show (first two weeks in Feb.) as well. The inn is closed June 15–September 25.

EL PRESIDIO INN BED AND BREAKFAST $$
297 N. Main Ave., 520/623-6151
The beautiful El Presidio Inn Bed and Breakfast in the Julius Kruttschnitt House, built in 1886 and remodeled over the years in various architectural styles, is one of the city's best small inns. It's located in "Snob Hollow" in the historic El Presidio neighborhood, on the same block where Tucson's wealthy pioneers used to live in their big mansions. The inn has one of the finest garden courtyards I've ever seen; it's so cool and lush that you may not get out of the inn to see the rest of Tucson. The inn has four rooms ($120, $130, and $150), two of which—the Carriage House and the Gate House—open onto the courtyard and have kitchenettes. The two small rooms inside the house have private baths. They only allow kids over 13 years old, and they don't allow pets or smoking. A two-nights minimum stay is required October–May.

HOTEL ARIZONA $
181 W. Broadway Blvd., 520/624-8711, www.thehotelarizona.com
A 301-room hotel right in the middle of

The Hotel Arizona is conveniently located downtown.

downtown just off I-10, Hotel Arizona ($89–119 d) is popular with business travelers and the convention crowd. This is really an ideal place to stay if you're in town for sightseeing, hiking, or excursions outside of Tucson, as it's centrally located and easily accessible to the main thoroughfares and the interstate. The average room is small but clean with a desk, a two-line phone, free wireless Internet, and a TV; bigger suite-style rooms (and access to a VIP lounge) are also available. The on-site Coyote Café and Bistro serves breakfast, lunch, dinner, and room service from a menu of American favorites with a hint of Southwestern spice. There's a heated outdoor pool and a comfortable, easy-going bar with a big-screen TV.

HOTEL CONGRESS ⑤
311 E. Congress St., 800/722-8848,
www.hotelcongress.com

Hotel Congress ($79–99 d, about $10 less in summer beginning at the end of May,) built in 1919, is listed on the National Register of Historic Places. Though the rooms are a bit creaky, the beds are comfortable and the historic atmosphere more than makes up for the lack of sumptuous amenities (plus, it's the best value in town if you seek personality in your sleeping quarters). There is noise some nights coming from the Club Congress downstairs—it's not too bad, but there is a slight thumping that comes through the walls. The club is a venue for alternative bands and alt-country bands from across the nation, and the Tap Room bar will make you feel like a cowboy on his day off. The Cup Café off the beautiful old lobby has an eclectic mix of gourmet and Southwestern-style food for breakfast, lunch, and dinner.

ROADRUNNER HOSTEL AND INN ⑤
346 E. 12th St., 520/628-4709, cell 520/940-7280,
www.roadrunnerhostelinn.com

The only hostel in Tucson, the Roadrunner (a block south of Broadway Blvd. downtown) is a clean and homey place to stay and offers the single best accommodations deal in the town ($20 for dorm, $40 for private room). They provide free linens and blankets, showers,

THE NIGHT THEY CAUGHT THE DILLINGER GANG AT THE HOTEL CONGRESS

A hotel fire, a fireman with a good memory and a taste for lurid reading matter, and the hubris of a gang of outlaws all conspired over a few days in 1934 to bring down Public Enemy Number One John Dillinger right here in the Old Pueblo.

On January 21, 1934, two members of outlaw John Dillinger's gang pulled into Tucson with their molls at their sides, meaning to meet up over the next several days with their notorious leader and lay low for a while in the relative warmth of the Sonoran Desert winter.

According to writer and former Tucson police officer Stan Benjamin, the gang wanted to rent a small house downtown, but the landlady had just waxed the floors and wouldn't let them move in until the next day. So they booked a few rooms at the Hotel Congress, built in 1919 to serve passengers on the Southern Pacific Railroad – its depot was right across the street.

Dillinger and his moll, Evelyn "Billie" Frechette, wouldn't arrive in town until a few days later, but by then the small Tucson police force already had suspicions about the gang's advance party, and it was these suspicions that would lead to Dillinger's arrest.

As Benjamin writes in an article that is so far the definitive work on the locally famous incident, "Without A Shot Fired: The 1934 Capture of the Dillinger Gang in Tucson" (a reprint of which is available at the Hotel Congress for $5), early in the morning of January 22, a fire broke out in the Hotel Congress's basement, and the three-story hotel had to be evacuated. A few of Tucson's friendly firemen helped the members of Dillinger's gang and their girlfriends down from a third-story room, and even returned to the smoky rooms to rescue the gang's luggage, which they later said was "very heavy" (eventually they found out that the bags contained several guns and over $20,000 in cash). At least the outlaws gave the firemen a $12 tip.

Unfortunately for the cocky bank robbers, however, those same firemen were, a few hours later, reading a copy of *True Detective Magazine,* in which they saw a "wanted" shot of the very men they'd helped out of the hotel. Once the police got wind of this, and after a separate tip from some businessmen who the

outlaws had tried to impress at a local bar the night before, the police began watching the gang's movements, which eventually led to Dillinger's capture at a rented house a few miles from the hotel.

If you want to learn more details about the capture beyond what Benjamin's fascinating article explains, check out the Arizona Historical Society Museum Downtown, which has an excellent display on the incident. Every year in January, the Hotel Congress and other venues host Dillinger Days, a celebration of 1930s popular culture and of Tucson's brief brush with national law-enforcement fame.

Dillinger wouldn't stay captured for long, but neither would he stay alive for long. After his capture in Tucson he was sent to jail in Indiana to await trial for murder. He had escaped from custody by March of 1934, and continued robbing banks with the gang until a shootout with the FBI sent him deep underground. In July of 1934, just about six months after his capture in Tucson, Dillinger was famously shot down by federal agents outside the Biograph Theater in Chicago.

Built in 1919, the Hotel Congress is still one of the most popular hangouts in Tucson.

HOTELS

laundry ($1 per load), and a large kitchen for guests to use. The four private rooms are small and a bit spare but for the money they are perfect; the three dorm rooms (one for just guys, one for women, and one that's co-ed) each sleep six on the usual bunk beds. They offer two computers hooked up to the Internet for guest use, plus free wireless throughout the place. There's a shady backyard patio for morning lounging with complimentary coffee or tea, and a living room with a big TV and lots of VHS and DVD movies to watch. They don't accept credit cards.

ROYAL ELIZABETH BED AND BREAKFAST INN 💲💲
204 S. Scott Ave., 877/670-9022, www.royalelizabeth.com

The Royal Elizabeth Bed and Breakfast Inn is in a beautiful home known as the Blenman House, built in 1878 in Tucson's El Presidio district. It's now on the National Register of Historic Places. There are six large rooms to choose from, all elegantly decorated in an Old World style, with big beds and footed standalone bathtubs. There's also a heated pool and spa and immaculate grounds. Rates run $155–285 a night for double occupancy, with a two-night minimum on weekends.

TUCSON MARRIOTT UNIVERSITY PARK 💲💲
80 E. 2nd St., 520/792-4100, www.marriott.com

This high-rise chain hotel ($169–365 d) is situated within a few steps of the University of Arizona, close to the Main Gate district with its dozens of shops, bars, and restaurants, and with easy access to both downtown and midtown. There are nine floors, and anything above, say, floor three affords 360-degree views of the valley and the mountains. The 233 rooms are nice enough, each with a large television, desk, sitting area, wet bar, and a big comfy bed; there are 17 suites if you need more room. Free wireless Internet is offered throughout, and there's an outdoor heated pool, a fitness center, a whirlpool, and more. It will cost you at least $11 per day to park here.

Midtown
Map 2

Midtown is a sprawling, rather amorphous district, but pretty much wherever you stay here you'll be near some kind of big strip mall or shopping plaza with restaurants, chain stores, and supermarkets. Staying in midtown is a good idea if you're looking for mid-range and affordable options, and it's where families with small children should look first.

🅲 ARIZONA INN 💲💲
2200 E. Elm St., 520/325-1541, www.arizonainn.com

This historic boutique hotel on a residential street in central midtown, founded in the 1930s by Arizona's first-ever congresswoman and still owned and operated by the same family, is the best place to stay in Tucson—as long as you have fairly deep pockets ($329–579 d; $195–309 d during the summer). They offer several different kinds of rooms, all

the 1930s-era Arizona Inn

© TIM HULL

HOTELS

© TIM HULL

The Arizona Inn features 14 acres of gardens in the heart of midtown Tucson.

of them decorated in the inimitable 1930s Southwestern-chic style. The standard room has wireless Internet, a king-size bed, and a television and DVD player, while the larger suites have patios, dry bars, and sitting areas. But you probably won't be spending a lot of time in the room, as the grounds and lobby have so much charm to offer—there's a 60-foot pool, old-school tennis court, and all kinds of quiet little corners in the verdant retreat-like setting behind the high pink walls.

DOUBLETREE HOTEL AT REID PARK ⑤⑤
445 S. Alvernon Way, 520/881-4200, www.doubletree1.hilton.com

This popular midtown chain (at Broadway and Alvernon just east of Reid Park) is centrally located and close to the golf courses, bike paths, and zoo at Reid Park. It has a huge enclosed courtyard with a very nice outdoor pool. Many of the 295 rooms ($119–139 d) have balconies that look out on the central courtyard, and they all have free high-speed wireless Internet and big plasma TVs. There are two restaurants

on-site—the Southwestern bar and grill called the Javelina Cantina, with a nice courtyard for chilling out with a margarita, and a steak house. This 14-acre hotel also has a fitness room, a whirlpool, and tennis courts. Pets are allowed. Rates go as low as $79 per night in the summer.

EMBASSY SUITES ⑤
5335 E. Broadway Blvd., 520/745-2700, www.embassysuites1.hilton.com

This big chain-hotel compound at the Williams Center in east midtown (Broadway and Craycroft) is perfect for families. Each of the spacious suites ($139–159 d) has two rooms and two TVs, and has the option of having up to three beds. Every night the friendly staff passes out free drinks and popcorn during the Manager's Reception, and in the morning you can order up a complimentary big breakfast (no mere muffin and coffee here). They've got a great pool and the lobby and lounge are decorated in an upscale, tasteful Southwestern style with big leather couches that you can just sink into. In summer the rates plummet and you can get a

HOTELS

suite for $109 or even lower. Check the website for all kinds of seasonal and themed deals.

FOUR POINTS BY SHERATON TUCSON UNIVERSITY PLAZA $$

1900 E. Speedway Blvd., 520/327-7341

A 150-room high-rise chain at the corner of Speedway and Campbell, the Four Points is within easy walking distance of the University of Arizona and as such is popular with visiting students and parents. It has a big heated outdoor pool, and the upper floors afford long looks at the desert and the mountains. The rooms ($113–157 d, less in the summer) are basic but clean; some of them have kitchens and many have balconies. There's free Internet access (though you have to ask for it) and cable TV, a decent American restaurant on-site, a bar, and a fitness room. There's no smoking allowed.

LODGE ON THE DESERT $$

306 N. Alvernon Way, 520/325-3366,
www.lodgeonthedesert.com

The Lodge on the Desert ($65–370 d) has changed hands and is undergoing a major $15 million expansion and renovation that isn't expected to be finished until at least mid-summer 2009. In March 2009 the manager said that they still have "more than half of the rooms" to finish, but added that guests aren't usually subjected to too much construction noise. The hotel's new lobby and restaurant are open, and they are beautiful, as are the hacienda-style rooms offering free wireless Internet, comfortable beds, and big cushy bathrobes. The grounds are green and private, and the patio lounge is one of the best in the city.

SAM HUGHES INN BED AND BREAKFAST $$

2020 E. 7th St., 520/861-2191, www.samhughesinn.com

A charming Spanish-revival bed-and-breakfast in midtown's quiet, tree-lined San Hughes neighborhood, this inn is within walking distance of the University of Arizona and is close to downtown. The inn has four distinctively decorated rooms ($90–130 d) that offer free wireless Internet and private bathrooms; the large rooms have refrigerators and televisions. The enclosed courtyard out back is something to see—green and cool and perfect for relaxing and watching the sun dip behind the towering mountains.

© TIM HULL

Four Points by Sheraton Tucson University Plaza is located near the University of Arizona.

The Foothills

Map 3

You're not likely to find a cheap room in this neighborhood, but you will find some of the world's most exclusive resorts. Visitors and émigrés have sought healing in Southern Arizona since at least the early 19th century. Any tubercular patient lucky enough to flee the crowded, disease-ridden tenements of the Northeast or the malarial bottomlands of the South was invariably advised to seek the high and dry air of the Southwest. The medicine of the 19th-century being what it was, physicians had little else but this general, somewhat specious advice to offer the scores of Americans who suffered from TB, fevers, dysentery, and other ailments of the chest and the blood.

Scholar Billy Jones, in his book *Health-Seekers in the Southwest 1817–1900,* estimates that some 20–25 percent of those who moved to the Southwest during the great migrations of the 19th and 20th centuries did so hoping to cure some ailment, creating a "Health Frontier" that, in Tucson, resulted in the haphazard construction of vast tent cities on the outskirts of town populated by consumptives and often destitute men and women not long for the world.

Medical science has since cured most of the diseases that once brought sickly travelers to the desert, but that hasn't stopped today's visitors from seeking health of a different breed. Tucson has long rivaled its ritzy northern neighbors Scottsdale and Sedona as a place where the afflicted, both physically and psychically, can find solace—usually very expensive solace.

CANYON RANCH ❸❸❸

8600 E. Rockcliff Rd., 520/749-9000, 800/742-9000, www.canyonranch.com

Perhaps the valley's most famous resort, Canyon Ranch is representative of what the other top resorts offer. Here you can not only pamper yourself silly with spa treatments (an activity sure to lead to optimum, albeit temporary, good health), but then it's off to appointments with a staff nutritionist, chiropractor, acupuncturist, and internist. A personal trainer will work with

you on keeping in shape long-term, while a meditation class will help you get in tune with your spirituality. After one of your three gourmet (but healthy) meals a day, you can attend lectures and classes on various topics in healthful living. For an experience so meaningful, it's not surprising that you're going to have to spend accordingly. A minimum three-night stay at Canyon Ranch is going to set you back $2,600–5,020 per person depending on accommodations. That's all-inclusive, however: For that price you get three gourmet meals a day, spa treatments galore, consultations with all the medical professionals on staff, and unlimited activities. The high season at Canyon Ranch is September 23–June 7, after which, as it is with all Tucson's resorts, prices drop rather dramatically.

◖ HACIENDA DEL SOL GUEST RANCH RESORT ❸❸❸

5601 N. Hacienda del Sol Rd., 520/299-1501, 800/728-6514, www.haciendadelsol.com

Founded in 1929 and displaying the elegant Spanish colonial architecture of a more

entrance to Hacienda del Sol Guest Ranch Resort

Celebrities such as Katharine Hepburn used to frequent the Hacienda del Sol Guest Ranch Resort.

© TIM HULL

civilized age, Hacienda del Sol gets my vote for the best foothills resort—not because it's the most inclusive or ritzy, but because it reflects more than any other local accommodations (save perhaps the Arizona Inn) the beauty and rustic-chic of the high-style Southwest of yesteryear. Each of the rooms ($109–515 d depending on the season) is distinctive, with custom-made furniture and a story all its own. The small, comparatively inexpensive Historic Rooms look out on the enchanting courtyard, with an inviting outdoor pool and hot tub. Like its younger foothills neighbors, this resort has a full-service spa, an excellent New American restaurant, a wonderful patio bar, riding stables, and more.

LA SIESTA MOTEL $

1602 N. Oracle Rd., 520/624-1192,
www.lasiestatucson.com

The Miracle Mile area, near Oracle Road, was the place to stay in Tucson during the golden age of the American motor court. The neighborhood fell into a bit of disrepute once the interstate took over (and it is still a bit of a sketchy neighborhood, though the city has long-term plans for revitalization), and few visitors venture to this part of the city anymore. That's changing a bit, however. The owners of this refurbished retro-motor court ($65–125 d) purchased the property about three years ago and have kept all the road-movie details while putting a modern scrub on the whole place. They call it a "slice of Americana." They rent out 13 rooms, some with kings, some with queens, others with kitchenettes. The most expensive room is the suite, with two bathrooms and a kitchen and even a private back patio. You have to make a reservation—no walk-ins. This is really one of the better deals in town, and the owners are friendly and seem to be committed to making this neighborhood a unique part of Tucson once again.

LOEWS VENTANA CANYON RESORT $$$

7000 N. Resort Dr., 520/299-2020, 800/234-5117,
www.loewshotels.com/hotels/tucson

One of the best things about this resort is its view—anywhere you stand on the grounds you get a long, clear look beyond the sweeping golf course off to the valley below. With a fabulous restaurant, a top-notch spa, tennis courts, hiking trails, and one of the most scenic golf courses in the Southwest, it's no wonder this world-renowned hotel and spa ($345–495 d depending on the season) was rated number 31 of the top 100 golf resorts in the nation by *Condé Nast Traveler.* The resort also has a popular star-gazing program and a desert setting you won't soon forget.

THE WESTIN LA PALOMA RESORT & SPA 💲💲💲
800 E. Sunrise Dr., 800/937-8461, www.westinlapalomaresort.com

Guests of this resort and hotel along Sunrise Drive in the foothills are allowed to use the facilities of the nearby country club, which has a 27-hole Jack Nicklaus–designed golf course. The rooms here ($199–319 d, $109–159 d in summer) are spacious and have private patios looking out over the desert, huge sink-in beds, wireless Internet, and some have fireplaces and sunken spa tubs. The nearby Elizabeth Arden Red Door Spa will pamper you silly after you play a few sets on one of 10 championship tennis courts. There are also indoor racquetball courts, a huge pool area, pilates and yoga studios, and an exercise room. Janos, one of the best restaurants in the state, is on-site.

WESTWARD LOOK RESORT 💲💲💲
245 E. Ina Rd., 520/297-1151, 800/722-2500, www.westwardlook.com

First built as a private home in 1912, this hacienda-style resort has Southwestern charm to spare. Though it has been built up and remodeled over time (including a multimillion-dollar facelift in 2008), the older, adobe portions still have the exposed vigas made from wood brought down from Mount Lemmon. The 241 guest rooms and suites ($139–339 d) have wireless Internet and plasma TVs and all the usual high-end luxuries, and the resort offers horseback riding, tennis, spa treatments, and 80 acres of desert foothills grounds with nature trails, stargazing programs, and exhibits about the desert's natural history and native peoples.

HOTELS

© TIM HULL

La Siesta Motel is a refurbished old motor court along the once tourist-friendly Oracle Road.

© TIM HULL

Loews Ventana Canyon Resort is one of the city's most popular high-end resorts.

WINDMILL INN $$$$

4250 N. Campbell, 520/577-0007,
http://windmillinns.com/tuc.htm

This small chain hotel at St. Philip's Plaza, at Campbell and River, is one of the few non-resort places to stay in the foothills. The rooms ($111–239 d) are fantastic, with a mini-fridge, wet bar, and cable TV, free wireless Internet, and continental breakfast. There's an exercise room, a heated outdoor pool and whirlpool, and bikes available for guests to use. The rooms are gathered around a poolside enclosed courtyard that feels private and serene even at this very busy intersection.

RETREATS FOR THE SOUL

If you're looking for a few days of quiet, spiritual contemplation, there are several monasteries and retreat centers in Southern Arizona to choose from.

The **Redemptorist Renewal Center** (7101 W. Picture Rocks Rd., 520/744-3400, www.desert renewal.org), about 12 miles west of downtown Tucson near Saguaro National Park West, offers personal retreats on their 120-acre campus in the foothills of the Tucson Mountains. For 40 years the Redemptorists, followers of St. Alphonsus Liguori, an 18th-century spiritualist who founded the Congregation of the Most Holy Redeemer, have offered personal retreats at this beautiful center. The center offers miles of hiking trails, a tranquil desert setting, and even petroglyphs left behind by the Hohokam Indians. According to the friendly, welcoming Redemptorists, "it is a place where a person may listen to the voice of God." Private retreats are offered here throughout the year. There are two seasons: In the low season, June–September and throughout December, a standard retreat home will cost you $80 per night for a single and $125 for a double; during the high season, January–May and October–November, prices go up just a bit, to $95 for a single and $125 for a double. They also offer many themed retreats and group activities. During both seasons there's a two-night minimum.

About 50 miles southeast of Tucson, in the lush San Pedro River Valley, the Benedictines at the **Holy Trinity Monastery** (760/433-1701, www.holytrinitymonastery.org) in St. David, a very green and shady historically Mormon village, welcomes retreatants and even RVers. The monastery's 132 acres have sheep, chickens, cows, pecan trees, a 1.3-mile bird sanctuary trail along the San Pedro, and lots of peace and quiet. For $50–80 a night, a married couple can rent one of 11 rooms on the property; or singles can stay in the Hermitage, where there's a suggested donation of $70 for one day, $300 for a week, or $1,250 for a month – if you've really got some issues to work through or a lifetime's worth of stress to slough off. The rooms here are small and private with very few frills and no television or radio. Meals are also available: The main meal of the day is $9 per person, or you can get three a day for $20. Sunday meals cost $12 and feast-day meals cost $15. Prepare for a quiet, prayerful, contemplative time: "In keeping with the tradition of monastic hospitality, guest house facilities are offered for monastic retreats," the Benedictines say. "All retreatants, coming either singly or in a group, are expected to participate in the monastic exercises of silence, solitude, simple living, community, and personal prayer." Holy Trinity may be one of the few monasteries in the world with an RV park on-site, called the **Monte Cassino RV Park** – its regulars are referred to as the "Holy Hoboes." There are 16 sites with full hookups and 10 with water and electric offered for $20 per night, $120 for a week, and $350 for a month. If you're interested in joining the ranks of the Holy Hoboes, you might want to plan far ahead, as many people return year after year.

Finally, there's the Benedictine **Santa Rita Abbey** (HC 1, Box 929, Sonoita, 520/455-5595, www.santaritabbey.org) near Sonoita, nestled in the foothills of the Santa Rita Mountains. It's about 48 miles from Tucson. You have to make a request to spend a retreat here, by either calling them or writing an email or a letter. The retreat house has a small kitchen and dining room where guests make and eat their own meals.

East Side and the Rincon Valley   Map 4

You'll find several small, secluded bed-and-breakfast-style inns surrounded by wild desert on the far east side, as well as one of the region's original dude ranches. These accommodations are for those who want to surround themselves with rhythms and sounds of the desert.

DESERT DOVE BED AND BREAKFAST ⊙⊙
1707 E. Old Spanish Trail, 520/722-6879, www.desertdovebb.com

The Desert Dove is the perfect place to stay if you want to be surrounded by wild desert, within walking distance of Saguaro National Park East (there's a trail going from the inn to the park). The two-room adobe bed-and-breakfast ($145 Oct.–May, $125 June–Sept.) has the atmosphere of a hand-built desert sanctuary, with a tranquil and shady yard crowded with mature desert vegetation—great for wildlife watching. The rooms are both decorated with antiques and interesting knickknacks and have private entrances and wireless Internet. There are no TVs, and neither kids, nor pets, nor smoking are allowed. Don't stay here unless you're looking for a bit of isolation and quiet—it's a half-hour or so drive to midtown from here. During the high season (Feb.–Mar.), you have to book more than one night.

◖ HACIENDA DEL DESIERTO BED AND BREAKFAST ⊙⊙
11770 E. Rambling Trail, 520/298-1764, www.tucson-bed-breakfast.com

A hiker's and bird-watcher's paradise east of town near Saguaro National Park East, Hacienda del Desierto is a wonderland of hacienda-style details and quiet comfort for anyone looking to escape to the desert for a few days. The four rooms ($124–279 d) are tastefully decorated with Southwestern, Mexican, and Spanish colonial touches, all with private baths, private entrances, and kitchenettes. The courtyard patio here is overflowing with greenery, and there's a private nature trail on the inn's 16 acres where you might be able to see a desert creature or two. TVs, DVD players, and Internet access are available, as are neuromuscular and aromatherapy massages.

HILTON TUCSON EAST ⊙⊙
7600 E. Broadway Blvd., 520/721-5600 www.hilton-tucson-east.com

A large chain hotel with 233 rooms about seven miles east of downtown (Broadway and Prudence), Hilton East is a good choice for business travelers and families with kids. It has wireless Internet, a restaurant and bar with a nice terrace, an exercise room, a heated pool and hot tub, a beautiful atrium lobby, and free parking. They offer a host of different packages (including one that has a pizza delivered to your room), but expect to pay around $143–218 for double occupancy, less in the summer.

TANQUE VERDE RANCH ⊙⊙⊙
14301 E. Speedway Blvd., 520/296-6275, www.tanqueverderanch.com

The dude ranch has been a venerable Southwestern tradition since at least the turn of the 20th century, and few places carry that tradition on with more style and fun than the folks at Tanque Verde Ranch, a historic all-inclusive resort-ranch on the east side. A ranch since 1868, and a dude ranch since 1908, this huge desert property is about a 30-minute drive east from downtown, at the base of the Rincon Mountains, and offers all kinds of Old West–style activities, so many that you likely won't leave the grounds much. It's not cheap; the 76 ranch house–style rooms and suites, many with fireplaces and patios, go for about $275–350 per person, per night. However, that price is all inclusive, and comes with three meals a day, horseback riding, outdoor BBQs, guided mountain biking, and more. There are big indoor and outdoor pools, hiking trails, and children's activities galore, as well as tennis courts and evening entertainment.

HOTELS

West Side and the Tucson Mountains   Map 5

HOTELS

The west side is dominated by the desert. Like the far east side, a stay out here will bring you close to nature, but keep you far from the madding crowd.

CASA TIERRA ADOBE
BED AND BREAKFAST INN $$
11155 W. Calle Pima, 520/578-3058,
www.casatierratucson.com

Take a scenic 30-minute drive west of downtown into the Tucson Mountains and you'll find one of the best small inns around on five beautiful and secluded desert acres. This enchanting hacienda-style inn has three rooms and a two-bedroom suite ($135–325 d depending on the season) and is a perfect place to stay for those wanting the tranquility of the wild desert relatively close to town. The Spanish colonial home is open and airy, with many patios and fountains and little nooks to discover; there's greenery everywhere and all kinds of astonishing little

details that show the owners really wanted to create a special place. Each room has a private bath and a refrigerator, and every morning the hosts serve up a gourmet vegetarian breakfast. There's a two-night minimum here.

JW MARRIOTT STARR PASS
RESORT & SPA $$$
3800 W. Starr Pass Blvd., 520/792-3500,
www.jwmarriottstarrpass.com

A high-end resort and golf club about 15 minutes west of downtown in a beautiful desert setting, Starr Pass has 75 well-appointed guest rooms and 35 suites ($229–519 d depending on the season and amenities), each with wireless Internet, patios, flat-screen TVs and much more. There's a 27-hole Arnold Palmer golf course here, surrounded by the wild desert. Among the resort's amenities are a full-service spa, a gourmet restaurant, a fitness center, and personal trainers on staff.

South Side   Map 6

The accommodations in south side are rather bleak. Unless you want to call the casinos home, or you're here on a quick business trip, think about staying in a different part of the city.

DESERT DIAMOND
HOTEL AND CASINO $$
7350 S. Nogales Hwy., 520/294-7777,
www.desertdiamondcasino.com

The rooms at this hotel and casino ($139–350 d) still have that new-room smell, as the whole complex was completely refurbished in late 2008. Each has a flat-screen TV, free wireless Internet, and a big pillow-top bed. The neighborhood around Desert Diamond is a bit bleak, but there's so much going on inside this adult playground that it hardly matters what the outside looks like. The hotel features a fitness center, a pool, a hot tub, and a convivial fire pit, while guests

have access to several restaurants, including an all-you-can-eat buffet, a coffee bar and a booze bar, a nightclub, and, of course, all the blackjack, poker, and slots you can afford to play.

HOLIDAY INN EXPRESS $
2548 E. Medina Rd., 877/863-4780
There are few if any independent accommodations with character and style in this neighborhood. There are of course half a dozen or more big, faceless chains here geared toward the business traveler; if you're looking to stay in this neighborhood, you'll have to choose one of these. I've found that the Holiday Inn Express chain offers a good value; they've all got comfortable clean beds, free wireless Internet, and a surprisingly well-stocked free breakfast come morning, all for around $75–100 (double occupancy) per night.

Greater Tucson Map 7

The deserts, mountains, and river valleys surrounding Tucson offer several memorable places to stay. None of them are particularly inexpensive, and most are high-end. If you want to be away from the city, or if you are visiting friends, parents, or grandparents in Green Valley, Tubac, or Oro Valley, consider one of the listings below.

Madera Canyon used to be dotted with summer homes and getaway cabins, but beginning in the 1970s the U.S. Forest Service tore them down and converted the treasured ecosystem into a federal recreation area. Now only a scattered few homes remain on historic mining claims. Three of the lasting structures are lodges that welcome visitors year-round.

AMADO TERRITORY INN ⑤⑤

3001 E. Frontage Rd., Amado, 520/398-8684, www.amado-territory-inn.com

A quaint little bed-and-breakfast inn ($130–250 d) along I-19 between Green Valley and Tubac (about 40 minutes south of Tucson), the Amado Territory Inn has rooms and suites with flat-screen TVs and refrigerators, as well as an art-filled lobby, tasteful decorating throughout, and fragrant, peaceful gardens. They offer some spa services, and even have a few rooms with whirlpool tubs. There are several restaurants near by, and it's close to the shopping and galleries in Tubac (plus there are a few galleries on-site) and the bird-watching and hiking of the Santa Ritas.

CHUPAROSA INN ⑤⑤

1300 Madera Canyon Rd., Madera Canyon, 520/393-7370, www.chuparosainn.com

The Chuparosa has three excellent modern rooms ($150–175 d), each with a big comfy bed, a kitchenette, and a private entrance. The inn has a lush on-site bird-watching area where hummingbirds hang out, hovering together around the many feeders set up around the grounds. There's a barbecue that the guests are allowed to use, and they serve a hearty continental breakfast, but you're on your own for lunch and dinner. This is probably the nicest place to stay in the canyon, and the hosts are experts on the canyon and can direct you to all the best trails and bird-watching areas. Kids are not allowed.

ESPLENDOR RESORT ⑤⑤

1069 Camino Caralampi, Rio Rico, 520/281-1901, www.esplendor-resort.com

About 50 miles south of Tucson along I-19, just north of Nogales and the border region, Esplendor sits on a hill overlooking the drylands below. It has a wonderful setting, a golf course, and basic rooms ($129–209 d) that are comfortable and clean. The pool area is magnificent, with comfy couches and lots of shade and friendly staff that will bring you rum and cokes poolside. The decor is all Spanish colonial—including the dresses worn by the waitresses in the dining room, which serves pretty good breakfasts. This is a fine resort, and it's a good option if you're going to be spending a lot of time along the border or in nearby Tubac or Green Valley.

HILTON TUCSON EL CONQUISTADOR GOLF & TENNIS RESORT ⑤⑤⑤

10000 N. Oracle Rd., 520/544-5000, www.hiltonelconquistador.com

About a half-hour drive north from Tucson, El Conquistador is a storied resort hotel nestled in the west-side foothills of the Santa Catalina Mountains (where they say bighorn sheep used to roam; don't miss seeing the huge life-like statue of a ram, an homage to what has been lost, out in front of this high-end resort). It's like its own city, and if you stay here ($209–518 d, $159–398 d in summer, lots of packages and deals offered year-round) you might not get into town proper for all the lazing around poolside you'll be doing. They offer amenities and services on par with the other top resorts in town, with 428 guest rooms and suites, a full-service spa, a 45-hole desertland golf course, a

Hilton Tucson El Conquistador Golf & Tennis Resort

water park with a 143-foot waterslide that the kids will freak over, 31 lighted tennis courts, five restaurants, horseback riding, and pretty much whatever else your pampered heart desires.

THE INN AT SAN IGNACIO $$

1861 W. Demetrie Loop, Green Valley, 520/393-5700, www.innatsanignacio.com

Green Valley is a quiet, largely age-restricted retirement haven with about 20,000 year-round residents, half a dozen golf courses, and a commanding view of the mighty Santa Rita Mountains a few miles to the east, where bird-watchers from all over the world go to complete their life lists. There are several lodges in Madera Canyon, about a 15-minute drive from Green Valley and the most popular spot in the range, but you have to either bring your own food or drive down the mountain every night for dinner if you choose one of those places. An alternative is this quiet inn ($129–169 d) near a golf course in Green Valley, which offers suites with kitchenettes, TVs, Internet, and private patios with views of the mountains. If you're a couple with split priorities—one loves golf, the other loves bird-watching and hiking—you'll both be happy here.

MADERA KUBO $

1259 S. Madera Canyon Rd., Madera Canyon, 520/625-2908, www.maderakubo.com

The A-frame Madera Kubo has four cozy cabins ($95) and a gift shop, but no food. The cabins are decorated with handmade furniture and a country aesthetic, and the hosts are a friendly family that has lived in the canyon for decades. The place has a slightly junky look when you first drive up, but once you look a little closer it reveals itself to be charming and lived in. You'll likely be sharing your stay with a few bird-watchers, who flock to the canyon from around the world.

MIRAVAL RESORT & SPA $$$

5000 E. Via Estancia Miraval, Catalina, 520/825-4000, 800/232-3969, www.miravalresorts.com

I know a young woman who spent three days

and nights at Miraval—a favorite spot of no less an authority on living life to the fullest than Oprah Winfrey—and when she returned to the real world she said that henceforth her life would be divided into just two chapters: before Miraval and after Miraval. For what you pay ($798–1,300 d minimum, probably more with added activities and such), one should be able to expect some sort of life-changing experience. This world-famous resort, on 400 acres backed by the Santa Catalinas, has 118 rooms, a full-service (and then some) spa, a whirlpool, sauna, Olympic-size lap pool, a full gym, an obstacle course, climbing wall, yoga and pilates centers, and much more. The rooms are very nice, but with all there is to do here you don't spend much time inside; still, most of the casita-style accommodations have TVs, DVD players, wireless Internet, and more.

SANTA RITA LODGE **$**

1218 S. Madera Canyon Rd., Madera Canyon, 520/625-8746, www.santaritalodge.com

This quaint mountain lodge offers several casitas and freestanding cabins with private decks ($95–115 d). The lodge, the oldest in the canyon, has beautiful grounds along Madera Creek and attracts birds with feeders and provides benches for viewing. There's also a gift shop, but no food, so bring your own or plan to eat in Green Valley, about 12 miles away. March through May the lodge can fix you up with an experienced birding guide by appointment. Tours start early and last about four hours ($20 pp).

TUBAC GOLF RESORT **$$$**

1 Otero Rd., Tubac, 520/398-2211, www.tubacgolfresort.com

This sprawling historic hacienda-style upscale resort ($140–265 d) has a popular lush golf course lined with casitas and rooms of various sizes and styles, two restaurants, a pool, hot tub, and other amenities. Over the last several years the resort has been going through a $40 million restoration. Check the website for great package deals; prices drop considerably in summer. It's a luxurious, elegant place to stay about 45 minutes from Tucson south on I-19 and within easy distance of the shops and galleries at Tubac and the trails of the Tumacácori Highlands and the Santa Rita Mountains.

TUBAC INN **$**

12 Burruel St., Tubac, 520/398-3178, www.tubaccountryinn.com

The artist's village of Tubac—the first settlement in what was to become Arizona—has all the shopping and art that enthusiasts of those activities could possibly want, and this tasteful, friendly bed-and-breakfast is right in the middle of it all. The small inn ($90–175 d depending on the season) is situated right in the heart of the village and offers suites with kitchenettes, TVs, and wireless Internet. Breakfast is served in a basket at your door every morning. Smoking is not allowed, nor are kids under 13 years old, nor pets of any age.

WHITE STALLION RANCH **$$**

9251 W. Twin Peaks Rd., 520/977-2624, www.whitestallion.com

This historic 3,000-acre dude ranch about a 30-minute drive northwest of downtown Tucson is one of several places in Southern Arizona where you can discover your inner cowpoke. It's in a gorgeous location at the base of the jagged Tucson Mountains and close to Saguaro National Park West. There are 41 guest rooms, many of them multiroom suites that are perfect for big families or friends traveling together, all decorated in that familiar Mexico-influenced ranch-house style. As it is with other dude ranches, the prices here are high but all inclusive. Expect to pay about $127–905 per person, per day, depending on the season and which room you choose; but that price includes three meals daily, horseback riding, various ranch activities, and even a ride to and from the airport.

HOTELS

EXCURSIONS FROM TUCSON

Just a few hours of scenic off-interstate driving east and south of Tucson, small historic mining towns, forested sky-island mountain ranges, underground fantasy worlds still being formed by slowly dripping water, a secret landscape where rocks stand to attention, and a bustling, colorful, exotic borderland await discovery.

Even if you're only in town for a week or so, set aside one or two days to explore both Cochise County to the east and Santa Cruz County to the south. Both counties straddle the U.S.-Mexico border and are still willfully haunted by the violent past of the old territory, and both are rather sparsely populated, dotted with a few old-timer ranches still scraping along, and even more mass-produced pueblo-revival and hacienda-style high-dollar dream homes owned by baby-boomer runaways. The

spirit and culture of Mexico pervades the towns of southeastern Arizona, but so does the crafty hippie ethos of the artists, artisans, and burnouts that have transformed once-moribund mining towns like Bisbee into tourist-friendly attractions. The legendary West of the imagination (along with a bit of real history as well) is on display in Tombstone; and the actual West, the one ruled by capitalists and their hard-rock-mining minions, is illuminated by headlamp-light on a tour deep underground. Also underground, Kartchner Caverns State Park, just an hour or so outside the city, beckons daytrippers to explore its otherworldly dripping-water innards, and its swirling colors and odd, thrilling mineral formations are nearly as memorable as the sweeping grassland deserts and high, isolated mountain ranges all around.

HIGHLIGHTS

LOOK FOR TO FIND RECOMMENDED EXCURSIONS.

Best Time Spent Underground: Enter the otherworldly caves at **Kartchner Caverns State Park,** which are still being formed by slowly dripping water and are home to bats and hanging multicolored formations (page 202).

Best Sweeping View of the Border-lands: Along the U.S.-Mexico border at **Coronado National Memorial** you can stand on a scenic overlook with expansive, wind-swept views of the San Pedro and San Rafael Valleys, all the way to Mexico (page 204).

Best Day Trip Turned Overnighter: Explore **Bisbee,** a quaint old mining boom-town that's now an enclave for artists, antiques shops, and several boutique hotels (page 207).

Best Native American Museum: Discover Native American cultures from pre-history all the way to the Chiricahua Apache and beyond at the **Amerind Foundation Museum,** one of the finest private ethnological collections in the nation (page 220).

Best Photo Opportunity in Southern Arizona: Make sure to get a photo of the magnificent forest of hoodoos and twisted rock high in the evergreen mountains at **Chiricahua National Monument** (page 220).

EXCURSIONS

© TIM HULL

Bisbee

PLANNING YOUR TIME

Any of the excursions suggested here can be done as a leisurely day trip from Tucson, leaving after breakfast and returning in late afternoon. A major part of any of these day trips is the drive itself, and it's best to avoid the interstate and take the scenic two-lane backroads. If you want to spend a few days exploring southeastern Arizona, hiking along the San Pedro

River or in the Huachuca Mountains, I'd suggest staying in Bisbee, where you'll find some of the best historic hotels and bed-and-breakfasts in the state, and making excursions from there. A trip to the Chiricahua Mountains from Tucson is definitely an all-day trip, and you really need to spend at least two days to truly enjoy this wonderful place. It's a long, empty drive to the Chiricahua National Monument,

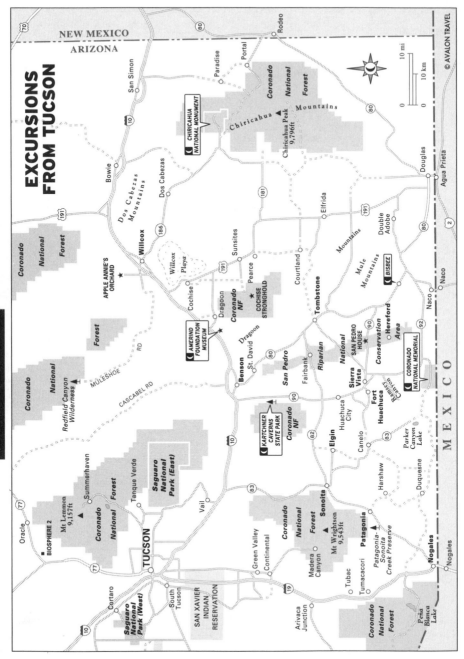

EXCURSIONS FROM TUCSON

© AVALON TRAVEL

EXCURSIONS

Set aside at least two days to explore the Chiricahua National Monument.

but at the end of it is one of the most spectacular sights this side of the Grand Canyon.

Let's say you only have one full day for excursions. In that case, head to Kartchner Caverns (1 hour from downtown Tucson) and Bisbee, taking the scenic route. It's a good idea to call ahead and reserve tickets to the caverns, though it's not as important to do so these days at it once was. Leave after breakfast, have lunch in Bisbee before heading to the caverns, and you'll be back in the Old Pueblo by dinner time, unless you fall in hopeless love with the off-kilter hillside town.

If you're headed down to Nogales and across the border, I'd recommend doing so around lunch or dinner time, as eating at one of the restaurants in the tourist district in Nogales, Mexico, is one of the joys to be had across the line. If you're across the line after dark, be careful. It's easy to get caught up in the scene—downing margaritas with lunch, then tequila shots, then some guy you don't know comes up from behind and in broken English offers to take you to a strip club…Remember that you've got an hour or so worth of driving north on I-19 to make it back to Tucson.

EXCURSIONS

Kartchner Caverns and the Huachuca Mountains

The Kartchner Caverns are still alive, forming slow and steady over eons as water drips and falls into a secret world beneath the Whetstone Mountains, about 40 miles east of Tucson. The State of Arizona spent 11 years and more than $30 million developing Kartchner Caverns State Park, and it shows. It's really one of the must-sees of a visit to Southern Arizona. The Huachuca Mountains, rising high above the charmless military town of Sierra Vista, home to a U.S. Army intelligence center, offer sky island forests, cool mountain hiking trails, subtropical birds found few other places in the nation, and some of the longest, clearest views of the borderlands you'll find. Ranging in elevation from 3,934 feet at the base to 9,455 feet at the top of Miller Peak, the Huachucas are another of Southern Arizona's signature sky island ranges. You'll see the common transition from semidesert grasslands at the base, up into arid scrub, onto mixed oak forests, and all the way up to cool ponderosa pine forests in the higher reaches. There are dozens of trails in the range, and labyrinths of dirt roads that lead deep into the outback.

Both of these areas can be visited as day trips, or even half-day trips, from Tucson, but if you want to spend some time hiking and exploring the mountains, there are a few excellent bed-and-breakfast-style inns nearby. The restaurant scene here is rather bleak, with the usual interstate-side chains and sprawlville corporate eateries (especially in Sierra Vista). I'd recommend bringing along food with you in the car, especially if you're going to be driving around the dirt backroads in the Huachucas or hiking at the Ramsey Canyon Preserve (and even if you're just going to the caverns).

SIGHTS
☾ Kartchner Caverns State Park

Kartchner Caverns (Hwy. 90, Benson, 520/586-2283 for reservations, 520/586-4100 for information, www.azstateparks. com, daily 7:30 A.M.–6 P.M., free w/tour reservation, $5/vehicle up to two people, $2 each additional person over 14) were discovered in the early 1970s by two cave-loving University of Arizona students. Gary Tenen and Randy Tufts knew right away that they had shimmied down a sinkhole in the Whetstone Mountains into caving immortality, as the small but "wet" cave—meaning that it is still forming drip by drip, in a very real sense "alive"—is one of the most spectacular water-on-rock formations of its kind. And yet the explorers managed to keep their find a secret for several years in an effort to protect it from cavers less responsible than themselves. They called it Xanadu, after the great English poet Samuel Taylor Coleridge's famous unfinished poem *Kubla Kahn,* a name given to the Throne Room's 58-foot main column, formed not so much by drips but by torrents of water flowing into

THE FIRST WORK OF SOUTHWESTERN LITERATURE

The impenetrable northern reaches of the Spanish Empire in Mexico were essentially unexplored by Europeans when Álvar Núñez Cabeza de Vaca found himself shipwrecked and lost in the grasslands and deserts of what is now the Southwestern United States and northern Mexico in the 1520s. And though he and his companions – one of them, Esteban, was a Moorish slave or indentured servant – probably never made it to Arizona proper, the tales they told of their adventures when they finally returned to civilization inspired subsequent discoveries in the great north.

In 1539 Fray Marcos de Niza and Esteban trekked north to discover the Seven Cities of Cíbola, rumors of which Esteban and Cabeza de Vaca had heard during their ordeal. Esteban scouted ahead and was eventually killed by the Indians, who lived not in golden cities but in regular old mesa-top pueblos not too different from those that still exist on Hopi reservations in Arizona and in the Rio Grande Valley of New Mexico. Nevertheless, de Niza's report suggested that the golden cities may indeed be a reality, and that was enough to inspire an ambitious expedition in 1540 led by Francisco Vasquez de Coronado in search of the reported riches. Coronado found none, but his expedition moved through what is now eastern Arizona.

Later in his life, after his return, **Cabeza de Vaca** wrote an account of his travails and journeys called *Adventures in the Unknown Interior of America,* which many consider to be the first work of Southwestern literature.

the cave over millennia, and the largest cave column in Arizona.

Eventually Tenen and Tufts told the property owners what they'd found, and the Kartchner family quickly joined those who wanted to see the cave preserved. A pre-tour film in the park's Discovery Center tells the whole story and explains what makes this cave so unique. There's also an interesting museum and a gift shop; just outside the Discovery Center a native-plant butterfly garden is worth a stroll.

There are two different tours you can take though the caverns. The **Big Room Tour** (1.5 hrs, $23 adult, $13 age 7–13, no children under 7) is offered only October 15–April 15—during the summer months a large colony of bats returns to the Big Room, as they have likely done for eons, to give birth to and rear their single pups. The **Rotunda/Throne Room Tour** (1.5 hrs, $19 adult, $10 age 7–13) is offered year-round and is more than enough to satisfy even the most discerning spelunker.

Because the cave is still "alive," much is made of its conservation. Visitors are warned repeatedly not to touch any of the formations, and guides are not shy about telling kids to stand back and keep their hands to themselves. The tour information is very repetitive if you've just watched the pre-tour movie.

If a tour of the cave isn't enough, the park offers campsites with electric hookups, water, a dump station, and restrooms with showers ($22).

Fort Huachuca and Sierra Vista

Much of the war against the Chiricahua Apaches was fought from Fort Huachuca, founded in 1877 in a canyon that had historically served as an escape route for one of the Southwest's final hold-out tribes. Currently the fort is a major center for military intelligence training; its stories, past and present, are told at two museums here. The main gate to get into the base of the fort is at Fry Boulevard and Highway 90 in Sierra Vista. Once you're let on the base, the guards will direct you to Building 41401, which houses the museums. The **Fort Huachuca Museum** (520/533-5736, Mon.–Fri. 9 A.M.–4 P.M., Sat.–Sun. 1–4 P.M., $2 suggested donation) has exhibits about army life on the Southwestern frontier, the famous battles with the Chiricahua Apaches, and the Buffalo Soldiers—African American cavalrymen whose story is one of the most fascinating of the West. The **U.S. Army Intelligence Museum** (520/533-5736,

Mon.–Fri. 9 A.M.–4 P.M., Sat.–Sun. 1–4 P.M., $2 suggested donation) tells the 200-year story of the army's underrated intelligence corps. Since September 11, 2001, foreign nationals have not been allowed on the base, even if they are just there to see the museums.

Sitting at the base of the Huachuca Mountains, the military town of Sierra Vista is the largest town in the valley and the fort's host, but has little charm in and of itself. There are a lot of chain hotels and restaurants, and it's close to the southern end of the San Pedro River. It makes a good base if you're planning on spending some quality time in the mountains, but otherwise it's just a drive-through.

Ramsey Canyon

You'll pass the Cornado National Forest Ranger Station as you head up to the 300-acre Ramsey Canyon Preserve, an easily accessible stream-influenced canyon protected by the **Nature Conservancy** (27 Ramsey Canyon Rd., 520/378-2785, www.nature.org, Mar.–Oct. daily 8 A.M.–5 P.M., Nov.–Feb. daily 9 A.M.–4 P.M.). This is a very popular area with bird-watchers, who come to see the more than 14 species of hummingbird and other avian species that stop over in the cool riparian canyon, fed by babbling Ramsey Creek, protected by high canyon walls, and crowded with sycamores, maples, and columbines.

The upper part of the canyon is within the **Miller Peak Wilderness Area.** Make sure you stop at the Nature Conservancy's excellent visitors center, which has maps, trail guides, books, T-shirts, and helpful, friendly volunteers. It's a good idea to get there early; this area is very popular and the parking lot only has 23 spaces—first-come, first-served.

To reach the preserve, take Ramsey Canyon Road west from Highway 92 south of Sierra Vista (6 miles south of Fry Blvd.); the preserve is at the end of the road, four miles west of the highway.

Also along Ramsey Canyon Road, before you reach the preserve, you'll find the **Arizona Folklore Preserve,** a quaint little theater along the creek where Arizona State Balladeer and

© TIM HULL

view of the borderlands from Coronado National Memorial

nationally known folky Dolan Ellis puts on acoustic folk concerts on Saturday and Sunday at 2 P.M. The shows are popular, so call ahead (520/378-6165, www.arizonafolklore.com) for a reservation.

◖ Coronado National Memorial

Named in honor of Spanish conquistador Francisco Vásquez de Coronado, who trudged north in 1540 searching for the Seven Cities of Cíbola—which turned out to be nothing more than a few hardscrabble pueblos—this beautiful landscape along the U.S.-Mexico border, on the southern end of the Huachuca Mountains, has a **visitors center** (Coronado Memorial Rd., 5 miles from Hwy. 92, 520/366-5515, www.nps.gov/coro, daily 9 A.M.–5 P.M.) with exhibits about its namesake, local history, and natural history. Three miles west of the visitors center is a scenic overlook at Montezuma Pass, with expansive views of the San Pedro and San Rafael Valleys and Mexico. You can have a picnic here and hike around on a number of trails leading to and from the lookout, but there's no camping allowed. To get there,

go south on Highway 92 about 20 miles to South Coronado Memorial Drive, then it's five miles to the visitors center. (At the visitors center you can purchase a map of the Huachucas with all the trails on it for $5.)

San Pedro Riparian National Conservation Area

This 58,000-acre preserve protects some 40 miles of the upper San Pedro River between St. David and the border. There are about 400 species of birds here, 82 mammal species, and 45 reptile and amphibian species, some of which you're likely to see if you stay vigilant and quiet while exploring. Beavers, once plentiful in the now nearly extinct riparian habitats of Southern Arizona, have been reintroduced here. The Friends of the San Pedro River have converted a 1930s-era ranch house—in the shade of a beautiful 120-year-old Fremont cottonwood tree—into the **San Pedro House** gift shop and bookstore (9800 Hwy. 90, 520/508-4445, daily 9:30 A.M.–4:30 P.M.), where you can pick up information and pamphlets for a self-guided river walk and other trails and get advice from the volunteers. Here you'll also find the **Murray Springs Clovis Site and Trail,** a kind of stone-age butcher shop frequented by Clovis people 8,000–11,000 years ago. Scientists have dug up the fossils of several huge extinct mammals here, some of which are currently housed at the Museum of Natural History in New York.

RESTAURANTS

There is not an impressive restaurant selection near Kartchner Caverns and in Sierra Vista, but there is one little place that is worth recommending, and it has a bit of an interesting history related to the nearby caverns. The **Horseshoe Café** (154 E. 4th St., Benson, 520/586-3303, daily 11 A.M.–9 P.M., $5–15) serves pretty good steaks, burgers, and Mexican favorites—including big, sloppy and tasty burritos. It's been around for something like 70 years and is right on Benson's main drag; it's decorated with all kinds of portraits of horses and a few antiques, but I can see how some people might consider it a borderline dive. At any

---

THE WESTERN DESERT

Southwest of Tucson, the vast desert homeland of the Tohono O'odham Indians stretches out, a hot wasteland where few dare to venture. You can reach this 4,400-square-mile borderland reservation via Highway 286 west of Tucson, but there isn't much out there except gorgeous, mostly untouched desert. Straddling the border, the reservation is a popular, albeit deadly, corridor for illegal immigrants heading north, and dozens die crossing the reservation every year – only the O'odham know how to live out here.

About 90 minutes west of Tucson along Highways 86 and 386 (follow the signs), you'll find another of Southern Arizona's famous observatories. **Kitt Peak National Observatory** (520/318-8726, www.noao.edu, daily 9 A.M.-3:45 P.M., $2 suggested donation) operates 23 telescopes – the world's largest collection – atop the 6,875-foot peak in the reservation's Quinlan Mountains. Docent-led tours are available at 10 A.M., 11:30 A.M., and 1:30 P.M. and last about an hour ($4 adult, $2.50 child 6-12), or you can pick up a pamphlet and take a self-guided tour. The visitors center has exhibits on astronomy and a gift shop selling star- and planet-related items and O'odham baskets. Far off to the west look for 7,700-foot Baboquivari Peak, the home of I'itoi, the tribe's sacred "elder brother" god.

The reservation capital, Sells, is a small outpost about 58 miles southwest of Tucson on Highway 86. There's a supermarket, a few businesses, offices, and a school. During the first weekend in February O'odham cowboys join in the All Indian Rodeo and Fair, during which locals set up food booths, play music, march in a parade, dance, and show off and sell their crafts. Continue through the thick desert west on Highway 86 and you'll ride into Ajo, a copper mining community with a few restaurants and a good place to see the scars that strip mining leaves open on the land.

South of Ajo on Highway 85, past the tiny town of Why, you'll find **Organ Pipe Cactus National Monument.** This rugged, beautiful monument along the border protects what amounts to pretty much all of the Organ Pipe cacti in North America, along with many other species of cactus, and is a popular area for seeing spring wildflowers in bloom. It has in the past been named one of the most dangerous national monuments in the country, as the area is a major drug-smuggling corridor, but it is safe to visit. Just make sure to lock your car and don't stray off the well-traveled park roads. The Kris Eggle Visitor Center (520/387-6849), named for a ranger who was killed during a shootout with drug smugglers, is open daily 8 A.M.-5 P.M. A campground with 208 sites has drinking water but no hookups or facilities ($12 per night). The 21-mile Ajo Mountain Drive, on a twisty dirt road that's usually passable, will take you into the monument's center, where you can see the goofy, many-armed cacti up close.

EXCURSIONS

rate, the food is filling and tastes good. Author Neil Miller, in his recent history of the caverns, reports that during the many years that Gary Tenen and Randy Tufts kept their discovery a secret, every time they would visit their secret cave they'd invariably stop at the Horseshoe for a bite to eat before returning to Tucson. For some reason, nobody in the restaurant seemed to think it was strange that the two spelunkers always came in covered in mud.

HOTELS

The riverside **Casa de San Pedro** (8933 S. Yellow Lane, Hereford, 520/366-1300, 888/257-2050, www.bedandbirds.com, $149–175 d) is a territorial-style home with a central courtyard, a pool, hot tub, and all kinds of activities geared toward bird-watchers and nature lovers. **Ramsey Canyon Inn** (29 Ramsey Canyon Rd., Hereford, 520/378-3010, www.ramseycanyoninn.com, $130–150 d) just outside the Ramsey Canyon Preserve, has six rooms named for hummingbird species, delicious breakfasts, and a setting that can't be beat.

PRACTICALITIES

If you're looking to put together a backpacking or camping adventure in the Huachuca range, talk to the staff at the **Coronado National Forest Sierra Vista Ranger District** (5990 S. Hwy. 92, Hereford, 520/378-0311). The **Benson Tourist Center at the Railway Depot** (249 E. 4th St., 520/586-2842) has a lot of local information, including historical displays and guides to the area's lesser-known sights.

Getting There and Around

There are a few different routes you can take to Kartchner Caverns and the Huachuca Mountains, but there's really only one way to get there: by car. Every now and again you might see a skinny bearded man pedaling slowly along the highway, weighted down with packs and bags, but the vast majority of day-trippers take their own car—or their own motorcycle, typically a late-model, possibly rented Harley piloted by a gray-haired retiree who was born to be wild but didn't know it until just a few months ago.

The easiest way to get to the caverns is to take I-10 east of Tucson to the Highway 90 exit, then head south on Highway 90 until you see the entrance to the park. From the park to the mountains, take Highway 90 south into Sierra Vista, then head for the hills. For a longer, more scenic route, take I-10 east to the Highway 83 exit, then follow 83 south through the grasslands on the east side of the Santa Rita Mountains. Turn east on Highway 82, then north or south on Highway 90, depending on whether you're headed for the caves or the peaks.

Bisbee and Tombstone

Tombstone, the sight of the most famous 30-second gunfight in history, calls itself the "town too tough to die," but it is really Bisbee that deserves that distinction. Bisbee's huge open-pit copper mine flourished for a few generations, and after it closed the quaint little town found new life among artists, writers, and countercultural escapists, while still maintaining its role as a county seat and government center. Today, Bisbee is actually growing, and there always seem to be new restaurants and stores opening in the quaint structures of Old Town.

Tombstone's mining boom—and it was mining, not cardsharps, gunfighters, and vigilantes, that put the town on the map—lasted only about seven years, from 1880 to 1887 give or take. These days Tombstone is a tourist trap, nothing more and nothing less.

Both former mining centers followed a similar economic cycle, however. Their impressive mineral wealth may have been found first by intrepid lone-wolf hard-rock miners, but the industry was very soon taken over by Eastern conglomerates owned by fat-cat "capitalists,"

© TIM HULL

Motorcyclists take to Southern Arizona's backroads every sunny weekend.

as that species was called back then (by a group that included the territory's then governor), and the hills were denuded of their ore by broken-backed miners making about $4 a day. That was until the corporations couldn't make the mines pay anymore, owing mostly to flooding, so they packed off and went looking for another place to dig and blast, leaving the town and laid-off workers to fend for themselves. And fend for themselves they both have done, inviting tourists from all over the globe to discover their unique charms.

BISBEE

The most charming town in Cochise County began life in the 1880s as a copper mining camp. Eventually several billion pounds of the useful ore would be taken out of the ground here, and by 1910 Bisbee was said to be the biggest city between the Midwest and West Coast.

Flooding in the 1,000-foot-deep tunnels and the boom and bust nature of the mining economy closed the mines by the 1970s, and

the town, with its labyrinthine staircases and cozy little bungalows built precariously on the slopes of the Mule Mountains, was nearly moribund when it was discovered by hippies, artists, and artisans, a group that funkified the town into what it is today. Retired miners, retirees from elsewhere, county government workers, and sons and daughters of the pioneers also call Bisbee home. **Old Town** (where you'll likely spend most, if not all, your time) is stuffed full of shops, galleries, restaurants, historic landmarks, and some of the best old hotels in the state. Perhaps the most fun to be had in Bisbee comes from just walking around, climbing the scores of off-kilter steps and exploring its back alleys and narrow streets.

Sights

Driving in on Highway 80, just after the intersection with Highway 92, you can stop at a turnout along the side of the road and witness the **Lavender Pit Mine** and the huge tailings surrounding the largest open-pit mine in the state, now closed. Bisbee is still proud of

EXCURSIONS

Bisbee, the most charming town in Cochise County, started as a copper-mining camp.

its history as the queen of all mining towns, and you can learn all about it at the **Bisbee Mining and Historical Museum** (Copper Queen Plaza, junction of Main St. and Brewery Gulch, 520/432-7071, www.bisbeemuseum. org, daily 10 A.M.–4 P.M., $4 adult, $1 child 4–16), housed in the building formerly occupied by the headquarters of the Copper Queen Consolidated Mining Company. Now an affiliate of the Smithsonian Institution, the museum has exhibits on local history and culture during territorial days, with an emphasis on the history and science of copper mining. You can see for yourself what it was like descending into the earth every day to coax the ore out of the mountain on the 75-minute **Queen Mine Tour** (478 N. Dart Rd., 520/432-2071, 866/432-2071, www.cityofbisbee.com/queenminetours, daily 9 A.M., 10:30 A.M., noon, 2 P.M., 3:30 P.M., $12 adult, $5 child 4–15). Retired miners lead these tours and will regale you with stories of what it was really like underground, as you ride deep beneath the earth on an old mine car, wearing a yellow slicker,

a hard hat, and a headlamp. It's about 47 degrees in the shaft, so think about taking something warm to wear. If you don't want to go under, consider going over—on the 90-minute, 11-mile **Surface Tour** (departs from the Queen Mine Tour office daily at 10:30 A.M., noon, 2 P.M., 3:30 P.M., $10), which takes you through the historic district and shows you the open pit while you sit back in a comfortable van.

Restaurants

Café Roka (35 Main St., 520/432-5153, www. caferoka.com, Wed.–Sat. 5–9 P.M., $14–24) has some of the best Italian food around with a tasteful, elegant multilevel interior. **Winchester's** (11 Howell Ave., 520/432-1910, daily 7 A.M.–10:30 A.M., 11 A.M.–2:30 P.M., and 5:30–9 P.M., $9–23) at the Copper Queen Hotel serves delicious American food and other dishes. The best breakfast in town can be found at the **Bisbee Breakfast Club** (75 Erie St., 520/432-5885, www.bisbeebreakfastclub.com, Mon. 7 A.M.–noon, Thurs.–Sun.

© TIM HULL

It's worth the wait for a table at the Bisbee Breakfast Club.

7 A.M.–2 P.M., $10 and under), serving huge American-style breakfasts, along with a bit of Mexican spice of course, in a refurbished old building on the largely abandoned historic block next to the huge pit. You might have to wait to get a table, but the food is worth it.

Shops

Old Town Bisbee has dozens of unique shops, and there always seem to be new ones opening. There are jewelry stores; shops selling local art and Mexican folk art; a book store (**Atalanta's Music & Books,** 38 Main St., 520/432-9976, daily 10 A.M.–6 P.M.) with a huge selection of mostly used tomes and some new, including a large section of books by local authors; a shop that sells only things made out of copper; and several multilevel antiques and junk shops that you can get lost in for hours.

Hotels and RV Parks

There are all manner of accommodations in Bisbee, and bed-and-breakfasts proliferate along the narrow, twisty roads of Old Town. The **Bisbee Grand Hotel** (61 Main St., 520/432-5900, 800/421-1909, www.bisbeegrandhotel.net, $79–175 d) is in a Victorian building in Old Town. It offers small well-decorated rooms with private baths, and a full breakfast served on the veranda. It has wireless Internet, and a saloon downstairs frequented by tourists and locals. The **The Copper Queen Hotel** (11 Howell Ave., 520/432-2216, www.copperqueen.com, $114–176 d) is an institution in Bisbee, built in 1902 and still in beautiful shape—but almost certainly haunted, as anyone in Bisbee will tell you. It has a pool, a saloon, and a restaurant.

For a truly unique experience, rent one of the 1950s vintage trailers at **Shady Dell RV Park** (1 Old Douglas Rd., 520/432-3567, www.theshadydell.com, $45–145 d), each beautifully refurbished and decorated. Many have polished chrome and wood interiors, and include black-and-white TVs and phonographs complete with 45-rpm singles from the era. Located on the premises is **Dot's Diner** (520/432-1112, $10 and under), a ready-made 10-stool diner from the 1950s where you can get great food daily 7 A.M.–2:30 P.M.

TOMBSTONE

Just outside the green and lush Mormon village of St. David, Highway 80 rises onto the dry scrubby plane where Ed Schieffelin struck silver in 1879, defying the soldiers who'd predicted he'd find only his own tombstone out there. The town of the same name became one of the largest, rowdiest, and deceptively sophisticated locales in the Southwest for a time, a place where legends were created daily by overheated newspapermen, and where a 30-second gunfight of dubious legality became a defining frontier myth. These days, about 1,600 residents still call Tombstone home, many of them retirees or people working in some capacity for the town's tourism industry, which attracts visitors, many of them from Europe, year-round.

Sights
BOOTHILL GRAVEYARD
Reportedly, many of Tombstone's gunfighters,

along with their victims, lay alongside prostitutes, settlers, and obscure passers-through in this hilltop graveyard (daily 7:30 A.M.–6 P.M., donations welcome). You can walk among the more than 300 uniformly bland and refurbished graves, and read short messages on some of them that illuminate what death was like on the frontier. It doesn't feel authentic in the least, despite claims to the contrary, but it is free. Boothill is just off Highway 80 at the north of end of town.

ALLEN STREET AND NATIONAL HISTORIC DISTRICT
In danger of losing the federal funding that accompanies National Historic Landmark status (legend in Tombstone has a tendency to trample true history for tourists' sake), the Tombstone city council in 2006 covered Allen Street with dirt to make visiting the town a more "authentic" experience. Closed to cars and lined with wood-plank sidewalks, Western kitsch shops, and even a few genuine historical attractions, Allen Street *is* Tombstone to most. There are several saloons and restaurants here, and faux-gunfighters and saloon girls (some of them with somewhat anachronistic tattoos) mill about next to the working stagecoach replicas of **Old Tombstone Historical Tours** (520/457-3018, $10 adult, $5 child).

The National Historic District includes several streets off of Allen, including Toughnut Street to the west, Freemont Street to the north, and 6th Street to the south.

Within this historic district you'll find the ***Tombstone Epitaph* Museum** (5th St., daily 9:30 A.M.–5 P.M., free), where you can see the original press used to print the perfectly named *Epitaph* newspaper, first published in 1880 and still going, and other printing-related exhibits. The **OK Corral and Historama** (Allen St., 520/457-3456, www.ok-corral.com, daily 9 A.M.–5 P.M., $7.50 with gunfight, $5.50 without) has all the information you'll need on the famous, albeit short, gunfight between the Earps and Clantons. You can see a rather tired and dusty historical reenactment of the fight, and watch a show narrated by Vincent Price, on the major events in Tombstone history.

Among the saloons in the district, the **Crystal Palace Saloon** and **Big Nose Kate's Saloon** are worth a look, with Kate's being a fine place to kick back a few and look at all the pictures on the walls if you have the time. Both are on Allen Street. One of the best sights on Allen is the **Bird Cage Theatre** (Allen and 6th Sts., 520/457-3421, daily 8 A.M.–6 P.M., $6 adult, $5 child 8–18), an 1881 dance hall, brothel, saloon, theater, and casino that has been spectacularly preserved. A self-guided

© TIM HULL

OK Corral and Historama

tour takes you through the building, which looks much as it did when it closed in 1889. On Freemont and 6th Streets, the **Tombstone Western Heritage Museum** (520/457-3800, Mon.–Sat. 9 A.M.–5 P.M., Sun. 12:30–5 P.M., $5 adult, $3 child 8–18) has may relics of Tombstone's past, including a few personal items once owned by the Earps.

TOMBSTONE COURTHOUSE STATE HISTORIC PARK

A more sober treatment of Tombstone's history is presented inside this preserved 1882 courthouse on 3rd and Toughnut Streets (520/457-3311, daily 8 A.M.–5 P.M., $4 adult, $1 child 7–13). The museum features artifacts, pictures, and ephemera from the territorial days, and there's a rebuilt gallows in the building's courtyard. Particularly interesting are the two nearly forensic accounts of the gunfight, each with slightly differing details.

ROSE TREE INN MUSEUM

Planted way back in 1885, this Lady Banksia, sent all the way from Scotland to Tombstone as a gift, is believed to be the world's largest rose tree at 8,700 square feet—it is listed in *Guinness World Records* as such. The white blossoms are usually at their best in early April. The small museum exhibits photos and furniture owned by the tree's planter, who moved to the territory in 1880 (4th and Toughnut Sts., daily 9 A.M.–5 P.M., $3).

Restaurants

Nellie Cashman Restaurant (5th and Toughnut Sts., 520/457-2212, daily 7:30 A.M.–9:30 P.M.) has good American food, and the **Lamplight Room** (198 N. 4th St., 520/457-3716, Fri.–Mon. 11:30 A.M.–8 P.M., Sun. 11:30 A.M.–7 P.M.) serves Mexican and American food for breakfast, lunch, and dinner daily. There are several eateries within the historic district, most of them serving cowboy- and Southwestern-style food.

Hotels

There are a few easy-to-locate chain hotels in Tombstone, and a variety of bed-and-breakfasts. The **Tombstone Boarding House B&B** (108 N. 4th St., 520/457-3716, 877/225-1319, www.tombstoneboardinghouse.com, $59–89 d) offers comfortable rooms in two adobe houses that date to the 1880s. The **Wild Rose Inn** (101 N. 3rd St., 520/457-3844, 866/457-3844, $79–89 d, $109 with private bath) is in a Victorian home built in the early 1900s.

PRACTICALITIES

The **Bisbee Chamber of Commerce & Visitor Center** (1 Main St., Copper Queen Plaza, Bisbee, 520/432-5421, 866/224-7233, www.bisbeearizona.com, Mon.–Fri. 9 A.M.–5 P.M., Sat.–Sun. 10 A.M.–4 P.M.) is where you'll find brochures on self-guided walking tours and loads of information on what to do and see in town. Parking isn't easy, especially on weekends, so it's a good idea to find a space, stick with it, and explore the town on foot.

In Tombstone, stop by the **Visitor Information Center** (4th and Allen Sts., 520/457-3929, daily 10 A.M.–4 P.M.), for a nearly overwhelming amount of information about the town and its sights. In March, Tombstone celebrates its founder during **Ed Schieffelin Territorial Days.** In April the **Tombstone Rose Tree Festival** shines the light on the record-making rose tree, and in May, Tombstone's most famous citizen gets his own party during **Wyatt Earp Days.** The anniversary of that infamous gunfight warrants a celebration every year in October.

Getting There and Around

The quickest way to get to Bisbee and Tombstone is to take I-10 east from Tucson for about 40 minutes to the exit for Highway 80. Take Highway 80 south through Tombstone, then keep going south until Highway 80 meets Highway 90; take Highway 90 east to Bisbee. For a longer, even more scenic drive, take I-10 east from Tucson and turn south on Highway 83, take Highway 82 east to Tombstone, then go south on 80, pick up 90, and head on into Bisbee.

EXCURSIONS

The Border Region

Any where you are in Cochise or Santa Cruz Counties, you're never more than a few miles from Mexico. Small towns like Bisbee and Douglas each have a Mexican twin right across the line (though they are fraternal twins—the Mexican counterparts are larger and more populous), and traffic between the two generally flows pretty easy. But the easiest, and in a sense the safest, way to visit our neighbors to the south for the day is to walk across the border at the Mariposa Port of Entry in Nogales, Arizona, about an hour south of Tucson on I-19. The Arizona side of what locals call Ambos Nogales ("both Nogales") is a somewhat sleepy government and produce-warehousing town with about 25,000 souls, while the sprawling industrial city just across the border teems with more than 500,000 residents.

THE BORDER SITUATION

In February 2009, the U.S. State Department renewed its travel alert for Mexico, particularly the border region. It was the third time in just over a year that the travel alert had been updated (alerts are typically reconsidered and updated every six months), and the move continued a debate among locals and visitors here in the borderlands as to whether the region is safe for American travelers.

"A number of areas along the border are experiencing rapid growth in the rates of many types of crime," the alert says (read the alert, and all the other information the U.S. State Department offers for U.S. travelers in Mexico, at http://travel.state.gov/travel/cis_pa_tw/cis/cis_970.html). "Robberies, homicides, petty thefts, and carjackings have all increased over the last year across Mexico generally, with notable spikes in Tijuana and northern Baja California. Ciudad Juarez, Tijuana and Nogales are among the cities which have recently experienced public shootouts during daylight hours in shopping centers and other public venues," the alert continues. "Criminals have followed and harassed U.S. citizens traveling in their vehicles in border areas including Nuevo Laredo, Matamoros, and Tijuana."

While it's true that there is violence along Arizona's border with Mexico related to drug trafficking and human smuggling, and indeed 2008 and 2009 were particularly bloody years in the larger border cities, including Nogales, Sonora, owing to the Mexican government's crackdown on the drug cartels and power plays among the cartels themselves, it's not typical for tourists to get caught in the middle.

In the tourist blocks of Nogales, Sonora, just beyond the port of entry, the biggest annoyance you are likely to encounter is the constant barking of the hard-selling shopkeepers.

"Common-sense precautions such as visiting only legitimate business and tourist areas during daylight hours, and avoiding areas where prostitution and drug dealing might occur, can help ensure that travel to Mexico is safe and enjoyable," the travel alert says – and that's pretty good advice. You may very well be approached by someone while you're strolling around the Nogales tourist district who will offer to take you to a strip club or get you drugs. It's up to you, obviously, but I wouldn't take them up on their offer – that seems a bit like asking for trouble.

There has been a lot of talk recently about Mexico being on the verge of becoming a "failed state." That is certainly an outlandish exaggeration, and one that most Mexican nationals would likely laugh off as gringo paranoia. Still, it's true that the lion's share of the illegal drugs that come into the United States do so over the U.S.-Mexico border in the Southwest. A rather large percentage of these drugs (mostly marijuana, cocaine, and methamphetamine) – not to mention undocumented mi-

Most visitors stick to the tourist-friendly blocks just beyond the port of entry. A good portion of the nation's produce passes through the port of entry in Nogales, Arizona, as does a large amount of illegal drugs.

NOGALES, SONORA

Nogales, Mexico, in the state of Sonora, is a modern factory and produce-shipping center, but it's also a very popular tourist destination. It's easy to get there: Just walk across the international border in downtown Nogales, Arizona,

after parking at one of the many pay lots (about $4 per day) near the port of entry. There's a tourist area of about a square mile just south of the border, with restaurants, curio shops and, if you want, drugstores. You can drive into Mexico, but the lines of cars driving north into the United States are long and slow. If you need a ride there are cabs everywhere and the drivers speak English; they, like everyone else who deals with tourists, take U.S. cash.

In recent years more and more merchants in Nogales's tourist district are competing

---

grants, though that flood has slowed recently along with the U.S. economy – is transported via I-19 from Nogales, to drop-houses in Tucson and Phoenix, from which they are distributed to the rest of the country. Moreover, borderland hikers and wilderness trekkers are likely to see evidence of the drug trade and human

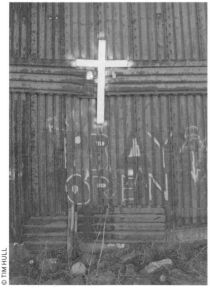
© TIM HULL
"graffiti" on the border fence

migration in the form of trash and blighted landscapes. But it is extremely unlikely that you'll get caught up in the illegal mix unless you willfully put yourself there.

Perhaps the mayor of Nogales, Sonora, Marco Antonio Martinez Dabdoub, said it best when he told the *Arizona Daily Star*, Tucson's leading daily, recently that "We can bet that if [tourists] come [to Nogales] 100 times, there won't be a single act of violence against them."

And before you go believing in all that "failed state" nonsense, consider that it is nearly impossible for a private citizen in Mexico to obtain a gun legally, and that, according to a variety of sources, something more than 90 percent of the gun violence along the border is perpetrated with guns smuggled *into* Mexico from the United States. And then there is also the matter of the supply-and-demand theory upon which our economy was supposedly founded. The demand for illegal drugs and low-wage workers in America is high; it always has been and it probably always will be. If not for the hungry market, would there be suppliers willing to stop at nothing to feed it?

If you find yourself across the border in Nogales and in need of help, contact the **U.S. Consulate** (Calle San Jose, Nogales, Sonora, Mexico tel. 01/631-311-8150, http://nogales. usconsulate.gov).

© TIM HULL

Nogales, Sonora

for fewer and fewer tourist dollars due to the economy, gas prices, and much publicized violence, making a slow, fun stroll along the narrow streets and souvenir-crowded shops an impossibility. Everybody puts on the hard sell these days, and the last time I was in Nogales to buy a bottle or two of Oaxacan mescal I was accosted at every step and begged repeatedly to have a look at this or that shop, all of which contain similar if not identical items. There's lots of leather and silver, Mexican handicrafts, Day of the Dead items, ceramics, Mexican vanilla, and cheap booze, but if you're not willing to deal with the incessant barking of the sometimes desperate merchants, you may want to avoid shopping here. But if you've never been to Mexico, this is an easy and generally safe way to do so. There are *farmacias* on every block, and dentist and doctor offices everywhere, and their services are offered for a fraction of the price of their American counterparts. Most of them have barkers standing outside, calling you to come in and spend your dollars.

Restaurants

The main north–south street is Obregon, two blocks west of the border-crossing station. Popular restaurants include **La Roca,** east of the railroad tracks in downtown; **El Toro,** a steak house about two miles south of the border on Lopez Mateos; and **La Palapa,** a no-frills seafood place about a mile and a half south on Lopez Mateos. **The Oasis** has an outdoor balcony overlooking where two main thoroughfares, Lopez Mateos and Obregon, merge—reminiscent of Times Square, but much smaller. Sit there, enjoy shrimp in a warm cheese sauce, and 7watch the traffic. And yes, you can drink the water, but most restaurants will put a water bottle on your table to encourage you to buy it in a bottle.

NOGALES, ARIZONA

This small town is named, like its cross-border sister, for the walnut trees that once thrived in the area. It has long been Santa Cruz County's seat, and the beautiful old neoclassical shiny-domed **Santa Cruz County Courthouse**

(2150 N. Congress Dr.), built in 1904 out of stone quarried locally, lends it a historic feel that belies the constant comings and goings of a border town. The **Old City Hall** building, built in 1914, now houses the **Pimería Alta Historical Society** (Grand Ave. and Crawford St., 520/287-4621, Wed.–Sun. 10 A.M.–4 P.M.), with several interesting exhibits and artifacts on the history of the region. The town's historic downtown along **Morley Avenue** has a few stores that were established in the early 1900s and are still being run by descendants of pioneer merchants.

Restaurants

With dozens of authentic Mexican restaurants within an easy walk across the border, don't spend too much time eating on the Arizona

HIKING IN THE TUMACÁCORI HIGHLANDS

The Tumacácori Highlands, northwest of Nogales, can best be accessed using exit 12 (Ruby Rd.) off I-19 just north of Nogales. West about 11 miles is **Peña Blanca Lake,** where bass and catfish can be lured in but not eaten because of high mercury content. There's a boat ramp and trail around the lake. Branch off on Forest Road 39 for the **White Rock Campground,** which has sites year-round, but no water ($5). Continue another five miles along Forest Road 39 to the trailhead for the **Atascosa Lookout Trail.** The popular steep trail to the 6,255-foot peak, a six-mile round-trip, takes you to a decommissioned fire lookout which, for a few months in 1968, was manned by writer Edward Abbey.

There's a sign pointing to the trailhead for the **Sycamore Canyon Trail** on Forest Road 39 about 10 miles in from Peña Blanca Lake. This trail leads deep into a watered canyon, with steep walls dotted with saguaro, white sycamore trees, and jagged rocks jutting out from above. It's a five-mile hike one-way to the U.S.-Mexico border, marked by a barbed-wire fence. The trail isn't always well marked, as the creek often overtakes it and you will certainly have to wade in parts. During the rainy season some sections may be impassable. The canyon is a major corridor for drug smuggling, and you are likely to see a lot of trash and other evidence of the trade.

This lush riparian canyon in the Tumacácori Highlands supports a rich array of flora and fauna.

EXCURSIONS

THE BORDERLAND
JAGUAR DETECTION PROJECT

Retired land surveyor and mountain-lion hunter Jack Childs and his wife, retired educator Anna Childs, founded the Borderland Jaguar Detection Project in 2001, several years after they'd become members of the very exclusive group of humans ever to see the roaring jungle cat in the wild. Researchers now believe, based on the work of the Childses and others, that the jaguar reaches the northernmost edge of its vast range in the misty, watered canyons of the neotropical Arizona borderlands.

As the Childses tell it in their book *Ambushed on the Jaguar Trail: Hidden Cameras on the Mexican Border,* the couple first encountered the jaguar while out riding mules in the Baboquivari Mountains, in the late summer of 1996, not really hunting so much as giving their lion hounds a chance to stretch their legs after being cooped up all summer. As hunting hounds will do, the dogs soon picked up a scent and followed it to its natural conclusion. But when the Childs arrived to see what beast the dogs had treed, expecting it to be a cougar, they found instead a spotted male jaguar resting calmly on a limb. Their lives were never the same.

The Childses cobbled together a few grants and donations to eventually begin their ambitious detection project, which is an ongoing and integral part of the efforts of the Arizona–New Mexico Jaguar Conservation Team. The couple, working with a few other researchers, place heat-and-motion-detecting "camera traps" in ideal jaguar habitat throughout the borderlands, and visit them regularly to change film and batteries. The project has been responsible for photographing, many times, two distinct male jaguars – called Macho A and Macho B – who stalk the canyons and mountains just north of the U.S.-Mexico border. The Childses have yet to photograph female jaguars, or to prove that Arizona's jaguars are anything but opportunistic wanderers, perhaps from a well-known resident population of male and female jaguars in the Sonoran wilds about 150 miles south of Douglas.

The Macho sightings have been enough to keep the project going, and that's as it should be. However, as the Childses' book makes clear, the longed-for jaguar is only one of more than 20 other large mammals that appear in the project's photographs – including *Homo sapiens.* Those photos show black bears playing and eating; cougars tussling around like house cats, marking their territory, and hunting; bobcats doing likewise; as well as various raccoons, coatis, skunks, foxes, ringtails, badgers, bovines, and many other borderland creatures doing what they do when we're not watching. These photographs show us a hidden, often nocturnal world of predator and prey, and a bustling dimension of the Arizona backcountry in which our own arbitrary borders have no meaning. The cameras have even photographed at least two species – the Gould's turkey and the Mexican brown-nosed opossum – that were thought to be all but gone from this region.

In a sad postscript to this story, in early 2009 Game and Fish officials out hunting for mountain lions and black bears to tag and collar as part of a large mammal research study came across Macho B and made a quick field decision to collar the jaguar in an effort to learn more about the elusive cats. A few weeks later the radio information sent from the collar suggested that Macho B was sick. Game and Fish veterinarians quickly moved in and discovered that Macho B was in the advance stages of kidney failure. The cat died a short time later while being treated at the Phoenix Zoo. I contacted the Childses shortly after the tragic event to express my sympathy, and this is what Jack had to say: "Macho B has left a great legacy. We will continue our quest for Macho C or maybe even Hema (female) A."

side. If you insist on eating in Arizona, try the steaks and Sonoran-style food at **Las Vigas Steak Ranch** (180 W. Loma St. at Fiesta Market off Arroyo Blvd., 520/287-6641), or the excellent Mexican food at **Cocina La Ley** (226 W. 3rd St., 520/287-4555).

PATAGONIA, SONOITA, AND ELGIN

With an average elevation between 4,000 and 5,000 feet, and average annual rainfall around 20 inches, the grasslands and creek beds of the "Mountain Empire" on the eastern side of the Santa Rita range are much cooler than Tucson, and the landscape is unlike any other in Arizona. The towns here are tiny, but they serve as an increasingly popular tourist spot, and little out-of-the-way inns are plentiful. In Patagonia, the largest town in the area with only about 800 people, there's a yellow train depot in the center of town, built in 1900, and a nearby butterfly garden. A few shops sell unique locally made items and other treasures.

There has been quite a proliferation of bed-and-breakfasts in this area over the last several years. You can find brochures for most of them at **Mariposa Books** (436 Naugle Ave., 520/394-9186), a great bookstore in Patagonia with a tourist information desk.

There are two ways to get to the grassland seas and cottonwood forests of the Mountain Empire, a historic ranching and mining district between the Santa Rita, Patagonia, Mustang, and Huachuca Mountains. If you're coming from the Santa Cruz Valley, take Highway 82 from Nogales 19 miles southeast to Patagonia and then on to Sonoita, where Highway 83 branches off north to I-10. If you're coming from Tucson, take I-10 east to Highway 83.

Patagonia Lake State Park

About seven miles south of Patagonia on Highway 82 is Southern Arizona's largest lake, 2.5-mile-long Patagonia Lake (400 Patagonia Lake Rd., 520/287-6965, daily 8 A.M.–10 P.M.), where you can fish for bass, bluegill, and catfish, and camp, rent a boat, swim, and lay around Boulder Beach, water ski (though not

on weekends), and hike around the 5,000-acre Sonoita Creek State Natural Area. The campground has 72 campsites and 34 hookups ($15 no hookup, $22 w/ water and electric), and there are boat launches, restrooms, showers, a dump station, and a camp supply store. In March crowds head to the park to see the annual Mariachi Festival. From Nogales head 12 miles northeast on Highway 82, then turn left at the sign and drive four miles to the park entrance.

Telles Grottos Shrine

Just southwest of Patagonia along Highway 82, near milepost 15.9, there's a shrine built into the rock face of the mountain. It's worth taking a few minutes to climb the steps and take a peek inside, where there will likely be candles burning and messages written to the dead. The shrine was built in the 1940s by the Telles family, whose matriarch vowed she would construct and keep up the shrine if her five boys returned safely from World War II. They did, and the shrine is still in use today.

There are shrines along roads all over Southern Arizona.

Wine Country

With soil and growing conditions often likened to those in Burgundy, France, the Sonoita-Elgin grasslands are becoming a well-known and well-reviewed wine-making region. It's fun to drive through the open landscape and sample wines, but consider taking along a designated driver.

In Sonoita just east of the crossroads on the east side of Highway 82 is the **Dos Cabezas Wineworks** (3248 Hwy. 82, 520/455-5141), open for tasting Friday–Sunday 10:30 A.M.–4:30 P.M. The tasting room and gift shop at **Sonoita Vineyards** (520/455-5893, www.sonoitavineyards.com), located three miles south of Elgin on the Elgin-Canelo Road, is open daily 10 A.M.–4 P.M. Also along Elgin Road is **Callaghan Vineyards** (336 Elgin Rd., 520/455-5322, www.callaghanvineyards.com), with a tasting room open Friday–Sunday 11 A.M.–3 P.M. The **Village of Elgin Winery** (520/455-9309, www.elginwines.com) has tastings daily 10 A.M.–5 P.M., and the **Rancho Rossa Vinyards** (201 Cattle Ranch Lane, Elgin, 520/455-0700, www.ranchorossa.com) is open Saturday–Sunday 10:30 A.M.–3:30 P.M., as well as Fridays from December to March. In April locals turn out in Elgin for the annual **Blessing of the Vine Festival;** check www.elginwines.com for details.

Patagonia-Sonoita Creek Preserve

The Nature Conservancy protects a Freemont cottonwood/Gooding willow riparian forest—one of the best and last remaining examples of this lush landscape in Arizona—on about 750 acres along perennial Sonoita Creek (520/394-2400, www.nature.org/arizona, Oct. 1–Mar. 31 Wed.–Sun. 7:30 A.M.–4 P.M., Apr. 1–Sept. 30 Wed.–Sun. 6:30 A.M.–4 P.M., $5 pp). This small green paradise has six miles of easy trails leading through the forest, with its 100-foot-tall 130-year-old cottonwoods—the biggest and oldest in the country—and along the creek. The birding here is excellent, and it's not uncommon to see deer, bobcat, toads, and frogs in this verdant preserve. Friendly

Conservancy volunteers lead nature walks every Saturday morning at 9 A.M. This is an extremely rare ecosystem, one that was once abundant in Southern Arizona but now has all but disappeared.

Restaurants

The Velvet Elvis Pizza Co. (292 Naugle Ave., Patagonia, 520/349-2102, Thurs.–Sun. 11:30 A.M.–8:30 P.M.) serves delicious gourmet pizza and has interesting pictures of the King and the Virgin. The **Steak Out Restaurant & Saloon** (3243 Hwy. 83, Sonoita, 520/455-5205, www.azsteakout.com, Mon.–Thurs. 5–9 P.M., Fri. 5–10 P.M., Sat.–Sun. 11 A.M.–10 P.M.) is hard to miss since it is the biggest building in town. They serve delicious steaks and ribs.

Hotels

The **The Sonoita Inn** (3243 Hwy. 82, Sonoita, 520/455-5935, www.sonoitainn.com) at the crossroads of Highway 82 and Highway 83 has 18 rooms with Western ambience, all with great views of the grasslands and mountains. The room rates are seasonal and vary depending on the time of the year. There are several chain hotels in Nogales, Arizona, along Mariposa Road and along Grand Avenue, both major thoroughfares. If you're looking for something special there's the historic **Hacienda Corona de Guevavi** (348 S. River Rd., Nogales, 520/287-6503, www.haciendacorona.com, $189–229 d), a historic inn along the Santa Cruz that once hosted John Wayne and other stars. The inn features murals by Salvador Corona, a famous artist and bullfighter, and offers bed-and-breakfast-style rooms and stand-alone casitas. It has a swimming pool and offers horseback riding, stargazing, and many other activities.

PRACTICALITIES

For visitor information go to the **Nogales-Santa Cruz Chamber of Commerce** (23 W. Kino Park Way, Nogales, 520/287-3685, www.nogaleschamber.com, Mon.–Fri. 9 A.M.–5 P.M.).

Although it's hassle-free to enter Mexico, coming back can present problems if you do not have a passport. American citizens now need a passport—no exceptions. There's a **U.S. Consulate** (Mexico tel. 01/631-311-8150 or 01/631-313-4797, from U.S. 011/52-631-313-4820, Mon.–Fri. 8 A.M.–5 P.M.) in Nogales, Sonora, on Calle San Jose, about five miles south of the border. If you get in trouble on the weekend you'll be stuck until Monday, since a consulate officer checks the Nogales, Mexico jail Monday through Friday only.

Getting There and Around

You need a car to get to Nogales and the border region, but I wouldn't recommend driving into Mexico—it takes too long to get back across the border and there's limited parking around the tourist district anyway. Take I-19 south to Nogales and follow the signs to the port of entry, then park at one of the safe and secure parking lots on the Arizona side (about $4 a day) and walk across. To get to the Mountain Empire, take I-19 to Nogales and then take Highway 82 northwest into the grasslands.

Willcox and the Chiricahua Mountains

These wondrous, storied mountains far east of Tucson, near the New Mexico border, comprise one of the most unique, diverse ranges in the state. Rugged and remote, this area is recommended primarily for its scenic qualities, unless you're a wilderness lover, a hiker, or a camper. The easiest way to see the mountains is to visit Chiricahua National Monument, where you can drive to the top of an overlook and behold an awesome view. On the way, stop off at the Amerind Foundation and learn about the Chiricahua Apache and other Native Americans, and in dusty, dilapidated Willcox you'll find a few quirky reminders of the old Southwest.

Though the former railroad and ranching town of Willcox has seen better days, the canyons, mountains, and grasslands around it are worth the 80-mile drive east on I-10 from Tucson. Willcox today has a few boarded-up buildings and abandoned motels along its main thoroughfare, but its **historic downtown** holds some interest and is worth a mosey. The famous singing cowboy Rex Allen grew up in the area, and a museum and an annual festival honor that fact. Willcox is also known as the place where Wyatt's brother Warren Earp met with a bullet in 1900, and was later buried in the Historic Willcox Cemetery.

SIGHTS
Historic Downtown and Railroad Avenue

This area used to be where life in Willcox happened, and even today it's the most interesting part of town. There's a shady, grassy park with a big bronze statue of native son Rex Allen, and across the street on Railroad Avenue the singing cowboy's life and career are celebrated at the **Rex Allen Arizona Cowboy Museum** (150 N. Railroad Ave., 520/384-4244, daily 10 A.M.–4 P.M., $2 single, $3 couple, $5 family), which also displays a **Cowboy Hall of Fame** honoring area ranchers and cowboys. Just down the sidewalk a bit is the **Willcox Commercial Store,** which claims to be the oldest continually operating store in the state. The **Willcox Rex Allen Theater,** a 1935 art deco movie house, still runs new movies on weekends, and at the end of Railroad Avenue is the **Southern Pacific Depot,** built way back in 1880 and now used by the City of Willcox. The depot's lobby has exhibits on the history of the area and the railroad, and Rex Allen narrates a video played on a loop (Mon.–Fri. 8:30 A.M.–4:30 P.M.) The small town honors their most famous native with **Rex Allen Days** the first week of October every year.

Just around the corner from Railroad Avenue, the **Chiricahua Regional Museum** (127 E.

EXCURSIONS

Maley, 520/384-3971, daily 10 A.M.–4 P.M.) exhibits mining artifacts, weapons used by Native Americans and the cavalry, and rocks and minerals found in the region. There's also an excellent display on the history of the Apaches.

Apple Annie's Orchard

The Sulphur Springs Valley outside of Willcox has the perfect growing conditions for the apple, peach, pear, and Asian pear orchards at Apple Annie's (2081 N. Hardy Rd., Willcox, 520/384-2084, www.appleannies.com, July 3–Oct. 31 daily 8 A.M.–5:30 P.M.). From July to late October every year people flock to the "u-pick" farm to pick and purchase fruit by the bucketful. The farm also serves delicious hamburgers and cowboy beans for lunch, and you can buy all kinds of homemade preserves, sauces, condiments, and pies in the farm store. Take I-10 to exit 340, turn west on Fort Grant Road, and travel five and half miles to the Apple Annie's sign.

A plaque at Cochise Stronghold tells the history of the Apache chief Cochise.

◖ Amerind Foundation Museum

On your way east on I-10 get off at the Dragoon exit (exit 318) to visit this excellent little museum (520/586-3666, www.amerind.org, daily 10 A.M.–4 P.M., June–Sept. closed Mon.–Tues., $4 adult, $3 child 12–18) in beautiful Texas Canyon. Established in 1937, the Amerind Foundation (Amerind is a contraction of American and Indian) preserves and studies Native American cultures from prehistory all the way to the Chiricahua Apache and beyond. It is commonly thought to hold one of the best private ethnological collections in the nation. The museum is fascinating, and the location, among the imposing boulders of Texas Canyon, makes it well worth the stop.

Cochise Stronghold

A bit farther east on I-10, exit 331 takes you to the former hideout of Cochise and his band in the Dragoon Mountains. (Head southeast on Highway 191, then west nine miles on Ironwood Road; the last four miles are on a dirt road.) The great Apache chief is said to be buried somewhere out here, but nobody knows where for sure. It seems an ideal place to hide, with plenty of bluffs from which to watch the plains for the oncoming army. There are a few easy trails at the Stronghold, including a short nature trail and a paved history trail with information about the Chiricahua Apache. A few campsites ($12) are sheltered by the same high boulders that once kept the Chiricahua hidden. If you want to hike deeper into the canyon, try the six-mile round-trip Cochise Stronghold Trail that veers off the nature trail.

◖ Chiricahua National Monument

This place simply has to be seen to be believed. Precarious rock spires jut into the sky in this strange, wonderful landscape, called the "Land of Standing-Up Rocks" by the Apache. About 38 miles southeast of Willcox (120 miles from Tucson) on Highway 186, the National Monument (520/824-3560, www.nps.gov/chir, daily 8 A.M.–4:30 P.M., $5 adult over 16) protects one of the most unique areas in Arizona. There's a visitors center two miles from the

© TIM HULL

The Chiricahua National Monument was named "Land of Standing-Up Rocks" by the Apache.

EXCURSIONS

monument entrance on Bonita Canyon Road, a paved two-lane road that you can drive up six gorgeous miles to **Massai Point** and one of the most spectacular overlooks this side of the Grand Canyon. The visitors center has an excellent free guide with information on all the trails within the monument, their length, and how to find the trailheads, and there's a free hikers shuttle available. You can camp at the Bonita Campground a half mile from the visitors center for $12 per night (no hookups). Bring your own food and water to this special place; there's none available for miles in any direction.

RESTAURANTS

The only town of any size in the area is Willcox, and the fare there is rather bleak. There are a few chains, but it's best to come prepared with your own food to take along in the car. The **Plaza Restaurant** (1190 W. Rex Allen Dr., Willcox, 520/384-3819) serves pretty good family-style American food and other dishes, and **Salsa Fiesta** (1201 W. Rex

Allen Dr., Willcox, 520/384-4233) has decent Mexican food.

HOTELS

There aren't a lot of non-chain places to stay out here, unless you're camping or you have your own rig. Willcox has a few interstate chains that are easy to find, and there are a few bed-and-breakfasts tucked away in the mountains. The bucolic **George Walker House** (2225 W. George Walker Lane, Portal, 520/558-2287, www.thegeorgewalkerhouse.com) in Portal, a small historic settlement in the Chiricahuas, offers wood stoves, wireless Internet, kitchens, and even a stocked fridge. The small inn is open to only one party at a time ($75–189 depending on how many people, up to seven) and is popular with bird-watchers and hikers. They recommend calling at least three months in advance for a reservation.

PRACTICALITIES

For information and advice on getting out into the less-accessible regions of the Chiricahua

© TIM HULL

Portal is a tiny town in the Chiricahua Mountains.

range, contact the **Douglas Ranger District** (1192 W. Saddleview Rd., 520/364-3468, Mon.–Fri. 8 A.M.–4:30 P.M.), 2.2 miles north of Highway 80 on Highway 191 in Douglas.

Getting There and Around

A trip to this area takes to you some fairly remote locals, so I'd recommend, just this once, shooting here as quick as you can along the 75-mile-per-hour I-10. It's an 82-mile drive to Willcox from Tucson, and from there it's another 35 miles to Chiricahua National Monument southeast along Highway 186. Gas up before you leave Willcox, and bring food and water and whatever else you think you might want. All the other sights in this section can be easily accessed off I-10 before you get to Willcox, and are well signed.

BACKGROUND

The Land

The Sonoran Desert is a deceptive landscape. The soft greens and yellows can appear monotonous, yet stop and look closely and they reveal staggering variety. It rains here only rarely, yet during the summer rainy season this arid land is positively lush. Once a year, in the spring, the land bursts with otherwise dormant wildflowers, like a one-night-only command performance. The region is dominated by desert, a flat land stretching out like a vast forgotten sea, yet increase your elevation into one of the region's sky islands and you will be hunting for tropical birds in a misty creek bed among oak and pine, or, if you go high enough, clamping on a pair of skis.

The Sonoran desert is a much more varied desert than others in North America. Southern Arizona, of which Tucson is the largest city by far—really the only metro area of any size—is often referred to by those who study the region's biomes, as the sky islands. The region's "sky island" mountain ranges, some of which reach heights of 10,000 feet above sea level or more, are high, isolated mountains looking out over a sea of arid desert, and as such they support an astonishing variety of plants and animals. It's often said that driving from the desert floor in Tucson, at around 2,000 feet above sea level, to the top of nearby Mount Lemmon, at

© TIM HULL

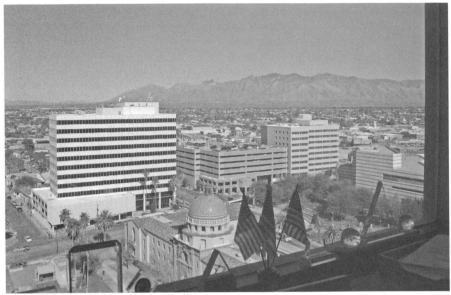

© TIM HULL

Tucson is the nation's 32nd-largest city.

just above 9,000 feet—about an hour's drive—is akin, biologically speaking, to traveling from Mexico to Canada. The region's mountain ranges—the Santa Catalina Mountains north of Tucson; the Santa Rita Mountains to the south, the Rincon Mountains to the east, the Huachuca Mountains to the southeast, and other ranges farther east near the New Mexico border—represent a transitional zone from the colder Rocky Mountains to the more tropical and subtropical Sierra Madre Occidental in Mexico. The mid-ranges of the mountains are dominated by Madrean evergreen woodlands or Mexican oak-pine woodlands. Sometimes the whole region is referred to as the Madrean Archipelago. On the slopes of these mountains, called the "bajada," scrub oak turns into desert trees, such as mesquite and palo verde, and at the base there are sometimes vast semidesert grasslands sweeping across the land.

And in the middle of all this natural diversity and beauty sits Arizona's second-largest city, Tucson, the county seat of Pima County. It's not always necessary to delineate the Tucson metro area from Pima County as a whole; indeed, Tucson is really the primary metropolitan hub for four counties in the southern section of Arizona—Pima County, Cochise County to the southeast, Pinal County to the northwest, and Santa Cruz County to the south.

Created in 1864 around the same time as the Territory of Arizona, Pima County has about 9,184 square miles with elevations that range from 1,200 feet to 9,157 feet on top of Mount Lemmon in the Santa Catalina range, which looms over the northern portion of Tucson and adds significantly to the dramatic, exotic look of the city. Nearly half of the land in Pima County—about 42 percent—is set aside as reservations for the Tohono O'odham, formerly called the Papago, and the Pascua Yaqui, a small tribe of indigenous people that moved north from Mexico seeking refuge from persecution in the early 20th century. As is common in Arizona, a state created by the federal government out of a vast region gathered together under the indefinite rubric of New Mexico, only about 13 percent of the land in

Pima County is privately owned. The rest, aside from the reservations, is either controlled by the state or the federal government. This, combined with the area's diverse natural wonders, is one of the main reasons Tucson has become a favorite spot for wilderness lovers and outdoorspeople.

Pima County has a population of about a million persons, about 530,000 of which live in the city of Tucson, making the Old Pueblo the nation's 32nd-largest city. Spread out and sprawling, Tucson comprises about 192 square miles, and sits at an elevation of 2,389 feet above sea level. The city is connected to the rest of the nation via I-10, and is connected to Mexico, just 60 miles south, by I-19.

CLIMATE

One of the hottest deserts in the world, the Sonoran differs from other arid regions in North America in that it has mild winters. There are only a few nights throughout the year when newscasters come on the air and breathlessly implore Tucsonans to bring their plants inside for fear of an overnight frost. According to the Center for Sonoran Desert Studies, nearly half the flora and fauna in the region are "tropical in origin." One of the defining climate characteristics of Tucson and the surrounding deserts and mountains is the unique bi-seasonal rain pattern. While Tucson typically receives less than 12 inches of rainfall annually—often much less; the region has been gripped by an ongoing drought for at least a decade—nearly all of the region's precipitation comes during just two brief rainy seasons. The most important of these is the summer rainy season, locally referred to as the monsoon, when, from July through to (hopefully) about mid-September, surges of wet, tropical air move up from the south and build over the mountain, creating often violent, localized thunderstorms, mostly in the late afternoon and early evening after a long, hot summer day. The most violent monsoon storms, sometimes called "gully washers" or flash floods, can swell the region's usually dry river beds and washes in a matter of minutes. To say that

IS IT GETTING EVEN HOTTER IN TUCSON?

According to at least one University of Arizona researcher, people have made it hotter in Tucson than it already was – and it was already the hottest desert in North America before we arrived en masse after World War II to begin changing the wilderness into car-centric, fossil fuel-dependent cities and suburbs. UA professor emeritus William Sellers, in a chapter on the state's climate in *Natural Environments of Arizona,* finds that the state's "minimum temperature averaged significantly higher during the 1953-2002 period than it did prior to the early 1940s." This is proof, Sellers writes, of the urban heat island effect, through which nighttime temperatures (which in other less-paved-over deserts tend to drop significantly, offering a cooling respite to the land while the sun is down) stay rather high because the heat is stored in buildings and asphalt. Indeed, Sellers finds that the average minimum temperature in the Phoenix area has increased by nearly seven degrees Fahrenheit since the early 1960s, while the average maximum temperature has gone up only about two degrees Fahrenheit in that time. Apparently we love the heat so much we never want it to cool down. Additionally, Sellers writes, average nighttime temperatures in the state's deserts were significantly lower prior to the 1940s than they are today. Temperatures as low as zero degrees Fahrenheit were recorded along washes in the Tucson area, and in 1937 Tucson's temperatures were below normal every day for a month. "The most likely cause for most of the increase in the average temperature in Arizona since the early 1940s is the rapid expansion in the population and the industrial development that occurred in the area during and following World War II," Sellers concludes.

these storms are "localized" is an understatement. It's a common joke in Tucson—though no less true for being a joke—that, during the monsoon, one can often observe rain falling in one's front yard but not in the back. One side of town can be awash in a flash flood, while a few miles away the sun is beating down clear and unbroken, without a cloud in the sky. The strength and, so to speak, success of the

monsoon can vary greatly from year to year. For example, according to data collected by the National Weather Service in Tucson, in 1964 the monsoon season yielded an amazing 13.84 inches of rain in Tucson; in 2004, however, the area received just 2.42 inches of rain during the same season. The winter rainy season lasts from roughly October to March, and is not as localized, nor as closely watched, as the monsoon.

A DESERT AT RISK

In a June 12, 2008, review in the *New York Review of Books,* physicist Freeman Dyson wrote, "Environmentalism, as a religion of hope and respect for nature, is here to stay. This is a religion we can all share, whether or not we believe that global warming is harmful."

Yet it seems most of us need a local connection and ground-level evidence to spur a lifestyle change. Desert dwellers can turn to the research of Travis Huxman, director of the University of Arizona's Biosphere 2 lab and an associate professor of ecology and evolution-

ary biology, to understand why going green matters. Huxman and his colleagues are using that infamous bubble in the desert north of Tucson to find out how climate change and drought are changing the very desert under our feet.

"Deserts are very sensitive to change; you see big impacts in deserts before you might see them somewhere else," Huxman said during an interview at his campus office. He says that in the desert most of the effects of climate change are reflected in the way soil

© TIM HULL

If winter brings a fair amount of precipitation to the desert, however, then the whole landscape explodes with dormant annual wildflowers, and the normally monotone landscape is transformed into a patchwork of colors.

ENVIRONMENTAL ISSUES

With its delicate and finely balanced biomes and some of the most dramatic and exotic scenery on earth, Arizona has over the generations been a haven, a laboratory, and a rallying point for environmentalists and ecologists. One of the biggest threats to the state's extremely varied ecosystems is growth; much of the desert has been paved over and crowded with homes, while the upland forests host droves of overbuilt homes just waiting for a wildfire to burn them to their foundations. There are no signs

moisture changes, and that he's finding more boom-and-bust soil water characteristics, which means that sometimes there is a lot of moisture and other times there is no moisture at all. This is all leading to a change in the kind of plants we see in the desert.

That means more scrub is growing in the desert, leading to a movement toward a grassland-type system that is dominated by nonnative species. That in turn causes an accelerated fire cycle and changes in biodiversity – changes, Huxman explained, to "the very desert landscape that makes this area so attractive to tourists, and [that lead to] less resilient landscapes for ranching and other uses of the desert." And that includes potentially catastrophic changes to the watershed.

This means that big, representative species of the Sonoran Desert, most notably the mighty saguaro, are living under a very real threat. We could lose the saguaro and other large components of the desert because of fires sparked by invasive grasses, which are spreading as a direct result of global climate change. It's happening in North America's other deserts as well. In the Mojave Desert to the west, the great Joshua tree is similarly threatened, says Huxman.

"I don't have a projection for how long it would take [for the desert to fundamentally change as a result of drought and climate change], but you can hardly drive a freeway through the North American deserts and not see this change and the impact of fire on these landscapes," Huxman says. "It's fairly obvious."

Though a survey of the Sonoran is yet to be done, an assessment of the Great Basin Desert found that some 40 percent of the landscape has been affected by nonnative grasses, leading to a significant change in the character of the desert. In Arizona, such changes are most evident in the high deserts of the state's north-central pine belt. There, the largest ponderosa pine forest in North America is on the verge of total collapse. The conifers are stressed due to drought, and that stress allows bark beetles and other killers to dig in, which in turn leaves this typically fire-resistant species ready to burn. And once they're gone, will they grow back, or has the ecosystem changed irrevocably? But that's not even the biggest problem, according to Huxman. What we don't know yet is how the water cycle will react if a single dominant species like the ponderosa pine is no longer part of the ecosystem. "That's the big research question," Huxman says. "How will all this affect water?...That's our problem on many different scales: How water and energy are related; so the most important thing we can do now is to remember that when we are thinking about energy efficiency, we are also thinking about water efficiency at the same time."

In other words, it's all related. When you turn off the lights, when you use a reusable tote instead of a throwaway bag, when you ride your bike to work, when you change to energy-saving lightbulbs – when you "go green" by making all those small, easy changes that are becoming so popular these days – you are also saving water. And water is one of the very few things that we all will always need.

that this trend is going to let up any time soon, either. The constant influx of people has led over the years to environmental problems far beyond the mere pavement of desert and clearing of forests. Growth and the state's founding impetus to glean profit from the land have led to the overpumping of groundwater and the damming and taming of most of the state's rivers. This has altered the green riverways so completely that many species of native fish are now as good as gone, and nonnative plants line the mostly dry riverbeds, crowding out native riverine flora like cottonwoods and willows.

Climate change, scientists say, is likely to increase the state's environmental woes, and, coupled with an ongoing drought that has been more or less eating away at the state for more than a decade, may lead to shortages on the Colorado River, water from which the vast majority of urban Arizonans, including Tucsonans, depend. Some scientists have recently predicted that Lake Mead may dry up by 2025, while others believe the current human culture in Arizona may, one day in the future, suffer the same collapse as did the Anasazi, the Hohokam, and other complex societies who have tried to make a go of it here, leaving behind the ruins of their rise and fall but not much else.

Flora and Fauna

FLORA
Wildflowers

In the early spring, especially after a rainy winter, the desert bajadas and valleys bloom with color as dormant wildflowers burst back to life. Various shades of photogenic whites, yellows, blues, reds, and purples contrast with the uniform rich green of the well-watered springtime desert to create a truly beautiful but ephemeral scenery. Some of the most common bloomers are the light-purple **Arizona Lupine,** the deep-yellow **Mexican Goldpoppy,** the dark-pink **Parry Pestemon,** and the virginal-white **Desert Lily.** In summer the northland meadows and grasslands bloom with wild color as well.

Trees, Cacti, and Bushes

Below 3,500 feet or so, the Lower Sonoran Life Zone predominates, characterized by **creosote, palo verde,** and **mesquite** trees on the plains and thick stands of various cacti and other dry-adapted plants on the slopes and bajadas. Arizona is the only state where three major deserts converge: The Sonoran stretches across the southern portion of the state and includes the Phoenix and Tucson areas, while the Mojave dominates on the western reaches. The Chihuahuan Desert of Mexico stretches north into southeastern Arizona.

Between 4,500 and about 7,000 feet you're in the Upper Sonoran Life Zone, characterized by scrub oak, piñon pine, juniper, manzanita, and sagebrush grasslands; this zone is often called the chaparral. The midlands of the state, at around 6,000 feet and higher, are marked by the transition zone, and this is where you start to see the beginnings of the vast ponderosa pine forests. Above 8,500 feet or so thick stands of evergreen conifers and white aspen are common. Above 9,500 feet or so, a height reached in Arizona primarily by climbing up towering mountains, the Subalpine Zone has tough Engelmann spruce and bristlecone pine, and above that it's all barren rocks and tundra.

The official Arizona state tree is the palo verde, a green-skinned desert dweller that can grow up to 25 feet high. The tree proliferates throughout the Lower Sonoran Life Zone and is often a close neighbor to the saguaro, the baby buds of which use the palo verde's cover to hide and grow. Other common desert trees are the ubiquitous mesquite, which has often been used for firewood and building, and its beans have nourished people and animals alike. Both the mesquite and the palo verde bloom yellow in the spring. Ironwood trees and drought-resistant evergreens grow along slopes

There are many species of agave growing in Arizona, and some reach the mammoth proportions of this one.

and washes in the desert. Bushy plants crowd the desert as well; creosote is everywhere, as is prickly **catclaw** and **rabbitbrush,** all of which bloom yellow. Adding a little red to the bloom time is the **ocotillo,** which is everywhere in the desert and resembles a sprouting group of pipe cleaners. Throughout the desert and into the chaparral of the transition zones you'll see several species of **agave,** an important plant to the human population in that it can be turned into mescal and tequila. The *Agave parryi,* or **century plant,** blooms only once, with a tall stalk of yellow flowers, before dying.

In the scrublands and chaparral and higher you'll see scrub oak, piñon pine, juniper, manzanita, and other brushy trees. In the high country, above 6,000 feet or so, you'll see ponderosa pine mainly. Higher still, in the montane forests at the highest elevations, fir, spruce and aspen forests dominate. Along many waterways, called riparian areas, are big cottonwoods and willows and sycamores.

FAUNA
Mammals

Arizona's official state mammal is the **ringtail,** a relative of the raccoon often called a Ringtail Cat or a Miner's Cat because of its rodent-eating proclivities. Its huge, bushy white-and-black-ringed tail is its identifying feature, but it's not likely you'll see one unless you're nocturnal. The **mountain lion** or cougar is found, and hunted, throughout the state; smaller **bobcats** are often seen lounging near water features in Sonoran Desert backyards, and scrawny **coyotes** can be spotted quickly crossing highways throughout the state. In the western deserts a few **bighorn sheep** still cling to the dry rocky cliffs.

A few different species of **jackrabbit** can be found all over, and **white-tailed** and **mule deer** live from the bottom of the Grand Canyon to the mountain heights and most places in between. **Pronghorn** live on the high grasslands in herds. The collared peccary, or javelina, is everywhere in the desert and the transition zone, so much so that they are considered pests to some. The **black bear** lives in the mountains throughout the state, and various species of **bats** come out in the Arizona night, responsible for pollinating and continuing the state's signature cactus forests.

Reptiles

The desert is known as the home of the rattler, a snake seen more and more these days as the suburban attack on the desert continues. There are a few species of rattlesnake found in Arizona. The **western diamondback,** which has lent its name to the state's world-champion baseball team, lives in the desert and the mountains and has deadly venom. His snakeskin is gray with brown, diamond-shaped splotches along the back and a series of black and white bands just above his rattle. As with nearly all animals, the diamondback will leave you alone if you afford it the same courtesy. The light-brown **western rattlesnake** lives throughout the state, and the **Arizona ridge-nosed rattlesnake,** a reddish-brown or gray hunter of rodents and lizards, lives in the woodlands of southeastern Arizona.

Several different species of **lizard** can be seen all over the lowlands, doing push-ups on hot rocks. The desert's most recognizable residents, these tiny left-over dinosaurs come in many shapes and sizes. One of the biggest is the fat and venomous **gila monster,** with its beady skin and languid looks. The monster can sometimes be seen sunning itself in and around Tucson. The only venomous lizard in the United States, it should be given a wide berth if encountered.

The slow and wise **desert tortoise** hides out from the desert sun in its burrow, and if it makes it past its soft-shell youth, when it's a favorite of predatory birds, it can live up to a hundred years or more. Frogs and toads in Arizona include the **Arizona treefrog,** a lime-green forest resident, and the **western spadefoot toad,** which lives in the desert in a burrow and is a blotchy greenish brown with gray tints.

Insects

The **bark scorpion** is the crabby, pinching demon of the desert underworld; its venom is dangerous if it finds its way to the blood. The **grand western cicada** makes a racket in the woodlands on summer evenings. The hirsute **desert tarantula** looks much meaner than it is, cruising about in the early morning and early evening. You're bound to encounter gnats and mosquitoes and other tiny pests in desert riparian areas and around upland lakes.

History

The Tucson region is one of the oldest continually inhabited areas in the United States; there's a record of human existence in the valleys and mountains of Southern Arizona going back some 12,000 years.

In the 1930s, University of Arizona archaeologists began an archaeological dig on the Tohono O'odham Reservation southwest of Tucson, in Ventana Cave, named for a nearby hole in a rock outcropping that resembles a window (*ventana* is Spanish for window). Over the course of the dig, the archaeologists found a record of more than 10,000 years of regular human use of the cave, including 39 bodies of "pottery-bearing" and even "pre-ceramic" peoples. While such hunter-gatherers living light on the land likely dominated this area for thousands of years, the first relatively complex culture to settle in the river valleys around Tucson—including the Santa Cruz River Valley south of the city, and the San Pedro River Valley to the southeast, were the Hohokam people. They lived in the region, farming using irrigation canals, from about A.D. 200 to about 1450.

By the time the Spanish arrived in what is now Southern Arizona, and what at the time was the far northern edge of the New World, the Hohokam were gone and their likely ancestors, the Tohono O'odham ("the desert people," called the Papago for centuries) and the Akmiel O'odham (the "river people," called the Pima for centuries), had settled in the Tucson area at the base of Sentinel Peak west of downtown and along the area's rivers, which in those times were likely year-round streams that provided an abundance of food and other resources. It is widely believed that the name Tucson came from the Pima word *schookson,* which roughly translates to "spring at the foot of Black Mountain"—the black mountain in this case being the basalt Sentinel Peak. The Spanish also found another group of indigenous people living in Southern Arizona, the Apache. An Athabaskan tribe that moved into the area a century or more before the Spanish arrived, the Apache were at that time a semi-nomadic, hunter-gatherer culture that had a habit of raiding their neighbors and drawing the unending ire of the Spanish, then the Mexicans, then the Americans, before finally being defeated by the U.S. Army after a long and bloody war. Their descendants now live on reservations in northeastern and central Arizona.

While the famed Coronado expedition to discover the mythical Seven Cities of Cíbola moved through southeastern Arizona in the 1540s, it wasn't until the 1690s, when the hardy Jesuit adventurer Father Eusebio Francisco Kino began his journeys into Southern Arizona and Sonora, that regular contact between the Spanish and the natives began. Kino brought cattle with him to the region for the first time, and established several long-lasting missions including San Xavier del Bac near Tucson, to this day still celebrating Mass in its dark, cool interior. By the 1750s the Spanish crown had established a presidio or fort at Tubac, which was moved to the Tucson valley in 1775. Southern Arizona comprised the northern reaches of the Spanish New World empire, though it was sparsely populated and a violent, dangerous place to live. Spanish cattle ranchers and other hardy settlers fought Apaches and others for the right to live in the region, but for decades the north would remain too isolated and too dangerous to grow much. The Mexicans won their independence from Spain in 1821 and so took over administration of the vast northlands. The wilderness was

PADRE KINO

More than 300 years after he first rode into this valley, the name Eusebio Francisco Kino still has meaning here.

The pious, intellectual, and exceedingly tough padre who, among many other accomplishments, established this region's world-renowned mission system and introduced cattle ranching to the Santa Cruz Valley, is a unifying figure in this culturally mixed locale.

"At a time when there is so much violence on both sides of the border, let this man of peace bring us together; let us remember a higher calling, and find it in Kino," said Gloria Alvillar, an organizer and member of the nonprofit group Patronato de Kino, who recently returned from a visit to the padre's hometown of Segno, Italy.

One of the stated goals of Patronato de Kino is to "promote Padre Kino to beatification," or sainthood – a process they hope to conclude by 2011, the 300th anniversary of Kino's death.

Raul Ramirez, the secretary of Patronato de Kino, said, "We think about him as a symbol of hope. In the Catholic tradition you pray to saints for intercession with God, and we think that Kino would be a good symbol of unity; he tried to unite the tribes of Pimería Alta, and we are looking at him as source of unity again."

The road to beatification, however, is a hard one. It may even be longer and more difficult than the thousands of arid and dangerous miles the padre traveled in the latter 1600s to arrive in what is now Southern Arizona and Northern Sonora, where he not only attempted to convert the native people to his way of thinking but also introduced new lifeways.

© TIM HULL

a mural by artist Bill Singleton inside El Presidio Real de San Agustín del Tucson

exploited somewhat for its resources, used for cattle ranching and placer mining by tough Mexican explorers, but mostly it was too far from the center of power and had too many dangerous Indians to be of much worth to the new nation.

In the later 1820s trappers, hunters, and mountain men like James Ohio Pattie, Antoine Leroux, and Pauline Weaver became some of the first Anglo-Americans to venture through Arizona, in search of beaver pelts. Such men would in turn guide the Army of the West and the Mormon Battalion through the state in 1846 and 1847 during the Mexican War.

After the war ended in 1848, much of what is now the Southwest became U.S. property, and in 1850 a huge area that included Arizona and New Mexico became the New Mexico Territory. In 1854 the land between the Gila River and the Mexican border—Southern Arizona, basically, some 29,644 acres—was added to the territory through the Gadsden Purchase at a price of about $10 million.

Beginning in 1849 and lasting for several years afterward, thousands of Americans passed through Arizona headed for gold and glory in California. Those hard-rock, hard-luck miners would return east to the state a few years later in search of the gold and silver most of them had failed to find on the coast. Several boundary, land, railroad, and scientific surveys of Arizona and the West during the 1850s brought this far corner of the continent greater attention and interest from the East.

It was the increasing mining activity in the state that, among other factors, led President Lincoln to establish the Arizona Territory in 1863, disconnecting it from the huge conglomerate of land called New Mexico. The capital was established at Prescott, in the state's mineral-laden midlands, and the East's economic exploitation of the land, albeit on a much smaller scale than it would eventually become, commenced. During the Civil War, Tucson was a Confederate hotbed for a time before being occupied by the U.S. Army. After the Civil War ended, immigration and exploration of the Southwest picked up considerably.

Still, when John Wesley Powell completed the first river-run through the Grand Canyon in 1869, the population of the territory was less than 10,000 persons.

Indeed, for may years before and after the Gadsden Purchase and the Civil War, Tucson remained a sparsely populated outpost in a far, forgotten corner of the world. When journalist J. Ross Browne made a journey through Arizona and Sonora with Charles Poston, of the first American pioneers to try his luck at mining and ranching in Southern Arizona, Browne had this to say about the far-flung outback (from a series of articles about the territory published in *Harper's Monthly* in 1864 and 1865):

At the period of its purchase Arizona was practically a terra incognita. Hunters and trappers had explored it to some extent; but their accounts of its resources and peculiarities were of a vague and marvelous character, according well with their wild habits of life. Few people in the United States knew anything about it, save the curious book-worms who had penetrated into the old Spanish records. An impression prevailed that it was a worthless desert, without sufficient wood or water to sustain a population of civilized beings. Mr. Gadsden was ridiculed for his purchase, and it was very generally believed that Congress, in expending ten millions of dollars for such an arid waste, had in view some ulterior project of extension, based upon the balance of power between the Northern and Southern states. It was even hinted that this was to be a grand reservoir for disappointed office-seekers, who could be effectually disposed of by means of Territorial appointments.

But settlers trickled in over the coming years, spurred here to cure their tuberculosis, or in search of treasure, adventure, science, or cheap land. Despite this, the territory remained a wild and dangerous place for most. The Apache, Navajo, and other tribes didn't feel they should have to give up the land they had conquered to white settlers, many of whom were looking to get rich quick by exploiting the land and then leave. From 1871 until the final surrender of Geronimo in 1886, the U.S. Army fought a brutal war with the Apache and other tribes. The Apache finally beaten, the territory moved one step closer to large-scale settlement and development.

From 1867 to 1877 Tucson was the capital of the Arizona Territory, until that distinction was handed over for good to the growing, largely American town of Phoenix about 100 miles north in the Salt River Valley. On March 20, 1880, the Southern Pacific Railroad arrived in Tucson and completely transformed the city, bringing in more people and materials than ever before. By 1882, with a population of about 8,000 persons, the once-isolated adobe village could boast gas lights and even a few telephones.

STATEHOOD AND BEYOND

Arizona became a state on February 14, 1912. The first half of the 20th century in Southern Arizona and the rest of the state was dominated by the era of reclamation. The federal government used taxpayer money to develop the state's water resources, damming rivers for irrigation, water storage, and hydroelectric power, creating a huge agricultural industry in the process. Phelps-Dodge and other mining giants ripped huge holes in the lands to extract low-grade copper, while American owners and managers on the whole treated the Mexican and Native American miners and pickers poorly, even criminally on many occasions.

At the same time, increasing numbers of residents and visitors began to realize that there was more to the fantastic Arizona landscape than profit and loss, and this era saw the rise of national parks and monuments, national forests, and state-level protection of important lands. Beginning around the 1920s boosters in Phoenix and Tucson and elsewhere began to see the economic benefits of attracting tourists to the sunny state, and by 1950 or so tourism had replaced the extractive industries in importance. During the two world wars the federal government set up training bases and military installations in the state that led to a growth spurt, and the advent of swamp coolers and air-conditioners stimulated a population boom in Arizona that has yet to really let up. By 1960 Tucson's population had nearly doubled in a decade's time, as it would continue to do over and over. Today, there are about a million people living in the dry basin, and they just keep coming.

Government and Economy

GOVERNMENT
Arizona's government has had a contrarian relationship with the federal establishment since before statehood. The state's entrance into the union was delayed for some time because the legislature, backed by a majority of the public, refused to give up a section of its constitution that allowed for the popular recall of judges. Today the bickering between the two continues over public-land issues and border control. The truth is that the federal government made Arizona, and it controls a good portion of the land in the state still. With history as an example, it's easy to see that had the federal government not protected huge portions of the state as national forests, monuments, parks, and wilderness areas, outside economic interests, mostly from the East, would have used them for their own profit, as they have the lion's share of Arizona's natural resources since long before statehood.

Like nearly everybody else, the state's government has, for most of its history, been interested in developing and taking from the land, and the various land-hungry interests who at one time or another were in favor—be they mining, agricultural, ranching, or military—have dictated policy. This is not true as much today as it has been in the past, however.

While Arizona is known today as a staunchly red (Republican) state, there are a few blue (Democrat) enclaves, notably Tucson and the Navajo Nation.

ECONOMY
Southern Arizona's economy for much of the past was ruled by the boom-and-bust realities of the extractive and agricultural industries. Worldwide prices, the fickleness of the market, and the constant threat of a destructive act of nature made economic life here before World War II a wild ride. Booms in the cattle industry in the 1890s and cotton before and during World War I created large industries in the state virtually overnight. The overgrazing of an aridland open range and monoculture agricultural took their individual tolls, however, and both cattle and cotton really only influenced life here on a major scale for a relatively short time. Of the state economy's well-known "Five C's"—copper, cotton, cattle, citrus, and climate—the others have fared better than cotton and cattle, both of which are now very minor elements of the state's economy. Copper mining, the state's claim to fame in economic circles for several generations, was nearly moribund until 2005, when worldwide prices hit record levels (thanks, in large part, to a global building boom centered in China, and the ubiquity of copper in consumer electronic products and other modern necessities), and previously mothballed pits have opened again and startup firms from outside the state are searching the desert for new pit sites. This may be just a blip on the overall economic radar screen, however. The extractive and agricultural industries are no longer the primary economic engines of Arizona and the West and haven't been for some time. According to a report by the Tucson-based Sonoran Institute released on September 29, 2006, fewer than 5 percent of the West's counties have more than 20 percent of employment in traditional extractive industries, and agriculture and ranching made up

just 4 percent of total employment in the west as of 2000. In the Tucson area in 2008, just 1.9 percent of workers were employed in mining and ranching, according to figures complied by the Pima Association of Governments.

A boom in single-family housing and urban and suburban development has enraptured the state for several decades, though as of this writing that boom has predictably gone bust. Still, despite its boom-and-bust ways the state has often been somewhat impervious to national economic slowdowns, primarily because of its always-steady growth. Growth fuels itself, and an economy that is growing is always perceived to be healthy. Between 2000 and 2006, Arizona's population grew by about 20 percent. The deep truth of the Arizona economy, and one that holds for the entire West, is that the service industry (much of it tourism-related), with its low wages and transient workers, is the hottest

running economic engine here and has been for many years. All over the West non-labor income like investments, disability, and retirement payments come in a close second to the service industry as a top economic driver. The median household income in Arizona is about $44,000 with 2.6 people per household. Some 15 percent of Arizonans live below the poverty line.

More locally, Tucson has a somewhat diverse economy, but much of it is based on the service industry. Something like 85 percent of the jobs here are service-related, according the Pima Association of Governments. Top employers in town include the University of Arizona, the city and county governments, and Raytheon, a company that makes weapons systems. The tourism industry is also a particularly robust employer in the Old Pueblo. The average annual income in the Old Pueblo is around $30,690, and the median household income is around $52,000.

People and Culture

Tucson has a few different faces. Exploring the city and its environs, it's difficult to escape constant reminders that not too long ago this land was considered not the southern end of the United States but rather the northern end of Mexico. Before that it belonged to Spain, before that the Tohono O'odham and the Apache, before that the Hohokam. For more than 10,000 years varied, sometimes contradictory, cultures have developed and adapted in this desert basin encircled by ragged ranges, and somehow they've mixed themselves up into a distinctive culture that one might call Southwestern. This is how it is in Tucson, where mixture is celebrated and studied, pulled apart, dissected, and turned around itself.

Many Tucson residents are émigrés, but there's definitely a much higher percentage of born-and-bred locals here than in Phoenix, Arizona's only other urban region of any size. Indeed, the majority of the state's 6.1 million residents live in Pima and Maricopa Counties, in and around the two large urban

areas of Phoenix and Tucson—about a million persons live in Pima County and some 3.7 million live in Maricopa. About 13 percent of Arizonans are over 65, but 26 percent are under 18. The former statistic is expected to rise significantly as more and more baby boomers retire and move to the Sunbelt, just as their parents did in the 1960s and 1970s. On par with nationwide averages, about 81 percent of Arizonans are high school graduates, and 24 percent have at least a bachelor's degree. A full 68 percent of Arizonans own their homes.

Tucson has a larger percentage of Mexican-American and other Latino residents than most other places. According to the U.S. Census Bureau, in 2000, Tucson's Hispanic population was 35.7 percent, compared to about 20 percent nationwide. Those numbers are expected to rise after the 2010 census is complete. According to a City of Tucson report, Latinos could once again become the majority population in Tucson by 2015.

THE TOHONO O'ODHAM TODAY

It's easy to forget that Native America persists, despite our best efforts to wipe it out over the last few centuries.

Here in the Southwest, where many native peoples and traditions are celebrated and studied, it's easier still to forget that those people are not quaint objects of purely academic interest, but real people who are everyday trying to survive in the post-modern world while holding on to some sense of their indigenous identity. The Tohono O'odham, who were already living in the Tucson valley when Capt. Hugh O'Conner rode north from Tubac in 1775 to establish El Presidio de San Agustín del Tucson, are one such native people.

According to **TOCA: Tohono O'odham Community Action** (520/383-4966, www.tocaonline.org), an O'odham-led nonprofit community development group, the "Desert People" have had mixed success in adapting to the modern world; it is a firm belief of such groups that going backward is the best way for the O'odham to move forward. For this, according to TOCA, they must return to the principals of *O'odham Himdag* ("The Desert People's Way").

They used to be called the Papago, a name given to them by the Spanish; there are about 28,000 members of the Tohono O'odham Nation, about 20,000 of which live on the sprawling desert reservation southwest of Tucson, a seemingly forbidding patch of Sonoran Desert the size of Connecticut that has been providing the Desert People with sustenance – though a hard-won sustenance to be sure – for eons.

These days, however, despite the fact that the O'odham operate two successful casinos near Tucson and are poised to build a huge casino-resort in the west of Phoenix, small-scale economic life on the reservation isn't exactly overflowing with plenty. TOCA says that the per-capita average income on the reservation is about $6,998 per year, far below the national average of about $22,000. Moreover, 50 percent or more of O'odham adults have Type II diabetes (the numbers for the U.S. as a whole are between 4 and 6 percent). TOCA goes on to say that fewer than half of reservation adults have even a high school education, putting them at the bottom of all Native American tribes in the United States in terms of education. And worse still, the group is worried that the Tohono O'odham language and their unique cultural traditions, ceremonies, and knowledge about the desert are in danger of dying out within a few generations.

In order to solve these seemingly insurmountable social realties, TOCA says it's committed to developing "indigenous solutions, rather than focus[ing] on the problems while importing the 'solutions' from the outside." But what does that mean in practice? Well, take for instance the diabetes problem, a health crisis of staggering proportions on the reservation today. In 1960 diabetes was completely absent from the reservation, TOCA says, adding that the cause of the epidemic over the last 50 years or so has been the "destruction of the traditional food systems and diet." Indeed, studies have shown that traditional O'odham foods like tepary beans, cholla cactus buds, wild spinach, corn, and squash served to regulate the O'odham's blood sugar, and that the sudden switch to a completely different diet over the last several decades has sent this age-old system out of whack. As a result of such studies, TOCA has begun to develop a food program that puts some of the old ways back into the O'odham diet. They've also instituted programs to revive the tribe's basket-weaving traditions, and to bring together youths and tribal elders in hopes that the Desert People's collective cultural memory survives for centuries to come.

If you're interested in learning more about the O'odham, their lifeways, their history, and their present, head west on Highway 86 across the reservation toward Sells and the **Tohono O'odham Nation Cultural Center and Museum** (520/383-0211, www.tonation-nsn. gov), in Topawa (seven miles south of Sells on Federal Route 19). It's about a 70-mile drive that'll probably take about two hours.

The Arts

Tucson is the arts capital of Arizona, though some might consider this a somewhat dubious distinction. There are scores of artists and artisans who call the desert home, and there are galleries throughout the Old Pueblo showing everything from your basic cowboy-and-Indian portraits to the cutting-edge avant-garde. World-famous Southwestern artists like Ted DeGrazia and Maynard Dixon have called the Old Pueblo home.

The city is awash in the arts and images of Mexico, and that nation's folk arts are particularly popular as both tourist souvenirs and local decor. Despite being hundreds of miles from the Navajo and Hopi Reservations in northeastern Arizona, Tucson is known throughout the Southwest as a center for Native American arts, and February's **Indian Arts Fair** on the grounds of the University of Arizona's Arizona State Museum is one of the largest and most popular events of its kind.

Tucson has a literary tradition going back to its early days, and in the early 20th century the

art gallery entrance in the foothills

nation's best-selling author, Harold Bell Wright, moved to the city because of sickness and later claimed that Tucson had saved his life. Perhaps the three best-known authors to have lived in the Old Pueblo are Edward Abbey, J. A. Jance, and Pulitzer-winning Barbara Kingsolver. Abbey, one of the west's most famous tricksters, polemicists, novelists, and nature writers, lived in Tucson off and on for many years, and is buried somewhere out in the desert southwest of the city in a secret grave. Jance is a best-selling mystery novelist whose plots often play out in Bisbee and Cochise County. Kingsolver, author of a trilogy of novels that take place in Tucson, among many other works, lived in Tucson for many years and even freelanced for the *Tucson Weekly,* a popular alternative weekly here. Another Old Pueblo writer with a national reputation is the great Charles Bowden, who used to be on the staff of the dying afternoon daily the *Tucson Citizen* and has over the last 20 years or more written several nonfiction works revealing the darker sides of the Sunbelt and the borderlands. Friends of mine who work the few local big-box bookstores like Borders and Barnes & Noble have reported somewhat regular sightings of two great American writers: Cormac McCarthy, author of several novels about the Southwest, including one, *Blood Meridian,* in which Southern Arizona figures briefly; and Larry McMurtry, author of the *The Last Picture Show, Lonesome Dove,* and many others.

Perhaps Tucson's most famous resident, though she doesn't live here full-time, is Linda Ronstadt, the beloved singer who hit her peak in popular music in the 1970s but continues to sing and tour and is a very popular figure in the Old Pueblo, as her family dates back here to territorial times.

The city's most robust arts-related economy has since the 1940s centered on the film industry. This has largely been the result of the building of **Old Tucson Studios,** and the popularity over much of the 20th century of the Western, for which Tucson and its environs often provided the iconic scenery.

CLEAR SKIES AND SUNSETS: TUCSON'S HOMEGROWN MOVIE INDUSTRY

If one is to take for truth a story often related, with minor variations, in most histories about the western march of the movie business, it may have been the myth of what the West was supposed to be that kept Arizona from becoming the western seat of the film industry instead of just a poor relation.

It is an apocryphal-sounding story about fate's privilege, a story that Bob Shelton, former owner of Old Tucson Studios – and the undisputed patriarch of Tucson's modern film industry – told me several years ago over lunch.

In 1914, he said, legendary producer Adolph Zuker sent Cecil B. DeMille and Samuel Goldwyn to Flagstaff, in Northern Arizona. Zuker had the year before bought the rights to *The Squawman,* a Broadway play with a typical Western theme. DeMille and Goldwyn, looking for alkaline flats and purple sage, stepped off the train into snow, finding themselves surrounded not by mesas and cacti but by white-capped mountains and near-alpine vistas. "I thought Arizona was a desert," one might have said to the other.

If they had traveled a day or so downstate to Tucson – then the principal urban area in the young state – they would have found exactly what they were looking for, and the climate and the variation might have persuaded them to set up shop, or so the speculation goes. But they didn't go south and they didn't stay in Flagstaff; instead, they headed farther west until they ran out of land. There they rented a barn and made the first full-length Western. Thus Hollywood was born and Arizona was passed over as a candidate for the western seat of a fledgling industry that would irrevocably transform the world.

That's not to say that the movie industry didn't come to Southern Arizona; it did, and to a certain extent it still does. There were a few films produced here in the early days, and a few studios set up offices, including those of the Al Jennings Production Company, which had an office here in 1918. Jennings was a former outlaw whose ambition was to release the Western bandit from the romantic sentimentality that dominated much of the media coverage of that famous, and to a large extent made-up, Western lifestyle. Such exceptions aside, however, after Hollywood was established not much happened here until Columbia Pictures came in 1939 and built Old Tucson, a purported replica of Tucson circa 1860. Columbia came to film an outdoor epic aptly titled *Arizona,* starring William Holden and Jean Arthur. Other productions trickled in, bringing a host of myth-making stars to a region that was already falling back on hackneyed stories of cowboys and Indians, outlaws and gunfighters, saloon girls and freedom, in its search for a national identity.

For a while Old Tucson fell into disrepair and near obscurity; then, in 1959, Shelton bought the land and put some money into the moldering complex. He opened for business in 1960. In Shelton, Tucson found its most active impresario: Today he is credited by many in the industry for single-handedly making Tucson, for a time, a major film location. When Tucson's film industry was at its peak, between the 1960s and the early 1990s, it was third only to Hollywood and New York in film production, and the community was doing $20 million in film business per year, according to Shelton: "It grew very substantially to the point where, at the peak of our prosperity, we could field three full film crews out of Tucson, and that was attractive to the industry. There was a time when I had John Wayne, Clint Eastwood, Lee Marvin, and Burt Lancaster all working on films at Old Tucson at the same time."

Shelton sold out eventually, and in 1995 the studio that for 60 years had "played a prominent role in shaping the world's perception of the Old West" (as Old Tucson's website brags) burned down. The fire took with it irreplaceable props and costumes and the last hopes of a local subculture created when the work was plentiful – a group of men and women who relied on Tucson's movie industry for work.

But the business had really been dying before the fire, as a phenomenon known as

© TIM HULL

camera crane on display at Old Tucson

"runaway production" started to take a toll. The film production money had started flowing north, to Canada, where the government had already created the Production Service Tax Credit, a stroke of genius that offered foreign film and television production companies tax breaks on production-labor expenses. The PSTC, coupled with further tax incentives offered in individual Canadian provinces, created a production-crew employment boom, and left a lot of film-industry workers in California – not to mention workers in smaller, ancillary markets like Tucson – out of work.

TUCSON ON-SCREEN

Plenty of forgettable Westerns, TV episodes, and commercials were made in Tucson, the "Hollywood of the desert." But among the hundreds of films made in and around Tucson since 1914's *The Return* are arguably many of the best Westerns ever made, as well as a few classics and indie favorites that have very little to do with cowboys and Indians. In this rather long list, gleaned from the Internet Movie Database (www.imdb.com), you are sure to find at least a few that you have already seen or will want to check out: *Ridin' Wild* (1925), *In Old Arizona* (1928), *Arizona* (1940), *Bells of Saint Mary* (1945), *Duel in the Sun* (1946), *Red River* (1948), *Broken Arrow* (1950), *Winchester '73* (1950), *The Violent Men* (1955), *Oklahoma!* (1955), *A Kiss Before Dying* (1957), *3:10 to Yuma* (1957), *Gunfight at the O.K. Corral* (1957), *The Badlanders* (1958), *Rio Bravo* (1959), *Lilies of the Field* (1963), *McLintock!* (1963), *El Dorado* (1966), *Hombre* (1967), *Andy Warhol's Lonesome Cowboys* (1968), *Easy Rider* (1969), *Rio Lobo* (1970), *Life and Times of Judge Roy Bean* (1972), *Alice Doesn't Live Here Anymore* (1974), *The Outlaw Josey Wales* (1976), *A Star is Born* (1976), *Revenge of the Nerds* (1984), *Three Amigos* (1986), *Can't Buy Me Love* (1987), *Major League* (1989), *Gas, Food, Lodging* (1992), *Bodies, Rest & Motion* (1993), *Tombstone* (1993), *Boys on the Side* (1995), *The Quick and the Dead* (1995), *Tank Girl* (1995), *Tin Cup* (1996), *The Postman* (1997), *Three Kings* (1999), *Jesus' Son* (1999), *Traffic* (2000), *Confessions of a Dangerous Mind* (2002), *Pumpkin* (2008).

ESSENTIALS

Getting There

BY AIR

Tucson International Airport (TIA, 520/573-8000, www.tucsonairport.org) hosts 10 major airlines (including American, Delta, Frontier, Continental, Southwest and Northwest, and Alaska Airlines) making approximately 60 departures every day. It's a small but efficient airport, with free wireless Internet access and daily nonstop flights to Seattle, Chicago, Dallas, Atlanta, Salt Lake, Denver, Houston, Minneapolis, Albuquerque, L.A., Vegas, San Diego, and San Francisco. If you're coming in from or headed to a city not on this list, it's likely you'll stop first at the state's major

airport, Sky Harbor International Airport, in Phoenix, and then desert-hop, as it were, about 45 minutes south (probably after waiting more than an hour or so at the terminal). If you find yourself at Sky Harbor and don't feel like boarding an absurdly short flight, you can rent a car there and make the easy hour-and-a-half drive down I-10 across the desert—though the scenery along I-10 is certainly not representative of what you're in for once you get to Tucson. Or, you can call **Arizona Shuttle Service** (520/795-6771, 520/795-6775, www. arizonashuttle.com), which offers 18 trips daily between Phoenix and Tucson.

If you're arriving or departing from TIA, remember that **Arizona Stagecoach** (520/881-4111, 520/889-1000, www.stagecoach.com) runs a 24-hour door-to-door shuttle to and from TIA. Life at TIA is not nearly as bad as it is at some of the nation's larger airports. Generally arrivals and departures at TIA are quick and easy, with relatively short lines; friendly, helpful people; and cheap, safe long-term parking. You can park at the airport's long-term lot for a mere $4 per day, and a free shuttle runs from the terminal to the parking area, or you can walk it if you're so inclined. There are always cabs waiting just outside the main entrance; expect to pay about $20 for a ride to midtown. To get to TIA from midtown take Campbell; this turns into the Kino Parkway south of Broadway. Follow road signs to Benson Highway, which leads to Tucson Boulevard and the airport entrance.

BY CAR

Road-trippers, whether from the east or the west, will arrive in Tucson via I-10. If you're coming from Sonora, Mexico, you'll come in on I-19, which merges with I-10 near downtown Tucson. A major road construction project is expected to keep most of the I-10 exits around Tucson closed on a revolving basis until 2010. If you're coming into town from the north or the east, keep an eye out for instructions on which exits are open, usually only one at a time. The best thing you can do is get off the interstate at the open exit, and then take the frontage road.

BY BUS

For bus service from Tucson to all points on the map there's the **Greyhound Bus Station** (471 W. Congress, east side of I-10, 520/792-3475, www.greyhound.com).

BY TRAIN

The **Amtrak Station** is downtown at 400 N. Toole Ave. (520/623-4442, www.amtrak.com).

Getting Around

PUBLIC TRANSPORTATION

The City of Tucson operates the **Sun Tran** (4220 S. Park Ave., 520/623-4301, www.suntran.com) bus line. It has stops all over the Old Pueblo and operates Monday–Friday 6 A.M.–7 P.M. and Saturday–Sunday 8 A.M.–5 P.M. Full fare is $1, with kids under five riding free.

DRIVING

If you're flying into Tucson and you don't have friends or relatives to chauffeur you around the typically sprawling Southwestern city, you'll need to rent a car. The airport has several counters from which to choose. If you're booking ahead try the locally owned **Adobe Car & Van Rental of Tucson** (3150 E. Grant Rd., 520/390-6708, 888/471-7951), which has a free pick-up service.

As for getting around the city by car, it's fairly easy if you keep in mind a few landmarks and general rules. Tucson is in a valley surrounded by mountains, with the mighty Santa Catalinas to the north, the Rincon Mountains to the east, and the Tucson Mountains to the west. Far south in the Santa Cruz Valley along I-19 are the Santa Rita Mountains. If you remember that the Santa Catalinas, the most imposing range around the valley, are to the north, it isn't too difficult to navigate Tucson. North of the city, on Oracle Road/Highway 77, are the small towns of Oracle, Oro Valley, and Catalina, all nestled in the backside foothills of the Santa Catalina Mountains. To the southeast is the old mining and ranching district of Vail and the Rincon Valley, now peppered with suburban housing developments, and beyond that the communities of Cochise County.

WHY IS IT SO DARK HERE?

If it seems a little darker in and around Tucson than in other places, there's a good reason for that. Up on **Mount Hopkins** in the Santa Rita range, the Smithsonian Institution operates the **Fred Lawrence Whipple Observatory,** a state-of-the-art telescope array used by scientists to study the beginnings of our universe. To assist this important research, and to help out other observatories across Southern Arizona, Pima County, Tucson, and Sahuarita have all passed ordinances that require special outdoor lighting, keeping the sky dark so that scientists can see (or at least attempt to see) ever-so-faint objects millions of light years away in space.

If you have a history of poor eyesight at night, it might be a good idea to let someone else do the driving after dark.

South on I-19 are the big open-pit copper mines, the bedroom community of Sahuarita, the retirement haven of Green Valley, the artists colony and shops of Tubac, and then on to the U.S.-Mexico border.

Most of the major intersections around Tucson are blessed with left-hand turn signals, so don't panic if you're in the back of a long line of cars wanting to turn left—your turn will come soon.

TAXIS

Cab rides can get expensive in Tucson because everything is so spread out. Expect to spend about $15 for a ride from midtown to restaurants and bars downtown or on 4th Avenue. There are plenty of rides to choose from. Try **AAA Yellow Cab Co./ Fiesta Taxi** (520/624-6611, 520/399-6062) or **All State Cab Company** (520/798-1111, 520/887-9000).

Tips for Travelers

TIME ZONE

Arizona is in the Mountain Time Zone, and is one of the few places in the country that does not switch over to Daylight Saving Time from the second Sunday in March to the first Sunday in November.

ACCESS FOR TRAVELERS WITH DISABILITIES

Many of the best sights in Tucson are accessible in one way or another to travelers with disabilities. For advice and links to other helpful Internet resources, go to **www.disabledtravelers.com,** which is run out of Arizona and is full of accessible travel information, though it's not specific to the state. The **National Accessible Travelers Database** may also be helpful. For questions specific to Tucson and Arizona, you may want to contact the state Department of Administration's **Office for Americans with Disabilities** (100 N. 15th Ave., Ste. 361, Phoenix, 602/542-6276, 800/358-3617, TTY: 602/542-6686, www.azada.gov).

GAY AND LESBIAN TRAVELERS

Tucson is no more or no less gay-friendly than most other cities its size, and the queer community is strong and diverse here. *The Tucson Observer* (520/622-7176, www.tucsonobserver.com) has news about the local gay community, politics, and national news. **Wingspan** (425 E. 7th St., 520/624-1779, www.wingspan.org) is the Old Pueblo's friendly and active GLBT community center. The **Tucson GLBT Chamber of Commerce** (520/615-6436, www.tucsonglbtchamber.org) publishes a free membership directory that's available at the visitors center at La Placita Village (110 S. Church Ave., 520/903-9900) downtown.

WHAT TO TAKE

Your Tucson-bound knapsack should include a few essential items, whether you're coming in spring, summer, or second spring. Definitely bring along a **swimsuit,** even if you're coming in January – most hotels have a heated pool and a hot tub. Bring **sunscreen** and a **hat** that casts a shadow over your face and your neck; even if it's not too hot out, that sun is always shining and its rays are dangerous. Bring **comfortable shoes** for walking, or even **hiking shoes** – you don't need big boots; a sporty low-top hiker will suffice for most hikes. Bring along a **small day pack** for carrying around snacks and drinks. You may want to invest in a good pair of **binoculars,** especially if you plan to do any bird-watching or other wildlife viewing. If you are an avid biker – road or mountain – you should definitely consider bringing your wheels along with you. Otherwise, you can easily rent one. If you're going to be here in the summer, pack **light, comfortable clothes,** but don't forget a **windbreaker** or other **light jacket;** if you're in the mountains after dark you may actually need it. Also bring along a pair of **flip-flops,** Tucson's official footwear, and wear them proudly with shorts or even jeans. A good map of the region is also helpful, though you can get one when you arrive. Make sure to bring your **camera.** You are definitely going to use it.

Health and Safety

West Nile and the Hanta virus are the long-shot threats to your health in Tucson and Arizona, and both can be avoided by taking precautions. Use insect repellant to ward off the former (which is spread by mosquitoes) and simply stay away from rodents, which may transmit the latter. Similarly rare are those infamous rattlesnake attacks. Keep an eye on the ground while you're hiking—if a snake, rattler or otherwise, is in your general vicinity, leave the area; that's the best way to avoid most snake bites. Also cover your ankles and keep your hands and feet out of dark holes. To avoid heat stroke and dehydration, very real threats in the summertime desert, stay out of the sun during the hottest part of the day; restrict your activity to early mornings and after sunset. Drink lots of water, and never go out into the desert alone or unprepared. Don't underestimate the heat and its power to drain your resources. Threats from humans come in all the usual forms. Lock your vehicle wherever you go, even in the most remote locations. Don't pick up hitchhikers, anywhere. Drug- and people-smuggling, and the violence that usually goes along with such activities, is common in areas along the U.S.-Mexico border in Southern Arizona.

HOSPITALS AND EMERGENCIES

Dial 911 for emergencies anywhere in Southern Arizona. **University Medical Center** (1501 N. Campbell Ave., 520/694-0111) is the top hospital in Southern Arizona and has the region's only Level 1 trauma center, so if you are seriously hurt anywhere in Southern Arizona you are likely to be treated by the capable staff there. It's located on a sprawling campus across Speedway, at Campbell, from the University of Arizona, and the two are, obviously, connected. On the eastern edges of midtown, Southern Arizona's largest health-care facility, **Tucson Medical Center** (5301 E. Grant, 520/327-5461, www.tmcaz.com), began life as a tuberculosis sanitarium, welcoming TB sufferers from all over the world to the desert's dry climate. These days TMC is where patients from all over the region, including Sonora, Mexico, will find themselves if they're having a difficult pregnancy, heart problems, and other serious health issues. Primarily because of its state-of-the-art newborn intensive care unit and extensive cardiac-care resources, TMC is a popular choice for middle- and upper-class Mexican nationals seeking a high level of care. A TMC nurse who works with newborns here told me recently that at least twice a month she'll work with a family from Mexico, usually well-to-do and fluent in English. On the city's west side, **St. Mary's Hospital** (1601 W. St. Mary's Rd., 520/872-3000, www.carondelet.org) is part of the large Carondelet Network, which also runs the east side's **St. Joseph's Hospital** (350 N. Wilmot Rd., 520/873-3000), and **Tucson Heart Hospital** (4888 N. Stone Ave., 520/696-2328). St. Mary's has 402 beds and is more than a century old (it started with only 12 beds). It has a full-service emergency room and a long list of services; St. Joseph's has 309 beds, an emergency room, and state-of-the-art comprehensive care; and Tucson Heart Hospital is an award-wining facility dedicated exclusively to heart disease.

Information and Services

MAPS AND TOURIST INFORMATION

Make sure to stop by the **Tucson Visitor Center** (110 S. Church Ave., 520/624-1817, Mon.–Fri. 9 A.M.–5 P.M., Sat.–Sun. 9 A.M.–4 P.M.). The bureau produces a helpful guide to the city you can pick up at the office or out in front when they're closed. There are scores of tourist pamphlets for the perusing. Park in the metered parking on Church Avenue in front of the Technicolor La Placita Village, which houses the center and a few shops and cafés.

The **Arizona Office of Tourism** (1110 W. Washington St., Ste. 155, Phoenix, AZ 85007, 602/364-3700, 866/275-5816, www.arizonaguide.com) will send you a free print or electronic version of the official state guide, and their website is full of information and lists of accommodations, events, and restaurants throughout the state. If you're planning to spend a lot of time in the state's national forests, you can get maps and information beforehand from the **National Forest Service, Southwestern Region** (333 Broadway SE, Albuquerque, NM 87102, 505/842-3292, www.fs.fed.us/r3), or from the websites for the individual forests, listed in the destination chapters of this book. The **Arizona BLM State Office** (1 N. Central Ave., Ste. 800, Phoenix, AZ 85004-4427, 602/417-9200, www.blm.gov/az/st/en.html) also has a lot of information on the state's wildlands, and the **Arizona State Parks Department** (1300 W. Washington, Phoenix, AZ 85007, 602/542-4174, www.pr.state.az.us) has information on all the parks managed by the state.

COMMUNICATIONS AND MEDIA
Internet Services

Please don't pay for wireless Internet access in Tucson. Even if your hotel doesn't provide free access to a wireless network (and nearly all the accommodations in this book do), there's sure to be a coffee house or restaurant near you that does. Even Jack-in-the-Box has free Wi-Fi. The City of Tucson has made pretty much the entire downtown area a wireless hot-spot. You can access the network around 101 North Stone Avenue at **Jacome Plaza** outside the main library, and nearby on Alameda Street near the Pima County Courthouse. You can also access a free wireless network throughout the Pima County complex along Alameda. If that's not enough, the **main library** downtown, and all of the myriad branch libraries around town, offer access to free wireless, as well as computers that can be used, with some restrictions, to access to the Internet.

If you've brought your laptop with you to town and it's acting up, don't call one of those high-priced corporate "geeks" to fix it. Instead, call **Student Experts** (520/762-6687, www.studentexperts.com), a local company that employs UA students who know their way around computers. Day or night, they'll race to your home or hotel and get you back to work in as little time as possible. I have used them several times, and they have always been professional and competent. And, best of all, they charge about half as much as the big guys.

Magazines and Newspapers

The morning daily newspaper the *Arizona Daily Star* (azstarnet.com) has a local focus but isn't provincial by any means. The weekly alternative tabloid the *Tucson Weekly* (www.tucsonweekly.com) is the place to go for news on arts, entertainment, politics, and local news; you'll find it free on red racks throughout the city. Distributed from green racks around the city (often right next to the *Tucson Weekly* rack) is one of the Old Pueblo's newest publications, *Tucson Green Times,* a monthly tabloid focusing on green living, sustainability, environmental politics, and more. If you want to know what's going on in Tucson in terms of sustainability—water harvesting, solar-energy research, alternative fuels, healthy living, etc.—this is a good place to start. *The Desert Leaf,* a free monthly distributed throughout the city at coffee houses, bookstores, and elsewhere, concentrates on the culture, lifestyles, and businesses of the foothills neighborhood, but really its editorial content is all over the map. Its articles will be helpful to anyone looking to learn about life in the high-end Southwest. *Tucson Lifestyles* magazine is a slick monthly with articles about local art and culture, real estate, restaurants, shops, and, of course, people. Every quarter a new edition of the slick *Tucson Guide* is released, stuffed full of interesting and informative articles on Tucson and the surrounding area, with an emphasis on all that is unique about this place. The weekly tabloid *Inside Tucson Business* covers the local

business community and is sold from racks and at newsstands and some bookstores.

You'll find all of the above publications, plus hundreds more from around the world, along with national and international newspapers, political and literary journals, paperbacks, cigars, pipe tobacco, and cigarettes, at **Crescent Tobacco Shop & Newsstand** (Downtown at 200 E. Congress St., 520/296-3102; on the east side at 7037 E. Tanque Verde Rd., 520/296-3102).

Radio and TV

I can't recommend that you tune in to any of the Old Pueblo's network affiliates for news. This is a small media market, often used as a brief stepping stone to something bigger by all those big-smile blondes and tall-and-handsome helmet-heads that television news producers prefer. In short, the local news programs in Tucson border on the laughable nearly all the time. Just don't watch them. The one exception I can recommend is the local PBS affiliate, KUAT Channel 6, operated on the campus of the University of Arizona. Every weeknight at 6:30 P.M. the smart news magazine *Arizona Illustrated* examines Tucson's life, politics, and culture in-depth, regularly presenting longish interviews and panel discussions with Southern Arizona politicians, movers-and-shakers, and journalists.

As for radio, the Tucson landscape is particularly bleak, filled with the corporate-run outlets with the same sounds, voices, and crude jokes you can hear in any city of moderate size. They are all there up and down the dial, and you won't have any trouble finding them. Venture onto the AM dial for several locally produced daily talk shows concentrating on politics and sports. The local NPR affiliate, KUAZ 89.1, also at the UA, broadcasts NPR from early in the morning with *Morning Edition,* and then continues throughout the day with *The Diane Rehm Show, Talk of the Nation, The World, Fresh Air,* and, at the end of the day, *All Things Considered.* After 7 P.M.

TUCSON'S COMMUNITY RADIO: KXCI 91.3 FM

Hidden away in an old brick house in Tucson's Armory Park historic district is one of the best radio stations in the West.

Since the early 1980s, **KXCI Community Radio** (220 S. 4th Ave., 520/622-5924 request line, 520/623-1000 office line, www.kxci.org) has been broadcasting an outrageously eclectic mix of music, news, and cultural programming that has contributed greatly to making Tucson a place where people slightly left of center feel welcome and comfortable. This full-time job is done by a staff of mostly volunteer, nonprofessional DJs, many of whom learn the ropes in a DJ class offered annually by the station.

Most weekdays the majority of daytime air is taken up by the Music Mix, a brew of new and old alternative rock, roots, country, Latino, jazz, electronica, world music, and classic pop that's so unpredictable you shouldn't be surprised to hear Willie Nelson followed by the White Stripes followed by a new tune from your favorite Afghan hip-hop artist.

Most nights there's a lineup of genre-specific shows. Mondays feature a "locals-only" broadcast that showcases the best of Tucson's fertile music scene, while on Tuesdays country-western, alternative country, and Americana rule. Wednesday is Latino night, and on Saturday you'll hear bluegrass in the morning and in the afternoon Kidd Squidd's Mystery Jukebox, during which the Kidd, who has an unmatched knowledge of music in all its forms, plays a few hours' worth centered around a creative theme.

Because KXCI is supported by grants and donations from listeners, there are no commercials and nobody is beholden to an absentee corporation dictating playlists. This can make for near daily discoveries of music that you didn't know was out there. Tune in to KXCI at 91.3 on the FM dial, or at www.kxci.org.

on weekdays KUAZ plays a good mix of jazz programming. If you enjoy an eclectic music mix and a news shows like *Democracy Now,* tune in to Tucson's community news station KXCI 91.3.

Public Libraries

The Pima County Public Library system has more than two dozen branches all over the county. The main branch in the vast system is downtown's **Joel D. Valdez Main Library** (101 N. Stone Ave., 520/594-5600, www.library.pima.gov, Mon.–Wed. 9 A.M.–8 P.M., Thurs. 9 A.M.–6 P.M., Fri. 9 A.M.–5 P.M., Sat. 10 A.M.–5 P.M., Sun. 1–5 P.M.), a center point of the Stone Avenue and Alameda Street business and government district with grassy knolls and public art around its central grounds. There's a parking garage directly under the library (look for the sign while heading either north or south on Stone); otherwise there are metered parking spots all around downtown which are free on the weekends. There are quite a few computers for public use at the main branch, and they have a large children's section and a program of kids' events that are very popular with local parents. Check out the library website for details and times. Of particular interest to visitors and tourists, the **Steinheimer Collection** at the main library is dedicated exclusively to books about Tucson, Arizona, and the Southwest. Additionally, every year a panel of Tucson librarians, writers, and book lovers presents a list of its favorite books about the Southwest published the previous year. For this year's list and those of past years check out www.library.pima.gov/books/swboy/index.cfm.

No matter which neighborhood you're in, you'll find a clean, well-stocked, and well-lit branch, with mostly friendly librarians and assistants ready to help, and a bank of Internet-ready computers. In midtown, there's the **Himmel Park Branch Library** (1035 N. Treat Ave., 520/791-4397, Mon.–Thurs. 10 A.M.–8 P.M., Fri. 10 A.M.–5 P.M., Sat. 9 A.M.–5 P.M., Sun. 1–5 P.M.) at Himmel Park, and it's fun to combine a walk around the green shady park with

© TIM HULL

The Joel D. Valdez Main Library is one of more than two dozen public libraries in Pima County.

a visit to the small branch. One of the newer branches, the **Martha Cooper Branch Library** (1377 N. Catalina Ave., 520/594-5315, Mon.–Thurs. 10 A.M.–8 P.M., Fri. 10 A.M.–5 P.M., Sat. 9 A.M.–5 P.M., Sun. 1–5 P.M.), is in a residential area a few miles east of Alvernon off Speedway Boulevard. On the east side, the **Kirk-Bear Canyon Branch Library** (8959 E. Tanque Verde Rd., 520/791-5021, Mon.–Thurs. 10 A.M.–8 P.M., Fri. 10 A.M.–5 P.M., Sat. 9 A.M.–5 P.M., Sun. 1–5 P.M.) and the **Murphy-Wilmont Branch Library** (530 N. Wilmot Rd., 520/594-5420, Mon.–Thurs. 10 A.M.–8 P.M., Fri. 10 A.M.–5 P.M., Sat. 9 A.M.–5 P.M., Sun. 1–5 P.M.) are both very popular. On the south side, check out the **El Pueblo Branch Library** (W. Irvington Rd., 520/791-4733, Mon.–Tues. 9 A.M.–6 P.M., Wed.–Thurs. 10 A.M.–6 P.M., Fri.

10 A.M.–5 P.M., Sat. 9 A.M.–5 P.M.), and on the west side there's the **Mission Branch Library** (3770 S. Mission Rd., 520/594-5325, Mon.–Thurs. 10 A.M.–8 P.M., Fri. 10 A.M.–5 P.M., Sat. 9 A.M.–5 P.M., Sun. 1–5 P.M.). Foothills residents spend a lot of time at the **Dusenberry-River Branch Library** (5605 E. River Rd., 520/594-5345, Mon.–Thurs. 10 A.M.–8 P.M., Fri.–Sat. 10 A.M.–5 P.M., Sun. 1–5 P.M.).

The University of Arizona has an excellent academic research library system that includes a huge main library, a science and engineering library, a law library, and a music and architecture library. Students, faculty, and alumni (not to mention residents willing to shell out about $100 a year for a "community user card") have access to the millions of books and other media here. Check out www.library.arizona.edu for details.

RESOURCES

Suggested Reading

HISTORY AND GENERAL INFORMATION

Bandelier, Fanny, trans. *The Journey of Álvar Núñez Cabeza de Vaca*. Chicago: Rio Grande Press, 1964. This strange first-person account marks the true beginnings of American literature. The conquistador spent years of privation with various northern Mexico Indian tribes after being shipwrecked near Florida in the late 1520s. He became a slave, a shaman, and a trader before finally finding his way back to civilization and inspiring the later "discovery" of the Southwest by the Spanish.

Barnes, Will C. *Arizona Place Names*. Tucson: University of Arizona Press, 1988. The life's work of a famous Arizonan who first came to the territory in 1854, this classic mixture of history, geography, and anecdote is a must-have for any serious Arizona explorer. First published in 1935, just a year before Barnes's death, the book represents more than 30 years of work by the author.

Castañeda, Pedro de, et. al. *The Journey of Coronado*. New York: Dover Publications, 1990. There are dozens of editions of this useful and fascinating collection of some of the original documents from the Coronado expedition, which moved through southeastern Arizona on the way north looking for the mythical Seven Cities of Cíbola. In this book, translated from the original Spanish version, you get the story as it happened, written by members of the expedition and others.

Griffith, James S. *Folk Saints of the Borderlands*. Tucson: Rio Nuevo Publishers, 2003; and *Beliefs and Holy Places*. Tucson: University of Arizona Press, 1992. Nobody explains the peculiar mixture of Catholicism and localized native beliefs that pervades the borderlands, creating new folk saints and holy places and infusing the land with meaning, better than "Big" Jim Griffith, a professor at the University of Arizona and the Old Pueblo's resident folklorist. Big Jim can often be seen on the local PBS affiliate, KUAT Channel 6, talking about the culture and legends of Pimería Alta.

Hart, John Bret. *Tucson: Portrait of a Desert Pueblo*. Woodland Hills, CA: Windsor Publications, Inc., 1980. This out-of-print coffee-table history of the Old Pueblo was sponsored by the Tucson Chamber of Commerce, but it's still a dependable, well-written account of the city's long history and has excellent historical photos throughout that really give one a sense of what the dusty old town was like not that long ago.

Miller, Neil. *Karchner Caverns: How Two Cavers Discovered and Saved One of the Wonders of the Natural World*. Tucson: University of Arizona Press, 2008. Miller tells the complete, thrilling story—based on interviews with nearly all those involved who are still living—of the long, secretive years in between the discovery of Kartchner Caverns by two young cavers and the opening of the $30 million show-cave more than a decade later. Along the way, he brings up some interesting questions about whether this cave should be open to the public at all.

Monahan, Sherry. *Tombstone's Treasures: Silver Mines and Golden Saloons.* Albuquerque: University of New Mexico Press, 2007. In a style that's more sedate and considered, though no less interesting, than what you'll find on Tombstone's dusty Allen Street, Monahan tells the real history of the world-famous mining camp.

Myal, Suzanne. *Tucson's Mexican Restaurants: Repasts, Recipes, and Remembrances.* Tucson: Fiesta Publishing, 1997. This book appears to be out of print, but it's still widely available online. It's an interesting and comprehensive guide to Tucson's Mexican restaurant scene, with several recipes from locally famous cooks. It's a bit out of date, but still a worthy guide to eating in Tucson.

Nequette, Anne M., and R. Brooks Jeffery. *A Guide to Tucson Architecture.* Tucson: University of Arizona Press, 2002. This is an easy-to-read and relatively comprehensive guide to all of Tucson's interesting and historic architecture. It also includes a good short general history of the region and its many architectural epochs.

Powell, Lawrence Clark. *Arizona: A History.* Albuquerque: University of New Mexico Press, 1990. A more recent edition of the book first published in 1976, Powell's history is not a definitive blow-by-blow, but rather a series of essays on various chapters in Arizona's history and culture. A much-admired Southwestern writer, librarian, and scholar, Powell lived in Tucson for many years. His *Southwest: Three Definitions* (Benson, AZ: Singing Wind Bookshop, 1990) is an excellent trilogy of essays on the landscape and culture of the Southwest.

Sheridan, Thomas. *Arizona: A History.* Tucson: University of Arizona Press, 1995. This is a very well-written and informative general history of the state, one of the better examples out there of New Western history. Also by Sheridan, an anthropologist and professor at the University of Arizona, *Los Tucsonenses: The Mexican Community in Tucson, 1854–1941* is a very readable and interesting account of the influence this community once held in the community, and what happened to the community in the wake of the Anglo takeover after the Gadsden Purchase.

Smith, Dean. *The Great Arizona Almanac: Facts About Arizona.* Portland, OR: WestWinds Press, 2000. Former newspaperman Smith compiled this almanac, with entries on Arizona history, travel, current events, famous residents, mileage charts, zip codes, and area codes. It's in dire need of a new edition, but is still very useful and interesting.

Sonnichsen, C. L. *Tucson: The Life and Times of an American City.* Norman: University of Oklahoma Press, 1982. A thorough telling of the Old Pueblo's long history from its founding as a presidio in 1776 up to the early 1980s.

NATURAL HISTORY AND TRAIL GUIDES

Brown, David E., and Carlos A. Gonzalez Lopez. *Borderland Jaguars.* Salt Lake City: University of Utah Press, 2001. The only comprehensive and complete book on the natural history of the borderland jaguar, this book includes a complete listing of the time, place, and circumstances of pretty much every jaguar sighting in Arizona from the 19th century until the turn of the 20th. Nearly all of those sightings resulted in the jaguar's death by gunshot, by the way.

Carter, Jack L., et al. *Common Southwestern Native Plants: An Identification Guide.* Silver City, NM: Mimbres Press, 2003. A thorough but easy-to-use guide to plants you're likely to see in Arizona; includes common species of the deserts, the forested mountains, and the plateau country.

Ffolliott, Peter F., and Owen K. Davis, eds. *Natural Environments of Arizona: From the*

Deserts to the Mountains. Tucson: University of Arizona Press, 2008. This recent collection of scholarly articles about the state's various biomes contains a lot of very up-to-date information about the sky islands and other natural wonders of Southern Arizona.

Grubbs, Bruce. *Desert Sense: Camping, Hiking & Biking in Hot, Dry Climates.* Seattle, WA: The Mountaineers Books, 2004. If you're going to be hiking or riding a bike in the desert, especially if you're doing it in the summer, consider picking up this or a similar book to familiarize yourself with desert survival beyond the basics of "bring water and wear a hat."

Hanson, Jonathan. *There's a Bobcat in My Backyard! Living With and Enjoying Urban Wildlife.* Tucson: The University of Arizona Press and the Arizona-Sonora Desert Museum, 2004. More than most cities its size, Tucson is within easy and quick access to wilderness, and the more we encroach on that wilderness with our commercial and residential growth, the more contact we have with wild animals. This charming, informative book tells us how to avoid unwanted contact with the desert's wild creatures as well as how to live with them, and watch them, for our own pleasure and edification.

Leavengood, Betty. *Tucson Hiking Guide.* Boulder,CO: Pruett Publishing Company, 1997. Widely available online, this is the best hiking guide to the most popular trails around the Tucson valley. It includes hikes in all of the area's sky island ranges, and many desertland treks as well. Leavengood is something of a grand dame of Tucson hiking, and she prefers long, many-mile all-day hikes. If this isn't really your bag, all of her hikes can be personalized and shortened quite easily.

Logan, Michael F. *The Lessening Stream: An Environmental History of the Santa Cruz River.* Tucson: University of Arizona Press, 2002. A professor paints an attractive and elegiac portrait of what the river used to be like and explains why it isn't that way anymore.

Olin, George. *50 Common Mammals of the Southwest.* Tucson: Western National Parks Association, 2000. An introduction to Arizona's mammals, this slim book with attractive illustrations is part of a series available throughout the state.

Quinn, Meg. *Wildflowers of the Southwest.* Tucson: Rio Nuevo, 2000. If you're going to be hiking in the desert in spring, pick up this guide to the many wildflowers that bloom throughout the state.

Valenzuela-Zapata, Ana G., and Gary Paul Nabhan. *Tequila: A Natural and Cultural History.* Tucson: University of Arizona Press, 2003. This slim history of one of Tucson's favorite liquids will tell you all you need to know about tequila and mescal: what they are, how they're made, and how they have influenced different Southwestern and Mexican cultures over time.

NATIVE AMERICANS

Jacoby, Karl. *Shadows at Dawn: A Borderlands Massacre and the Violence of History.* New York: Penguin, 2008. This book is part of a recent mini-rush of scholarly works about the Western Apache and the brutal Camp Grant Massacre of the 1871, which saw more than 100 sleeping Apache women and children slaughtered by a coalition of Anglo, Mexican, and Tohono O'odham leaders who wanted the band wiped out. This is a fascinating, well-researched book about a violent, shameful period of history that most Tucsonans, let alone Americans, know little about.

Nabhan, Gary Paul. *The Desert Smells Like Rain: A Naturalist in Papago Country.* San Francisco: North Point Press, 1982. Tucson-based ethnobiologist Nabhan writes with passion and verve about the Tohono O'odham and their desert homeland southwest of Tucson. This is a very readable, sometimes poetic account of this little-known people, form their ancient history to almost the present day, with a concentration on the unique adaptations they've made to the desert's harsh patterns.

Record, Ian. *Big Sycamore Stands Alone: The Western Apaches, Aravaipa, and the Struggle for Place.* Norman: University of Oklahoma Press, 2008. Record's is the best book I've ever read about the Apache. He includes a diversity of Apache voices from the past as well as the present, and native voices, until quite recently, have always been the one rather obvious element missing from most studies of Native Americans.

Spicer, Edward H. *Cycles of Conquest: The Impact of Spain, Mexico, and the United States on the History of the Indians of the Southwest, 1533–1960.* Tucson: University of Arizona Press, 1962. The long title of this monumental, classic study by a late professor of anthropology at the University of Arizona pretty much explains what it's about. It's a long, detailed book that chronicles the impact of the colonizers on all of Arizona's tribes, and the chapters on the O'odham and the Apache are excellent.

Stockel, Henrietta H. *Shame and Endurance: The Untold Story of the Chiricahua Apache Prisoners of War.* Tucson: University of Arizona Press, 2004. We've all heard of Geronimo, but few people know the story of how he and his people ended their days in captivity in Oklahoma, far from their beloved borderland home. This book is an eye-opening account of yet another shameful deed done to Arizona's indigenous people.

LITERATURE

Bowden, Charles. *Blue Desert.* Tucson: University of Arizona Press, 1986; and *Frog Mountain Blues.* Tucson: University of Arizona, 1987. Bowden's essays, reportage, and nature writing chronicle the darker side of the Sunbelt.

McCarthy, Cormac. *Blood Meridian, or the Evening Redness in the West.* New York:

Vintage, 1985. McCarthy, the finest living American writer, chronicles the brutal and bloody days when the Mexican government put out a $100 bounty for Apache scalps in Southern Arizona. It's a beautiful, violent, and disturbing novel, but one that will never leave your consciousness. There's even a scene that takes place at the Mission Tumacácori in the Santa Cruz Valley south of Tucson.

Shelton, Richard. *Crossing the Yard: Thirty Years as a Prison Volunteer.* Tucson: University of Arizona Press, 2007. *Going Back to Bisbee.* Tucson: University of Arizona Press, 1992. Shelton is a world-renowned, award-winning poet and creative nonfiction author and longtime University of Arizona professor. *Crossing the Yard* chronicles his decades-long efforts to teach creative writing classes in Arizona's notoriously hard-core prison system. *Going Back to Bisbee* is the story of a job he had teaching school in the small mining town in the 1950s, and includes the natural and human history of the region.

Silko, Leslie Marmon. *Almanac of the Dead.* New York: Simon and Schuster, 1991. Large sections of this Southwestern epic take place in Tucson, but it is a dark, rather dirty and underground Tucson that Silko conjures in this ambitious, rollicking novel about native peoples struggling with the past and the modern world. Born at the Laguna Pueblo in New Mexico, Silko received the MacArthur Foundation "Genius" grant and has lived in the Old Pueblo.

Wallace, David Foster. *Infinite Jest.* New York: Little Brown and Co., 1996. The author killed himself, at age 46, in 2008, but before that he wrote this epic story about addiction, America, tennis, and the funniest movie of all time. Portions of this huge novel take place in the Old Pueblo, and Wallace was enrolled in the University of Arizona's Creative Writing Program for a few semesters long ago.

Internet Resources

GENERAL INFORMATION
Arizona Office of Tourism
www.arizonaguide.com

If you're going to be traveling elsewhere in Arizona (and you should), check out the informative website of the state's tourism authority; there's a lot of information on Southern Arizona here as well.

Arizona-Sonora Desert Museum Center for Sonoran Desert Studies
www.desertmuseum.org/center

This website has a variety of interesting information on the desert's natural history and flora and fauna.

Bisbee Chamber of Commerce
www.bisbeearizona.com

This site has a lot of information about Bisbee, one of the top Southern Arizona attractions outside of Tucson, including a very comprehensive list of the town's many inns, restaurants, and shops.

City of Tucson
www.tucsonaz.gov

Tucson's city government Web hub has, one would hope, all the information you'll ever need on the goings-on of the town council, the mayor, parks and recreation, and the sewer department. There's also information that is likely more useful to the visitor, including a calendar of events, a bus schedule, and directions to every park in town.

Cochise County
www.cochise.az.gov

If you're doing any day-tripping southeast of Tucson in Cochise County, this official county website may help you get a feel for the area, and it has links to a plethora of information.

Metropolitan Tucson Convention and Visitors Bureau
www.visittucson.org

This is Tucson and Southern Arizona's official tourism site. It's got a lot of information on it, and some really beautiful images of the desert and the city.

Pima County
www.pima.gov

Similar in scope and subject matter to the City of Tucson site, Pima County's is even more comprehensive, including links to all kinds of information on living in and visiting the wider Tucson region, including a database through which you can check the food safety ratings of every restaurant in the county.

Santa Cruz County
www.co.santa-cruz.az.us

Tubac, Tumamacacori, Patagonia, and Nogales are all great places to visit in tiny rural Santa Cruz County, about 45 minutes south of Tucson on I-19. This county website has information about everyday life along the border.

NEWS AND CULTURE
Arizona Daily Star
www.azstarnet.com

Tucson's morning daily is free on this site, with news and information on all of Southern Arizona.

Arizona Republic
www.azcentral.com

If you want to know what's happening in Arizona outside of the Tucson region, check out the state's largest newspaper, free online every day; the site also has a robust Arizona travel guide and a useful dining and entertainment section.

Green Valley News
www.gvnews.com
A twice-weekly newspaper covering the Santa Cruz Valley; they regularly print stories about Tubac, Madera Canyon, and the Santa Rita Mountains.

Inside Tucson Business
www.azbiz.com
This weekly tabloid covers the business community in Tucson and Southern Arizona.

Nogales International
www.nogalesinternational.com
This twice-weekly paper covers the small border town of Nogales as well as the Mountain Empire communities.

Phoenix New Times
www.phoenixnewtimes.com
This site is the best place to go for entertainment and cultural listings and alternative news and commentary about life in the Valley of the Sun.

Sierra Vista Herald
www.svherald.com
Check out this site for information and news about Bisbee, the Huachuca Mountains, and all of Cochise County.

Tucson Weekly
www.tucsonweekly.com
Southern Arizona's best source of alternative news, political blogs, and cultural and entertainment news and listings.

Index

Restaurants Index

Nightlife Index

Ain't Nobody's Bizness: 116
Bar Toma: 109
Blanco Tacos + Tequila: 109
Bob Dobb's: 102
Boondock's Lounge: 114
Buffet, The: 105
Bum Steer: 106
Cactus Moon Café: 111
CataVinos: 117
Che's Lounge: 110
Clicks Billiards: 103
Club Congress: 114
C-Note Lounge: 111
Cow Pony Bar and Grill: 104
Danny's Babaquiveri: 106
Dirtbags: 106
District Tavern, The: 102
DV8: 112
Elle: A wine country restaurant: 117
El Parador: 112
Fenderskirts: 104
Hut, The: 114
IBT's: 116

Kon Tiki: 110
Maloney's: 102
Maverick, The: 113
Music Box Lounge: 110
Nimbus Brewing Company: 115
North on 4th: 107
O'Malley's: 102
Pearl Nightclub: 113
Plush: 115
Red Room at the Grill: 115
Shanty, The: 102
Sharks: 113
Shelter, The: 108
Smoke Cigar Patio and Bar: 110
Sports on Congress: 105
Surly Wench: 103
Tap Room, The: 108
Vaudeville Cabaret: 115
Wildcat House: 114
Wooden Nickel Tavern: 103
Woody's: 116
World Famous Golden Nugget: 107
World Sports Grille: 105

Shops Index

AJ's Fine Foods: 168
Antigone Books: 166
Antigua de Mexico: 171
Arizona Mercantile: The Museum Store at the Arizona Historical Society: 163
Bahti Indian Arts: 163
Bohemia: 160
Bon Boutique: 171
Bookmans: 166
Book Stop, The: 166
Broadway Village: 174
Buffalo Exchange, The: 170
Casas Adobes Plaza: 174
Clues Unlimited: 167
Community Food Bank Farmers Market: 173
Copper Country Antiques: 160
Creative Venture Craft Mall: 160
Crizmac Tucson Marketplace: 160
Del Sol: 161
Desert Vintage and Costume: 170

Downtown Farmers Market and Arts and Crafts Mercado: 173
Elizabeth Arden Red Door Salon: 165
El Presidio Mercado: 173
Food Conspiracy Co-op: 168
Foothills Mall, The: 174
4th Avenue: 175
Gadabout Salon and Spa: 165
Grant Road Antiques District: 175
Grey Dog Trading Company: 163
J. Gilbert Footwear: 170
Kid's Center, The: 169
La Encantada: 175
La Placita: 175
La Plaza Shoppes : 176
Lost Barrio: 176
Main Gate Square: 177
Maya Palace: 170
Mexican Garden, The: 161
Mexican Tile and Stone Co.: 172

Hotels Index

www.moon.com

DESTINATIONS | ACTIVITIES | BLOGS | MAPS | BOOKS

MOON.COM is all new, and ready to help plan your next trip! Filled with fresh trip ideas and strategies, author interviews, informative blogs, a detailed map library, and descriptions of all the Moon guidebooks, Moon.com is all you need to get out and explore the world—or even places in your own backyard. As always, when you travel with Moon, expect an experience that is uncommon and truly unique.

MAP SYMBOLS

▦ Expressway	◖ Highlight	✗ Airfield	↧ Golf Course
▦ Primary Road	○ City/Town	✈ Airport	℗ Parking Area
▦ Secondary Road	◉ State Capital	▲ Mountain	▰ Archaeological Site
▫ Unpaved Road	⊛ National Capital	✦ Unique Natural Feature	⚱ Church
- - - - Trail	★ Point of Interest		⛽ Gas Station
⋯⋯ Ferry	• Accommodation	☍ Waterfall	⬭ Glacier
▭ Railroad	▼ Restaurant/Bar	⬥ Park	▨ Mangrove
▬ Pedestrian Walkway	▪ Other Location	⬤ Trailhead	▨ Reef
▥ Stairs	Λ Campground	⛷ Skiing Area	▨ Swamp

CONVERSION TABLES

$°C = (°F - 32) / 1.8$
$°F = (°C \times 1.8) + 32$
1 inch = 2.54 centimeters (cm)
1 foot = 0.304 meters (m)
1 yard = 0.914 meters
1 mile = 1.6093 kilometers (km)
1 km = 0.6214 miles
1 fathom = 1.8288 m
1 chain = 20.1168 m
1 furlong = 201.168 m
1 acre = 0.4047 hectares
1 sq km = 100 hectares
1 sq mile = 2.59 square km
1 ounce = 28.35 grams
1 pound = 0.4536 kilograms
1 short ton = 0.90718 metric ton
1 short ton = 2,000 pounds
1 long ton = 1.016 metric tons
1 long ton = 2,240 pounds
1 metric ton = 1,000 kilograms
1 quart = 0.94635 liters
1 US gallon = 3.7854 liters
1 Imperial gallon = 4.5459 liters
1 nautical mile = 1.852 km

MOON TUCSON

Avalon Travel
a member of the Perseus Books Group
1700 Fourth Street
Berkeley, CA 94710, USA
www.moon.com

Editors: Michelle Cadden, Erin Raber
Series Manager: Erin Raber
Copy Editor: Amy Scott
Graphics and Production Coordinator:
   Elizabeth Jang
Cover Designer: Elizabeth Jang
Map Editor: Albert Angulo
Cartographers: Lohnes & Wright, Chris Markiewicz,
   Kat Bennett

ISBN-13: 978-1-59880-208-5
ISSN: 2150-9751

Printing History
1st Edition — December 2009
5 4 3 2 1

Front cover photo: Mission San Xavier del Bac
   © Tim Hull
Title page photo: Sonoran still life (DeGrazia Gallery
   in the Sun) © Tim Hull

Interior color photos: page 2 (left) *calavera* (skeleton),
(middle) Casa Molina restaurant matador and bull,
(right) carving in San Xavier; page 18 (thumbnail)
mural by Melchor Ramirez at César Chávez Park,
(lower left) Mexican and South American folk arts in
Tubac, (lower right) cholla in the Sonoran Desert. All
photos pages 2 – 24 © Tim Hull.

Printed in Canada by Friesens

KEEPING CURRENT

If you have a favorite gem you'd like to see included in the next edition, or see anything
that needs updating, clarification, or correction, please drop us a line. Send your
comments via email to feedback@moon.com, or use the address above.